THE CHALLENGE OF

Effective Speaking

Thirteenth Edition

Rudolph F. Verderber
University of Cincinnati

Kathleen S. Verderber
Northern Kentucky University

Australia · Canada · Mexico · Singapore

Spain · United Kingdom · United States

THOMSON

WADSWORTH

THOMSON

™

WADSWORTH

The Challenge of Effective Speaking, Thirteenth Edition
Rudolph F. Verderber, Kathleen S. Verderber

Publisher: Holly J. Allen
Editor: Annie Mitchell
Senior Development Editor: Greer Lleuad
Assistant Editor: Darlene Amidon-Brent
Editorial Assistant: Trina Enriquez
Senior Technology Project Manager: Jeanette Wiseman
Senior Marketing Manager: Kimberly Russell
Marketing Assistant: Andrew Keay
Advertising Project Manager: Shemika Britt
Project Manager, Editorial Production: Mary Noel
Art Director: Maria Epes
Print Buyer: Karen Hunt

Permissions Editor: Sarah Harkrader
Production Service: Cecile Joyner/The Cooper Company
Text Designer: Jerry Wilke
Action-Step Icons: © 2004, Mark Fox/BlackDog
Photo Researcher: Stephen Forsling
Copy Editor: Peggy Tropp
Cover Designer: Ross Carron
Cover Images: © 2004, Mark Fox/BlackDog
Cover Printer: Coral Graphic Services
Compositor: G&S Typesetters, Inc.
Printer: Courier Corporation/Kendallville

For more information about our products, contact us at:
Thomson Learning Academic Resource Center
1-800-423-0563
For permission to use material from this text or product, submit a request online at **http://www.thomsonrights.com**.
Any additional questions about permissions can be submitted by email to **thomsonrights@thomson.com**.

Library of Congress Control Number: 2004 114809

Student Edition: ISBN 0-534-64697-2

Annotated Instructor's Edition: ISBN 0-495-00011-6

Thomson Higher Education
10 Davis Drive
Belmont, CA 94002-3098
USA

Asia (including India)
Thomson Learning
5 Shenton Way
#01-01 UIC Building
Singapore 068808

Australia/New Zealand
Thomson Learning Australia
102 Dodds Street
Southbank, Victoria 3006
Australia

Canada
Thomson Nelson
1120 Birchmount Road
Toronto, Ontario M1K 5G4
Canada

UK/Europe/Middle East/Africa
Thomson Learning
High Holborn House
50-51 Bedford Row
London WC1R 4LR
United Kingdom

Latin America
Thomson Learning
Seneca, 53
Colonia Polanco
11560 Mexico
D.F. Mexico

Spain (including Portugal)
Thomson Paraninfo
Calle Magallanes, 25
28015 Madrid, Spain

Brief Contents

Part Four Adapting to Other Occasions and Formats

Detailed Contents

3 Effective Listening 32

Part Two Principles

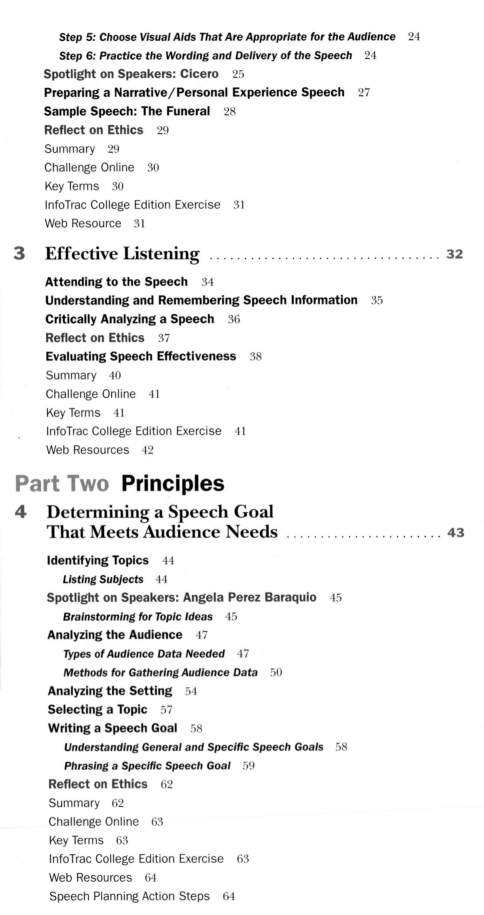

4 Determining a Speech Goal That Meets Audience Needs 43

7 Organizing and Outlining the Speech Body 111

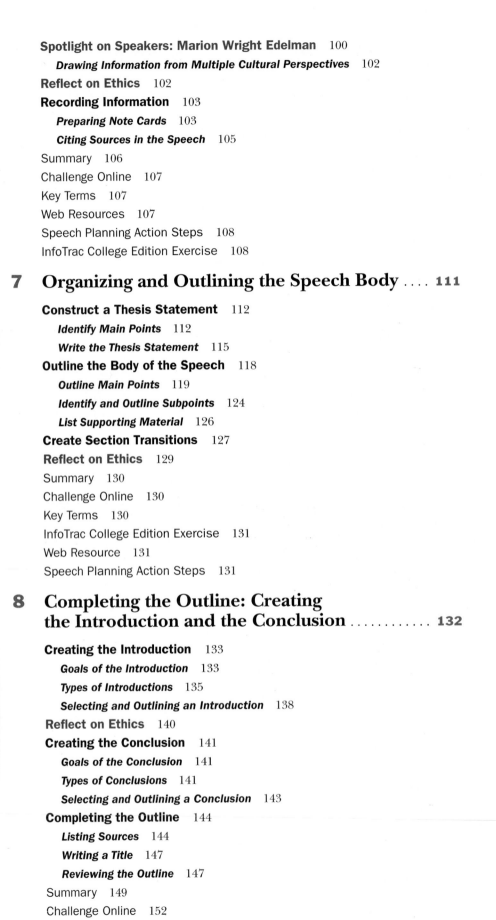

8 Completing the Outline: Creating the Introduction and the Conclusion 132

9 Constructing and Using Visual Aids 154

10 Practicing Speech Wording 174

11 Practicing Delivery 190

Part Three Informative and Persuasive Speaking

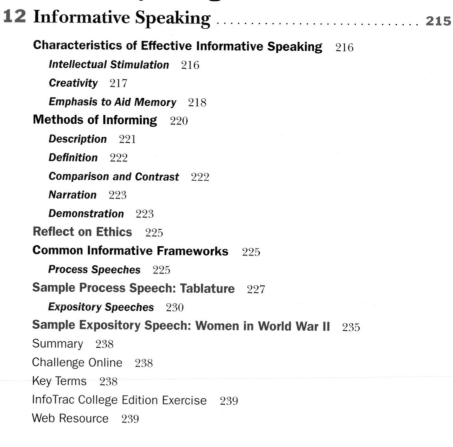

Part Four Adapting to Other Occasions and Formats

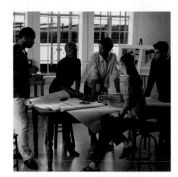

Preface

Wow! A thirteenth edition! We are so grateful to have the opportunity to bring to you the latest edition of *The Challenge of Effective Speaking*. In 1970, when Rudy published the first edition of this book, he shared with his colleagues his solution to the speech instructor's dilemma: How could students master a great deal of information and at the same time present competent speeches early in the academic term? The results have been gratifying. Not only has *Challenge* become a classic, but the book's approach to teaching and mastering public speaking in the college classroom—radical thirty-five years ago—has become the standard in the discipline.

What continues to make this text the standard to which other texts respond is how we have adapted the Verderber method to meet the needs of successive classes of college students. When we begin a revision, we carefully consider feedback from instructors across the country who inform us about the changing needs of their students. We also review the latest scholarship and read countless speeches given by community leaders. We then revise the book to reflect what we learned. In each edition our goal is to make *The Challenge of Effective Speaking* a better tool for teaching the current generation of students how to give effective speeches. We believe that this thirteenth edition clarifies, updates, and refines the speech preparation process to reflect the speaking challenges likely to be encountered by today's students when they move beyond the classroom.

When we finished writing this edition we were surprised by how substantially we had revised the material. Yet we believe that we have retained the essence of what has made the text a favorite teaching tool. We are very excited about the changes and hope you will find that they make your students even better able to master effective public speaking. Let's take a look at the changes and the key features of the text.

New to This Edition

This new edition incorporates many conceptual and pedagogical changes, including the following significant chapter revisions:

Chapter 1: Introduction to Public Speaking takes a new and unique approach to introducing students to public speaking. This chapter introduces a conceptual framework of the public speaking process that focuses students on the characteristics and processes of public communication. It highlights the role that speech preparation plays in speaking effectiveness. In the past we began our discussion of public speaking by using a general communication model. These models, while instructive, have become ill suited to helping students understand the "audience-speaker-context" dynamic and how this dynamic applies to whether the student gives an effective or ineffective speech.

In this edition we have created a model that explains this dynamic and shows that speech effectiveness is determined by how well the speaker is able to understand and adapt the message of the speech to the audience and the context during the speech preparation and speech-making processes. We believe this conceptual foundation provides a better starting point for novice speakers.

Chapter 2: Developing Confidence through the Speech Planning Process has been extensively revised. The discussion of speech apprehension provides both short-term tactics and long-term strategies for combating nervousness. The chapter emphasizes how effective preparation can mitigate apprehension, and it introduces the six Speech Planning Action Steps that can be used to prepare an effective speech. The chapter then provides a first-speech assignment so students can get early practice in setting a speech goal, adapting to an audience, gathering supporting information, organizing a speech, preparing visual aids, and practicing a short narrative speech.

Chapter 4: Determining a Speech Goal that Meets Audience Needs includes more in-depth treatment of the audience analysis process, including a systematic description of the various approaches to collecting audience demographic and audience attitudinal information.

Chapter 5: Adapting to Audiences has been completely reconceptualized and describes specific methods a speaker can use to make sure that speech material is adapted to a specific audience. This chapter includes methods for demonstrating that the material is relevant to the audience, ensuring that the audience comprehends the message, establishing common ground, displaying goodwill, illustrating speaker credibility, acknowledging audience attitudes, and adjusting to language and cultural differences.

Chapter 6: Researching Information for Your Speech has been revised to reflect the ways in which electronic research databases, electronic indexes, and Internet-based resources have changed how speakers do secondary research. The chapter assumes that students will do computer-mediated research and explains how to use the tools at their disposal to access the information they seek.

Chapter 9: Constructing and Using Visual Aids has been updated to prepare students for the real-world expectation of providing professional-quality visual aids.

Chapter 10: Practicing Speech Wording has been simplified and provides more examples so students can understand how to use language to develop ideas that are clear, vivid, and appropriate.

Chapter 12: Informative Speaking has been substantially revised so that it focuses not simply on different types of informative speeches, but rather on different methods of informing that can be used to develop a main point in any informative speech. These methods of informing include description, definition, comparison and contrast, narration, and demonstration. Each method is explained and exemplified. Two of the most common types of informative speeches, the process speech and the expository speech, are discussed in depth, and speech assignments and sample speeches of both speech types are provided.

Chapter 13: Persuasive Speaking: Reasoning with Your Audience is the first of two chapters on persuasive speaking. Together these chapters present an integrated approach that helps students understand how logical reasoning, emotional appeals, and speaker credibility can work together in the persuasive process. This chapter is devoted to teaching students the basics of verbal reasoning. It discusses how initial audience attitudes toward a subject affect the choice of persuasive speaking goal, describes and exemplifies the types of persuasive propositions, explains how to choose reasons and support, teaches how to use the Toulmin approach to developing sound arguments, and lays out common reasoning fallacies that speakers should avoid. Toward the end of the chapter, five persuasive organizational patterns are presented. The chapter ends with the assignment of a speech to convince.

Chapter 14: Persuasive Speaking: Motivating the Audience, the second chapter on persuasive speaking, is grounded in the Elaboration Likelihood Model (ELM) of Petty and Cacioppo. In this chapter we begin by acquainting students with the ELM so they understand how logical reasoning, emotional appeals, and speaker credibility affect audience beliefs and behavior. We describe how speakers can use emotional appeals to increase audience involvement with their proposition. The ELM model suggests that involved audiences are more likely to listen to, think about, and carefully evaluate a speaker's arguments. We then suggest that speakers should demonstrate credibility, especially good will, in order to increase the likelihood that listeners who are not involved will comply with the speaker. Next we explain how speakers can motivate audience members to take action by providing incentives that fill unmet needs. We also explain the motivated sequence organizational pattern. Finally, we provide guidelines for ethical persuasive speaking. The chapter concludes with the assignment of a speech to actuate.

Chapter 15: Ceremonial Speaking: Speeches for Special Occasions has been revised so that students first explore audience expectations for each type of ceremonial speech, then specific strategies and tips to consider as they prepare a ceremonial speech. A discussion of toasts has been added because a toast may be the first ceremonial speech that many students are asked to give.

New and Revised Features

+ **The Speech Planning Action Steps** that guide students through an orderly speech preparation process reflect the hallmark of the Verderber method. These sequential activities structure the tasks that students must complete to prepare effective speeches. Over the years, we have heard again and again from instructors that when they require their students to complete and submit the Speech Planning Action Steps, the quality of their students' speeches improves markedly. Almost every Action Step is accompanied by a sample student response to the activity. The Action Step activities that appear in the text can also be completed online at The Challenge of Effective Speaking Web site, and many of the activities can be completed by using Speech Builder Express™, a web-based outlining and organization tool that coaches students through key parts of the speech preparation process.

+ **A new feature box, Spotlight on Speakers,** introduces students to well-regarded public speakers with a variety of backgrounds and experiences, including Susan B. Anthony, Marian Wright Edelman, and Bono. These short vignettes feature both contemporary and historically important speakers, highlighting the characteristics of their speaking that have led to their success.

+ **New sample student speeches** are accompanied by sample preparation activities, including adaptation plans and complete-sentence outlines. In this edition, we have included some new speeches and have brought back the classic "Open Your Eyes" persuasive speech in response to feedback from instructors who use the book. With each speech, we provide extensive marginal comments about the speech, comparing what the speaker did with the concepts and guidelines discussed in the chapter.

+ **The Reflect on Ethics case studies** have been more thoroughly integrated into each chapter. These short cases depict ethical dilemmas faced by speakers as they prepare and deliver speeches. Questions at the end of each case encourage students to think through the ethical issues. The cases can be used for short writing assignments or for brief class discussions.

In addition, the thirteenth edition includes the following updated technological features, all highlighted at the end of each chapter in the Challenge Online section:

✦ **The Challenge of Effective Speaking CD-ROM** is packaged free with each new book. This dynamic multimedia learning tool brings the text content to life with video clips of full-length sample student speeches, many of which are featured in the text. Icons throughout the text refer students to the CD-ROM and prompt them to watch, listen to, and evaluate the speeches. By watching these speeches, students can prepare for their own speech performance and provide effective feedback to their peers. Students are encouraged to evaluate and critique the speeches directly on the CD-ROM and then compare their evaluations with those of the authors'. The Challenge CD-ROM also provides access to The Challenge of Effective Speaking Web site, InfoTrac College Edition, and Speech Builder Express.

✦ The extensive and revamped **Challenge of Effective Speaking Web site** provides students with a multitude of text-specific learning aids, including video clips from sample student speeches that highlight examples of specific speech elements. From the Web site students can download speech checklists as well as complete the Action Step activities online, e-mail them to their instructors if requested, and compare their responses with models provided by the authors. The Web site also features study aids such as chapter outlines, flash cards and other resources for mastering glossary terms, and chapter quizzes that help them check their understanding of key concepts.

✦ **Web Resource Web links and InfoTrac College Edition activities** have been integrated into the text to expand skills practice and learning online. These Web Resources are highlighted in the text with colored text and icons and are easily accessed from The Challenge of Effective Speaking Web site. All the links are monitored to ensure that they remain active.

✦ Many Speech Planning Action Steps can be completed with **Speech Builder Express,** a dynamic online speech organization and outlining tool. This interactive software enables students to complete speech assignments and generate a complete speech outline, including a works cited section. During interactive sessions, students can create goal and thesis statements, identify main points and supporting material, choose organizational patterns, and plan visual aids. All the Speech Builder Express activities are formatted according to the principles discussed in this text, and students can get help at any time through an online "tutor" feature that provides the relevant text material as an onscreen prompt. All work from a session can be saved and used in subsequent work periods.

Supplementary Materials

In addition to The Challenge of Effective Speaking CD-ROM and Web site, the thirteenth edition is accompanied by a suite of integrated resources for students and instructors.

Student Resources

+ **InfoTrac® College Edition.** An easy-to-use online library is also packaged with each new edition. A *free* four-month subscription to this extensive easy-to-use database of reliable, full-length articles (not abstracts) from hundreds of top academic journals and popular sources is ideal for helping students master online research and is especially useful when students are preparing speeches.

+ **Opposing Viewpoints Resource Center.** This online center helps expose students to all sides of today's most compelling social and scientific issues, from genetic engineering to environmental policy, prejudice, abortion, health care reform, violence in the media, and much more. The result is a dynamic online library of current events topics—the facts as well as the arguments as articulated by the proponents and detractors of each position.

+ **Speech Builder Express Student Guide.** This student-friendly guidebook offers students assistance with using Speech Builder Express speech outlining and organizing software. Students will receive help on selecting an appropriate organizational pattern, preparing a thorough and effective speech outline, incorporating visual aids, and much more.

+ **Student Workbook.** This workbook provides numerous practical, hands-on activities that apply the concepts presented within the text. The workbook contains a summary of each chapter, the Speech Planning Action Step activities, a research journal, outlining activities and worksheets, copies of the speech evaluation forms included in the text, and Internet activities.

+ **Election 2004: Speeches from the Campaign.** This timely CD-ROM includes both full and excerpted speeches from the 2004 campaign for president of the United States. Students can view speeches from the Democratic and Republican conventions as well as a variety of other speeches throughout the campaign.

+ **The Art and Strategy of Service Learning Presentations** *by Rick Isaacson and Jeff Saperstein, both at San Francisco State University*. This handbook can be bundled with the text and is an invaluable resource for students in the basic course that integrates or is planning to integrate a service learning component. The handbook provides guidelines for connecting service learning work with classroom concepts and advice for working effectively with agencies and organizations. The handbook also provides model forms and speeches for students to use throughout the course.

+ **A Guide to the Basic Course for ESL Students** *by Esther Yook, Mary Washington College*. Available bundled with the text, this guide assists the non-native speaker. Features FAQs, helpful URLs, and strategies for accent management and overcoming speech apprehension.

Instructor Resources

+ **Instructor's Resource Manual with Test Bank.** This indispensable manual features changes from the twelfth edition to the thirteenth edition, information about evaluating speeches and helping students overcome speech anxiety, sample syllabi, chapter-by-chapter outlines, summaries, suggested lecture and discussion topics, classroom exercises, and assignments, as well as a comprehensive test bank with answer key.

- **ExamView®.** A user-friendly assessment and tutorial system that makes it easy to create, deliver, and customize tests and study guides (both print and online) in minutes. Features all of the test items found in the Instructor's Resource Manual.

- **Multimedia Manager for Communication: A Microsoft® PowerPoint® Presentation Tool.** Available to qualifying adopters. The Multimedia Manager features hundreds of images, text, and cued CNN® videos that can be used to create the ideal lecture presentation. This CD-ROM also features pre-designed Microsoft® PowerPoint® lectures that can be customized or used as is.

- **WebTutor™ Toolbox on WebCT and Blackboard.** WebTutor Toolbox is preloaded with content and available using the access code when packaged with this text. WebTutor Toolbox pairs all the content of the text's rich book companion Web site with all the sophisticated course management functionality of a WebCT or Blackboard product. Materials (including online quizzes) can be assigned, and the results can flow automatically to a gradebook.

- **JoinIn™ on TurningPoint®.** Available to qualifying adopters. Book-specific JoinIn™ content for Response Systems tailored to the Verderbers' text can be used to assess student progress with instant in-class quizzes and polls. Book-specific questions can be posed, and students' answers can be displayed seamlessly within Microsoft® PowerPoint® slides, in conjunction with any "clicker" hardware.

- **Student Speeches for Critique and Analysis.** Available to qualifying adopters. This multivolume video series offers both imperfect and award-winning sample student speeches. The speeches presented in this text are available in this series. Students can watch, critique and analyze a variety of speeches, including speeches of introduction, impromptu, persuasive, and informative speeches. Select speeches feature non-native English speakers and the use of visual aids.

- **Wadsworth Communication Video Library.** Available to qualifying adopters. The Video Library includes a variety of instructional videos as well as the Great Speeches video series.

- **CNN Today: Public Speaking Videos and DVDs.** Available to qualifying adopters. These videos and DVDs feature riveting footage from CNN, the world's leading 24-hour global news television network. CNN® Today Videos and DVDs show students the relevance of course topics to their everyday lives. Organized by topics covered in a typical course, these videos and DVDs are divided into short segments—perfect for introducing key concepts. High-interest clips are followed by questions designed to spark class discussion.

- **The Teaching Assistant's Guide to the Basic Course** *by Katherine G. Hendrix, University of Memphis.* Based on leading communication teacher training programs, the guide covers general teaching and course management topics as well as specific strategies for communication instruction, such as providing effective feedback on performance, managing sensitive class discussions, and conducting mock interviews.

Acknowledgments

In this day and age, a basic textbook is the result of the efforts of many people, and we would like to thank all of those whose work has made this edition possible. While we are ultimately responsible for the content of the book, this Thirteenth Edition is the result of a wonderful team effort. We begin by thanking the students who have graciously allowed us to publish the speeches they gave in class. We also want to thank our colleagues around the globe who have used previous editions, and especially those who have offered feedback and insights into how the text could better meet the needs of their students. We are especially grateful to the following people who formally participated in providing the comments upon which our revision plan was based: Merry Buchanan, University of Central Oklahoma; Suzanne Buck, University of Houston; June Butts, Broward Community College; James M. Gotcher, Austin Peay State University; Stephanie L. Hood, Pasadena City College; Cheryl A. Moody, Southwestern Illinois College; Pamela J. Reid, Copiah-Lincoln Community College; Ken Sherwood, Los Angeles City College; Kristina N. Tabor, University of Cincinnati; Kathryn Wylie-Marques, John Jay College; and B. K. Whetstone Smith, Houston Community College.

We thank Cheryl Moody of Southwestern Illinois College, who wrote the annotations for the *Challenge* Annotated Instructors' Edition; the author of the Instructor's Resource Manual with Test Bank; and the author of the Student Workbook.

We have been blessed to have a wonderful team of Wadsworth professionals to work with. We want to thank our publisher, Holly Allen; acquisitions editor, Annie Mitchell; senior development editor, Greer Lleuad; assistant editor, Darlene Amidon-Brent; editorial assistant, Trina Enriquez; production project manager, Mary Noel; senior technology project manager, Jeanette Wiseman; and senior marketing manager, Kim Russell. We also want to acknowledge the work of Cecile Joyner of The Cooper Company, who along with Greer Lleuad keeps our projects on track, on time, and on budget.

Finally we want to thank our family, who puts up with our periodic unavailability. We especially want to acknowledge the grandchildren, Anna, Ethan, and Abbey, whom we love so much and to whom we dedicate this edition.

Introduction to Public Speaking

Public Speaking Is
an Audience-Centered Process

■ Audience

■ Context

■ Speaker

■ Speech Planning Process

■ Speech Making Process

■ Speech Effectiveness

Public Speaking Skills
Empower

Public Speaking Challenges
Us to Behave Ethically

The Effective Public Speaker
Is Competent

*All the great speakers were bad
speakers at first.*

Ralph Waldo Emerson, "Power," *The Conduct of Life,* **1860**

When Tom Simmons, a candidate for council, was invited to speak at the University Forum, he presented his views on the role of government in education.

As Marquez, Bill, and Glenna drove home from the movie they had seen, Bill said he thought the movie deserved an Academy Award nomination and asked the others if they agreed. Marquez listened carefully and then gave two reasons why he thought the movie failed to portray characters realistically.

As Heather and Gavin were eating dinner, Heather tried to explain why she was upset with the attention he was paying to Susan.

At the monthly meeting of the Engineering Department, Nancy Bauer, a purchasing clerk, gave a speech on how to fill out the new online requisition form all engineers would be using when ordering parts for newly designed machines.

Who would you identify in these four situations as giving a speech? You're probably thinking that since Tom and Nancy knew that they were expected to speak to a group, they prepared ahead, so they certainly were giving a speech. True. But isn't it likely that since Heather had been thinking about Gavin's attentiveness to Susan for a while, she had prepared ahead as well? And since Marquez was asked a direct question, didn't he have to come up with an answer that made sense, an answer that he had probably been mulling over as he watched the movie?

The point? This course focuses on developing your public speaking skills, but you will be able to draw on these skills across a variety of settings, including work-related meetings, personal business transactions (such as negotiating to buy a new car), and personal relationships. In short, practicing public speaking skills will help you present your ideas more informatively and more persuasively in any setting.

In this chapter, we begin by describing the communication process that occurs during a speech. Then we consider how building public speaking skills empowers us, challenges us to behave ethically, and builds competence.

Public Speaking Is an Audience-Centered Process

More than 2000 years ago, the Greek philosopher Aristotle observed, "The audience is the end and object of the speech." What he meant was that the eloquence of your words is irrelevant if the words are not heard by, are not understood by, or do not affect the people to whom you are speaking. The same is true today. As a speaker, you have a specific goal in mind that you want to achieve when you speak. How effective you are at attaining that goal will depend on whether people in your audience listen to, understand, and perhaps act on what you say.

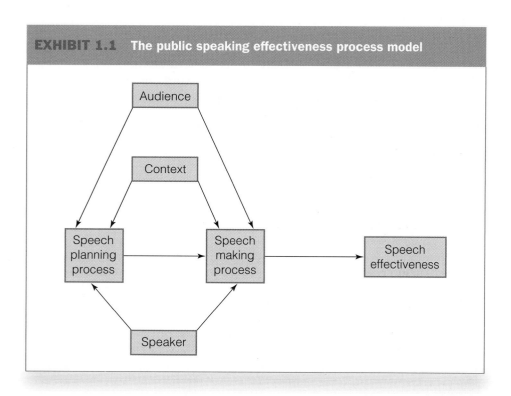

EXHIBIT 1.1 The public speaking effectiveness process model

The Public Speaking Effectiveness Process Model (Exhibit 1.1) depicts the central role played by your audience during both speech planning and speech making. During the speech planning process, your careful analysis of the audience, the speaking context, and your speech planning skills will guide you as you develop your speech action plan. During the speech making process, you can use the audience feedback you receive to alter your planned speech so that your audience is better able to listen, understand, or be motivated to act. Let's briefly discuss each element of this model: audience, context, speaker, speech planning process, speech making process, and speech effectiveness.

Audience

The **audience** is the specific group of people to whom your speech is directed. An effective speech planning process begins with studying your audience. **Audience analysis** is a study made to learn about the diverse characteristics of audience members and then, based on these characteristics, to predict how audience members are apt to listen to, understand, and be motivated to act on your speech. Armed with an understanding of your specific audience, you are in a better position to develop a speech plan whose specific goal, organizational pattern, and examples, statistics, and other supporting material are suited to your particular audience's needs. For example, if the audience analysis reveals that most audience members are under 25, a speaker who has decided to speak on the internment of Japanese Americans during World War II may need to provide more detailed background information than would need to be provided to an audience whose members were adults during World War II.

During the speech making process, your audience members give you **audience feedback**—nonverbal and occasionally verbal cues that indicate audience members' reactions to what the speaker is saying. If you pay attention to these cues, you can deviate from your speech plan in order to help meet audience

audience the specific group of people to whom the speech is directed

audience analysis a study made to learn about the diverse characteristics of audience members and then, based on these characteristics, to predict how audience members are apt to listen to, understand, and be motivated to act on your speech

audience feedback nonverbal and verbal cues that indicate audience members' reaction to what the speaker is saying

needs that the feedback communicates. For example, after quickly defining a key term and giving a short example, Ethan notices a number of audience members looking quizzical. Even though he had not planned to do so, Ethan should use this feedback and redefine the term using simpler words and even give another detailed example. In this way, he alters his speech plan to meet a need he has identified through audience feedback.

Context

context the physical, cultural, historical, and psychological factors in the setting in which your speech is presented

physical setting the location, size of room, seating arrangement, distance between audience and speaker, time of day, room temperature, and lighting

cultural setting the values, beliefs, meanings, and social mores of specific groups of people to which your audience members belong

historical setting events that have already occurred that are related to your speech topic, to you as a speaker, to previous speeches given by you with which audience members are familiar, or to other encounters that audience members have had with you

psychological setting the feelings, attitudes, and beliefs of individual audience members that affect how your speech message is perceived

The **context** is comprised of physical, cultural, historical, and psychological factors in the setting in which your speech is presented. The context affects how your audience members perceive the speech.

The **physical setting** includes location, size of room, seating arrangement, distance between audience and speaker, time of day, room temperature, and lighting. These factors work together to create a physical context that can aid or detract from your speech. For example, if an audience of 50 people listens to a speech you present in a dimly lit hall with a capacity of 500 people where you are on a raised platform at a distance from the audience and use a microphone, they are likely to perceive you as impersonal and find it difficult to remain attentive to what you are saying. But an audience of 50 that listens to you give that same speech in a well-lit room designed for 60 people, where you stand within five feet of the first row and use only a small lectern to hold a few notes, is likely to perceive you as personable and is likely to pay better attention to what you say.

The **cultural setting** is comprised of the values, beliefs, meanings, and social mores of specific groups of people to which your audience members belong that help members of that group form and interpret messages. During the speech preparation process, you will try to understand how your cultural background meshes with that of your audience and adapt the speech message to ensure that it can be accurately interpreted within your audience members' cultural frame. Because early U.S. immigrants came from western European countries, U.S. public speaking practices have been rooted in western European culture. Today, we are a more diverse country with more heterogeneous cultural backgrounds. As a result, you may no longer expect that the members of your audience subscribe to western European imperatives. Understanding not only who is in the audience, but also how their cultural background differs from yours, is important during speech preparation and presentation. For example, in western European culture, feedback to speakers is primarily nonverbal. It would be considered rude for an audience member to speak out during a public address. In African American and other cultural settings, however, it is common for audience members to provide verbal feedback during a speech. Generally, this feedback is affirming and encouraging to the speaker. To learn more about cultural differences in approaches to persuasion, complete the InfoTrac College Edition exercise at the end of this chapter.

The **historical setting** is comprised of events that have occurred prior to the speech that are related to your speech topic, to you as a speaker, to previous speeches given by you with which audience members are familiar, or other encounters that audience members have had with you. The historical setting can predispose an audience toward or against your topic or you as a speaker. For example, a speech on police–community cooperation given by the long-established local president of the Fraternal Order of Police is likely to be viewed differently than if a newly elected president gives a similar speech.

The **psychological setting** is comprised of the moods, feelings, attitudes, and beliefs of the individual audience members that affect how your speech message is perceived. As you prepare your speech, you need to consider how individual audience members' psychological makeup is likely to affect how they listen to your speech. For example, a professor who has just returned a test on which most students performed poorly may have a rough time engaging their attention in the lecture that follows. Student audience members may feel resentment toward the professor and have trouble listening to what is being said.

Speaker

The **speaker** is the source or originator of the speech. As the speaker, what you discuss and the language you use to express those ideas will depend on your own interests, beliefs, background, and public speaking skills. You will choose topics that you care about, know something about, and want to inform or persuade others about. The experiences you have had will influence the attitudes and beliefs that you express in the speeches you give. For example, after a drunk driver killed her daughter, Candace Lightner began speaking out about the lenient treatment afforded those who drove drunk. Her speeches on this issue led her to become a cofounder of MADD, Mothers Against Drunk Driving. Although your speeches may not lead you to found a social movement, how well you communicate your ideas will depend on your public speaking skills. In this course, you will learn the skills you will need to craft and deliver speeches and presentations that are effective.

speaker the source or originator of the speech

Speech Planning Process

Whereas most of our day-to-day interactions occur without much forethought on our part, most of the speeches and presentations that we give are based on preparation that we do beforehand. The **speech planning process** is the system that you use to prepare a speech. All of us have heard lectures, speeches, and presentations that were disorganized, boring, and difficult to follow. We may have even commented that the speaker needed to do more to prepare. In this course, you will learn a proven six-step process that will enable you to plan speeches that will be effective. The six steps in this process are (1) selecting a specific speech goal that is appropriate for your audience and occasion, (2) developing a strategy for audience adaptation, (3) gathering and evaluating information to use in your speech, (4) organizing and developing information into a well-structured outline, (5) choosing visual aids that are appropriate for your audience, and (6) practicing your speech wording and delivery.

speech planning process the system that you use to prepare a speech

Speech Making Process

Once you have carefully prepared your speech, you still have to deliver it to your audience. **Speech making** is this process of actually presenting a speech to the intended audience. Although you may be nervous before an audience, the planning you have done will give you confidence and allow you to focus on helping the audience to understand your message rather than focusing your attention on your discomfort. During your presentation, you will be conscious of what you have planned to say, but you will also respond to audience feedback and adjust to how your audience is receiving what you are saying. When you are well prepared, you will be comfortable deviating from your planned material to expand on definitions, offer additional examples, or vary your pace in response to audience members' needs.

speech making the process of presenting a speech to the intended audience

Speech Effectiveness

When you give a speech, your goal is to communicate with your audience members. You will be effective if, when you have finished speaking, the members of your audience have remained attentive, have understood what you have said, remember the main ideas you have spoken about, and are motivated to use what they have learned from you. Thus, **speech effectiveness** is the extent to which audience members listen to, understand, remember, and are motivated to act on what a speaker has said.

In order to be effective, then, you must present information in a way that captures and holds the attention of audience members. In this course, you will learn a variety of techniques for holding attention. For example, you may want to use a story to illustrate a point in your speech, since most of us perk up and listen when someone says, "that reminds me of a story. . . ."

Not only do you want the audience to listen to what you are saying, but you want them to understand. Most of us have had the unfortunate experience of sitting through a lecture in which we worked hard and paid attention, but after class when we tried to do our homework, we found that we really didn't understand the information that had been presented. Crafting presentations that the audience can understand depends on an accurate audience analysis during speech planning and continues with responding to audience feedback during speech making. During this course, you will learn how to use your audience analysis to help you prepare messages that your audience will understand.

Similarly, if when you have finished speaking the audience members look at each other and say, "I really enjoyed that speech, but I can't remember what was said," the speech cannot be considered effective. In this course, you will also learn how to help audience members remember the major ideas that you are presenting. For example, you may want to repeat key ideas as a way of emphasizing their importance, and you will learn how to use short summary statements as well.

Finally, in some of the speeches that you will give, your goal will be to have the audience act on what you have said. Although an audience may listen to, understand, and remember the major ideas in a speech whose goal is to have audience members become organ donors, to be effective the speech should also result in at least some members' actually signing donor cards, or at least becoming more accepting of the idea. In this course, you will learn the principles of persuasion and how to prepare speeches that are likely to affect the way that audience members think, feel, and act.

Public Speaking Skills Empower

You may be taking this course because it is required, but we believe this may be the single most important course you take during your college career. Why? Because developing public speaking skills empowers you in four ways.

First, developing public speaking skills empowers you to communicate complex ideas and information in a way that all members of the audience can understand. Many of us have had the experience of understanding something but being unable to explain it clearly to others. Most of us have had an unfortunate experience with a teacher who "talked over our heads." The teacher understood the material but was unable to express it clearly to us. When we can express our ideas clearly, we are more likely to share them. When others understand our ideas, they learn from us.

Second, developing public speaking skills empowers you to influence the

---

speech effectiveness the extent to which audience members listen to, understand, remember, and are motivated to act on what a speaker has said

Frederick Douglass

This Fourth of July Is Yours, Not Mine

The U.S. Constitution makes it clear that we are to be a nation of free people. Yet throughout much of the nineteenth century, Frederick Douglass felt anything but free. Born into slavery and separated from his parents at birth, Douglass managed to escape and then devoted his life to addressing the moral, legal, and ethical issues of this wicked social system. Douglass saw in speech making a way to empower himself and his people who were still enslaved. Much sought after as a lecturer, Douglass was invited to give a speech in 1852 in Rochester, New York, at a Fourth of July celebration where the audience was primarily white.

In his speech "The Meaning of July Fourth for the Negro," Douglass gives a powerful oration on the meaninglessness of this day. In this short exerpt notice how Douglass uses the irony of this situation to his advantage:

> Your high independence only reveals the immeasurable distance between us. The blessings in which you, this day, rejoice, are not enjoyed in common. The rich inheritance of justice, liberty, prosperity and independence, bequeathed by your fathers, is shared by you, not by me. The sunlight that brought light and healing to you, has brought stripes and death to me. This Fourth July is yours, not mine. You may rejoice, I must mourn.

Through this moral appeal Douglass shares his personal testimony and alludes to his vision for change. Like Douglass, you too can be *empowered* by the speaking process. Frederick Douglass's vision and his single voice earned him the respect and honor of many, including an appointment as adviser to President Lincoln. But more important, his strong words helped bring about change—an amendment—to a constitution that claimed liberty for all.

attitudes and behavior of other people. We seem to be trying constantly to influence others. Have you ever tried to get a classmate to lend you her notes? Or tried to get an airline to change a reservation without charging a fee? Have you tried to get your boss to give you an extra shift at work? Or tried to get a professor to change a grade you received? When we thoughtfully articulate the reasons for our positions and requests, others are more likely to comply with our wishes. Public speaking skills equip us to fashion arguments that others may find compelling.

Third, mastering public speaking skills empowers you to achieve your career goals. Studies show that for almost any job, one of the most highly sought-after skills in new hires is oral communication skills.[1] So, whether you aspire to a career in business, industry, government, education, or almost any other field you can name, communication skills are likely to be a prerequisite to your success. Moreover, most jobs require people to present oral reports and proposals and to train coworkers. Although you might be hired on the basis of your technical competency, your ability to earn promotions will depend on your ability to communicate what you know to others, including your boss, your clients, and your colleagues in other departments.

Fourth, public speaking skills empower you to participate in our democratic processes. Free speech is a hallmark of our democracy. The strategies and policies our government adopts are a direct result of the debate that occurs across the nation and in our executive, legislative, and judicial branches of government.

When you are equipped with sound public speaking skills, you will have the confidence to speak out in town hall meetings and other settings and voice your ideas on important public issues.

Public Speaking Challenges Us to Behave Ethically

ethics a set of moral principles that are held by a society, group, or individual that differentiate right from wrong and good behavior from bad behavior

Today, as in times past, we expect a speaker to behave ethically. **Ethics** are a set of moral principles that are held by a society, group, or individual that differentiate right from wrong and good behavior from bad behavior. (To read a thorough discussion about ethics and what they involve, check out Web Resource 1.1: The Basics of Ethics. Use your Challenge CD-ROM to access this Web Resource at the Challenge Web site. Select the chapter resources for Chapter 1, then click on "Web Resources.") Regardless of whether the setting for your speeches is a classroom, a boardroom, the campaign trail, or the floor of a legislative body, you have ethical responsibilities to your listeners.

Speakers are ethical when they conform to standards of moral behavior that are expected in public speaking situations. What standards are we expected to conform to? Five generally agreed upon standards are honesty (not to lie, cheat, or steal); integrity (holding sound moral principles); fairness (behaving justly); respect (showing consideration); and responsibility (being accountable). If you look at these closely, you'll see that these terms are quite general and abstract. But there are two specific behaviors that are fundamental to ethical speaking:

1. Ethical speakers tell the truth. Telling the truth is showing honesty in behavior. An audience expects that what you tell them will be true—not made up, not your personal belief presented as fact, and not an exaggeration. If, during or after your speech, members of your audience doubt the accuracy of something you have said, they are likely to reject all of your ideas. To make sure that what you say is truthful, you will want to research your topic carefully and present both sides of controversial issues accurately.

crediting ideas giving the sources of information you use

2. Ethical speakers fully credit sources for their ideas. Fully **crediting ideas**—giving the sources of the information you use—is ethical. Presenting others' ideas as your own or refraining from identifying questionable sources is unethical. For instance, saying "The overwhelming majority of people have a pessimistic view of ethics and morality in this country" is less ethical than saying "According to a Gallup poll cited in a June 28, 2003, *Christian Century* article, 'Seventy-seven percent of Americans rated current ethics and morality as fair or poor.'"[2]

plagiarism stealing and passing off the ideas and words of another as one's own or using a created production without crediting the source

In many cases, failing to cite sources is **plagiarism**—stealing and passing off the ideas and words of another as one's own or using a created production without crediting the source. Unfortunately, plagiarism is too common. According to a 2002–03 survey of 3,500 graduate students at U.S. and Canadian universities, "23%–25% of students acknowledged one or more instances of 'cutting and pasting' from Internet sources and/or published documents."[3] Moreover, 38% of undergrads admit to committing such online plagiarism in the past year (2003).[4] In the classroom setting, plagiarism can lead to failing an assignment or the course, or being suspended from school. In public speaking settings, it can undermine speaker credibility, result in lawsuits, and ruin promising careers.

How can you recognize and avoid plagiarism? Caroline McCullen cites three common methods of plagiarism:[5]

1. If you change a few words at the beginning, in the middle, or at the end of the material, but copy much of the rest, you are plagiarizing.

2. If you paraphrase the unique ideas of another person and do not credit that person, you are plagiarizing.

3. If you purchase, borrow, or use a speech prepared by another and present it as original, you are plagiarizing.

Crediting sources is also important because where ideas originate is often as important as the ideas themselves. For example, the faith that an audience may place in a statistic on global warming will depend on the source. If the statistic comes from an article by a renowned scientist in a respected peer-reviewed journal, it is likely to have more credibility than if it comes from the personal Web page of someone with unknown credentials. Ethical speakers are careful to acknowledge the sources of controversial ideas, especially when the information is damaging to an individual or institution.

Throughout this text, we will continue to discuss ethical standards for public speaking. Likewise, we will consider more specific ethical issues as we discuss topic selection, audience analysis, selection and use of supporting information, construction and use of visual aids, speech language, delivery, reasoning, use of emotional appeals, establishing credibility, and refutation.

Most of the ethical principles we will present are drawn from what is commonly accepted to be ethical behavior in the United States. But we will note where standards differ across cultures and how these differences lead to alternative ethics. Because ethical behavior is central to public speaking, in each chapter you will find a Reflect on Ethics box like the one shown here. These short cases challenge you to think through your ethical responsibilities as a speaker.

To learn more about ethics, check out the Web site for the Markkula Center for Applied Ethics at Santa Clara University. Use your Challenge CD-ROM to

A person cannot choose and act rationally without some explicit or implicit ethical system. Jimmy Carter has always been praised for his ethical standards.

REFLECT ON ETHICS

Bernice, who volunteers at the battered women's shelter, has been asked to speak this evening at a meeting of the local Kiwanis Club about the need for private donations. Although Bernice has a great deal of factual material at her disposal and has her speech pretty well prepared, she thinks her speech would have a lot more power if she could use some real experiences to make her speech more persuasive. As she thinks about various experiences she has heard about, she considers using Angela's story. Angela, a middle-aged mother, has been staying at the shelter with her three children since she was released from the hospital. She provides an excellent example of the heartbreaking situations that battered women face. Bernice knows that the stories of people at the shelter are confidential, but she thinks that Angela would give her permission to tell her story. However, Angela is at a doctor's appointment and will not be back at the shelter before Bernice is scheduled to speak.

How should Bernice proceed if she cannot contact Angela? Explain.

access **Web Resource 1.2: Ethics Connection** at the Challenge Web site. Select the chapter resources for Chapter 1, then click on "Web Resources."

The Effective Public Speaker Is Competent

communication competence the perception that communication behavior is appropriate and effective

Prof. Brian Spitzberg, a noted communication scholar, defines **communication competence** as the perception that communication behavior is appropriate and effective.[6] When we apply this definition to public speaking, we can say that audiences will perceive you as competent if your speeches are appropriate to the situation and effective in achieving their goals.

What should be of the greatest comfort to you is that you don't have to have been born a great speaker. Public speaking competence is learned.[7] The goal of this course is to help you understand and develop the specific skills that lead to effective speaking. We know that you are unlikely to become a great orator. But we also know that the speech planning process you will learn will help you become better at giving speeches. The speech planning process you will learn is broken into easy-to-follow action steps. In Part Two of the text, you will be introduced to each of these steps as you prepare for your first graded speech assignment. In Part Three, the action steps will be adapted to specific types of informative and persuasive speeches, and in Part Four, you will see how to adapt them to other formats and speaking situations. Each speech assignment you complete will require you to repeat the steps, but each time you will acquire additional information, so that by the time you have finished this text, you will have applied the steps to a variety of speaking goals and become adept at using this step-by-step process.

© Frank Siteman/PhotoEdit

People aren't born knowing how to speak competently. Public speaking is a learned activity.

Summary

Public speaking is important to success in nearly every walk of life. Speeches—oral presentations that are usually given without interruption—occur at formal occasions where an audience has assembled expressly to listen, in less formal employment contexts, and during our informal daily conversations.

Public speaking is an audience-centered process that occurs in a context comprised of physical, cultural, historical, and psychological factors. The speaker uses a six-part speech plan process that includes selecting a goal, developing a strategy for audience adaptation, gathering and evaluating information, organizing the information, choosing visual aids, and practicing speech wording and delivery. How effective a speech is depends on how well audience members listen to, understand, remember, and are motivated to act on what the speaker has said.

Public speaking skills empower us to communicate ideas and information in a way that all members of the audience can understand, enabling us to influence the attitudes and behaviors of others, to achieve career goals, and to participate in our democratic society.

Public speaking challenges us to behave ethically. Ethics—a set of moral principles that differentiate right from wrong and good behavior from bad behavior—rely on standards of honesty, integrity, fairness, respect, and responsibility. Specifically, ethical speeches tell the truth and fully credit sources for their ideas to avoid plagiarism.

Finally, engaging in public speaking challenges us to be competent—that is, to speak in a way that is both appropriate and effective—by following the speech planning process necessary for giving effective informative and persuasive speeches as well as speeches for special occasions.

CHALLENGE ONLINE

Now that you've read Chapter 1, use your Challenge of Effective Speaking CD-ROM for quick access to the electronic study resources that accompany this text. Your CD-ROM gives you access to InfoTrac College Edition, Speech Builder Express, and the Challenge of Effective Speaking Web site. When you get to the Challenge of Effective Speaking home page, click on "Student Book Companion Site" in the Resource box at right to access the online study aids for this chapter, including a digital glossary, review quizzes, and the chapter activities.

KEY TERMS

At the Challenge of Effective Speaking Web site, select chapter resources for Chapter 1. Print a copy of the glossary for this chapter, test yourself with the electronic flash cards, or complete the crossword puzzle to help you master the following key terms.

audience (3)   **context** (4)
audience analysis (3)   **physical setting** (4)
audience feedback (3)   **cultural setting** (4)

historical setting (4)	**speech effectiveness** (6)
psychological setting (4)	**ethics** (8)
speaker (5)	**crediting ideas** (8)
speech planning process (5)	**plagiarism** (8)
speech making (5)	**communication competence** (10)

INFOTRAC COLLEGE EDITION EXERCISE

Diversity has a significant influence on how we communicate with others. This is especially important for businesses. Use your Challenge of Effective Speaking CD-ROM to access InfoTrac College Edition. In the Subject Guide, type "intercultural communication" and then click on Search. Then, under "intercultural communication," click on "view periodicals." Scroll down to the article titled "Cross Cultural Awareness" by Lee Gardenswartz and Anita Row, March 2001. Open the article and scroll to the section titled "Role of Culture." Look for suggestions for communicating with employees of diverse cultures. Then read the whole article, or a similar article, for additional suggestions on dealing with diversity issues.

WEB RESOURCES

Access the Web resources for this chapter online at the Challenge of Effective Speaking Web site. Select the chapter resources for Chapter 1, then click on "Web Resources."

1.1 The Basics of Ethics (8)   **1.2 Ethics Connection** (10)

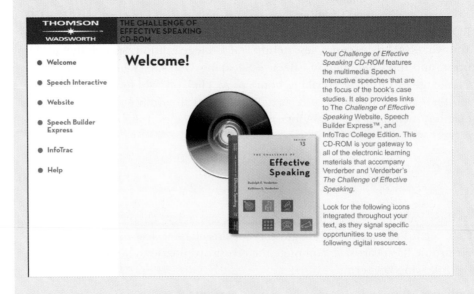

Developing Confidence through the Speech Planning Process

2

© Joel Gordon

Courage is resistance to fear, mastery of fear,
not absence of fear.

Mark Twain, *Pudd'nhead Wilson*

Professor Montrose begins class by saying "Let's look at some of the key points of the chapter that you were assigned to read for today." He then points to Paul and asks, "What were the keys to solving the Kingston problem effectively?" Paul, sputtering and turning red, begins to sweat and stammers, "Well, uh, I guess that, well. . . ." Montrose then points to the next student and asks, "Sylvia, what would you say about this?" Sylvia looks at Prof. Montrose and answers, "According to the text, there are three steps involved." She goes on to list the steps and then discuss each of the three.

You might think, "Poor, Paul. He just got so nervous when Montrose pointed at him and asked him the question that he couldn't remember a thing." And it may be that he did suffer from severe speech anxiety—or stage fright. But then why was Sylvia able to look Montrose in the eye, tell him there seem to be three steps, and then discuss each? One answer might be "Well, she doesn't suffer stage fright, so she was able to answer the question." Again, that might well be true. But there's another answer as well: Paul hadn't prepared well for class, while Sylvia had not only read the text material but had also outlined the key points and reviewed them over a cup of coffee before class.

Recall the title of this chapter: "Developing Confidence through the Speech Planning Process." Although nervousness or stage fright is normal in public settings, such as a class, even the most frightened person whose heart is pounding will perform better when he or she is well prepared.

In this chapter we begin by explaining what scholars call "speech apprehension" and what you might call "stage fright." Then we discuss how careful preparation can help you develop confidence when you speak. At the end of the chapter we consider the narrative speech, a common first speech assignment in this course.

Understanding Public Speaking Apprehension

public speaking apprehension a type of communication anxiety; the level of fear a person experiences when anticipating or actually speaking to an audience

People have feared speaking in public since they first began doing it. And those who teach others to speak have been concerned with helping students overcome their fears almost as long. **Public speaking apprehension,** a type of communication anxiety, is the level of fear a person experiences when anticipating or actually speaking to an audience. Almost all of us have some level of public speaking apprehension, but about 15 percent of the U.S. population experiences high levels of apprehension.[1] Yet this apprehension hardly ever stops people from speaking! In our teaching career we have only had two students whose stage fright was so severe that they could not complete a speech. One walked to the front of class, looked at the audience, and ran back to his seat. The other paused, turned pale, sat down, and then walked back to her seat. Today we can also benefit from a significant wealth of research studies that have identified methods for helping us overcome our nervousness.

Signs of Speech Apprehension

The signs of pubic speaking apprehension vary from individual to individual, and symptoms range from mild to debilitating. Symptoms may include physical, emotional, and mental reactions. Physically, you may experience stomach upset (or butterflies), flushed skin, sweating, shaking, lightheadedness, rapid or heavy heartbeats, and verbal disfluencies including stuttering and vocalized pauses ("like," "you know," "ah," "um"). Emotionally, you may feel anxious, worried, or upset. You might also experience specific negative ideas or thought patterns. For example, a highly apprehensive person might dwell on thoughts such as "I'm going to make a fool of myself" or "I just know that I'll blow it."

Luckily, the level of public speaking apprehension we experience seems to vary and gradually decreases as we speak. Researchers have identified three phases of reaction that we proceed through: anticipation reaction, confrontation reaction, and adaptation reaction.[2] Exhibit 2.1 visually depicts this cycle.

Anticipation reaction is the level of anxiety you experience prior to giving the speech, including the nervousness you feel while preparing and waiting to speak. Your **confrontation reaction** is the surge in your anxiety level that you feel as you begin your speech. This level begins to fall about a minute or so into your speech and will level off at your prespeaking level about five minutes into your presentation. Your **adaptation reaction** is the gradual decline of your anxiety level that begins about one minute into the presentation and results in your anxiety level's declining to its prespeaking level in about five minutes. Research has found that most of us experience moderate levels of both anticipation and confrontation reactions.[3] So, it's normal to be nervous before you speak.

There are many ways to measure your level of public speaking apprehension. Exhibit 2.2 presents one short survey that is widely used by researchers. You can complete the six questions and score them to gauge your level of apprehension.

anticipation reaction the level of anxiety you experience prior to giving the speech, including the nervousness you feel while preparing and waiting to speak

confrontation reaction the surge in your anxiety level that you feel as you begin your speech

adaptation reaction the gradual decline of your anxiety level that begins about one minute into the presentation and results in your anxiety level's declining to its prespeaking level in about five minutes

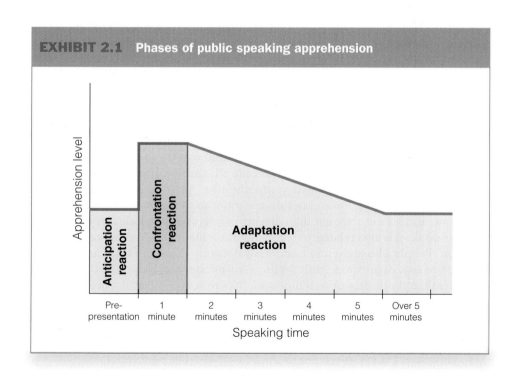

EXHIBIT 2.1   Phases of public speaking apprehension

Causes of Speech Apprehension

The causes of pubic speaking apprehension are still being studied, but several causes have been suggested. These include apprehension because of biologically based temperament, previous experiences, and level of skills.

BIOLOGICALLY BASED TEMPERAMENT

First, recent research has found that some public speaking apprehension may be inborn. This "communibiological" explanation proposes that for some of us public speaking apprehension stems from our temperament, which is neurobiological in origin. According to this theory, two aspects of inherited temperament, extroversion/introversion and neuroticism, blend together to create higher levels of public speaking apprehension.[4] People who are more extroverted experience lower levels of public speaking apprehension than do people who are introverted. Extroverted people generally are more sociable, lively, active, assertive, dominant, and adventuresome than are introverted people. Public speaking apprehension level is also related to the temperamental characteristic called "neuroticism." People who are temperamentally neurotic experience greater levels of general anxiety, depression, guilt feelings, shyness, mood swings, and irrational thoughts than do those whose temperaments are more stable. According to the communibiological theory, public speaking apprehension is likely to be higher for those of us who are both more introverted and more neurotic. Does this mean that if you are temperamentally predisposed toward high public speaking apprehension then you are doomed to be ineffective in your speaking efforts? Of course not, but it does suggest that you will be "working against the grain" and may need special help in learning how to control some of the negative aspects of your temperament.[5]

PREVIOUS EXPERIENCE

Second, our level of public speaking apprehension may also be a result of the reinforcement we received from our previous speaking efforts.[6] From reading aloud during second grade to giving an oral report in science class to accepting a sports award at a banquet, we have all had many "public speaking" experiences. How well we performed in past situations is likely to affect how apprehensive we are about speaking in public now. If your second-grade teacher humiliated you when you read aloud, or if you flubbed that science report, or if friends laughed at your acceptance speech, you will probably be more apprehensive about speaking in public than if you had been praised for earlier efforts. The public speaking apprehension that we feel because of our past experiences, though uncomfortable, does not have to handicap our future performances. There are strategies we can use as we prepare to speak that will help us reduce our apprehension and be more effective. We will discuss some of these strategies in the next section.

LEVEL OF SKILLS

A third cause of public speaking apprehension that we believe is most important comes from having underdeveloped speaking skills. This "skill deficit" theory was the earliest explanation for apprehension and continues to receive the attention of researchers. It suggests that most of us become apprehensive because we don't know how to (or choose not to) plan or prepare effectively for a public presentation.

Effective speech planning is an orderly process that is based on a set of skills. When we do not know or apply these skills, we are likely to have higher anticipatory reaction levels. On the other hand, when we have become skilled at using the six-step speech planning process and when we use it carefully to prepare for a presentation, our preparation will give us confidence so our anticipation reaction will be lower than if we were ill prepared. The goal of this course is to help you become skilled and, in so doing, help you to become a more confident speaker.

Although most speakers confess to nervousness at the prospect of giving an important speech, the goal is not to eliminate nervousness but to learn how to cope with it.

© Chuck Savage/Corbis

Ideal Level of Apprehension

Many of us believe that we would be better off if we could be totally free from nervousness and apprehension. But based on years of study, Prof. Gerald Phillips has concluded that nervousness is not necessarily negative. He noted that "learning proceeds best when the organism is in a state of tension."[7] In fact, it helps to be a little nervous to do your best: If you are lackadaisical about giving a speech, you probably will not do a good job.[8]

Because at least some tension is constructive, the goal is not to eliminate nervousness but to learn how to cope with it. According to

Phillips, studies that followed groups of students taking speaking courses found that nearly all of them still experienced tension, but almost all of them had learned to cope with the nervousness. Phillips concludes that "apparently they had learned to manage the tension; they no longer saw it as an impairment, and they went ahead with what they had to do."[9] So let's look at how you can cope with stage fright and apprehension and use it to your advantage.

Overcoming Public Speaking Apprehension

Because our public speaking apprehension has multiple causes, there are several general methods that can help us reduce our anxiety and several specific techniques we can use to manage our nervousness.

General Methods

Some methods are targeted at reducing the apprehension that results from our worrisome thoughts and irrational beliefs. Other methods are aimed at reducing the physical symptoms of anxiety that we experience. Still others focus on helping us overcome the skill deficiencies that lead to our anxiety. In this section we consider four common methods for reducing public speaking apprehension.

1. Communication orientation motivation (COM) techniques are designed to reduce anxiety by helping us adopt a "communication" rather than a "performance" orientation toward our speeches.[10] According to Michael Motley, public speaking anxiety is increased when we hold a **performance orientation,** viewing public speaking as a situation that demands special delivery techniques in order to impress our audience "aesthetically"[11] or viewing audience members as hypercritical judges who will be unforgiving about even our minor mistakes. On the other hand, if we approach public speaking from a **communication orientation,** we view our speech as just an opportunity to talk with a number of people about a topic that is important to us and to our audience. When we have a communication orientation, we are focused on getting our message across to people in our audience rather than on how the people in our audience are judging or reacting to us as a speaker.

So, one method to use to reduce public speaking apprehension is to give performance-oriented individuals a basic understanding of public speaking apprehension, helping them understand how their performance orientation adds to their apprehension, and working with them so that they consciously adopt a communication orientation. When we recognize that public speaking is very much like casual conversations, in which we focus on our message and the people who are listening, and when we recognize that our audience is concerned with understanding the content of the speech, not with judging us, we have adopted a communication rather than performance orientation and our anxiety at speaking will be lowered.

2. Visualization is a method that reduces apprehension by helping us develop a mental picture of ourselves giving a masterful speech. Like COM techniques, visualization helps us overcome the mental and emotional causes of apprehension. Joe Ayres and Theodore S. Hopf, two scholars who have conducted extensive research on visualization, have found that if people can visualize themselves going through an entire speech preparation and speech making process, they will have a much better chance of succeeding when they are speaking.[12]

communication orientation motivation (COM) techniques designed to reduce anxiety by helping the speaker adopt a "communication" rather than a "performance" orientation toward the speech

performance orientation viewing public speaking as a situation demanding special delivery techniques in order to impress an audience aesthetically or viewing audience members as hypercritical judges who will be unforgiving about even our minor mistakes

communication orientation viewing a speech as just an opportunity to talk with a number of people about a topic that is important to the speaker and to the audience

visualization a method that reduces apprehension by helping speakers develop a mental picture of themselves giving a masterful speech

systematic desensitization a method that reduces apprehension by gradually having people visualize increasingly more frightening events

Visualization has been used extensively with athletes to improve sports performances. In a study of players trying to improve their foul-shooting percentages, players were divided into three groups. One group never practiced, another group practiced, and a third group visualized practicing. As we would expect, those who practiced improved far more than those who didn't. What seems amazing is that those who only visualized practicing improved almost as much as those who practiced.[13] Imagine what happens when you visualize and practice as well!

By visualizing the process of speech making, not only do people seem to lower their general apprehension, but they also report fewer negative thoughts when they actually speak.[14] So, you will want to use visualization activities as part of your speech preparation. To complete a visualization activity that will help you prepare your speeches, use your Challenge of Effective Speaking CD-ROM to access **Web Resource 2.1: Visualizing Your Success.** This audio activity will guide you through a visualization in which you will imagine that you successfully accomplish the complete speech preparation and presentation process. And for even more information about visualization, complete the InfoTrac College Edition exercise at the end of this chapter.

3. Systematic desensitization is a method that reduces apprehension by gradually having people visualize increasingly more frightening events. Individuals first learn procedures for relaxation, then learn to apply these to each of the anxiety-producing events that they visualize and so learn to remain relaxed when they encounter these anxiety-producing situations in real life.[15] This method is used to help people overcome the physical symptoms of public speaking apprehension. Since "relaxing" is easier said than done, these programs focus on teaching you deep muscle relaxation procedures. The process involves consciously tensing and then relaxing muscle groups in order to learn to recognize the difference between the two states. Then, while in a relaxed state, you imagine yourself in successively more stressful situations—for example, researching a speech topic in the library, practicing the speech out loud to a roommate, and finally giving a speech. The ultimate goal of systematic desensitization is to have us transfer the calm feelings we attain while visualizing to the actual speaking event. Calmness on command—and it works.

4. Public speaking skills training is the systematic teaching of the skills associated with the processes involved in preparing and delivering an effective public speech with the intention of improving speaking competence as a means of reducing public speaking apprehension. Skills training is based on the assumption that some of our anxiety about speaking in public is due to our realization that we do not know how to be successful, that we lack the knowledge and behaviors to be effective. Therefore, if we learn the processes and behaviors associated with effective speech making, then we will be less anxious.[16] Public speaking skills include those associated with the processes of goal analysis, audience and situation analysis, organization, delivery, and self-evaluation.[17]

All four of these methods for reducing public speaking apprehension have been successful at helping people reduce their anxiety. Researchers are just beginning to conduct studies to identify which techniques are most appropriate for a particular person. A study conducted by Karen Kangas Dwyer suggests that

public speaking skills training systematic teaching of the skills associated with the processes involved in preparing and delivering an effective public speech with the intention of improving speaking competence as a means of reducing public speaking apprehension

If people can visualize themselves going through an entire process, they will have a much better chance of succeeding when they are in the situation.

© Jeff Greenberg/PhotoEdit

the most effective program for combating apprehension is one that uses a variety of techniques but individualizes them so that the techniques are used in an order that corresponds to the order in which the individual experiences apprehension.[18] So, for example, if your immediate reaction when facing a speaking situation is to think worrisome thoughts ("I don't know what I'm supposed to do," "I'm going to make a fool of myself"), which then lead you to feel nervous, you would be best served by first undergoing skills training or COM techniques. Another person who immediately feels the physical sensations of apprehension (such as nausea and rapid heartbeat) would benefit from first learning systematic desensitization techniques before working with visualization or receiving skills training. So, to reduce your public speaking apprehension you may need to use all four techniques, but use them in an order that matches the order in which you experience apprehension.

Specific Techniques

Along with the four general methods just discussed as ways of systematically overcoming public speaking apprehension, public speaking instructors generally recommend several specific techniques to novice speakers.

1. Allow sufficient time to prepare. During the first few days of class you will receive a course syllabus, a plan for what will occur in class each day. Your instructor will let you know both how many and what kinds of speeches you will be giving this term. Armed with this information, you can develop a schedule based on preparing each speech over one or two weeks. If you have a topic at least a week or ten days prior to your assigned presentation, you should be able to allow enough time to prepare for your speech.

2. Practice your speech aloud. When you practice your speech aloud, you get comfortable hearing yourself talk about your topic. You identify sections of the speech where your ideas may not flow and where you need to do additional preparation. By the third or fourth time you have practiced aloud, you will notice your delivery becoming easier and you will gain confidence in your ability to present your ideas to others.

Many successful speakers not only practice aloud alone, but also practice in front of trusted friends who serve as a "practice" audience and give the speaker feedback. On the night before your speech, review your speech plan immediately before you go to sleep. That way, as you sleep your mind will continue to prepare.

3. Choose an appropriate time to speak. In some classes, the date on which you speak will be assigned but the order of speakers for the day is voluntary. Some students become more nervous when they sit and listen to others, so they are better off speaking early in the class period. Other students find that listening to their peers calms them, so they are better off speaking later in the class period. If given a chance, choose to speak at the time that is optimal for you.

4. Use positive self-talk. Immediately prior to getting up to speak, coach yourself with a short "pregame pep talk." Remind yourself about the importance of what you have to say. Remember all the hard work you have done to be prepared and recall how good you are when you are at your best. Remind yourself that nervousness is normal and useful. Tell yourself that you are confident and ready.

5. Face the audience. Face the audience with confidence. When it is time, walk purposefully to the front. Take a second or two to look at the audience. Take a deep breath as you smile and begin your well-rehearsed introduction.

6. Focus on sharing your ideas. Although you may feel nervous, your audience is unlikely to "see" it. Continue to focus on sharing your ideas with the audience rather than focusing on your nerves.

Gaining Confidence through Effective Speech Planning

Whether you are a marketing account manager presenting an advertising campaign idea to your corporate clients, a coach trying to motivate your team in its game with your arch rival, or a student giving a speech in class, you will have more confidence in your likelihood of success when you have developed an effective **speech plan**—a strategy for achieving your goal.

speech plan a strategy for achieving your goal

An effective speech plan is the result of a six-step process:

1. Selecting a specific speaking goal that is appropriate for the audience and occasion
2. Understanding your audience and adapting to it
3. Gathering and evaluating information to use in the speech
4. Organizing and developing ideas into a well-structured speech outline
5. Choosing visual aids that are appropriate for the audience
6. Practicing the speech wording and delivery

In the next section of this book, you will learn the skills associated with each of these steps. As you practice the skills, you will gain confidence in your ability to present your ideas effectively. Let's briefly preview what you will learn in each step.

Step 1: Select a Speech Goal That Is Appropriate for the Audience and Occasion

Your **speech goal** (or speech purpose) is a statement of what you want your audience to know, believe, or do. To arrive at such a goal, you begin by selecting a topic. Regardless of whether you are a renowned speaker or are preparing your very first speech, the advice is the same: Choose a topic that you know something about and that interests you or is important to you. Although there could be times in your life when you must speak on a topic that is unfamiliar to you, in this class *and* in the great majority of real-life speaking experiences, you will be speaking on topics that meet these tests.

speech goal a statement of what you want your listeners to know, believe, or do

Because your speech will be given to a particular audience, before you get very far you need to think about your specific audience: Who are they? What do they need to know about your topic? What do they already know? To answer these questions, you need to make a preliminary audience analysis based on their gender, culture, average age, education level, occupation, income level, and group affiliation. As you study these factors, you can assess the kinds of material the audience is likely to know and the information they are likely to respond to.

Likewise you also need to consider your setting: What is the size of the audience? When will the speech will be given? Where will the speech be given? What is the time limit for the speech? What is the specific assignment? Since you will be speaking in the same classroom all term, you can determine any peculiarities of the room that you need to take into consideration. Most important for this first speech are the size of the audience and your time limit.

Once you have a topic and have analyzed the audience and setting, you can phrase your speech goal. Every speech has a general and a specific goal. For most of your in-class speeches, your general goal is likely to be assigned to you. You will probably be giving either an informative speech, in which you want your audience to understand information, or a persuasive speech, in which you want your audience to believe something or act in a particular way. For an icebreaker speech, your goal is likely to be to have the audience enjoy your personal experience. But in a nonclassroom setting, your general goal is based on what is appropriate for your particular audience on the particular occasion.

Your specific speech goal articulates exactly what you want your audience to understand, believe, or do. For instance, for an informative speech, Glen, a member of the basketball team, might phrase his goal, "I want my audience to understand how to shoot a jump shot." Ling, an art history major, might phrase her goal, "I want the audience to have an appreciation of Ming porcelain."

Step 2: Understand Your Audience and Adapt to It

audience adaptation presenting ideas verbally, visually, and vocally in a way that will help the audience relate to them

Once you have a clear speech goal, you begin the task of understanding your specific audience and how to adapt your speech to it. **Audience adaptation** means presenting ideas verbally, visually, and vocally in a way that will help the audience relate to them. As you prepare for a speech, you will consider your specific audience's needs and seek to meet these needs continually as you develop your ideas.

For any speech, it is important to consider the audience's initial level of interest in your goal, their ability to understand the content of the speech, and their attitude toward you and your topic.

If you believe your audience has very little interest in your speech topic, you will need to adapt to them in order to help them understand why the topic is important to them. For instance, if Ling is talking with an audience that she believes has very little interest in understanding Ming porcelain, she may pique their interest by recounting how someone took an old vase to the *Antiques Road Show* TV program and discovered that it was from the Ming period and worth $40,000!

Suppose you were giving a speech on rationing during World War II. Your adaptation challenges would differ between the audience pictured here and an audience composed of young college students.

Not only will you need to adapt your speech by piquing audience interest, but if you believe that your audience doesn't know much about your topic, you will want to provide the basic information they need to understand your speech. For instance, if Ling is speaking to an audience that is unfamiliar with porcelain, she may need to explain briefly how porcelain is made and how it differs from other pottery before they will be able to understand how to identify Ming era vases.

Finally, you will need to adapt to your audience's initial attitudes toward your topic. If Kelly has chosen to speak on repealing the death penalty, she will need to understand where her audience stands on this topic before she begins. If the majority of her audience is pro–death penalty, then as she prepares she will adapt by selecting arguments and evidence that can be accepted by the audience.

Step 3: Gather and Evaluate Information to Use in the Speech

For most of your speeches, you will need additional information from research sources. You will also want to use some humorous, exciting, or interesting experiences and stories to illustrate your points. When you select a topic, although you already know something about, you will usually need more information that you can get from printed or interview sources. Regardless of the sources of your information, you will need to evaluate the information you gather and select the items that you deem to be valid and truthful. The more you know about your topic, the easier it is to evaluate the information you uncover in your research. For instance, Nora, who rides on the local volunteer Life Squad, will be able to give a better speech on CPR than a person with no practical experience who has learned about CPR from reading and interviewing others. Why? Because in the course of her volunteer work, Nora has actually used this skill and has real experiences to draw from. Likewise, as a student of art history, Ling is able to explain the characteristics of Ming porcelain because she has studied it in her History of Chinese Art class.

For your major class assignments, you may draw material from your own knowledge and experiences, observations, interviews, surveys, and research.

Step 4: Organize and Develop Ideas into a Well-Structured Speech Outline

You begin the process of organizing your speech by identifying the three or four major ideas you want your audience to remember. If the audience understands and remembers these main points, you will have achieved your speech goal. These main points are written in full sentences. Once you have identified these key ideas, you will combine them with your speech goal into a succinct thesis statement that describes specifically what you want your audience to understand when you are done speaking.

Main points must be carefully worded, and then they must be arranged in an organizational pattern that helps the audience understand and remember them. Two of the most basic organizational patterns are chronological and topical order. In later chapters, we'll consider several types of organization that you may want to use in your informative and persuasive speeches. Chronological means following an order that moves from first to last. So, Nora, who is planning to speak on how to perform CPR on a child, will organize her speech following the steps (what is done first, second, and third) involved in administrating CPR. In some circumstances, you may find that your speech is best presented topically. Topical means following an order of headings. For instance, Ling, who decides to inform her audience about the three characteristics that distinguish Ming vases from others, might choose to talk about the characteristic in ascending order with the most important characteristic last.

Having identified, phrased, and ordered the main points, you are now ready to outline the body of the speech. Although it is tempting to work out a speech as it comes to mind, speeches are not essays, and you will be more effective if you prepare a thorough outline.

After you have outlined the body of the speech, which includes noting elaborations, you can outline your introduction and conclusion. Your introduction should both get attention and lead into the body of the speech. Because there are never any guarantees that your audience is ready to pay full attention to the speech, an effective introduction draws the audience into what you are saying.

In your conclusion you will want to remind the audience of your main points and do so in a creative way that helps the audience remember them.

When you think you are done, review the outline to make sure that the parts are relevant to your goal. A written outline allows you to test the logic and clarity of your proposed organization. In Chapters 7 and 8 you will learn how to develop a complete outline comprised of the introduction, the main points, major subpoints of the body and key support, section transitions, and the conclusion, plus a list of sources. The length of your outline will depend on the length of your speech. In a speech of three to five minutes, the outline may contain up to 50 percent or more of the words in the speech; for a five- to eight-minute speech, up to 33 to 50 percent. And in speeches given in public later in life (often 30 to 45 minutes), the speech outline may contain as little as 20 percent of the words.

Although an expert who has spoken frequently on a topic may be able to speak effectively from a mental outline or a few notes, most of us benefit from the discipline of organizing and developing a complete speech outline.

Step 5: Choose Visual Aids That Are Appropriate for the Audience

"One picture is worth a thousand words" is an old saying with a lot of wisdom. So, even for a very short speech, you may decide to create a visual aid that will help clarify, emphasize, or dramatize what you say. Because audiences understand and retain information better when they have received that information through more than one sense, objects, models, charts, pictorial representations, projections, and computer graphics maximize the effect of high-quality information.

As you get ready to practice your speech, you will want to make sure that you consider when to use visual aids, how long to use them, and how to show visual aids so that everyone can see them.

Step 6: Practice the Wording and Delivery of the Speech

In your practice sessions you need to choose the wording of main points and supporting materials carefully. If you have not practiced various ways of phrasing your key ideas, you run the risk of missing a major opportunity for communicating your ideas effectively. In practice sessions work on clarity, vividness, emphasis, and appropriateness of language.

Although a speech is comprised of words, how effective you will be is also largely a matter of how well you use your voice and gestures in delivering your speech. You will want to present the speech enthusiastically, with vocal variety and emphasis, using good eye contact (look at members of the audience while you are speaking).

Very few people can present speeches effectively without considerable practice. The goal of practice is to give you confidence that you can talk comfortably with your audience and accomplish your speech goal within the time limit. Don't try to memorize the speech. Trying to memorize your speech is likely to add to your stage fright since you now may rightly fear forgetting what you planned to say. Instead, deliver your speech extemporaneously, that is, practiced until the ideas of the speech are firmly in mind, but varying the wording from practice to practice and in the actual delivery. Engaging in effective practice sessions enables you to become comfortable with your main points, the supporting material you use to explain them, and the transitioning from one point to another. We will consider detailed information about methods of practice in Chapter 11.

Exhibit 2.3 summarizes the six action steps of an effective speech plan in outline form. These steps will be explained in Part Two of this book. As you read, you will see specific speech preparation activities that are related to each action step. By completing all of these activities you will gain confidence in your ability to be effective when you give your speech.

SPOTLIGHT ON SPEAKERS

Cicero

Do As the Romans

As you study the speech planning process, you should be aware that these canons (or rules) date back to ancient Rome. Like many philosophers of his time, the great statesman, politician, and orator Marcus Tullius Cicero (106 B.C.–43 B.C.) had much to say about effective public speaking and issues of speech invention, arrangement, language, and delivery. Included in his recommendations were the following:

On invention/research: "Before beginning, prepare carefully."

On invention/speech goals: "The aim of Forensic Oratory is to teach, to delight, to move."

On invention/goodwill: "We were born to unite with our fellow men, and to join in community with the human race."

On language: "We should be as careful of our words as of our actions, and as far from speaking ill as from doing ill."

On arrangement/time: "When you wish to instruct, be brief. . . . Every word that is unnecessary only pours over the side of a brimming mind."

On faulty reasoning and evidence: "It is the act of a bad man to deceive by falsehood."

On poor speaker credibility: "Praise coming from so degraded a source, was degrading to me, its recipient."

On delivery: "They are eloquent who can speak of low things acutely, and of great things with dignity, and of moderate things with temper."

On delivery: "Great is our admiration of the orator who speaks with fluency and discretion."

On delivery: "A good orator is pointed and impassioned."

On confidence: "Confidence is that feeling by which the mind embarks in great and honorable courses with a sure hope and trust in itself."

Compare Cicero's quotes to the guidelines you're using for your speeches. Do you challenge yourself to be "classically" effective, as he suggests?

1 | Goals

I. Determine a speech goal

2 | Audience

II. Develop a strategy for audience adaptation

3 | Research

III. Gather information

4 | Organization

IV. Organize and develop your material

5 | Visual Aids

V. Create visual aids

6 | Delivery

VI. Practice speech wording and delivery

I. **Select a specific speech goal that is appropriate for the audience and occasion. (Chapter 4)**
   A. Select a topic from a subject area you know something about and that is important to you.
   B. Analyze your audience to assess their familiarity with and interest in your topic.
   C. Consider how your speech setting affects what is appropriate for you to talk about.
   D. Develop a speech goal statement tailored to your audience and the occasion.

II. **Understand your audience and plan to adapt to it. (Chapter 5)**
   A. Understand audience diversity.
   B. Understand audience interests so that material relates to them.
   C. Adjust content so it is appropriate for your audience's current understanding of this topic.
   D. Understand your audience's attitude toward your topic.
   E. Determine how you will establish your credibility with your audience.

III. **Gather and evaluate information you can use to reach your speech goal. (Chapter 6)**
   A. Survey manual and electronic sources of information and evaluate the quality of the information found.
   B. Observe and interview sources of information.
   C. Record on note cards information that is relevant to your specific speech goal.

IV. **Organize and develop ideas into a well-structured speech outline. (Chapters 7 and 8)**
   A. Write a thesis statement that identifies the specifics of your speech goal.
   B. Outline main points as complete sentences that are clear, parallel, and meaningful.
   C. Choose an organizational pattern that orders the main points in a way that aids audience understanding.
   D. Create section transitions to help the audience follow your organization.
   E. Create an introduction that gets attention, sets the tone, creates goodwill, builds your credibility, and leads into the body of the speech.
   F. Create a conclusion that both summarizes the material and leaves the speech on a high note.
   G. Review and complete the speech outline.

V. **Choose visual aids that are appropriate for the audience.**
   A. Consider drawings, maps, charts, and graphs
   B. Make sure your printed elements are large enough to be seen—use upper- and lowercase letters.
   C. Plan when to use visual aids and how to show them so that everyone can see them. (Chapter 9)

VI. **Practice the speech wording and delivery.**
   A. Practice until the wording is clear, vivid, emphatic, and appropriate. (Chapter 10)
   B. Practice until the delivery is enthusiastic, vocally expressive, fluent, spontaneous, and direct. (Chapter 11)
   C. Continue practicing until you can deliver it extemporaneously within the time limit. (Chapter 11)

Preparing a Narrative/
Personal Experience Speech

The **narrative/personal experience speech** is a presentation in which you recount an experience you have had and the significance you attach to that experience. Your professor is likely to assign an ungraded first speech to help you "get your feet wet." This first speech is designed to give you a chance to talk with your class without the pressure of a grade. It is an excellent opportunity for you to try out the basic speech preparation action steps we have just introduced. Let's look at how Eric Wais applied these steps to prepare his speech "The Funeral."

narrative/personal experience speech a presentation in which you recount an experience you have had and the significance you attach to that experience

The first step is to develop a speech goal that meets audience needs. For his personal experience speech assignment, Eric Wais considered several experiences that he thought the class would enjoy hearing about. For his topic, he finally chose the story of Dan's funeral.

Eric thought that his class would enjoy and relate to his experience, which dramatized what happens when people don't really know what they are talking about.

He knew that the speech would be for an audience of about fifteen classmates who were all traditional-age college students, that the assignment was a narrative/personal experience speech, and that the time limit was two to three minutes.

His general goal was to dramatize. Specifically, Eric wanted the audience to appreciate what can happen when the speaker knows less about the subject than do members of the audience.

His strategy for audience adaptation included using personal pronouns and other means of creating common ground by telling his personal experience. He also tried to be as specific as possible in relating the details so that the audience would have a clear and vivid mental picture of the events.

Because it was a personal experience narrative, Eric didn't need additional research; he only needed to reconstruct the details of his funeral experience.

Eric organized and developed his story in a way that dramatized his goal. He began his speech with a description of his friend, then recounted the funeral experience, and concluded by reinforcing the point of his story.

When you use narratives/personal experiences as a speech or in a speech, remember the following elements:

+ **A narrative usually has a point to it, a climax to which the details build up.** Think carefully about the point of your story and make sure it is appropriate.

+ **A narrative is developed with supporting details that give background to and embellish the story so that the point has maximum effect.** Try to select and develop details that heighten the impact.

+ **Narrative drama can be increased by using dialogue.** Dialogue gives an audience the experience of "being there" and increases their interest and involvement.

+ **A narrative is often is emotional.** Most narratives dramatize because they recount emotional incidents. They may be funny, tragic, or frightening, but effectively told personal experiences establish an emotional bond between speaker and audience.

Although Eric used no visual aids, some narratives can be enhanced with pictures of the event described, and of course effective narratives use language and nonverbals to paint vivid pictures of what happened. Eric used clear and vivid language to tell his story. He also practiced his speech several times until he was comfortable with his ability to tell the story.

Preparing a Narrative/Personal Experience Speech

Prepare a two- to three-minute personal experience (narrative) speech. Think about experiences you have had that were humorous, suspenseful, or dramatic that dramatized something that is important to you, and select one that you think your audience would enjoy hearing about.

The sample speech that follows is an example of a student speech that was given to meet this assignment. Use your Challenge of Effective Speaking CD-ROM to watch a video clip of Eric presenting his speech in class. Click on the Speech Interactive icon in the menu at the left, then click on Speech Menu in the menu bar at the top of the screen. Select "Narrative/Personal Speech: The Funeral" to watch the video (it takes a minute for the video to load).

Although the narrative speeches are not graded, you can identify some of the strengths of Eric's speech by using your CD-ROM to prepare an evaluation checklist and an analysis. You can then compare your answers to those of the authors. To complete the checklist electronically, click on Evaluation in the menu bar at the top of the screen. To prepare your feedback electronically, click on Analysis in the menu bar. To compare your answers to those provided by the authors, click the "Done" button.

SAMPLE SPEECH

The Funeral

About two years ago, my friend Dan moved to Minneapolis and about two months later he died in a motorcycle accident. It wasn't anybody's fault—he skidded on a patch of oil. But he left a lot of friends here and everyone took the news really hard. Dan was just so full of life—he really was a great guy to be around, always telling jokes, singing songs, his bands. He was a great guy to hang out with. He had "King of Saturday Night" tattooed across his back in giant letters. And that's how we all really liked to think of him. He was the guy you always wanted to spend your Saturday nights with because he knew how to have a great time.

So it was hard on all of us when we found out. The funeral was very difficult. We all showed up. It was really rough—it was really hard seeing him in the casket like that so quiet and so unlike we remembered him. They had taken out all of his piercings and they had covered up all of his tattoos for his family. But, uh, you know, it was still the Dan we all knew. It was just really hard to see him like that.

The crowd at church was actually a pretty funny group. The first couple of rows in church were all Dan's family, all middle-aged, middle-class white people in their suits and ties. And then the rest of the church was just a crazy assortment of people—blue hair, tattoos, and whatever anyone could come up with for nice funeral clothing— which in a lot of cases was just a clean T-shirt and a pair of jeans. That's all some people could do. And no one really minded. The service was really emotional, and, uh, it was really hard on all of us. Everyone was taking it really hard. And for a lot of us that wasn't really normal—we weren't really used to going through that with each other.

Um, but toward the end of the service, the priest stood up to give his eulogy. We were all crying and trying not to cry. He stood up and said, "I know Dan was a musician. And I think if Dan was here today, he'd want to sing us a song." And like I said we were all kind of busy with our own thoughts. We knew that this guy had never met Dan and didn't know him. But we were willing to put up with—we were willing to go along with it. But he paused, and he took out a sheet of paper and he said, "I think Dan would sing this song in particular for his friends and family. 'Did you ever know that you're my hero? You're everything I wish I could be.'" And he just said it so matter-of-factly that as soon as I heard it, I started laughing. I couldn't stop myself. And I felt awful about it, but I couldn't stop. And he just kept reading this song. The idea of Dan sitting on his motorcycle with tattoos and a cigarette hanging out of the corner of his mouth or standing up with one of his bands and singing this Bette Midler song was just so absurd to me that I just couldn't help just laughing out loud. And as the priest kept reading the lyrics to this awful song, I looked around and everyone in the back of the church was just screaming laughing—falling out of their seats laughing, rolling in the aisles. And the priest had no idea what was so funny. And the family certainly didn't think anything was funny about it. But, I think we all knew that it was the way Dan would have wanted it;—if he was there he would have been laughing right along with us. It was one big last joke for him and it's really my last memory of Dan, and I can't think of a better way to say good-bye. ∎

REFLECT ON ETHICS

Paul is scheduled to give his first speech—one in which he is supposed to talk about a personal experience he has had. Paul realizes that his nervousness is being heightened by the personal nature of the topic, because he thinks his experiences are really ordinary and he will bore the class. Suddenly he remembers his high school buddy James. Now James was a wow—and man, did he have the stories. So Paul thinks, hey, I'll just pretend that the "dead rat incident" happened to me. After all, no one knows it didn't. So, Paul develops his speech around this experience that James had. It's a great story, he delivers it well, and he receives an excellent response from his professor and class.

Is it ethical for Paul to relate the experience as his? Explain.

Summary

This chapter discusses speech apprehension, how careful preparation can help you develop confidence when you speak in public, and how to prepare for a first speech assignment.

Public speaking apprehension is the level of fear a person experiences when speaking. Signs of speech apprehension include physical, emotional, and cognitive reactions that vary from person to person. The level of apprehension varies over the course of speaking. The causes of speech apprehension include biologically based temperament, previous experience, and levels of skills.

Several methods are available for overcoming public speaking apprehension. General methods include communication orientation motivation (COM) techniques, visualization, systematic desensitization, and public speaking skills training. Specific techniques include allowing sufficient time to prepare, practicing the speech aloud, choosing an appropriate time to speak, using positive self-talk, facing the audience with confidence, and focusing on sharing your ideas.

Gaining confidence through effective speech planning reduces public speaking apprehension and increases speaking effectiveness. An effective speech plan is the product of six action steps. People are most likely to gain confidence in speaking by following this six-step process. The first step is to select a specific goal that is appropriate for the audience and occasion. The second step is to understand your audience and adapt material to it. The third step is to gather and evaluate information to use in the speech. The fourth step is to organize and develop ideas into a well-structured speech outline. The fifth step is to choose visual aids that are appropriate for the audience. And the sixth step is to practice the speech until delivery is enthusiastic, vocally expressive, fluent, spontaneous, and direct.

A good opening assignment is a narrative/personal experience speech in which you recount an experience you have had and the significance you attach to it. A narrative is a speech that has a point to it, a climax to which the details build up. It is developed with supporting details that give background to and embellish the story so that the point has maximum effect. A narrative often includes dialogue and is often humorous.

CHALLENGE ONLINE

Now that you've read Chapter 2, use your Challenge of Effective Speaking CD-ROM for quick access to the electronic study resources that accompany this text. Your CD-ROM gives you access to Eric's speech on pages 28–29, an evaluation checklist and analysis questions to help you identify the strengths of his speech, InfoTrac College Edition, Speech Builder Express, and the Challenge of Effective Speaking Web site. When you get to the Challenge of Effective Speaking home page, click on Student Book Companion Site in the Resource box at the right to access the online study aids for this chapter, including a digital glossary, review quizzes, and the chapter activities.

KEY TERMS

At the Challenge of Effective Speaking Web site, select chapter resources for Chapter 2. Print a copy of the glossary for this chapter, test yourself with the electronic flash cards, or complete the crossword puzzle to help you master the following key terms.

public speaking apprehension (14)
anticipation reaction (15)
confrontation reaction (15)
adaptation reaction (15)
communication orientation motivation (COM) (18)
performance orientation (18)
communication orientation (18)

visualization (18)
systematic desensitization (19)
public speaking skills training (18–19)
speech plan (21)
speech goal (21)
audience adaptation (22)
narrative/personal experience speech (27)

Visualization has been recognized as a means of improving performance in many areas, most specifically in athletics. Use your Challenge of Effective Speaking CD-ROM to access InfoTrac College Edition. Click on Subject Guide and type the words "visualization (mental images)," then click on View Periodical References, where more than seventy-five articles are listed. Scroll down and open the article "Visualization for Construction of Meaning during Study Time: A Quantitative Analysis" by Lauren Cifuenes and Yichuan Jane Hsieh, *International Journal of Instructional Media*, Summer 2003, v30 i3, or a similar article. Look specifically for suggested procedures for using visualization.

WEB RESOURCE

Access the Web resource for this chapter online at the Challenge of Effective Speaking Web site. Select the chapter resources for Chapter 2, then click on "Web Resources."

2.1 Visualizing Your Success (19)

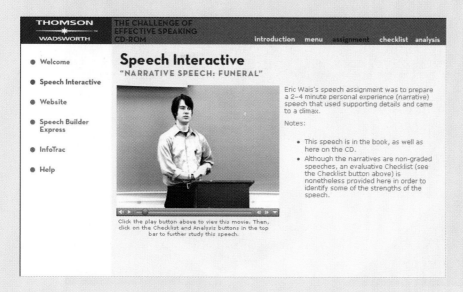

3

Effective Listening

© Colin Anderson/Brand X Pictures/Alamy Images

*A good listener tries to understand thoroughly
what the other person is saying.*

Kenneth A. Wells, *Guide to Good Leadership*

When Professor Norton finished her point on means of evaluating social legislation, she said, "Let me remind you that the primary criterion is the value to the general public at large, not the profit people can make from exploiting legislation."

As Ben, Shana, and Tim were walking from the class, Ben said, "I was glad to hear that Norton recognized the importance of making profit from social legislation."

"That wasn't her point," said Shawna. "She said that the emphasis is on the value to the general public."

"I'm sure she emphasized profitability," responded Ben. "Tim, what do you think she said?"

"Man, I don't even know what you're talking about. I was thinking about my math test this afternoon."

Does this conversation sound familiar to you? Have you had times when you'd swear that you heard right when you didn't? If your answer is "Not me," then we congratulate you, for this example illustrates three of the most common listening problems: missing what was said, hearing it but misunderstanding, and not listening or not remembering what was said.

In the last chapter we previewed the speech planning process that you will learn to use to prepare speeches. In this chapter we discuss listening, the other set of skills that you will be practicing and hopefully improving in this course.

According to the International Listening Association, "**Listening** is the process of receiving, constructing meaning from, and responding to spoken and or nonverbal messages."[1] Listening is important because of our time spent communicating, 50 percent or more is spent listening.[2] Although all of us have spent a great deal of time learning to read and write, less than 2 percent of us have had any formal listening training.[3] Yet effective listening is a key to success in most occupations. To read more about the importance of listening in various careers, read the InfoTrac College Edition article described at the end of this chapter.

listening the process of receiving, constructing meaning from, and responding to spoken and/or verbal messages

How effective are your listening skills? To find out, complete an inventory of your listening skills. Use your Challenge of Effective Speaking CD-ROM to access **Web Resource 3.1: Listening Inventory.** The information you glean from this inventory can help you pinpoint the specific skills you need to improve.

In this class, in addition to learning about how to prepare and deliver effective speeches, you will also become more effective at listening to the speeches of others. During this term, you will give perhaps five or six speeches, but you will probably hear more than sixty. As you listen to these speeches, you can practice the skills of effective listening.

In this chapter we describe how you can (1) improve your attention when listening to speeches, (2) improve your understanding and memory of the information you have heard, (3) critically analyze what has been said, and (4) assess the effectiveness of a speech. Finally, we will explain how, by giving effective post-speech feedback, you can fulfill your responsibilities to your classmates.

Attending to the Speech

attending paying attention to what the speaker is saying regardless of extraneous interferences

Attending is paying attention to what the speaker is saying regardless of extraneous interferences. Poor listeners have difficulty exercising control over what they attend to, often letting their mind drift to thoughts totally unrelated to the speech. Remember Tim's response to the question of which interpretation was more on target? "Man, I don't even know what you're talking about. I was thinking about my math test this afternoon." Consider your own experiences listening to speeches, such as your professors' class lectures. Are there times when you daydream about something else? Likewise, are there times when the speaker's mannerisms, such as throat clearing or pacing, distract you?

Four techniques can help us maintain our attention when we are listening to speeches (or to classroom lectures).

1. Get physically and mentally ready to listen. Suppose that a few minutes after class begins your professor says, "In the next two minutes, I'm going to cover some material that is especially important—in fact, I can guarantee that it will be on the test." What can you do to increase your attention? Well, physically you can alter your posture and sit upright in your chair, lean slightly forward, and stop any random physical movement. You can also look directly at the professor, because by making eye contact you increase the amount of information you get.[4] You can also react mentally by focusing all of your attention on what the professor is saying and blocking out the miscellaneous thoughts that are constantly passing through your mind.

2. Suspend judgment while you hear the speaker out. Far too often, we let a person's mannerisms and words "turn us off." If you find yourself upset by a speaker's ideas on gay marriage, abortion, or any controversial topic, instead of tuning out or getting ready to fight, work that much harder to listen objectively so that you can understand the speaker's position before you respond. Likewise, even when a speaker uses language that is offensive to you, you need to persevere and not be distracted. If we are not careful, we may become annoyed when a speaker mutters, stammers, or talks in a monotone. We need to focus instead on what is being said and overlook the speaker's disfluency.

3. Adjust to the listening goals of the situation. When you are listening to an after-dinner speaker for pleasure, you can afford to listen without much intensity. Unfortunately, many people approach all speech situations as if they were listening to pass time. But in public forums, in business settings, and in class, your goal is to understand and retain information or to listen critically to be able to evaluate what speakers say and how they say it. In the remainder of this chapter, we consider guidelines for adjusting your listening to meet the demands of these goals.

4. Identify the benefits of attending to the speaker's words. At times we do this almost automatically, especially when your professor says something like, "Pay attention to this explanation—I'll tell you right now, it will be the basis for one of the major test questions." But even if such a statement is not made, you can provide your own motivation. As you listen, ask yourself why and how you might use the specific information in the near future. For instance, you may be able to use the information in a discussion with your friends, or to help you solve work-related problems, or to personally improve. Identifying benefits can motivate you to apply each of the three previous behaviors even more regularly.

Understanding and Remembering Speech Information

The second aspect of listening to speeches is to understand and remember what the speaker is saying. **Understanding** is the ability to assign accurate meaning to what was said. **Remembering** is being able to retain and recall information that you have heard. Both understanding and remembering are facilitated by the use of active listening behaviors. **Active listening** includes identifying the organization of ideas, asking questions, silently paraphrasing, attending to nonverbal cues, and taking notes. To help you both understand better and retain more, let's consider these five active listening behaviors.

1. Determine the speaker's organization. Determining the organization helps you establish a framework for understanding and remembering the information.[5] In any extended message, an effective speaker has an overall organizational pattern for the information being presented. This organization includes a goal, the main points that develop the goal, and details that are presented to develop the main points. Effective listeners mentally (or physically) outline the organization so that when the speech is over they can cite the goal, the main points, and some of the key details.

For instance, during a PTA meeting, Gloria Minton, a teacher, gives a short presentation on the problem of bullying. Her goal is to explain what can be done in school to deter this behavior. In her speech she presents two main ideas: what teachers can do, and what students who are being harassed can do. She gives examples, statistics, and specific recommendations to develop each of the points she has made. When she is done, the audience members who have listened carefully are able to remember her goal and state steps that teachers and bullied students can take. Audience members may or may not remember the specific examples and statistics that she used to develop each point.

Although effective speakers organize their speeches so that it is easy to identify their goal, key points, and details, not all speakers are well organized. As a result, we as listeners have to pay close attention to grasp the main ideas. As you listen to a speech, ask yourself "What does the speaker want me to know or do?" (goal); then ask "What are each of the main points?"; and finally, ask "What details explain or support each of the main points?

In classroom lectures, feel free to ask the professor to supply any information you believe has not been presented clearly. (With student speeches or major speeches you hear in other settings, you are unlikely to be able to ask such questions.)

2. Ask yourself questions. As we have seen, asking yourself questions helps you identify key aspects of the speech. But asking yourself questions can also help you determine whether enough information was presented. For instance, if a speaker says "Swimming is an activity that provides exercise for almost every muscle," active listeners might inwardly question "How?" and then pay attention to the supporting material offered or request it if the speaker does not supply it.

3. Silently paraphrase key information. Silent paraphrases help listeners understand material. A **paraphrase** is a statement in your own words of the meaning you have assigned to a message. It is not simply repeating what has been said. After you have listened to a message, you should be able to summarize your understanding. So after the speaker explains the criteria for judging diamonds, you might say to yourself, "In other words, it's a trade-off—the bigger the diamond, the poorer the quality." If you cannot paraphrase a message, either the message was not clearly explained or you were not listening carefully enough.

understanding the ability to assign accurate meaning to what was said

remembering being able to retain and recall information that you have heard

active listening identifying the organization of ideas, asking questions, silently paraphrasing, attending to nonverbal cues, and taking notes

paraphrase a statement in your own words of the meaning you have assigned to a message

Note taking is an important method for improving your memory of what you have heard in a speech.

4. Attend to nonverbal cues. You can interpret messages more accurately by also observing the nonverbal behaviors accompanying the words. So, regardless of the topic, you should pay attention to the speaker's tone of voice, facial expression, and gestures. For instance, the director of parking might tell a freshman that he stands a good chance of getting a parking sticker for the garage, but the sound of the person's voice may suggest that the chances are not really that good.

5. Take good notes. Note taking is a powerful method for improving your memory of what you have heard in a speech. Not only does note taking provide a written record that you can go back to, but also by taking notes you take a more active role in the listening process.[6] In short, whenever you are listening to a speech, take notes.

What constitutes good notes varies by situation. For a short speech, good notes may consist of a statement of the goal, a brief list of main points, and a few of the most significant details. For a lengthy and rather detailed presentation (such as a class lecture), good notes will not only record the goal and the main points, but will also include sub-points of main points and more detailed statements of supporting material. Outlining is a useful note-taking strategy because it creates the structure of the information you have received and want to retain. Outlining helps you distinguish among main points, subpoints, and supporting material.

Ideally, the notes you produce will be similar to the outline notes that the speaker used. You can test your ability to attend, understand, and retain what you hear by using your Challenge of Effective Speaking CD-ROM to access **Web Resource 3.2: Listening Test.** Select the chapter resources for Chapter 3, then click on "Web Resources."

Critically Analyzing a Speech

As we have seen, to get the most out of a speech we must not only pay attention to what is said but must also do what we can to understand and remember it. But good listening doesn't stop here. The third step in effective listening is **critical analysis** of a speech—the process of evaluating what you have heard in order to determine its completeness, usefulness, and trustworthiness. Critical analysis is especially important when the speaker expects you to believe, support, or act on what was said. If you don't critically analyze what you hear, you risk going along with ideas that violate your values. When you analyze a speech, consider the following:

critical analysis the process of evaluating what you have heard in order to determine a speech's completeness, usefulness, and trustworthiness

1. **Speaker credibility**
   How did the speaker gain expertise on this subject?
   Does the speaker appear to be knowledgeable?
   What did the speaker do or say that made you believe what was said?
   Why should you trust this speaker?

2. **Information quality**

Did the speaker convey enough high-quality information to ensure understanding?

Did the speaker present enough examples and other supporting details and explanations to enable us to apply the information?

Did the speaker present facts to support the ideas, or just opinions?

Did the speaker identify the sources of the ideas, facts, and other material that was presented?

Did the speaker present both sides of controversial issues?

Was enough information or evidence presented to support controversial ideas?

3. **Organizational logic**

Were the speaker's ideas well ordered?

Did they follow logically from one another?

Were important ideas missing that should be considered?

4. **Emotional message**

What specific emotions, if any, was the speaker appealing to during the speech?

Was the emotional appeal supported by high-quality information?

Was there an ethical use of emotional appeal?

By critically analyzing the speaker's credibility, the quality of information presented, the logic of the organization used, and the emotional overtones of the message, effective listeners thoughtfully consider if they understand, believe, support, and/or want to act on what they have learned in the speech.

Exhibit 3.1 summarizes effective and ineffective listening behaviors related to attending to what is said, understanding and remembering information, and critically analyzing the speech.

REFLECT ON ETHICS

As they were returning from a rally at the University Field House in which they heard candidates for the two congressional districts that surrounded the university, Nikita asked Lance what he thought of the speech given by Steve Chabot, the Republican candidate for office in the first district.

"Chabot, he's just like any Republican, he's going to make sure that big business is all right."

"I didn't hear him talking about big business. I thought he was talking about the importance of limiting the amount of federal government intrusion in state matters."

"Sure, that's what he said, but we know what he really meant."

"I asked you what you thought of the speech. What ideas did he present that turned you off?"

"Listen, you don't really have to listen to any Republican speaking. Everyone knows that Republicans are for big business and only Democrats are going to watch out for people like us."

1. Is Lance's failure to listen critically an ethical issue? If so, why?
2. If Lance really had been listening critically, what should he be discussing with Nikita?

EXHIBIT 3.1 Effective and ineffective listening behaviors

	Effective listening behavior	Ineffective listening behavior
Attending to the speech	Physically and mentally focusing on what is being said, even when information doesn't seem relevant	Seeming to listen, but looking out the window and letting your mind wander
	Adjusting listening behavior to the specific requirements of the situation	Listening the same way regardless of type of material
Understanding/ remembering speech information	Determining organization by identifying goals, main points, and supporting information	Listening to individual bits of information without regard for structure
	Asking yourself questions to help you identify key aspects of the speech	Seldom or never reconsidering what was said
	Silently paraphrasing to solidify understanding	Seldom or never paraphrasing
	Seek out subtle meanings based on nonverbal cues	Ignoring nonverbal cues
	Taking good notes	Relying on memory alone
Critically analyzing speeches	Assessing speaker credibility, information quality, organizational logic, and emotional nature of messages	Relying on gut reactions to the speech

Evaluating Speech Effectiveness

In many situations outside of the classroom, attending, understanding and retaining information, and critically analyzing the speech are sufficient. But at times, particularly in class, we want to or are called upon to **evaluate speech effectiveness**—to determine how well you believe a speaker meets key criteria, or put another way, to grade the speech.

The ultimate test of a speech's effectiveness is how well it accomplishes its goal. Yet an overall judgment of a speech's effectiveness can be tricky to make. For example, in class we will likely be asked to rank the speeches we've heard—which did we think was best, and so on. For speeches outside of class we may be asked (or we may want to determine) whether we would say "the speech was excellent," or "it was one of the best we've heard," or "the speech was OK," or in some cases, "the speech was just not worth listening to."

Although it is important to know how to evaluate speech effectiveness, it is also useful to know how to use that information to give meaningful postspeech feedback to others in class. One goal of postspeech feedback is to praise efforts at meeting the particular criteria. The better we are at emphasizing successful efforts, the more likely students who are speaking next are likely to try to emulate those efforts. The second goal of postspeech feedback is to show ways that students could have done even better on primary criteria. We should operate under the assumption that all students are trying to use skills effectively. But regardless of how well students might have done with various skills, they are likely to be able to do even better. Thus the postspeech feedback can give specific examples of

evaluation of speech effectiveness how well you believe a speaker meets key criteria

When critiquing classmates' speeches, begin with positive comments, because people are likely to continue behaviors for which they have been praised.

how students could have done even better. Although this kind of feedback is useful to those who have spoken, it is especially useful for those who will be speaking next time.

Notice that we always begin with positive feedback, because people are likely to continue doing things they are praised for. Be sure to make your comments as specific as you can. Instead of saying "Mary sounded very enthusiastic," you might say "Mary's delivery was particularly good; she did an excellent job in varying pitch and emphasizing key words."

After everyone has had a chance to share examples of what was well done, it is equally important to offer suggestions for what the speakers might have done to make their speeches even better. Notice we don't say what was bad. But regardless of how good a speech is, it can always be made better. Even an "A" speech can be improved. As with positive feedback, it is useful to phrase advice for improvement very specifically. Although you might start by saying "I think speakers could have done even better with sectional transitions," you will want to continue with a statement such as "I particularly liked the way Jack said, 'Now that we've seen one way to test whether a diamond is real, let's consider a second way.' I would like to have heard more of those kinds of statements in the speeches." This specific, constructive phrasing, shows speakers how they can do even better in their next speeches.

The following are the **general criteria**—criteria that we can use as a starting point for evaluating any speech. As a general guide, evaluation of speech effectiveness is determined by how well you believe a speaker has met these criteria.

general criteria criteria that we can use as a starting point for evaluating any speech

1. **Content of the speech**

   Does the speaker seem to have expertise in the subject areas?

   Does the speaker have high-quality sources for the information given in the speech?

   Does the speaker reveal the sources of the information?

   Are visual aids appropriate and well used?

   Does the speaker establish common ground and adapt the content to the audience's interests, knowledge, and attitudes?

2. **Organization of the speech**

   Does the introduction of the speech get attention, build, and lead into the topic?

   Has the speaker stated a clear goal for the speech?

   Are the main points of the speech clearly stated, parallel, and meaningful?

   Do transitions lead smoothly from one point to another?

   Does the information presented explain or support each of the main points?

   Does the conclusion summarize the main points and end the speech on a high note?

3. **Language of the speech**

   Is the language clear?

   Is the language vivid?

   Is the language emphatic?

   Is the language appropriate?

4. **Delivery of the speech**

   Does the speaker sound enthusiastic?

   Does the speaker show sufficient vocal expressiveness?

   Is the presentation spontaneous?

   Is the presentation fluent?

   Does the speaker look at the audience?

   Were the pronunciation and articulation acceptable?

   Does the speaker have good posture?

   Does the speaker have sufficient poise?

As we will see later in this text, for each speech you give this term (and for the different kinds of speeches you will hear in real-life situations), there are additional criteria you will want to consider. For instance, to evaluate an informative demonstration speech effectively, the criteria you use may need to include evaluations of the visual aids used in the demonstration and how well the demonstration followed a sequential order; in contrast, the criteria you use to evaluate a persuasive speech of conviction would include evaluating the reasons given and the evidence in support of those reasons.

For each type of speech that you study in this text, we will provide a specific checklist you can use to evaluate this type of speech. The customized critique sheets will include the primary criteria (specific skills) your instructor is expecting speakers to demonstrate in this particular speech as well as general criteria, skills that speakers will attempt to meet in all speeches. For instance, for your first major speech assignment (see Chapter 11), the primary criteria on the checklist include how well organized the speech is and how well it is delivered.

Summary

Listening is the process of receiving, constructing meaning from, and responding to spoken and/or nonverbal messages. Effective listening in public speaking settings is an active process that requires the skills of attending, understanding and remembering, analyzing critically, and evaluating speech effectiveness.

Attending (hearing) effectiveness is sharpened by getting ready to listen, hearing the speaker out regardless of your thoughts or feelings, adjusting attention to the listening goals of different situations, and identifying benefits of attending to the speaker.

Understanding and remembering are enhanced by determining the speaker's organization, asking rhetorical questions, silently paraphrasing, paying attention to nonverbal cues, and taking good notes.

Critical analysis is the process of determining how truthful, useful, and trustworthy you judge a speaker and the speaker's information to be. Critical analysis requires assessing the speaker's credibility, judging the quality of the information sources, evaluating the organization and information sources of the speech, and understanding the emotions and emotional appeals used.

In public speaking classes, effective listeners provide feedback by critiquing the speeches of others. Because overall speaking effectiveness is complex, effective critics base their evaluation on how well the speaker meets the specific criteria related to the type of speech that has been given. Effective feedback includes citing specific strengths of speeches and ways that speakers can improve.

CHALLENGE ONLINE

Now that you've read Chapter 3, use your Challenge of Effective Speaking CD-ROM for quick access to the electronic study resources that accompany this text. Your CD-ROM gives you access to InfoTrac College Edition, Speech Builder Express, and the Challenge of Effective Speaking Web site. When you get to the Challenge of Effective Speaking home page, click on "Student Book Companion Site" in the Resource box at the right to access the online study aids for this chapter, including a digital glossary, review quizzes, and the chapter activities.

KEY TERMS

At the Challenge of Effective Speaking Web site, select chapter resources for Chapter 3. Print a copy of the glossary for this chapter, test yourself with the electronic flash cards, or complete the crossword puzzle to help you master the following key terms.

listening (33)
attending (34)
understanding (35)
remembering (35)
active listening (35)

paraphrase (35)
critical analysis (36)
evaluation of speech
    effectiveness (38)
general criteria (39)

INFOTRAC COLLEGE EDITION EXERCISE

Use your Challenge of Effective Speaking CD-ROM to access InfoTrac College Edition. Using the key words "listening skills" in the Subject Guide, search for the article "Is Anyone Listening (Listening Skills in the Corporate Setting)," by Jennifer J. Salopek, or a similar article. Although 80 percent of a group of businesspeople indicated that listening is important, this article points out that they also rated the skill as most lacking in business employees (Salopek, *Training and Development*, September 1999). How does the article answer the question "Why don't we listen better?" What suggestions for improving listening mentioned in the article do you find most beneficial?

WEB RESOURCES

Access the Web resources for this chapter online at the Challenge of Effective Speaking Web site. Select the chapter resources for Chapter 3, then click on "Web Resources."

3.1 Listening Inventory (33)　　　　　　　**3.2 Listening Test** (36)

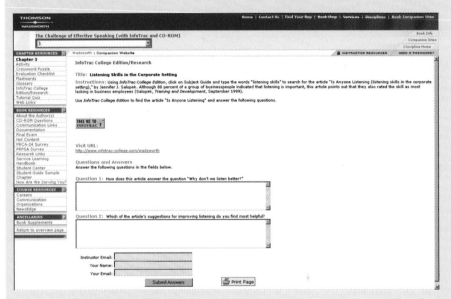

Determining a Speech Goal That Meets Audience Needs

The secret of success is constancy to purpose.
Benjamin Disraeli, speech, June 24, 1870

Determining a speech goal that meets audience needs

A. Brainstorming for topics
B. Analyzing your audience
C. Analyzing your setting
D. Articulating your goal by determining the response that meets audience needs

Donna Montez is a marine biologist. She knows that her audience wants to hear her talk about marine biology, but she doesn't know what aspect of the topic she should focus on.

Romeo Brown has been invited to speak to a student assembly at the inner-city middle school he attended. He has a lot he could say to these students who are so much like him, but he really wants them to understand what they need to do now in order to have a shot at going to college.

Dan Wong is taking a public speaking class. His first speech is scheduled for two weeks from tomorrow. As of today, he doesn't have the foggiest idea what he is going to talk about.

In real-life settings, people are invited to speak because they have expertise on a particular subject or have some relationship to the audience. Nevertheless, choosing exactly what to speak about is usually left in the hands of the speaker. So, although Donna and Romeo may have an inkling about what the audience expects, they, like Dan, will need to take the first action step, which is to determine a specific speech goal that is adapted to the audience and setting.

In this chapter we will explain each of the five substeps that help speakers with this task. These five substeps are identifying topics, analyzing your audience, understanding the speech setting, choosing a topic, and finally, developing a specific speech goal. Although we have to discuss each task separately, in practice they overlap and can be completed in a different order.

Identifying Topics

What do you know? What has interested you enough so that you have gained some expertise? Our speech topics should come from subject areas in which we already have some knowledge and interest. What is the difference between a subject and a topic? A **subject** is a broad area of expertise, such as movies, cognitive psychology, computer technology, or the Middle East. A **topic** is a narrow, specific aspect of a subject. So, if your broad area of expertise is movies, you might feel qualified to speak on a variety of topics such as how the Academy Awards nomination process works, the relationships between movie producers, directors, and distributors, or how technology is changing movie production.

In this section you will learn how to identify subject areas in which you have interest and knowledge and then, from those subject areas, to identify and select potential specific topics that you can use for the speeches you will be assigned to make in class.

subject a broad area of expertise, such as movies, cognitive psychology, computer technology, or the Middle East

topic some specific aspect of a subject

Listing Subjects

You can identify potential subjects for your speeches simply by listing those areas that (1) are important to you and (2) you know something about. These areas will probably include such things as your vocation or area of formal study (major, prospective profession, or current job), your hobbies or leisure activities, and special interests (social, economic, educational, or political concerns). So, if retailing is your actual or prospective vocation, skateboarding is your favorite activity, and problems of illiteracy, substance abuse, and immigration are your special concerns, then these are subject areas from which you can identify topics for your speeches.

At this point, it is tempting to think, "Why not just talk on a subject I know an audience wants to hear about?" But in reality, all subject areas can interest an audience when speakers use their expertise or insight to enlighten the audience on a particular subject.

Exhibit 4.1 contains subjects that students in two classes at the University of Cincinnati listed under (1) major or vocational interest, (2) hobby or activity, and (3) issue or concern.

Brainstorming for Topic Ideas

Recall that a topic is a specific aspect of a subject, so from one subject, you can list numerous topics by **brainstorming**—an uncritical, nonevaluative process of generating associated ideas. When you brainstorm, you list as many ideas as you can without evaluating them. Brainstorming allows you to take advantage of the basic commonsense principle that just as it is easier to select a correct answer to a multiple-choice question than to think of the answer to the same question without the choices, so too it is easier to select a topic from a list than to come up with a topic out of the blue.

Under the subject of tennis, for example, a person who plays tennis as a hobby might be able to brainstorm a list of fifteen, twenty, or more topics such as types of serves, net play, types of courts, player rating systems, and equipment improvements, to name just a few. From these lists of topic ideas, you will be able to

brainstorming an uncritical, nonevaluative process of generating associated ideas

Major or Vocational Interest	Hobby or Activity	Issue or Concern
communication	soccer	crime
disc jockey	weightlifting	governmental ethics
marketing	music	environment
public relations	travel	media impact on society
elementary teaching	photography	censorship
sales	mountain biking	same-sex marriage
reporting	hiking	taxes
hotel management	volleyball	presidential politics
physics	tennis	cloning
fashion design	genealogy	global warming
law	backpacking	child abuse
human resources	horseback riding	road rage
computer programming	sailing	illiteracy
nurse	swimming	effects of smoking
doctor	magic	women's rights
politics	gambling	abortion

develop speeches not only for this course but also for other settings in which you might give speeches. By completing Speech Planning Action Step 1, Activity 1A: Brainstorming for Topics, you can develop a list of topic ideas that you can use for your speeches in this class.

To brainstorm for potential topics, follow the three steps in Speech Planning Action Step 1, Activity 1A. To see a sample of what one student who completed this exercise came up with, see the Student Response to Activity 1A.

For additional details on how to use brainstorming for developing topics, read "Brainstorming by Yourself," available through InfoTrac College Edition. Use your Challenge of Effective Speaking CD-ROM to access Web Resource 4.1: Brainstorming.

SPEECH PLANNING   ACTION STEP 1

1 | Goals

ACTIVITY 1A **Brainstorming for Topics**

The goal of this activity is to help you identify prospective topics for speeches.

1. Divide a sheet of paper into three columns. Label column 1 with your vocation or major, such as Acting; label column 2 with a hobby or an activity, such as Chess; and label column 3 with a concern or an interest, such as Water Pollution.
2. Working on one column at a time, brainstorm a list of at least fifteen related topics for each column.
3. Place a check mark next to the three topics in each list that you would most enjoy speaking about.
4. Keep the lists for future use in choosing a topic for an assigned speech.

You can go online to print out a worksheet that will help you complete this activity. Use your Challenge of Effective Speaking CD-ROM to access Action Step Activity 1A.

ACTIVITY 1A Brainstorming for Topics

Vocation or major	Hobby or activity	Concern or interest
Geology	*Lacrosse*	*Environment*
faults	✓ *history*	✓ *habitat destruction*
folds	*rules*	*rain forests*
✓ *volcanoes*	*equipment*	*extinctions*
earthquakes	*helmet*	*jaguars*
oil	*pads*	*air pollution*
gems	*Crosse*	*water pollution*
✓ *diamond tests*	✓ *skills*	*fertilizers*
fossils	*ball*	✓ *oil wells*
Hopper crystals	*field*	*industrialization*
Morrison formation	*players*	*overpopulation*
geophysics	*midfield*	*Washington salmon*
archeology	*goalie*	✓ *littering*
soil	✓ *strategy*	*lakes*
✓ *hydrology*	*break-away*	*rivers*
drilling	*attack*	*ozone layer*

Analyzing the Audience

Because speeches are given for a particular audience, before you can finally decide on your topic you need to understand who will be in your prospective audience. **Audience analysis** is the study of the intended audience for your speech. During your audience analysis you will want to develop a demographic profile of your audience that includes age, gender, socioeconomic background, race, ethnicity, religion, geographic uniqueness, and language. You will also want to understand audience members' knowledge of and attitudes toward your topic. This information will help you choose from your topic lists one that is appropriate for most audience members. You will also use your audience analysis in **audience adaptation**—the process of tailoring your information to the specific speech audience. To read an interesting article on the importance of careful audience analysis, use your Challenge of Effective Speaking CD-ROM to access Web Resource 4.2: Defining Your Audience.

audience analysis the study of the intended audience for your speech

audience adaptation the process of tailoring your information to the specific speech audience

Types of Audience Data Needed

The first step in analyzing the audience is to gather audience demographic data and subject-specific information to determine in what ways audience members are similar to and different from you and from each other.

DEMOGRAPHIC INFORMATION

From demographic information you will be able to make educated inferences about how familiar the audience is with your subject area and their attitudes toward it. You will want demographic information about the age, education, gender, income, occupation, race, ethnicity, religion, geographic uniqueness, and language of your audience. You will also want to know about the audience mem-

Effective speakers use audience age to predict interest in and attitudes toward their topic. What might you conclude about this audience's attitudes toward and interest in the topic of child care?

© Davis Barber/PhotoEdit

bers' level of knowledge and attitude toward your subject. Exhibit 4.2 presents a list of questions to answer when acquiring demographic information about an audience.

SUBJECT-RELATED AUDIENCE DATA

Not only will you want to understand the demographic makeup of your audience, but you will also want to learn about the average knowledge level your audience members have on your subject, their interest in the subject, their attitudes toward the subject, and their perceptions of your credibility. Let's take a closer look at each of these.

1. Audience knowledge. What can you expect your average audience member to already know about your subject? What topics are likely to provide new information for most of them? It is important that you choose a topic geared to the background knowledge you can expect audience members to have. When you choose a topic that most audience members already know about, you will have to be really creative or you will bore them. On the other hand, if you choose a topic for which your audience has insufficient background, you will have to provide it or risk frustrating, confusing, or losing them. For instance, if your subject is music, you can expect that an audience of traditional-age college students will know the general history of rock and roll, including the major performers. So the topic "A Brief History of Rock and Roll" is unlikely to offer them much new information. However, a speech on the contributions of girl bands to the development of rock and roll would draw on the audience's background knowledge but offer information that is new to most audience members.

2. Audience interest. How attracted are audience members likely to be to your subject? For instance, suppose you would like to speak on the subject of cancer drugs. If your audience is made up of health care professionals, you can assume that because of their vocations they will be curious about the subject. But if your audience is this beginning public speaking class, then unless they have had a personal experience with cancer they may not naturally relate to your subject, so you will need to choose a topic that can capture their interest or work hard as you develop your speech to overcome their disinterest.

EXHIBIT 4.2   Demographic audience analysis questions

Age. What is the age range of your audience, and what is the average age?

Education. What percentage of your audience has a high school, college, or postgraduate education?

Gender. What percentage of your audience is male? female?

Socioeconomic Background. What percentage of your audience comes from high-, middle-, or low-income families?

Occupation. Is a majority of your audience from a single occupational group or industry, or do audience members come from diverse occupational groups?

Race. Are most members of your audience of the same race, or is there a mixture of races?

Ethnicity. What ethnic groups are represented in the audience? Are most audience members from the same cultural background?

Religion. What religious traditions are followed by audience members?

Geographic Uniqueness. Are audience members from the same state, city, or neighborhood?

Language. What languages do a significant number of members of the audience speak as a first language? What language (if any) is common to all audience members?

Knowledge of Subject. What can I expect that the audience already knows about my subject? How varied is the knowledge level of audience members?

Attitude toward Subject. What can I expect my audiences' feelings to be about my subject?

3. Audience attitude toward the subject. How does your audience feel about your subject? This is especially important when you want to influence their beliefs or move the audience members to action.

You can determine your audience's attitudes toward your subject directly by surveying them, which we will discuss in the next section. If you cannot survey the audience directly, you might try to see if published opinion polls related to your subject are available. Then you can estimate your audience members' attitudes by studying these opinion polls and extrapolating their results to your audience. To access links to two respected polling organizations, use your Challenge CD-ROM to access Web Resource 4.3: Public Opinion Polls. Finally, in some cases you will be forced to estimate the audience's attitudes from the occasion and the demographic information you have acquired. For instance, if your subject is affirmative action, you can infer that an audience of African American and Latino working-class people is likely to favor it, whereas an audience of professional-class white men is likely to be against it.

Once you understand your audience's attitude toward your subject, you can choose a topic that will allow you to influence rather than alienate the audience. For example, suppose you want to speak on the subject of gay rights and you have determined that your audience is somewhat hostile to the subject. In this case you might choose to speak on the topic of preventing gay bashing rather than tackle the more sensitive issue of gay marriage. Or, should you choose to speak on legalizing gay marriage, your awareness of audience attitudes should guide how you develop your speech.

Even Conan O'Brien must consider his audience's knowledge of, interest in, and attitudes toward various subjects when he plans his opening monologue.

credibility the perception that you are knowledgeable, trustworthy, and personable

survey a questionnaire designed to gather information directly from people

two-sided items survey items that force the respondent to choose between two answers, such as yes/no, for/against, or pro/con

multiple-response items survey items that give the respondent several alternative answers from which to choose

4. **Audience attitude toward you as a speaker.** Will your audience recognize you as a subject matter expert? Will they know that beforehand, or will you have to establish your credibility as you speak? **Credibility** is based on the perception that you are knowledgeable (have the necessary understanding that allows you to explain the topic well), trustworthy (are being honest, dependable, and ethical), and personable (show enthusiasm, warmth, friendliness, and concern for audience members). You will want to choose a topic that allows the audience to perceive you as credible and to believe that you know what you are talking about.

Methods for Gathering Audience Data

1. **You can collect data through surveys.** Although it is not always possible, the most direct way to collect audience data is to survey the audience. A **survey** is a questionnaire designed to gather information directly from people. Some surveys are done as interviews; others are written forms that are completed by the participants. The four kinds of items or questions most likely to be used in a survey are called two-sided, multiple-response, scaled, and open-ended.

✦ **Two-sided items** force the respondent to choose between two answers, such as yes/no, for/against, or pro/con. Suppose you wanted to understand your audience members' attitudes on the subject of TV. You might phrase several questions with two-sided answers, such as:

Do you believe that prime-time TV shows contain too much violence?

_____ Yes _____ No

Do you watch any of the *Law and Order* TV shows?

_____ Yes _____ No

Two-sided items are easy to use in an interview, and the answers are easy to sort during analysis.

✦ **Multiple-response items** give the respondent several alternative answers from which to choose. These items are especially useful for gathering demographic data. For example:

Which best describes your religious tradition?

_____ Protestant   _____ Evangelical   _____ Catholic

_____ Jewish   _____ Buddhist   _____ Muslim

_____ atheist   _____ other

Multiple-response items can also be used to assess the extent of knowledge that audience members have about a topic. For example, a speaker might assess audience members' knowledge about diamonds with the following question:

Please indicate what you know about diamonds by placing an "X" next to each topic you already know about.

_____ How to value a diamond

_____ How diamonds are made

_____ How to tell the difference between a diamond and a fake

_____ Blood diamonds

+ **Scaled items** measure the direction and/or intensity of an audience member's feeling or attitude toward something. For example:

> Indicate the extent to which you agree or disagree with the following statement:
>
> There is too much violence on prime-time TV.
>
> ___ Strongly   ___ Agree   ___ Neutral   ___ Disagree   ___ Strongly
>   agree   disagree

Scaled items can also be used to assess audience interest in a subject. For example:

> Please indicate, by circling the appropriate response, how interested you are in learning about each of the following.
>
> How to value diamonds:
>
> _____ Very interested _____ Somewhat interested _____ Uninterested
>
> How diamonds are cut:
>
> _____ Very interested _____ Somewhat interested _____ Uninterested
>
> Blood diamonds:
>
> _____ Very interested _____ Somewhat interested _____ Uninterested

+ **Open-ended items** encourage respondents to elaborate on their opinions without forcing them to answer in a predetermined way. These items yield rich information, but the wide variety of responses make them difficult to analyze. For example, to determine what you would need to do to establish your credibility on the subject of TV violence you might ask:

> How can you tell if someone is an expert on TV violence?

2. You can gather data through informal observation. If you are familiar with members of your audience (as you are with members of your classroom audience), you can get much of the significant data about them through informal observation. For instance, after being in class for even a couple of sessions, you should be able to estimate the approximate age or age range, the ratio of men to women, and their racial makeup. Because you are all in college, you know the educational level. From clothing and other cues, you can estimate the socioeconomic background. As you listen to your classmates talk, you will learn more about their interest in, knowledge of, and attitudes about many issues.

3. You can gather data by questioning the person who invited you to speak. When you are invited to speak to a group you are unfamiliar with, ask your contact person to answer the demographic questions in Exhibit 4.3. Even when the person cannot provide answers to all of the questions, the information you get will be helpful. If necessary, probe your contact person to at least estimate answers for those demographics that are likely to be most important for your topic. For instance, you may be speaking on a topic for which audience education level is especially important.

4. You can make educated guesses about audience demographics and attitudes. If you can't get information in any other way, you will have to make educated guesses based on such indirect information as the general makeup of the people who live in a specific community and belong to a group like this, or the kinds of people who are likely to attend the event or occasion. Suppose, for example, that you are asked by a nonprofit group you support to give a speech on volunteer opportunities with this charity to a meeting of high school guidance

scaled items survey items that measure the direction and/or intensity of an audience member's feeling or attitude toward something

open-ended items survey items that encourage respondents to elaborate on their opinions without forcing them to answer in a predetermined way

counselors who oversee community service projects for students. You can infer a number of things about audience members. First, all will be college-educated high school counselors from your city. They will all speak English. There are likely to be more women than men, and their ethnic backgrounds can be assumed to be similar to that of your community. They will be interested in your topic, but their knowledge of the specific opportunities at your agency will vary.

EXHIBIT 4.3   Audience analysis summary form

My subject is _____

Data were collected:

___ by survey

___ by direct observation

___ by questioning the person who invited me

___ by educated guessing

Demographic Data

1. The average audience member's education level is ___ high school ___ college ___ postgraduate.

2. The ages range from ___ to ___. The average age is about ___.

3. The audience is approximately ___ percent male and ___ percent female.

4. My estimate of the average income level of the audience is ___ upper ___ middle ___ lower.

5. Most audience members are of ___ the same occupation/major (which is _____) ___ different occupations/majors.

6. Most audience members are of ___ the same race (which is _____) ___ a mixture of races.

7. Most audience members are of ___ the same religion (which is _____) ___ a mixture of religions.

8. Most audience members are of ___ the same nationality (which is _____) ___ a mixture of nationalities.

9. Most audience members are from ___ the same state ___ the same city ___ the same neighborhood ___ different areas.

10. Most audience members speak ___ English as their first language ___ English as a second language (ESL).

Subject-Specific Data

1. The average audience member's knowledge of the subject will be ____ extensive ____ moderate ____ limited, because _____.

2. The average audience member's interest in this subject is likely to be ____ high ____ moderate ____ low, because _____.

3. The average audience member's attitude toward my subject is likely to be ____ positive ____ neutral ____ negative, because _____.

4. My initial credibility with the audience is likely to be ____ high ____ medium ____ low, because _____.

Whether you survey your audience, rely on informal observation, question the person who invited you to speak, or make educated guesses about audience demographics and subject-related information, you will want to record the information in a form that is convenient to use. Exhibit 4.3 presents an audience analysis summary form you can use to summarize your findings.

Now that you understand audience analysis, you can complete Speech Planning Action Step 1, Activity 1B: Analyzing Your Audience. To see an example of what a completed survey might look like, see the Student Response to Activity 1B.

SPEECH PLANNING   ACTION STEP 1

1 | Goals

ACTIVITY 1B Analyzing Your Audience

1. Decide on a method for gathering audience data.
2. Collect the data.
3. Copy or duplicate the Audience Analysis Summary Form (Exhibit 4.3).
4. Use the information you have collected to complete the form.
5. Write two short paragraphs to describe your initial impression of audience demographics, knowledge, and attitudes toward your subject.
6. Save the completed form. You will refer to this audience analysis information throughout the speech planning process.

You can download a copy of this form at the Challenge of Effective Speaking Web site. Use Your Challenge of Effective Speaking CD-ROM to access the chapter resources for Chapter 4, then click on Audience Analysis Summary Form.

STUDENT RESPONSE   ACTION STEP 1

1 | Goals

ACTIVITY 1B Analyzing Your Audience

Audience Analysis Summary Form
Demographic Data
1. The average audience member's education level is ___ high school _X_ college ___ postgraduate.
2. The ages range from _19_ to _24_. The average age is about _20_.
3. The audience is approximately _65_ percent male and _35_ percent female.
4. My estimate of the average income level of the audience is ___ upper _X_ middle ___ lower.
5. Most audience members are of _X_ the same occupation/major (which is *communication students*) ___ different occupations/majors.
6. Most audience members are of _X_ the same race (which is *white*) ___ a mixture of races.
7. Most audience members are of _X_ the same religion (which is *Judeo-Christian tradition*) ____ a mixture of religions.

(continued)

8. Most audience members are of _X_ the same nationality (which is *American*) ___ a mixture of nationalities.
9. Most audience members are from ___ the same state ___ the same city ___ the same neighborhood _X_ different areas.
10. Most audience members speak _X_ English as their first language ___ English as a second language (ESL).

Summary description of key audience characteristics: *From these data I conclude that most audience members are similar to each other and to me. We are all students at U.C. Most of us are around 20 years old, which suggests that we have a common generational view. Since U.C. is a commuter school, most of us are probably middle to lower socioeconomic class. There are more men than women in the class, and we are mostly white middle-class Americans. Although we have some religious diversity, most of us come from Judeo-Christian religious traditions.*

Subject-Specific Data
1. The average audience member's knowledge of the subject will be ___ extensive ___ moderate _X_ limited, because *my audience members are mostly communication students, not geology or mineralogy students.*
2. The average audience member's interest in this subject is likely to be ___ high _X_ moderate ___ low, because *without encouragement, they have no need to know about this subject. Mineralogy is hardly a trendy subject.*
3. The average audience member's attitude toward my subject is likely to be ___ positive _X_ neutral ___ negative, because *they don't really have any information about the topic.*
4. My initial credibility with the audience is likely to be ___ high ___ medium _X_ low, because *this is our first speech and they don't know I am a geology major whose family owns a jewelry store.*

Summary: *Most audience members don't know a lot about diamonds and have only moderate interest in the subject, although it is not a controversial subject.*

Analyzing the Setting

setting the location and occasion for a speech

The location and occasion make up the speech **setting.** The answers to several questions about the setting should guide your topic selection and other parts of your speech planning.

   1. What are the special expectations for the speech? Every speaking occasion is surrounded by expectations. At an Episcopalian Sunday service, for example, the congregation expects the minister's sermon to have a religious theme. Likewise, at a national sales meeting the field representatives expect to hear about new products. For your classroom speeches, a major expectation is that your speech will meet the assignment. Whether the speech assignment is defined by purpose (to inform or to persuade), by type (expository or demonstration), or by subject (book analysis or current event), your topic should reflect the nature of that assignment.

   2. What is the appropriate length for the speech? The time limits for classroom speeches are usually quite short, so you will want to choose a topic that is narrow enough to be accomplished in the time allotted. "Two Major Causes of Environmental Degradation" can be presented in five minutes, but "A History of Human Impact on the Environment" cannot. Problems with time limits are not peculiar to classroom speeches. Any speech setting includes actual or implied time limits. For example, the expected length for the sermon in a Protestant Sunday service may be twenty to thirty minutes; the expected length for a homily in a Roman Catholic Mass may be only ten minutes.

The setting of your speech should guide the topic you select.

3. How large will the audience be? If you will be speaking to a small audience (fewer than fifty people), you will be physically close enough to them to talk in a normal voice and to move about. In contrast, if you will be speaking to a large audience, you will probably need a microphone, and you'll be less likely to be able to move about.

4. Where will the speech be given? Because classrooms vary in size, lighting, seating arrangements, and the like, consider the factors that may affect your presentation. In a long, narrow room, you may need to speak louder than usual to reach the back row. In a dark room, make sure the lights are on and that the blinds or shades are open to bring in as much light as possible.

Venues outside of school settings offer even greater variations in conditions. Ask for specific information about seating capacity, shape, number of rows, nature of lighting, existence of a speaking stage or platform, distance between speaker and first row, and so on, before you speak. If possible, visit the place and see it for yourself.

5. When will the speech be given? A speech given early in the morning requires a different approach from one given right after lunch or in the evening. If a speech is scheduled after a meal, for instance, the audience may be lethargic, mellow, or even on the verge of sleep. As a result, it helps to insert more "attention-getters" (examples, illustrations, and stories) to counter potential lapses of attention.

6. Where in the program does the speech occur? If you are the only speaker or the featured speaker, you have an obvious advantage—you are the focal point of audience attention. In the classroom, however, and at some rallies, hearings, and other events, there are many speeches, and your place on the schedule may affect how you are received. For example, if you go first, you may need to "warm up" the listeners and be prepared to meet the distraction of a few audience members' strolling in late. If you speak last, you must counter the tendency of the audience to be weary from listening to several speeches.

7. What equipment is necessary to give the speech? For some speeches, you may need a microphone, a chalkboard, an overhead or slide projector and screen, or a hookup for your laptop computer. In most instances, speakers have some kind of speaking stand, but it is wise not to count on it. If the person who has invited you to speak has any control over the setting, be sure to explain what you need—but always have alternative plans in case what you have asked for is unavailable. It is frustrating to plan a computer PowerPoint presentation, for example, and then discover that there's no place to plug in the computer!

Complete Speech Planning Action Step 1, Activity 1C: Analyzing the Setting. Analyze the setting so that you understand your setting and take it into consideration as you choose your topic and develop your speech. To see how one student completed this activity, see the Student Response to Activity 1C.

SPEECH PLANNING   ACTION STEP 1

1 | Goals

ACTIVITY 1C Analyzing the Setting

The goal of this activity is to help you understand your speech setting. Fill in answers to the following questions:

1. What are the special expectations for the speech? _____

2. What is the appropriate length for the speech? _____

3. How large will the audience be? _____

4. Where will the speech be given? _____

5. When will the speech be given? _____

6. Where in the program does the speech occur? _____

7. What equipment is necessary to give the speech? _____

Write a short paragraph mentioning which aspects of the setting are most important for you to consider in speech preparation and why.

You can complete this activity online, print it out, and, if requested, e-mail it to your instructor. Use your Challenge of Effective Speaking CD-ROM to access Action Step Activity 1C.

STUDENT RESPONSE   ACTION STEP 1

1 | Goals

ACTIVITY 1C Analyzing the Setting

1. What are the special expectations for the speech? *informative or persuasive*
2. What is the appropriate length for the speech? *4–6 minutes*
3. How large will the audience be? *13–15 people*
4. Where will the speech be given? *614 Dyer*
5. When will the speech be given? *9:30 a.m., Tuesday*
6. Where in the program does the speech occur? *I will try to go first.*
7. What equipment is necessary to give the speech? *Overhead and chalkboard*

Time is certainly important: four to six minutes is not really very long. Also, I want to make sure that I am one of the first speakers.

Selecting a Topic

Armed with your topic lists and the information you have collected on your audience and setting, you are ready to select a topic that will be appropriate to the audience and the setting.

You will want to select a topic that is appropriate for your audience members and the setting. As you review your list of topics, compare each to your audience profile. Are there some topics that are too simple for this audience's knowledge base? Too difficult? Are some topics likely to be more interesting to the audience? How do the audience's age, ethnicity, and other demographic features mesh with each topic? By asking these and similar questions, you will be able to identify topics that are appropriate for the audience. Then consider the setting. Are some topics too broad for the time allotted? Are there topics that won't meet the special expectations? Answers to these and other questions will help you identify the topics that are appropriate to your setting. Speech Planning Action Step 1, Activity 1D: Selecting a Topic will aid you in selecting your topic. To see how one student responded to this activity, see the Student Response to Activity 1D.

| 1 | Goals | **SPEECH PLANNING** | ACTION STEP 1 |

ACTIVITY 1D Selecting a Topic

Use your responses to Action Step Activities 1A, 1B, and 1C to complete this activity.

1. Write each of the topics that you checked in activity 1A on the lines below:

_____ _____ _____

_____ _____ _____

_____ _____ _____

2. Using the information you compiled in Activity 1B, the audience analysis, compare each topic to your audience profile. Eliminate topics that seem less appropriate. Write each of the topics that remain on the lines below:

_____ _____ _____

_____ _____ _____

_____ _____ _____

3. Using the information you compiled in Activity 1C, your analysis of the setting for this speech, compare each of the remaining topics to your setting profile. Eliminate topics that seem less appropriate. Write each of the topics that remain on the lines below:

_____ _____ _____

_____ _____ _____

_____ _____ _____

4. Each of the remaining topics is appropriate to your audience and setting; you can be confident that you can develop an appropriate speech from any of these. So, from the topics that remain, select the one that you are most excited about sharing with others. My topic will be _____.

You can go online to complete this activity and print out a worksheet that will help you select your topic. Use your Challenge of Effective Speaking CD-ROM to access Action Step Activity 1D.

ACTIVITY 1D Selecting a Topic

1. Write each of the topics that you checked in Activity 1A on the lines below:

volcanoes   *history of lacrosse*   *habitat destruction*
diamond tests   *lacrosse skills*   *oil wells*
hydrology   *lacrosse strategy*   *littering*

2. Using the information you compiled in Activity 1B, the audience analysis, compare each topic to your audience profile. Eliminate topics that seem less appropriate. Write each of the topics that remain on the lines below:

volcanoes   *lacrosse skills*   *habitat destruction*
diamond tests   *lacrosse strategy*

3. Using the information you compiled in Activity 1C, your analysis of the setting for this speech, compare each of the remaining topics to your setting profile. Eliminate topics that seem less appropriate. Write each of the topics that remain on the lines below:

diamond tests   *lacrosse skills*   *habitat destruction*

4. Each of the remaining topics is appropriate to your audience and setting; you can be confident that you can develop an appropriate speech from any of these. So, from the topics that remain, select the one that you are most excited about sharing with others. My topic will be *diamond tests*.

Writing a Speech Goal

Once you have chosen your topic, you are ready to identify and write the general speech goal you hope to achieve in the speech and then the specific goal that is tailored to the audience and the setting.

Understanding General and Specific Speech Goals

general goal the overall intent of the speech

The **general goal** is the overall intent of the speech. Most speeches intend to entertain, to inform, or to persuade, even though each type of speech may include elements of other types. Consider the following examples: Conan O'Brien's opening monologue is intended to entertain, even though it may include material that is seen as persuasive. Likewise, John Kerry's political campaign speeches were intended to persuade, even though they also may have been very informative.

The general goal is usually dictated by the setting, particularly the occasion. (In this course, your instructor is likely to specify it.) Most speeches given by adults as part of their job or community activities have the general goal of informing or persuading. But occasionally, such as when giving a toast at a wedding, the purpose is to entertain.

specific goal a single statement that identifies the exact response the speaker wants from the audience

Whereas the general goal is often determined by the setting in which a speech is given, the **specific goal**, or specific purpose of a speech, is a single statement that identifies the exact response the speaker wants from the audience. For a speech on the topic "Evaluating Diamonds," one might state the specific goal as "I would like the audience to understand the four major criteria used for evaluating a diamond." For a speech on "Supporting the United Way," a specific goal might be stated "I would like the audience to donate money to the United Way." In the first example, the goal is informative: The speaker wants the audience to understand the criteria. In the second example, the goal is persuasive: The speaker wants to convince the audience to donate money.

Phrasing a Specific Speech Goal

The setting (or in the case of this class, the assignment) usually dictates the nature of your general speech goal. A specific speech goal, however, must be carefully crafted because it lays the foundation for organizing the speech.

The following guidelines can help you craft a well-worded specific goal.

1. Write a draft of your general speech goal using a complete sentence that specifies the type of response you want from the audience. Julia, who has been concerned with and is knowledgeable about the subject of illiteracy, drafts the following statement of her general speech goal.

I want my audience to understand the effects of illiteracy.

Julia's draft is a complete sentence, and it specifies the response she wants from the audience: *to understand* the effects of illiteracy. Her phrasing tells us that she is planning to give an informative speech.

2. Revise the statement (and the infinitive phrase) until it indicates the specific audience reaction desired. If your objective is to explain (to inform), the infinitive that expresses your desired audience reaction could be "to understand," "to recognize," "to distinguish," or "to identify." If you see the goal of your speech as changing a belief or calling the audience to action, then your general goal is persuasive and can be reflected by the use of such infinitives as "to believe," "to accept," "to change," or "to do." If Julia wanted to persuade her audience, her specific goal might be worded:

I want my audience to believe that illiteracy is a major problem.

3. Make sure that the goal statement contains only one idea. Suppose Julia had first written

I would like the audience to understand the nature of illiteracy and its effects on the individual and society.

This statement is not a good specific goal because it includes two distinct ideas: understanding the nature of illiteracy and understanding the specific effects that may follow from being illiterate. Either one is a worthy goal—but not both in one speech. Julia needs to choose one of these ideas. If your goal statement includes the word "and," you have more than one idea.

4. Revise your statement until it describes the precise focus of your speech (the infini-

In deciding on a general speech goal, you will have to balance your desires against the needs of your audience and the setting.

© Royalty-free/Corbis

tive phrase articulates the complete response you want from your audience). Julia's draft "I want my audience to understand the effects of illiteracy" is a good start, but the infinitive phrase "to understand the effects of illiteracy" is vague. Exactly what about illiteracy is it that Julia wants her audience to understand?

At this point Julia may need to begin doing some research in order to focus her ideas and refine her goal statement. But assuming that Julia already knows about how illiteracy handicaps people in the workplace, she might rephrase her specific goal to read

> I want the audience to understand three ways illiteracy hinders a person's effectiveness in the workplace.

This statement meets the criteria for being a good specific goal statement because it indicates the specific desired audience reaction and it contains only one explicit idea that is the focus of the speech.

 A good specific goal statement is important because it will guide the research you do as you prepare the speech. Once you have completed your research, you will expand your specific goal statement into a thesis statement, which will be the foundation on which you will organize the speech. To find and analyze a speaker's goal in a speech, complete the InfoTrac College Edition exercise at the end of this chapter.

Exhibit 4.4 gives several additional examples of general and specific informative and persuasive goals.

By completing Speech Planning Action Step 1, Activity 1E: Writing a Specific Goal, you will develop a well-written specific goal statement for your speech. To see how one student responded to this activity, see the Student Response to Activity 1E.

EXHIBIT 4.4   General and specific speech goals

Informative Goals

General goal: To inform the audience about techniques of handwriting analysis.

Specific goal: I want the audience to understand the differences between two major techniques graphologists use to analyze handwriting.

General goal: To inform the audience about forms of mystery stories.

Specific goal: I want the audience to be able to identify the three basic forms of mystery stories.

Persuasive Goals

General goal: To persuade the audience that drug testing by businesses should be prohibited.

Specific goal: I want the audience to believe that required random drug testing of employees by businesses should be prohibited.

General goal: To persuade the audience to donate to a food bank.

Specific goal: I want to persuade the audience to make a donation of five dollars or more to Second Harvest.

	SPEECH PLANNING	ACTION STEP 1
1	Goals		

ACTIVITY 1E Writing a Specific Goal

Type of speech: _____

1. Write a draft of your general speech goal using a complete sentence that specifies the type of response you want from the audience.
2. Revise the infinitive to make it reflect the specific audience response you desire.
3. Check the number of ideas expressed in the statement. If the statement contains more than one idea, select one and rewrite the statement.
4. Improve the statement so that it describes the precise focus of your speech.

Write the final draft of the specific goal:

_____

_____

_____

You can complete this activity online with Speech Builder Express, a speech outlining and development tool that will help you complete the action steps in this book to develop your speech. See the end of this chapter for instructions on how to access Speech Builder Express.

	STUDENT RESPONSE	ACTION STEP 1
1	Goals		

ACTIVITY 1E Writing a Specific Goal

Type of speech: *informative*

1. Write a draft of your general speech goal using a complete sentence that specifies the type of response you want from the audience.

   I want the audience to have an understanding of the skills necessary to play the game of lacrosse.

2. Revise the infinitive to make it reflect the specific audience response you desire.

   I want the audience to recognize the skills necessary to play the game of lacrosse.

3. Check the number of ideas expressed in the statement. If the statement contains more than one idea, select one and rewrite the statement.

   I want my audience to recognize the basic skills necessary to play the game of lacrosse.

4. Improve the statement so that it describes the precise focus of your speech.

   I want my audience to recognize the three basic skills needed to begin playing lacrosse.

Write the final draft of the specific goal:

I want my audience to recognize the three basic skills necessary to play the game of lacrosse.

Although Glen and Adam were taking the same speech course, they were in different sections. One evening when Adam was talking with Glen about his trouble finding a topic, Glen mentioned that he was planning to speak about home pages. Because the number of different speech goals from this topic seemed unlimited, he didn't see any harm in showing Adam his bibliography, so he brought it up on his computer screen.

As Adam was looking at it, Glen went down the hall to get a book he had lent to a friend earlier that morning. While Glen was away, Adam thought he'd take a look at what else Glen had in the file. He was soon excited to see that Glen had a complete outline on the goal "I want the class to understand the steps in designing a home page." Figuring he could save himself some time, Adam printed the outline; he justified his action on the basis that it represented a good start that would give him ideas. As time ran short, Adam decided to just use Glen's outline for his own speech.

Later in the week Glen's instructor happened to be talking to Adam's about speeches she had heard that week. When she mentioned that Glen had given a really interesting speech on home pages, Adam's teacher said, "That's interesting. I heard a good one just this morning. Now what did you say the goal of the speech you heard was?" When the goals turned out to be the same, Glen's instructor went back to her office to get the outline that she would be returning the next day. As the two instructors went over the outlines, they saw that the two speeches were exactly the same. The next day, they left messages for both Adam and Glen to meet with them and the department head that day.

1. What is the ethical issue at stake?
2. Was there anything about Glen's behavior that was unethical? Anything about Adam's?
3. What should be the penalty, if any, for Glen? For Adam?

Summary

The first step of effective speech preparation is to identify a topic. You begin by selecting a subject that is important to you and that you know something about, such as a job, a hobby, or a contemporary issue of concern to you. To arrive at a specific topic, brainstorm a list of related words under each subject heading. When you have brainstormed at least fifteen topics under each heading, you can check the three specific topics under each heading that are most meaningful to you.

The second step is to analyze the audience to decide how to shape and direct your speech. Audience analysis is the study of the intended audience for your speech. Gather specific data about your audience to develop a demographic profile that includes age, education, gender, background, occupation, race, ethnicity, religion, geographic uniqueness, language, knowledge of subject, and attitude toward subject. At times, you may want to validate your predictions by surveying your classroom audience using two-sided, multiple-response, scaled, or open-ended items or questions. You may also gather data through informal observation, by questioning the person who invited you to speak, and by making educated guesses about audience demographics and attitudes.

The third step is to analyze the setting of the speech, which will affect your overall speech plan, by asking such questions as: What are the special expectations for the speech? What is the appropriate length for the speech? How large will the audience be? Where will the speech be given? When will the speech be given? Where in the program does the speech occur? What equipment is necessary to give the speech?

The fourth step is to select a topic that is appropriate for your audience members and the setting.

The final step is to write your speech goal. The general goal of a speech (the overarching purpose) is to entertain, to inform, or to persuade. The specific goal is a single statement that identifies the exact response the speaker wants from the audience. Writing a specific speech goal involves the following four-step procedure: (1) Write a first draft of your speech goal using a complete sentence that specifies the type of response you want from your audience. (2) Revise the statement (and the infinitive phrase) until it indicates the specific audience reaction desired. (3) Make sure that the goal statement contains only one idea. (4) Revise your statement until it describes the precise focus of your speech.

CHALLENGE ONLINE

Now that you've read Chapter 4, use your Challenge of Effective Speaking CD-ROM for quick access to the electronic study resources that accompany this text. Your CD-ROM gives you access to InfoTrac College Edition, Speech Builder Express, and the Challenge of Effective Speaking Web site. When you get to the Challenge of Effective Speaking home page, click on "Student Book Companion Site" in the Resource box at the right to access the online study aids for this chapter, including a digital glossary, review quizzes, and the chapter activities.

KEY TERMS

At the Challenge of Effective Speaking Web site, select chapter resources for Chapter 4. Print a copy of the glossary for this chapter, test yourself with the electronic flash cards, or complete the crossword puzzle to help you master the following key terms.

subject (44)	**two-sided items** (50)
topic (44)	**multiple-response items** (50)
brainstorming (45)	**scaled items** (51)
audience analysis (47)	**open-ended items** (51)
audience adaptation (47)	**setting** (54)
credibility (50)	**general goal** (58)
survey (50)	**specific goal** (58)

INFOTRAC COLLEGE EDITION EXERCISE

Use your Challenge of Effective Speaking CD-ROM to access InfoTrac College Edition. Click on PowerTrac. Press on "Key Word" and drag down to "Journal Name." Enter the search term "Vital Speeches." View the speeches that come up and find a speech on a topic that interests you. Read the speech and identify the speaker's goal. Was the goal clearly stated in the introduction? Was it implied but clear? Was it unclear? Consider how this analysis can help you clarify your own speech goal.

WEB RESOURCES

Access the Web resources for this chapter online at the Challenge of Effective Speaking Web site. Select the chapter resources for Chapter 4, then click on "Web Resources."

4.1 Brainstorming (46)   4.3 Public Opinion Polls (49)
4.2 Defining Your Audience (47)

SPEECH PLANNING ACTION STEPS

Access the Action Step activities for this chapter online at the Challenge of Effective Speaking Web site. Select the chapter resources for Chapter 4, then click on the activity number you want. You may print out your completed activities, and you should save your work so you can use it as needed in later Action Step activities.

1A Brainstorming for Topics (46)   1D Selecting a Topic (57)
1B Analyzing Your Audience (53)   1E Writing a Specific Goal (61)
1C Analyzing the Setting (56)

To access Speech Builder Express, use the username and password included on your Challenge of Effective Speaking CD-ROM. Speech Builder Express is a Web-based speech outlining and development tool that will help you complete the Action Steps in this book to develop your speech. In this chapter, you can use this tool to complete Action Step Activity 1E: Writing a Specific Goal. When you log onto Speech Builder Express, you'll be prompted to set up an account with your username and password.

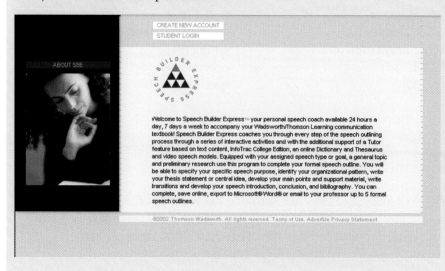

Once you've logged on and created an account, you can start on your speech outline by choosing a speech type. In this way you can create and save up to five speech outlines.

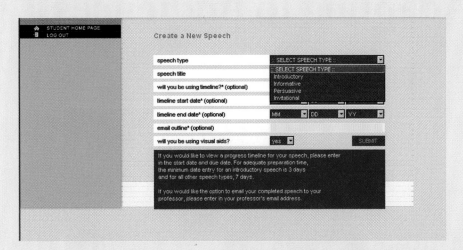

To work on your specific goal, select "Speech Goal" from the left-hand menu and follow the instructions to write and test your specific speech goal. To review information about specific goals, click on the "Tutor" button to read short reminders from this chapter.

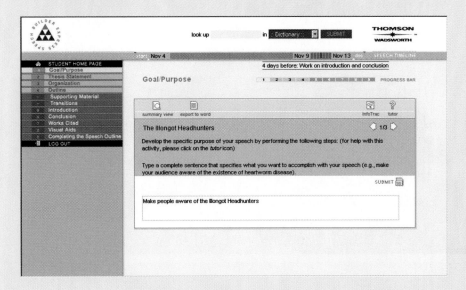

5

Adapting to Audiences

© Justin Sullivan/Getty Images

You persuade a man only insofar as you can talk his language by speech, gesture, tonality, order, image, attitude, idea, identifying *your ways with his.*

Kenneth Burke, *A Rhetoric of Motives*, 1950

Nathan had asked his friend George to listen to one of his speech rehearsals. As he finished the final sentence of the speech, "So, watching violence on TV does affect children in at least two ways—it not only desensitizes them to real violence, it also influences them to behave more aggressively," he asked George, "So, what do you think?"

"You're giving the speech to your classmates, right?"

"Yeah."

"And they're mostly mass media majors?"

"Uh-huh."

"Well, it was a good speech, but I didn't hear anything that showed that you had media majors in mind."

2 | Audience   ACTION STEP 2

Identifying opportunities for audience adaptation

Nathan may have chosen his topic with his audience in mind, but as he prepared he forgot that an effective speech is one in which what is said is geared to the specific audience. In the previous chapter we saw how audience and setting considerations help you to choose a speech topic. In this chapter we describe how you can use the audience analysis to tailor what you will say in the speech to the audience who will listen to it. The second Speech Planning Action Step is to identify audience adaptation strategies.

Audience adaptation is the process of customizing your speech to your specific audience. Your concerns about adapting to your audience will inform your research efforts, your choice of main points to cover in the speech, the supporting material that you will use to develop those points, and even the jokes you might want to tell. So the blueprint for adaptation that you create during Action Step 2 is the foundation for the work that follows. In the rest of this chapter we will describe the issues of adaptation, including demonstrating relevance, ensuring information comprehension, establishing common ground, gaining credibility, adjusting to the audience's initial attitudes, dealing with cultural and language differences, and forming a specific plan of adaptation.

audience adaptation the process of customizing your speech material to your specific audience

Relevance

The first issue that speakers face is demonstrating **relevance**—adapting the information in the speech so that audience members view it as important to them. Listeners pay attention to and are interested in ideas that have a personal impact ("What does this have to do with me?") and are bored when they don't see how what is being said relates to them. Effective speakers help members see importance by demonstrating the timeliness, proximity, and personal impact of the ideas in the speech.

relevance adapting the information in the speech so that audience members view it as important to them

Demonstrate Timeliness

Information has **timeliness** when it is useful now or in the near future. Speakers can increase the relevance of the information they present by showing how it is timely. For example, in a speech to a traditional college-age audience on the cri-

timeliness showing how information is useful now or in the near future

Reactions such as applause, laughter, head nodding, and smiles are all signs that your audience is relating well to what you are saying.

teria for evaluating the quality of diamonds, a speaker could quickly establish the topic's relevance to the audience with this introduction:

> Most of us have dreamed about shopping for that special diamond that will seal our relationship to our beloved for all time, but the day when the dream becomes a reality is no longer far away. And if you want to make sure that your dream doesn't become a nightmare, you'll want to learn how to evaluate the quality of a diamond.

Demonstrate Proximity

proximity relevance to personal life space

Listeners are more likely to be interested in information that has **proximity** to them—that is, it is relevant to their personal life space. Psychologically we are more interested in information that affects our "territory" than to information that is remote from us. So we are likely to be more attentive to information when it is related to our family, neighborhood, city, state, or country. The more "distant" the information, the less it interests us.

As you prepare to speak, you will want to consider how to make your information more proximal for your audience. You have probably heard speakers say "Let me bring this close to home for you . . . " and then make their point by using a local example. As you research your speech, you will want to look for statistics and examples that are proximal for your audience. For example, if you give a speech on the difficulties the EPA is having cleaning up Super Fund sites, you will want to visit the "Where You Live" page at the EPA's Web site to see what is being done at Super Fund sites in your area, or access your local newspaper's files to see if there have been any recent articles on local sites.

Demonstrate Personal Impact

When you present information on a topic that can have a serious physical, economic, or psychological impact on audience members, they will be interested in what you have to say. For example, notice how your classmates' attention picks up when your instructor says that what is said next "will definitely be on the test."

Your instructor understands that this economic impact (not paying attention can "cost") is enough to refocus most students' attention on what is being said.

As you research and prepare your speech, you will want to find and incorporate ideas that create personal impact for your audience. In a speech on toxic waste, you might show a serious physical impact by providing statistics on the effects of toxic waste on the health of people in your state. You may be able to demonstrate serious economic impact by citing the cost to the taxpayers of a recent toxic waste cleanup in your city. Or you might be able to illustrate a serious psychological impact by finding and recounting the stresses faced by one family (that is demographically similar to your audience) with a long-term toxic waste problem in their neighborhood.

Information Comprehension

Although your audience analysis helped you to select a topic that was appropriate for your audience's current knowledge level, you will still need to adapt the information you present so that audience members can easily follow what you are saying and remember it when you are through. Six techniques that can aid you are orienting or refamiliarizing the audience with basic information, defining key terms, creating vivid examples to illustrate new concepts, personalizing information, comparing unfamiliar ideas with those the audience recognizes, and using multiple methods of development.

Orient Listeners

When listeners become confused or have forgotten basic information, they lose interest or do not understand what is being said. Therefore, you will want to quickly review the basic ideas that are critical to understanding the speech. For example, if your speech concerns U.S. military involvement in Iraq, you can be reasonably sure that everyone in your audience is aware that the United States and Great Britain were participants in the coalition, but many may not remember the other countries that participated. So before launching into the roles of various countries, remind your listeners by listing the nations that have provided troops, and where they have been stationed.

There may be some audience members who do not need the reminder, so to avoid offending them by appearing to talk down to them, and to save face for those who need the reminder, you should acknowledge that they probably already remember the information. Phrases such as "As you will remember," "As we all probably learned in high school," and "As we have come to find out" are ways of prefacing reviews so that they are not offensive.

Define Key Terms

Words have many meanings, so you should ensure audience members' comprehension of ideas by defining key terms that may be unfamiliar to them or are critical to understanding your speech. This becomes especially important when you are using familiar words whose commonly accepted meanings have been altered. For instance, in a speech on the four major problems faced by functionally illiterate people in the workplace, it will be important to your audience to understand what you mean by functionally illiterate. So, early in the speech you can offer your definition: "By 'functionally illiterate,' I mean people who have trouble accomplishing simple reading and writing tasks."

Illustrate New Concepts with Vivid Examples

Vivid examples help audience members understand and remember abstract, complex, and novel material. One vivid example can help us understand a complicated concept. So, as you prepare your speech, you will want to adapt by finding or creating real or hypothetical examples and illustrations to help your audience understand new information you present. For example, in the previous definition of functionally illiterate, the description "people who have trouble accomplishing simple reading and writing tasks" can be made more vivid by adding the following example: "For instance, a functionally illiterate person could not read and understand the directions on a prescription label that states 'Take three times a day with a glass of water. Do not take on an empty stomach.'"

Personalize Information

personalize to present information in a frame of reference that is familiar to the audience

We **personalize** information by presenting it in a frame of reference that is familiar to the audience. Devon, a student at the University of California, is to give a speech on how the Japanese economy affects U.S. markets at the student chapter of the American Marketing Association. He wants to help his audience understand geographic data about Japan. He could just quote the following statistics from the 2004 *World Almanac*:[1]

> Japan is small and densely populated. The nation's 128 million people live in a land area of 146,000 square miles, giving them a population density of 877 persons per square mile.

Although this would provide the necessary information, it is not adapted to an audience comprised of college students in California, a large state in the United States. Devon can easily adapt the information to the audience by putting in terms that are familiar to this student audience.

> Japan is a small, densely populated nation. Its population of 128 million is nearly half that of the *United States*. Yet the Japanese are crowded into a land area of only 146,000 square miles—roughly the same size as *California*. Just think of the implications of having half the population of the United States living *here in California*, where 30 million people—about one-fifth of that total—now live. In fact, Japan packs 877 persons into every square mile of land, whereas in the *United States* we average about 74 persons per square mile. Overall, then, Japan is about 12 times as crowded as the *United States*.

This revision adapts the information by personalizing it for this audience. Even though most Americans do not have the total land area of the United States on the tip of their tongue, they do know that the United States covers a great deal of territory. Likewise, a California audience would have a sense of the size of their home state compared to the rest of the nation. Personalized information is easier for audience members to understand and remember, so as you research and prepare your speech, you will want to look for ways to personalize the information. In order for Devon to personalize his information, he had to get ahold of the statistics on the United States and California. If Devon were speaking to an audience from another part of the country, he could adapt to them by substituting information from that state.

Compare Unknown Ideas with Familiar Ones

When you understand who is in your audience, you can help them with new ideas by making comparisons to things with which they are familiar. So, as you prepare your speech, you will want to identify places where you can use adaptive compari-

© Louie Psihoyos/Corbis

Sometimes we can personalize information with a visual aid like this one that compares the size of a dinosaur egg, which is unfamiliar to most audience members, with the commonly seen chicken egg.

sons. For example, if I want an audience of Generation Xers to feel the excitement that was generated when telegrams were first introduced, I might compare it to the change that was experienced when e-mail became widely available. In the speech on functional illiteracy, if you want the audience of literates to sense what functionally illiterate people experience, you might compare it to the experience of surviving in a country where one is not fluent in the language:

> Many of us have taken a foreign language in school. So, we figure that we can visit a place where the language is spoken and "get along," right? But when we get to the country, we are often appalled to discover that even the road signs are written in this "foreign" language! And we can't quite make them out, at least not at sixty kilometers an hour! I was in France last summer, equipped with my three years of high school French, and I saw a sign that indicated that the train station I was looking for was "à droit"—"to the right," or is it "to the left"? I knew it was one or the other. Unfortunately, I couldn't remember and took a shot that it was to the left. Bad move. By the time I figured it out, I was ten miles in the wrong direction and ended up missing my train. At that moment I could imagine how tough life must be for functionally illiterate people. So many "little details" of life require the ability to comprehend written messages.

Use Multiple Methods for Developing Ideas

Because your audience members learn differently, you will want to adapt by using a variety of types of development when presenting new information. This will increase the likelihood that each member of your audience will be able to understand and remember what you are explaining. Some people learn best with detailed explanations, some need precise definitions or vivid examples, others learn through statistics, and still others will benefit from a well-designed visual aid.

Let's look at how you might use multiple methods to develop an idea. Suppose the point you are trying to make is this: For the large numbers of Americans who are functionally illiterate, understanding simple directions can be a problem. Here's an example that develops this idea:

> For instance, a person who is functionally illiterate might not be able to read or understand a label that says "Take three times a day after eating."

Now look at how much richer the meaning becomes when we build the statement by adding statistics and additional examples:

> A significant number of Americans are functionally illiterate. That is, about 35 million people, or about 20 percent of the adult population, have serious difficulties with common reading tasks. They cannot read well enough to understand how to prepare a dish from a recipe, how to assemble a simple toy from the printed instructions, or which bus to catch from the signs at the stop. Many functionally illiterate people don't read well enough to follow the directions on a prescription that reads "Take three times a day after eating."

To be able to offer multiple types of development geared to the needs of your audience, you will want to identify various items of different types so that you have choices about how to develop your ideas.

Common Ground

Each person in the audience is unique, with different knowledge, attitudes, philosophies, experiences, and ways of perceiving the world. Your listeners may or may not know others in the audience. So it is easy for them to assume that they have nothing in common with you or with other audience members. Yet when you speak, you will be giving one message to that diverse group. **Common ground** is the background, knowledge, attitudes, experiences, and philosophies that are shared by audience members and the speaker. Effective speakers use the audience analysis to identify areas of similarity and then apply the adaptation techniques of using personal pronouns, asking rhetorical questions, and drawing on common experiences to create common ground.

common ground the background, knowledge, attitudes, experiences, and philosophies that are shared by audience members and the speaker

Use Personal Pronouns

personal pronouns "we," "us," and "our"—pronouns that directly link the speaker to members of the audience

The simplest way of establishing common ground is to use **personal pronouns**—"we," "us," and "our"—to directly link the speaker to members of the audience. For example, in a speech to an audience whose members are known to be sympathetic to legislation limiting violence in children's programming on TV, notice the effect of using a personal pronoun:

> I know that most people are worried about the effects that violence on TV is having on young children.

> I know that most of us worry about the effects that violence is having on young children.

By using "us" instead of "people," the speaker includes the audience members and thus gives them a stake in listening to what follows.

Ask Rhetorical Questions

rhetorical questions questions phrased to stimulate a mental response rather than an actual spoken response on the part of the audience

A second way to develop common ground is to pose **rhetorical questions**—questions phrased to stimulate a mental response rather than an actual spoken response on the part of the audience. Rhetorical questions create common ground by alluding to information that is shared by audience members and the speaker. They are often used in the introduction to a speech, but can also be effective as transitions and in other parts of the speech. For instance, notice how this transition, phrased as a rhetorical question, creates common ground:

> When you have watched a particularly violent TV program, have you ever asked yourself, "Did they really need to be this graphic to make the point?"

Rhetorical questions are meant to have only one answer that highlights similarities between the speaker and audience members and leads them to be more interested in the content that follows. So, as the speaker, you should choose rhetorical questions that are in line with the information you have gleaned from the audience analysis. You don't want audience members to silently answer in a way opposite to the way you intend. When this happens, instead of listening to your speech, audience members may begin silently debating what you say.

Draw from Common Experiences

A third way of developing common ground is selecting and presenting personal experiences, examples, and illustrations that embody what you and the audience have in common. For instance, in a speech about the effects of television violence, you might allude to a common viewing experience:

> Remember how sometimes at a key moment when you're watching a really frightening scene in a movie you may quickly shut your eyes? I remember doing that over and over again. I vividly remember slamming my eyes shut during the snake scenes in *Indiana Jones.*

In this example, the audience members recall their own personal moment of fear and then relate it to the snake scene experience of the speaker.

To be able to create material that draws on common experiences, you must study the audience analysis to understand how you and audience members are similar in the exposure you have had to the topic or in other areas that you can then compare to your topic. For example, suppose you are going to give a personal experience speech on skydiving. If most of your audience members have never jumped out of a plane, it would be difficult for them to imagine the sensation unless you can create a common grounding experience. So you might try relating the immediate sensation on leaving the plane to a more common experience:

> The first thing you feel when you finally jump is that stomach-in-the-mouth sensation that is similar to something we've all experienced when we have lurched because we've missed a step going down a staircase or when we have momentarily gone airborne in a car from approaching the crest of a hill too fast.

credibility the confidence that an audience places in the truthfulness of what a speaker says

Speaker Credibility

Credibility is the confidence that an audience places in the truthfulness of what a speaker says. There are several theories as to how speakers develop credibility. You can read a summary of these theories by accessing Web Resource 5.1: Holistic Theory of Speaker Credibility.

Some famous people are widely known as experts in a particular area and have proven to be trustworthy and likable. When these people give a speech, they don't have to adapt their remarks to establish their credibility. For example, in January 2004 when Alan Greenspan, Chairman of the Federal Reserve Bank of the

United States, spoke before the Bundesbank in Berlin, Germany, on the subject of the United States trade deficit, no one listening would have questioned his credibility.

However, most of us, even though we may be given a formal introduction that attempts to acquaint the audience with our credentials and character prior to our speech, will still need to adapt our remarks to build audience confidence in the truthfulness of what we are saying. Three adaptation techniques can affect how credible we are perceived to be: demonstrating knowledge and expertise, establishing trustworthiness, and displaying personableness.

Demonstrate Knowledge and Expertise

knowledge and expertise how well you convince your audience that you are qualified to speak on the topic

When the audience perceives you to be a knowledgeable expert, it will perceive you as credible. Their assessment of your **knowledge and expertise** depends on how well you convince them that you are qualified to speak on this topic. You can demonstrate your knowledge and expertise through direct and indirect means.

You establish your expertise directly when you disclose your experiences with your topic, including formal education, special study, demonstrated skill, and your "track record." For example, in a speech on the criteria for evaluating a diamond, Brian could share his long-term fascination with precious stones by telling his audience:

> I've been interested in diamonds since I was ten when, during a visit to family in South Africa, we toured a diamond mine. Since then, I've worked part-time in a booth in the diamond district here in New York and now I'm studying geology here at NYU with the intent of becoming a registered gemologist and working in the industry.

Of course, in order to make claims like this, you have to have had experiences that give you "standing" to speak on your topic. This is why it was critical for you choose a topic you knew something about. When you can demonstrate your personal involvement with your topic, your audience begins to trust that you understand the material you are presenting. Needless to say, you will be perceived as more credible if you demonstrate to the audience that you have real experience with your topic.

Audience members will also assess your expertise through indirect means, such as how well prepared you seem and how much you demonstrate your first-hand involvement by using personal examples and illustrations. Audiences have an almost instinctive sense of when a speaker is "winging it," and most audiences distrust a speaker who does not appear to have command of the material. Speakers who are overly dependent on their notes or who hem and haw, fumbling to find ways to express their ideas, undermine the confidence of the audience. On the other hand, when your ideas are easy to follow and clearly expressed, audience members perceive you to be more credible.

Similarly, when the audience hears a speech in which the ideas are developed through specific statistics, high-quality examples, illustrations, and the personal experiences of the speaker, they are likely to view the speaker as credible. Recall how impressed you are with instructors who always seem to have two or three perfect examples and illustrations and who are able to recall statistics without looking at their notes. Compare this to your experiences with instructors who seem tied to the textbook and don't appear to know much about the subject beyond their prepared lecture. In which instance do you perceive the instructor to be more knowledgeable?

Therefore, as you prepare, you will want to adapt what you say so that you directly and indirectly demonstrate your expertise and knowledge.

Establish Trustworthiness

A second way to enhance your credibility as a speaker is to directly establish your **trustworthiness**—the extent to which the audience can believe that what you say is accurate, true, and in their best interests. The more your audience sees you as trustworthy, the more credible you will be. People assess others' trustworthiness by judging their character and their motives. So, you can establish yourself as trustworthy by following ethical standards and by honestly explaining what is motivating you to speak.

As you plan your speech, you need to consider how to demonstrate your character—that you are honest, industrious, dependable, and a morally strong person. For example, when you credit the source of your information as you speak, you confirm that the information is true—that you are not making it up—and you signal your honesty by not taking credit for someone else's ideas. Similarly, if you present the arguments evenly on both sides of an issue, instead of just the side you favor, audience members will see you as fair-minded.

How trustworthy you are seen to be will also depend on how the audience views your motive. If people believe that what you are saying is self-serving rather than being in their interest, they will be suspicious and view you as less trustworthy. Early in your speech, then, it is important to show how audience members

The audience's perception of your trustworthiness results from their assessment of your character and your apparent motives for speaking.

will benefit from what you are saying. For example, in his speech on toxic waste, Brandon might describe how one community's ignorance of toxic waste disposal dangers allowed a toxic waste dump to be located in their community and the serious health issues that subsequently arose. He can then share his motive by saying something like this: "My hope is that this speech will give you the information you need to thoughtfully participate in decisions like these that may face your community."

By adapting your material so that it highlights your character and pure motives, you can establish your trustworthiness.

trustworthiness the extent to which the audience can believe that what you say is accurate, true, and in their best interests

Display Personableness

We have more confidence in people that we like. **Personableness** is the extent to which you project an agreeable or pleasing personality. The more your listeners like you, the more likely they are to believe what you tell them. We quickly decide how much we like a new person based on our first impression of him or her. Although first impressions can be inaccurate, we still use them. And first impressions are based on what we infer about people from what we see, such as how they are dressed, how physically attractive we find them, how well they speak, whether they smile and appear friendly or not, and how they carry themselves.

personableness the extent to which you project an agreeable or pleasing personality

"Kendra, I heard you telling Jim about the speech you're giving tomorrow. You think it's a winner, huh?"

"You got that right, Omar. I'm going to have Bardston eating out of the palm of my hand."

"You sound confident."

"This time I have reason to be. See, Prof. Bardston's been talking about the importance of audience adaptation. These last two weeks that's all we've heard—adaptation, adaptation."

"What does she mean?"

"Talking about something in a way that really relates to people personally."

"OK—so how are you going to do that?"

"Well, you see, I'm giving this speech on abortion. Now here's the kick. Bardston let it slip that she's a supporter of Right to Life. So what I'm going to do is give this informative speech on the Right to Life movement. But I'm going to discuss the major beliefs of the movement in a way that'll get her to think that I'm a supporter. I'm going to mention aspects of the movement that I know she'll like."

"But I've heard you talk about how you're pro-choice."

"I am—all the way. But by keeping the information positive, I'll make her think I'm a supporter. It isn't as if I'm going to be telling any lies or anything."

1. In a speech, is it ethical to adapt in a way that resonates with your audience but isn't in keeping with what you really believe?
2. Could Kendra have achieved her goal by using different methods? How?

Politicians running for office provide excellent (and at times humorous) examples of adapting in order to be liked. When a candidate takes off his jacket and tie, rolls up his sleeves, and dons a baseball cap emblazoned with "AFL-CIO" before speaking to a rally of union workers to solicit their votes, he is trying to be "like them" in order to be liked. As a speaker trying to build credibility with an audience, you should look for ways to adapt your personal style to one that will help the audience like you and perceive you as credible.

Besides dressing in a way that is appropriate for the audience and occasion, you can increase the chances that the audience will like you by smiling at individual audience members before beginning your remarks and by looking at individuals as you speak, acknowledging them with a quick nod. You can also demonstrate personableness by using humor, especially self-deprecating remarks.

Initial Audience Attitudes

initial audience attitudes predispositions for or against a topic, usually expressed as an opinion

Initial audience attitudes are predispositions for or against a topic, usually expressed as an opinion. Meeting initial audience attitudes means framing a speech in a way that takes into account how much audience members know and their attitude toward the topic. As part of your audience analysis, you identified the initial attitude that you expected most of your audience members to have toward your topic. During your speech preparation, you will be challenged to adapt the material you plan to present so that it takes this attitude into account.

Although adapting to listeners' attitudes is obviously important for persuasive speeches, it is also important for informative speeches. For example, although a speech on refinishing wood furniture is meant to be informative, you may face an audience whose initial attitude is that refinishing furniture is difficult and complicated, or you may face an audience of young homeowners who are addicted to HGTV and who are really looking forward to your talk. Although the process you describe in both instances would be the same, how you approach explaining the steps in furniture refinishing would need to take the audience's initial disposition into account. Suppose you know that you have an audience of young new homeowners and have found out through a simple show of hands that most of them enjoy watching HGTV. Then you will want to play upon their interest as you speak, perhaps even making reference to some of the most popular shows on HGTV. If, however, you have an audience that initially views refinishing furniture as complicated and boring, then you will need to adjust what you say so that you develop their interest and convince them that the process is really simpler than they initially thought. In Chapter 13, Persuasive Speaking: Reasoning with Your Audience, we will examine strategies for dealing with listeners' attitudes in depth.

Language and Cultural Differences

Western Europeans' speaking traditions inform the approach to public speaking we discuss in this book. However, public speaking is a social and cultural act, so, as you would expect, public speaking practices and their perceived effectiveness vary. As they prepare and present speeches, speakers from various cultures and subcultures draw on the traditions of their speech communities, and speakers who address audiences comprised of people from ethnic and language groups different from their own face two additional challenges of adaptation: being understood when speaking in a second language, and having limited common experiences on which to establish common ground.

Overcome Linguistic Problems

When the first language spoken by the audience is different from that of the speaker, audience members often cannot understand what the speaker is saying because of mispronunciations, accents, vocabulary mistakes, and idiomatic speech meaning. Fear of making these mistakes can make second-language speakers self-conscious. But most audience members are more tolerant of mistakes made by second-language speakers than they are of those made by native speakers. Likewise, most audience members will work hard to understand a second-language speaker.

Nevertheless, second-language speakers have an additional responsibility to make their speech as understandable as possible. You can help your audience by speaking more slowly and articulating as clearly as you can. By slowing your speaking rate, you give yourself additional time to pronounce what seem like awkward sounds and choose words whose meanings you know. You also give your audience members additional time to "adjust their ear" so that they can more easily process what you are saying.

One of the best ways for you to improve when you are giving a speech in a second language is for you to practice the speech in front of friends and associates who are native speakers. These "trial audience members" should be instructed to take note of words and phrases that are mispronounced or misused. Then they can work with you to correct the pronunciation or to choose other words that better express your idea. Also keep in mind that the more practice you get speaking in the language, the more comfortable you will become with the language and with your ability to relate to audience members.

Choose Culturally Sensitive Material

Although overcoming linguistic problems can seem daunting, those whose cultural background is significantly different from that of their audience members also face the challenge of having few common experiences from which to draw. Much of our success in adapting to the audience hinges on establishing common ground and drawing on common experiences. But when we are speaking to audiences who are vastly different from us, we must learn as much as we can about the culture of our audience so that we can develop the material in a way that is meaningful to them. This may mean conducting additional library research to find statistics and examples that will be meaningful to the audience. Or it may require us to elaborate on ideas that would be self-explanatory in our own culture. For example, suppose that Maria, a Mexican American exchange student, is giving a personal narrative speech for her speech class at Yeshiva University in Israel on the *quiencianera* party she had when she turned 15. Because students in Israel don't have any experience with the Mexican coming-of-age tradition of *quiencianera* parties, they would have trouble understanding the significance of this event unless Maria was able to use her knowledge of the Bar Mitzvah and Bat Mitzvah coming-of-age ritual celebrations in Jewish culture and relate it to those.

Forming a Specific Plan of Audience Adaptation

You now understand the challenges that speakers face in developing and maintaining audience interest and understanding, and you have read about the adaptation techniques that can overcome these challenges. You have also completed your audience analysis. So, you are ready to think about the adaptation challenges you will face in your speech as well as how you might adapt to them. At this point in your preparation process, identifying the challenges you face with your audience and planning how you might meet them will provide a guide to direct your research efforts and aid you as you develop the speech. Your adaptation plan should answer the following questions:

1. **How relevant will the audience find this material to be?** How can I demonstrate that the material is timely, proximate, and has personal impact for the members of this audience?

2. **How can I make it easier for audience members to comprehend the information I will share?** Given this topic and audience, what ideas will the audience need to be oriented to? What key terms will I need to define? What new concepts might be developed through vivid examples? What new ideas might I want to compare to ones the audience is already familiar with? How can I personalize the information I present?

3. **What common ground do audience members share with each other and with me?** How and where can I use personal pronouns, rhetorical questions, and common experiences to enhance the perception of common ground?

4. **What can I do to enhance my credibility?** How did I develop my expertise on this topic, and how can I share that with the audience? How can I demonstrate my trustworthiness as I speak? What will I do to help the audience to find me personable so they will like me?

5. **What is my audience's initial attitude toward my speech topic likely to be?** What can I do to create or enhance audience interest in my topic or sympathy for my argument?

6. **What language or cultural differences do audience members have with each other and with me?** If I will be speaking in a second language, how do I plan to increase the likelihood that the audience will understand me? What cultural differences do I need to be sensitive to, and what culturally appropriate material do I need to search for and use?

SPEECH PLANNING　　　　　ACTION STEP 2

2 | Audience

ACTIVITY 2 Identifying Opportunities for Audience Adaptation

In order to identify opportunities for audience adaptation to lay a groundwork for applying information from the next several chapters, state your potential topic and then answer the following questions.

Potential topic: _____

1. How relevant will the audience find this material to be?
2. How can I make it easier for audience members to comprehend the information I will share?
3. What common ground do audience members share with each other and with me?
4. What can I do to enhance my credibility?
5. What is my audience's initial attitude toward my speech topic likely to be?
6. What language or cultural differences do audience members have with each other and with me?

You can complete this activity online, view another student sample of this activity, and, if requested, e-mail your completed activity to your instructor. Use your Challenge of Effective Speaking CD-ROM to access Action Step Activity 2.

To see how one student responded to this activity, see the Student Response to Activity 2.

ACTIVITY 2 Identifying Opportunities for Adaptation

Topic: *The criteria for evaluating diamonds*

1. How relevant will the audience find this material to be?

Initially they are not likely to see it as relevant.

How can I demonstrate that the material is timely, proximate, and has personal impact to the members of this audience?

Because they are in their early 20s, I can make the information timely and give it personal impact by putting it in the context of buying an engagement ring. I can make it proximate by using examples of people in this area who have been ripped off because they didn't know what to look for.

2. How can I make it easier for audience members to comprehend the information I will share?

I will orient the audience by reminding them of the different diamond shapes. I figure most people know these, but may have forgotten some of them. I will need to define terms such as cut, clarity, occlusion, and carat. I think that I will need to create vivid examples and personalize some of the more technical information I present. I will know better how to do this once I have decided on all of the main ideas I will present.

3. What common ground do audience members share with each other and with me?

Because most audience members are my age and are from the same national culture, we share areas of common ground that I can draw on. First, a diamond engagement ring is part of our shared culture. We are all about the same age, so we are looking for life mates and may be in the market for a diamond soon. So, using personal pronouns and rhetorical questions to create common ground will be pretty easy. We are different in that I have a very strong interest in gemstones, and I will have to work hard not to become too technical and to assume that audience members are more knowledgeable than they are.

4. What can I do to enhance my credibility?

As I am introducing my speech, I need to work in my credentials. I need to tell the audience that I became interested in diamonds when I got to tour a diamond mine in South Africa while we were visiting family. I also need to share that I work for a jeweler and that I am majoring in geology. I can demonstrate trustworthiness by making sure that I tell the audience where the standards for evaluating diamonds came from. Although I have several friends who will be in the audience, most of the audience does not know me, so I will try to be personable by getting to the presentation early to meet and talk with audience members as they arrive.

5. What is my audience's initial attitude toward my speech topic likely to be?

Most audience members will be only mildly interested in the topic when I begin, but by tying the information to buying an engagement ring, I hope to pique their interest.

6. What language or cultural differences do audience members have with each other and with me?

I will not be speaking in a second language, but I will need to be careful not to use too many technical terms that as a geology major I am comfortable with, but would be "jargon" to my audience. Although most audience members are U.S. nationals, there are three foreign students in class whose cultural engagement practices may not include the giving of a diamond ring. To adapt to them without singling them out, I may say something like "As we all know, in the U.S. it is tradition that when we become engaged the woman receives a diamond ring from the man."

Summary

Audience adaptation is the process of customizing your speech material to your specific audience.

The first stage of audience adaptation is to help the audience see the relevance of your material by demonstrating timeliness (showing how the information is useful now or in the near future), demonstrating proximity (showing relevance to personal life span), and demonstrating personal impact on audience members.

The second stage is to increase audience comprehension of information by orienting listeners, defining key terms, creating vivid examples to illustrate new concepts, presenting information in a frame of reference that is familiar to the audience, personalizing information, comparing unknown ideas with familiar ones, and using multiple methods for developing ideas.

The third stage is to develop common ground by using personal pronouns, asking rhetorical questions, and drawing from common experiences.

The fourth stage is to build speaker credibility by demonstrating knowledge and expertise, establishing trustworthiness, and displaying personableness.

The fifth stage is to meet initial audience attitudes by framing the speech in a way that takes into account how much audience members know and where they stand in their attitudes on that topic.

The sixth stage is to take into account language and cultural differences by overcoming linguistic problems and choosing culturally sensitive material.

The final stage is to complete a written strategy that specifies what actions you will take. Effective speakers are able to use adaptation tactics to develop unique speeches sharing a common speech goal but tailored to the specific needs of different audiences.

CHALLENGE ONLINE

Now that you've read Chapter 5, use your Challenge of Effective Speaking CD-ROM for quick access to the electronic study resources that accompany this text. Your CD-ROM gives you access to InfoTrac College Edition, Speech Builder Express, and the Challenge of Effective Speaking Web site. When you get to the Challenge of Effective Speaking home page, click on "Student Book Companion Site" in the Resource box at the right to access the online study aids for this chapter, including a digital glossary, review quizzes, and the chapter activities.

KEY TERMS

At the Challenge of Effective Speaking Web site, select chapter resources for Chapter 5. Print a copy of the glossary for this chapter, test yourself with the electronic flash cards, or complete the crossword puzzle to help you master the following key terms.

audience adaptation (67)   **proximity** (68)
relevance (67)   **personalize** (70)
timeliness (67)   **common ground** (72)

INFOTRAC COLLEGE EDITION EXERCISE

This chapter has stressed the importance of tailoring your speech to your audience. Use your Challenge of Effective Speaking CD-ROM to access InfoTrac College Edition. Click on PowerTrac. Under Search Index, choose Author. Type "Grazian, Frank" in the entry box and click Submit. After reading the article "Gaining Knowledge about the Audience Is Vital," see if you can explain Grazian's stated formula, "[The audience's] expectation of reward relates to the [listening] effort required." In addition, write down what you consider to be one or two key points of the article. Then, when you are listening to speeches in class or in public, evaluate if the speakers have tailored their speeches to the audience as effectively as they could have.

WEB RESOURCE

Access the Web resource for this chapter online at the Challenge of Effective Speaking Web site. Select the chapter resources for Chapter 5, then click on "Web Resources."

5.1 Holistic Theory of Speaker Credibility (73)

SPEECH PLANNING ACTION STEP

Access the Action Step activity for this chapter online at the Challenge of Effective Speaking Web site. Select the chapter resources for Chapter 5, then click on the activity number you want. You may print out your completed activities, and you should save your work so you can use it as needed in later Action Step activities.

2A Identifying Opportunities for Adaptation (79)

Action Step Activities

Title: Action Step 2.2 Adapting to the Audience

Instructions: The goal of this activity is to develop specific strategies for adapting your speech to your audience.

Questions and Answers
Answer the following questions in the fields below.

Question 1: Write the specific speech goal.

Question 2: Review your results from Speech Preparation Activity 1.2 in Chapter 4.

Question 3: Working with these data, write an audience adaptation strategy in which you include specifics about how you will adapt to that audience. Consider the following questions: A. How will you speak directly to the audience? B. How will you build and maintain interest in your speech goal? C. How will you adapt your material so that it is appropriate to your audience members' current level of knowledge? D. How will you build and maintain your credibility? E. How will you adapt your material to your audience's initial attitude toward your speech goal?

Instructor Email:
Your Name:
Your Email:

Submit Answers   Print Page

6

Researching Information for Your Speech

Locate and Evaluate Information Sources

- Personal Knowledge, Experience, and Observation
- Books, Articles, and General References
- Internet Resources
- Surveys
- Interviews
- Skimming to Determine Source Value
- Criteria for Judging Sources

Identify and Select Relevant Information

- Factual Statements
- Expert Opinions
- Elaborations
- Drawing Information from Multiple Cultural Perspectives

Record Information

- Preparing Note Cards
- Citing Sources in the Speech

© Bruce Ayres/Stone/Getty Images

An empty bag cannot stand upright.
Benjamin Franklin, *Poor Richard's Almanac*, 1740

Jeremy was concerned. He was scheduled to give his first speech in a week, but he hadn't begun to find information. When he was in high school, he had written a term paper on media violence, and he was really taken with the subject. Just a couple of months ago he had read a recent article in a magazine at the doctor's office, but he couldn't remember the issue of the magazine the article was in. He hadn't kept a copy of his term paper, but he was still really interested in the subject. But he wasn't sure exactly what to do to find the information he would need for a speech.

3 | Research   ACTION STEP 3

Gather Information

A. Locating and evaluating information sources
B. Preparing note cards
C. Citing sources

Jeremy's experience is not unlike that of many of us. We have strong opinions that we've formed over time as we have read and interacted with others, but we don't have the sources that support our knowledge or viewpoints at our fingertips. So when we decide to present these ideas in a public forum, we need to do some research.

You are likely to be assigned three or more major speeches during this term, and you are likely to find yourself in need of information to prepare those speeches. In this chapter we explain the many ways you can use to locate information sources, identify and select relevant information, and prepare to cite key sources in your speech.

Locate and Evaluate Information Sources

How can you quickly find the best information related to your specific speech goal? It depends. Speakers usually start by assessing their own knowledge, experience, and personal observations. Then they move on to an electronic search for relevant books, articles, general references, and Web sites. They also look for publicly available surveys, or conduct their own, and interview knowledgeable people.

Personal Knowledge, Experience, and Observation

If you have chosen to speak on a topic you know something about, you are likely to have material that you can use as examples and personal experiences in your speech. For instance, musicians have special knowledge about music and instruments, entrepreneurs about starting up their own businesses, and marine biologists about marine reserves. So Erin, a skilled rock climber, can draw material from her own knowledge and experience for her speech on "Rappelling Down a Mountain."

For many topics, the knowledge you've gained from experience can be supplemented with careful observation. If, for instance, you are planning to talk about how a small claims court works or how churches help the homeless find shelter and job training, you can learn more by attending small claims sessions or visiting a church's outreach center. By focusing attention on specific behaviors and taking notes on your observations, you will have a record of specifics that you can use in your speech.

Careful observation is an often overlooked research strategy. In addition to facts, observation can provide the kinds of specific details that make your topic come alive for an audience.

© Richard Hamilton Smith/CORBIS

Books, Articles, and General References

Most speakers use information found in books, articles, and other specialized sources. In the past speakers located books and articles by going to the library's card catalog (which listed all books) and to indexes and periodical catalogs (which listed magazines and journals). Today both books and periodicals are cataloged in electronic databases that can be accessed online at the library and/or over the Internet. Because electronic library systems and procedures change frequently to incorporate advances in technology, you can avoid losing time and frustrating yourself if you ask a librarian for help. Librarians are "free" resources, experts who can demystify a kinky research problem as well as direct you to short courses or workshops designed to make your research endeavors both productive and efficient.

BOOKS

If your topic has been around for more than six months, there are likely to be books written about it. Most libraries have their book holdings listed in an online catalog by title, author, and subject. Although you may occasionally know the title or author of a book you want, more often you will be looking for books using a subject label, such as "violence in the mass media."

In addition to being able to search by author, title, and subject, most online catalogs now allow you to search by entering "keywords." Even with this user-friendly system, you may find it useful to brainstorm for keywords to use in the search. For instance, Jeremy wanted to find information on the subject "violence in the mass media." With a few minutes of brainstorming, he came up with several keyword designations that brought a variety of "hits"—that is, books available. Notice the different number of hits he found using different keywords:

media violence 95

violence in mass media 57

violence television 88

Under "violence in mass media," one book listed was *The 11 Myths of Media Violence*. Exhibit 6.1 shows the information about the book that was in the database.

EXHIBIT 6.1 Library card (online catalog)

Author:	Potter, W. James	
Title:	The 11 myths of media violence	
Pub Info:	Thousand Oaks, CA: Sage Publications, c2003	
Location	**Call No.**	**Status**
Langsam stacks	P96 V5 P678 2003	Available
Description:	xviii, 259p.; 24 cm	
Note:	Includes bibliographical references (p. 229–249) and index	
Subject:	Violence in mass media	
OCLC#:	51095835	
ISBN:	0761927344 (hard)	
LCCN	2002008802	

Not all of the information will be useful to you. But you certainly will want to note the book's *location* (many libraries have multiple branch locations and not all books are available at all locations), *call number* (the book's physical "address" in the library), and *status* (whether it is immediately available for use or on loan to someone else, archived, or otherwise unavailable).

Another bit of useful information, found under "Note," is whether the book includes bibliographical references and an index. In addition to the information it contains, a book on your topic often leads you to additional sources. For instance, Exhibit 6.1 shows that the *11 Myths* book has twenty pages of bibliographical references, so Jeremy might find several excellent additional sources just from this book's bibliography.

In addition to searching the online database for books, you can use the call number for one book to physically locate other books on the same subject. For example, having found the *11 Myths* book through an electronic search, when Jeremy goes to the library to retrieve it, he will find that other books on that topic have very similar call numbers (in this case, P96 V5 P678 2003) and are shelved together. He can then quickly thumb through them to check their usefulness.

ARTICLES

Articles are published in **periodicals**—magazines and journals that appear at fixed periods. The information in periodical articles is often more current than that published in books, because many periodicals are published weekly, biweekly, or monthly. So, a periodical article is likely to be a better source if a topic is one that's "in the news." Articles are also likely to be the best source of information for highly specialized topics where there may not be sufficient information for books.

periodicals magazines and journals that appear at fixed periods

Most libraries subscribe to electronic databases that index periodical articles. Check with your librarian to learn what electronic indexes your college or university subscribes to. Here are three frequently available databases that index many popular magazines such as *Time* and *Newsweek* as well as some of the popular academic journals such as *Communication Quarterly* and *Journal of Psychology:*

✦ **InfoTrac College Edition** is the electronic index that you can access from the Internet this semester if you purchased a new copy of this textbook. InfoTrac College Edition indexes about 18 million articles in popular magazines and academic journals. See the end of this chapter for how to access and use InfoTrac College Edition.

✦ **InfoTrac University Library** is an expanded version of the InfoTrac College Edition. Available online through most college and university libraries, it provides access to several hundred additional popular magazines and academic journals.

+ **Periodical Abstract,** another electronic database available online in most college and university libraries, provides access to articles in more than one thousand popular magazines and academic journals.

Offerings of these online catalogs are likely to vary from place to place, so it is wise to check with a librarian to see which of these and other catalogs you have access to at your university library.

When using most online indexes, you begin by entering the subject heading that you are researching. The search of an index's database will result in a list of articles that are related to your subject. From these, you can then choose to read or print the individual articles or use the list of citations to locate hard copies of the original articles in your library's periodical section.

For instance, Rhonda has identified the drug "Ecstasy" as a topic under the heading of "designer drugs" on her brainstorming list. Rhonda's tentative speech goal is "I want my audience to understand the dangers of the drug Ecstasy." Working from her computer at home, Rhonda opens up InfoTrac College Edition and types in "ecstasy." She finds 221 periodical references, including the following:

Ecstasy rise. (Drugs) (Brief Article) Robyn Colman, Adrian Colman. *Youth Studies Australia,* June, 2004, v.23 i2 p.4(1)

FDA warns against Green Hornet, an herbal ecstasy: considered unapproved Rx. (News) (Brief Articles) Kerri Wachter. *Family Practice News,* May 1, 2004, v.34 i9 p.5(1)

Estimating the prevalence of Ecstasy use among club rave attendees. George S. Yacoubian Jr., Julia K Deutsch, Elizabeth J. Schumacher. *Contemporary Drug Problems,* Spring, 2004, v.31 il p.163(15)

Rhonda finds that the complete text of each of these articles can be printed on her own printer. At the University of Cincinnati college library, Rhonda could open the extended InfoTrac University Library index or Periodical Abstracts and find article lists that include some of these same articles as well as others.

At times a search may identify articles that cannot be downloaded to your own printer. You will need to go to your library's journal and magazine index to see whether the library has hard copies of the journal articles you want. Then you can manually access those journals.

Newspapers

Newspaper articles are excellent sources of facts about and interpretations of both contemporary and historical issues. At a minimum, your library probably holds both an index of your nearest major daily newspaper and the *New York Times Index.*

Three electronic newspaper indexes that are most useful if they are available to you are (1) the *National Newspaper Index,* which indexes five major newspapers: the *New York Times, Wall Street Journal, Christian Science Monitor, Washington Post,* and *Los Angeles Times;* (2) *Newsbank,* which provides not only the indexes but also the text of articles from more than 450 U.S. and Canadian newspapers; and (3) InfoTrac College Edition's *National Newspaper Index.*

In addition to books and articles, a variety of general references are useful sources for some speech material. At the library, general references are shelved together in a reference room or on reference shelves.

Encyclopedias

An encyclopedia can be a good starting point for research. Encyclopedias give an excellent overview of many subjects, but you certainly should never limit your research to encyclopedias. General encyclopedias contain short articles about a wide variety of subjects. In addition, there are many specialized encyclopedias to choose from in areas such as art, history, religion, philosophy, and science. For instance, a college library is likely to have the *African American Encyclopedia, Latino Encyclopedia, Asian American Encyclopedia, Encyclopedia Britannica, Encyclopedia Americana, World Book Encyclopedia, Encyclopedia of Computer Science, Encyclopedia of Women, Encyclopedia of Women in American Politics,* and many more.

Many libraries have encyclopedias available online, and some encyclopedias can be accessed from the Internet. For a list of encyclopedias that are available on the Web, use your Challenge of Effective Speaking CD-ROM to access Web Resource 6.1: Online Encyclopedias.

STATISTICAL SOURCES

Statistical sources present numerical information on a wide variety of subjects. When you need facts about demography, continents, heads of state, weather, or similar subjects, access one of the many single-volume sources that report such data. Two of the most popular sources in this category are *The Statistical Abstract of the United States* (now available online), which provides numerical information on various aspects of American life, and *The World Almanac and Book of Facts.* You will find almanacs and other statistical resources at your library in the reference section. For links to Web-based statistical sources, use your Challenge of Effective Speaking CD-ROM to access Web Resource 6.2: Statistics Online.

BIOGRAPHICAL REFERENCES

When you need accounts of a person's life, from thumbnail sketches to reasonably complete essays, you can turn to one of the many available biographical references. In addition to full-length books and encyclopedia entries, consult such books as *Who's Who in America* and *International Who's Who.* Your library is also likely to carry *Contemporary Black Biography, Dictionary of Hispanic Biography, Native American Women, Who's Who of American Women, Who's Who Among Asian Americans,* and many more. You can also access some biographical information online. For links to Web-based collections of biographical references, use your Challenge of Effective Speaking CD-ROM to access Web Resource 6.3: Online Biographical References.

BOOKS OF QUOTATIONS

A good quotation can be especially provocative as well as informative, and there are times when you want to use a quotation from a respected person. *Bartlett's Familiar Quotations* is a popular source of quotes from historical as well as contemporary figures. But many other collections of quotations are also available. Some you may find at your library include *The International Thesaurus of Quotations, Harper Book of American Quotations, My Soul Looks Back, 'Less I Forget: A Collection of Quotations by People of Color, The New Quotable Woman,* and *The Oxford Dictionary of Quotations.* For links to Web-based collections of quotations, use your Challenge of Effective Speaking CD-ROM to access Web Resource 6.4: Quotations Online.

U.S. GOVERNMENT PUBLICATIONS

Some government publications are especially useful for locating primary sources. The *Federal Register* publishes daily regulations and legal notices issued by the executive branch and all federal agencies. It is divided into sections, such as rules and regulations and Sunshine Act meetings. Of special interest are announcements of hearings and investigations, committee meetings, and agency decisions and rulings. The *Monthly Catalog of United States Government Publications* covers publications of all branches of the federal government. It has semiannual and annual cumulative indexes by title, author/agency, and subject. For links to several frequently used U.S. federal government documents, use your Challenge of Effective Speaking CD-ROM to access **Web Resource 6.5: Government Publications Online.** Online documents for other countries and for states and cities can be found by using a search engine.

Internet Resources

Internet an international electronic collection of thousands of smaller networks

In addition to printed resources (some of which you can access online), you may find resources for your speech that are only available on the **Internet,** an international electronic collection of thousands of smaller networks. The World Wide Web (WWW) is one network that houses information on a broad range of topics. You can access the Internet through your college or university library, campus computer labs, or your own personal computer. Public libraries also usually provide Internet access. On the Internet you can access electronic databases, bulletin boards, and scholarly and professional electronic discussion groups, as well as Web sites and Web pages that are authored by individuals and groups.

To find information on your topic you will use a search engine, a program that locates information that is housed on the Web. Google, InfoSeek, Excite, Hot-Box, and AltaVista are some of the more popular search engines. You use search engines by typing in keywords for your topic. If you want to be more effective, find out which computer symbols help limit and focus your search. For example, if Jeremy uses AltaVista and puts quotation marks around the words "media violence," he will only get hits in which these two words appear together. If he does not use quotation marks, he will get hits in which either word appears, which will produce lots of "hits" that aren't really relevant to his speech.

newsgroup (bulletin board) an electronic gathering place for people with similar interests

Just as there are different types of print resources, so too there are several types of electronic resources. A **newsgroup** or **bulletin board** is "an electronic gathering place for people with similar interests."[1] To communicate in a newsgroup, a user posts a message (called an article) about some topic that is appropriate for the site. Other users read these articles and, when so disposed, respond. The result is a kind of ongoing discussion in which users (ten, fifty, or maybe even hundreds) may participate. The Internet offers "more than 58,402 different sites that send and receive newsgroups."[2] Today many college classes require students to share their ideas and opinions about course-related topics in class-specific newsgroups. Bulletin boards and newsgroups maintained by scholarly organizations can be a source of new information that has yet to be published in other sources.

HOSTED WEB SITES

Most commercial and nonprofit organizations host Web sites that provide information on the organization and on issues of interest to the organization and its members. For example, the Sierra Club Web site at http://sierraclub.org/ provides updates on a variety of environmental issues. Hosted Web sites can be comprised of numerous Web pages and may also provide links to other related sites.

PERSONAL WEB PAGES AND BLOGS

Personal Web pages and blogs are created and maintained by individuals who can post any information they choose. On the personal sites or blogs of some noted scholars, you can find links to their professional papers. On other personal sites and blogs, you can find posts that support causes or points of view advocated by the site creator.

Surveys

A **survey** is a canvassing of people in order to get information about their ideas and opinions, which are then analyzed for trends. Surveys may be conducted in person, over the phone or Internet, or in writing. At times you will be able to find surveys that have been conducted by other people or organizations that provide information relevant to your topic; at other times you may want to conduct your own survey. If you decide to conduct your own survey, use your Challenge of Effective Speaking CD-ROM to access Web Resource 6.6: Conducting Surveys, which will provide you with important tips for collecting good information.

survey a canvassing of people in order to get information about their ideas and opinions, which are then analyzed for trends

Interviews

Like media reporters, you may get some of your best information for your speech from **interviewing**—the skillful asking and answering of questions. How relevant interviewing is to getting information for your speech will of course depend on your topic. To be effective, you'll want to select the best person to interview and have a list of good questions to ask.

interviewing the skillful asking and answering of questions

SELECTING THE BEST PERSON

Somewhere on campus or in the larger community are people who have expertise in the topic area of your speech and who can provide you with information. Usually a few telephone calls will lead you to the person who would be best to talk with about your topic. For instance, for a speech on "The Effects of Media Violence on Viewers," Jeremy could interview a professor of mass communication or sociology who studies violence in the media. When you have decided whom you should interview, make an appointment—you cannot walk into an office and expect the prospective interviewee to drop everything just to talk to you. Be forthright in your reasons for scheduling the interview. Whether your interview is for a class speech or for a different audience, say so.

If you are trying to get an interview with someone on campus, you might proceed as follows:

> Hello, my name is _____. I am taking a college course in fundamentals of speech, and I'm preparing a speech on the effects of mass media violence on viewers. I understand that you are an expert on this subject. If possible, I'd like to make an appointment to talk with you. Would you be available to talk with me for fifteen or twenty minutes during the next few days?

At the end of the conversation, thank the person, repeat the date and time of the interview, and confirm the office location. If you make the appointment more than a few days ahead, it is usually wise to call the day before the interview to confirm the appointment.

In general you should not waste your expert's time by asking questions whose answers can be easily obtained through print or electronic sources. Try to formulate a list that stays on the subject so that you can get the information you need without taking up too much time.

How many questions you plan to ask depends on how much time you have for the interview. Keep in mind that you never know how a person will respond. Some people are so talkative and informative that in response to your first question they answer every question you were planning to ask in great detail; other people will answer each question with just a few words.

Early in the interview, plan to ask some questions that can be answered easily and that will show your respect for the person you are interviewing. In an interview with a professor, you might start with background questions such as "How did you get interested in doing research on the effects of media violence?" The goal is to get the interviewee to feel at ease and to talk freely.

The body of the interview includes the major questions you have prepared. You may not ask all the questions you planned to, but you don't want to end the interview until you have the important information you intended to get. The questions are designed to get the information necessary to achieve your goal.

Before interviewing the expert, make sure that you have done other research on the topic. Interviewees are more likely to talk with you if you appear informed; moreover, familiarity with what has been written on the subject will enable you to ask better questions.

WRITING GOOD QUESTIONS

The heart of an effective interviewing plan is a list of good questions. They are likely to be a mix of open and closed questions, both primary and follow-up, phrased to be neutral rather than leading.

Primary questions are those main-point questions that the interviewer plans ahead of time. **Follow-up questions** are designed to pursue the answers given to primary questions. Although some follow-ups are planned ahead by anticipating possible answers, more often than not they are composed as the interview goes along. Some ("And then?" "Is there more?") encourage further comments; others ("What does 'frequently' mean?" "What were you thinking at the time?") probe; still others ("How did it feel to get the prize?" "Were you worried when you didn't find her?") plumb the feelings of the interviewee. All are designed to motivate a person to enlarge on an answer.

Open questions are broad-based questions that ask the interviewee to provide perspective, ideas, information, or opinions as the question is answered ("What kinds of people are likely to be most affected by television violence?" "What are some kinds of behaviors that viewers exhibit as a result of viewing violence?" "What would you recommend be done about violence on TV?" "What research studies would you recommend?"). Open questions enable the interviewer to find out about the person's perspectives, values, and goals, but they do take time to answer.[3]

Closed questions are narrowly focused and require only very brief answers. Some require a simple yes or no ("Are young children affected by TV violence more than older children?"); others only a short response ("What behavior seems to be most affected by television violence?"). By asking closed questions, interviewers can control the interview and obtain large amounts of information in a short time. On the other hand, the closed question seldom enables the interviewer to know why a person gave a certain response, nor is the closed question likely to yield much voluntary information.[4]

For the most part, questions should be phrased neutrally. **Neutral questions** are phrased in ways that do not direct a person's answers—for example, "Do you believe television violence has a major effect on children's behavior?" By contrast, **leading questions** are phrased in a way that suggests the interviewer has a preferred answer—for example, "Television violence has a major effect on children's behavior, doesn't it?"

Exhibit 6.2 lists some of the questions you might ask to get information on the effects of television violence on viewers.

CONDUCTING THE INTERVIEW

The following guidelines provide a framework for ensuring an effective interview.

1. Be courteous during the interview. Start by thanking the person for taking the time to talk to you. Throughout the interview, respect what the person says regardless of what you may think of the answers.

---

primary questions questions the interviewer plans ahead of time

follow-up questions questions designed to pursue the answers given to primary questions

open questions broad-based questions that ask the interviewee to provide perspective, ideas, information, or opinions

closed questions narrow-focus questions that require only very brief answers

neutral questions questions phrased in ways that do not direct a person's answers

leading questions questions phrased in a way that suggests the interviewer has a preferred answer

---

Background Information

How did you get interested in doing research on effects of media violence?

Findings

Does your research show negative effects of television violence on viewers?
Are heavy viewers more likely to show negative effects than light viewers?
Have you found evidence that shows major effects on aggressiveness?
   Desensitization?
Have you found evidence that shows effects on civility?
How is violence on TV changing?
How are these changes likely to impact heavy viewers?

Action

Are effects great enough to warrant limiting viewing of violent programming for
   children?
Do you have any recommendations that you would offer the viewing public?

2. Listen carefully. In addition to listening to what is said, also pay attention to how it is said. A person's tone of voice, facial expression, and gestures often communicate as much or more than what the person says. If you don't understand, take time to ask questions. If you're not sure you understand, tell the person what you think he or she meant, such as "If I understand you correctly, you're saying that older and younger children react differently to television violence."

3. Keep the interview moving. Although some people will get so involved that they will not be concerned with the amount of time spent, most people will have other important business to attend to.

4. Make sure that your nonverbal reactions—facial expressions and gestures—are in keeping with the tone you want to communicate. Maintain good eye contact with the person. Nod to show understanding. And smile occasionally to maintain the friendliness of the interview.

PROCESSING THE INTERVIEW

Because your interview notes were probably taken in an outline or shorthand form and may be difficult to translate later, sit down with your notes as soon as possible after the interview and make individual note cards of the information you want to use in the speech. If at any point you are not sure whether you have accurately transcribed what the person said, take a minute to telephone the person to double-check. You do not want to risk your credibility by misquoting an expert.

Skimming to Determine Source Value

Because you are likely to uncover far more information than you can use, you will want to skim sources to determine whether or not to read them in full. **Skimming** is a method of rapidly going through a work to determine what is covered and how.

skimming a method of rapidly going through a work to determine what is covered and how

If you are evaluating an article, spend a minute or two finding out whether it really presents information on the exact area of the topic you are exploring and whether it contains any documented statistics, examples, or quotable opinions. (We will examine the kind of information to look for in the next section.) If you are evaluating a book, read the table of contents carefully, look at the index, and skim pertinent chapters, asking the same questions as you would for a magazine article. Skimming helps you decide which sources should be read in full, which should be read in part, and which should be abandoned. Minutes spent in such evaluation will save hours of reading.

If you are using an electronic periodical index, you may be able to access short abstracts for each article identified by your search. Reading these abstracts can help you decide which sources you want to read in their entirety. Once you have the sources in hand, however, you still need to follow a skimming procedure.

Criteria for Judging Sources

When you rely on printed sources for the information in your speech, you can have some confidence that the information you are using is reliable if it has been published by a reputable publishing house and chosen by professional librarians to be part of the collection. You should be more cautious in using information that you find on the Internet because it contains information from a wide variety of sources and no one oversees the accuracy of the information or honesty of the people who produce it.

For instance, as the authors of *Researching Online* note, "While the universality of the Internet can be good in that it allows previously marginalized voices to be heard, it also adds a new layer of difficulty for researchers."[5] What does this mean? Editors of academic articles and books "have always made it a relative certainty that any source in a college library meets a basic standard of reliability and relevance." They go on to say, "Since the Internet lacks those gatekeepers, you're just as likely to encounter uninformed drivel there as you are to find a unique resource that's unavailable in any other form."[6]

With this warning in mind, it's important for you to critically evaluate the information and authorship of the material you find. In evaluating any source, you

Interviews are a good source of personal narratives that can be used to support key ideas.

© E. Crews/The Image Works

will want to use three criteria that have been suggested by a variety of research librarians: authority, objectivity, and currency.

AUTHORITY

The first test of a resource is the expertise of its author and/or the reputation of the publishing or sponsoring organization. A Web site that doesn't acknowledge the source of the information presented should be viewed skeptically. On the Internet, the first filter of quality is the type of URL. Those ending in ".gov" (governmental), ".edu" (educational), and ".org" are noncommercial sites with institutional publishers. The URL ".com" indicates that the sponsor is a for-profit organization. The second test of information is the qualifications of the source or the author. When an author is listed, you can check the author's credentials through biographical references or by seeing if the author has a home page listing professional qualifications. Use the electronic periodical indexes to see whether the author has other related articles that show expertise, or check the Library of Congress to see whether the author has published books in the field.[7]

At some sites you will find information that is anonymous or credited to someone whose background is not clear. In these cases your ability to trust the information depends on evaluating the qualifications of the sponsoring organization. If you do not know whether you can trust the source, then do not use the information.

OBJECTIVITY

A second test of the information is how impartially it is presented. All authors have a viewpoint, but you will want to be wary of information that is overly slanted. Web documents that have been created under the sponsorship of some business, government, or public interest groups should be carefully scrutinized for obvious biases or good "public relations" fronts. For example, commercial Web sites may include corporate histories and biographical essays on founders that present the company and founders in a favorable light. So you will need other sources to give you a more accurate picture of both the company's and founders' strengths and weaknesses. Similarly, although the Sierra Club is a well-respected environmental organization, the articles found on its Web site are unlikely to present a balanced discussion of the pros and cons of controversial environmental issues.

To evaluate the potential biases in articles and books, read the preface, or identify the thesis statement. These often reveal the authors' point of view. When evaluating a Web site with which you are unfamiliar, look for the purpose of the Web site. Most home pages contain a purpose or mission statement that can help you understand why the site was created. Armed with this information, you are in a better position to recognize the biases that may be contained in the information. Remember, at some level all Web pages can be seen as "infomercials," so always be concerned with who created this information and why.[8]

CURRENCY

In general, newer information is more accurate than older. So when evaluating your sources, be sure to consult the latest information you can find. One of the reasons for using Web-based sources is that they can provide more up-to-date information than printed sources.[9] But just because a source is found online does not mean that the information is timely. To determine how up-to-date the information is, you will need to find out when the information was placed on the Web and how often it is revised. Many authors post this information at the end of the page. If there are no dates indicated and no indications for checking the accuracy, the information should not be used.

Even some recent publications use old information. With statistics, especially, you want to know not only when the statistics were published, but also when the data were collected. If, for instance, you are talking about the number of women in Congress, you don't want to be using data that are more than two years old. Because congressional elections occur every two years, even data from a recent publication could be wrong.

Web Resource 6.7: Analyzing Information Sources provides information on additional criteria you can use to evaluate your sources.

SPEECH PLANNING	ACTION STEP 3
3 | Research	

ACTIVITY 3A **Locating and Evaluating Information Sources**

The goal of this activity is to help you compile a list of potential sources for your speech.

1. Identify gaps in your current knowledge that you would like to fill.
2. Identify a person, an event, or a process that you could observe to broaden your personal knowledge base.
3. Brainstorm a list of keywords that are related to your speech goal.
4. Working with paper or electronic versions of your library's card catalog, periodical indexes (including InfoTrac College Edition), and general references discussed in this chapter, find and list specific resources that appear to provide information for your speech.
5. Using a search engine, identify Internet-sponsored and personal Web sites that may be sources of information for your speech.
6. Identify a person you could interview for additional information for this speech.
7. Skim the resources you have identified to decide which are likely to be most useful.
8. Evaluate each resource to determine how much faith you can place in the information.

You can complete this activity online, print it out, and, if requested, e-mail it to your instructor. Use your Challenge of Effective Speaking CD-ROM to access Action Step Activity 3A.

STUDENT RESPONSE	ACTION STEP 3
3 | Research	

ACTIVITY 3A **Locating and Evaluating Information Sources**

Speech goal: *I would like the audience to understand three tests that can be used to tell if a diamond is real.*

1. Identify gaps in your current knowledge that you would like to fill.

   Since I'm a geology major and have worked with testing, I am familiar with the kinds of works I'll need to fill any gaps in knowledge.

2. Identify a person, an event, or a process that you could observe to broaden your personal knowledge base.

   An event I could observe is a geology teacher's explaining to a freshman-level class how to identify rocks and minerals.

3. Brainstorm a list of keywords that are related to your speech goal.

diamonds, diamond testing, geology

4. Working with paper or electronic versions of your library's card catalog, periodical indexes (including InfoTrac College Edition), and general references discussed in this chapter, find and list specific resources that appear to provide information for your speech.

Fundamentals of Geology, Earth Structure, Earth System History, Principles of Sedimentology and Stratigraphy, The Solid Earth, Manual of Mineralogy

5. Using a search engine, identify Internet-sponsored and personal Web sites that may be sources of information for your speech.

http://wwwmcli.dist.maricopa.edu.aaim/linear/Lo.html

6. Identify a person you could interview for additional information for this speech.

I could interview my mineralogy teacher, John Farver.

7. Skim the resources you have identified to decide which are likely to be most useful.

8. Evaluate each resource to determine how much faith you can place in the information.

Identify and Select Relevant Information

The information that you find in your sources that you will want to use in your speech may include factual statements, expert opinions, and elaborations.

Factual Statements

Factual statements are those that can be verified. "A recent study confirmed that preschoolers watch an average of 28 hours of television a week," "The Gateway Solo laptop comes with a CD-ROM drive," and "Johannes Gutenberg invented printing from movable type in the 1400s" are all statements of fact that can be verified. One way to verify whether the information is factual is to check it against material from another source on the same subject. Never use any information that is not carefully documented unless you have corroborating sources.

factual statements information that can be verified

EXAMPLES

Examples are specific instances that illustrate or explain a general factual statement. One or two short examples such as the following are often enough to help make a generalization meaningful.

examples specific instances that illustrate or explain a general factual statement

> One way a company increases its power is to buy out another company. Recently Kroger bought out Fred Meyer Inc. to make it the largest grocery firm in the country.

> Professional billiard players practice many long hours every day. Jennifer Lee practices as much as ten hours a day when she is not in a tournament.

Examples are useful because they provide concrete details that make a general statement more meaningful to the audience.

Although most of the examples you find will be real, you may find hypothetical examples you can use. **Hypothetical examples** are specific instances based on reflections about future events. They develop the idea "What if . . .?" In the following excerpt, John A. Ahladas presents some hypothetical examples of what it will be like in the year 2039 if global warming continues.

hypothetical examples specific instances based on reflections about future events

> In New York, workers are building levees to hold back the rising tidal waters of the Hudson River, now lined with palm trees. In Louisiana, 100,000 acres of wetland are

steadily being claimed by the sea. In Kansas, farmers learn to live with drought as a way of life and struggle to eke out an existence in the increasingly dry and dusty heartland. . . . And reports arrive from Siberia of bumper crops of corn and wheat from a longer and warmer growing season.[10]

Because hypothetical examples are not themselves factual, you must be very careful to check that the facts on which they are based are accurate.

Three principles should guide your use of examples. First, the examples should be clear and specific enough to create a clear picture for the audience. Consider the following generalization and supporting example.

> **Generalization:** Electronics is one of the few areas in which products are significantly cheaper today than they were in the 1980s.

> **Supporting example:** In the mid-1980s, Motorola sold cellular phones for $5,000 each; now a person can buy a Motorola cellular phone for under $90.

With this single example, the listener has a vivid picture of tremendous difference in about a twenty-year period.

Second, the examples you use should be representative. If cellular phones were the *only* electronics product whose prices had dropped so much over that same period, this vivid example would be misleading and unethical. Any misuse of data is unethical, especially if the user knows better.

Third, use at least one example to support every generalization.

STATISTICS

statistics numerical facts

Statistics are numerical facts. Statistical statements, such as "Only 5 out of every 10 local citizens voted in the last election" or "The cost of living rose 0.6 percent in January 2003," enable you to pack a great deal of information into a small package. Statistics can provide impressive support for a point, but when they are poorly used in the speech, they may be boring and, in some instances, downright deceiving. Here are some guidelines for using statistics effectively.

1. Use only statistics whose reliability you can verify. Taking statistics from only the most reliable sources and double-checking any startling statistics with another source will guard against the use of faulty statistics.

Use statistics from only the most reliable sources, and double-check any startling statistics with another source.

2. Use only recent statistics so that your audience will not be misled. For example, if you find the statistic that only 9 of 100 members of the Senate, or 9 percent, are women (true in 1999), you would be misleading your audience if you used that statistic in a speech. If you want to make a point about the number of women in the Senate, find the most recent statistics. Check for both the year and the range of years to which the statistics apply.

3. Use statistics comparatively. By themselves, statistics are hard to interpret. When we present comparative statistics, they are easier to understand.

In a speech on chemical waste, Donald Baeder points out that chemicals are measured in parts per billion or even parts per trillion. Notice how he goes on to use comparisons to put the meaning of the statistics in perspective:

> One part per billion is the equivalent of one drop—one drop!—of vermouth in two 36,000 gallon tanks of gin and that would be a very dry martini even by San Francisco standards! One part per trillion is the equivalent of one drop in two thousand tank cars.[11]

4. Do not use too many statistics. Although statistics may be an excellent way to present a great deal of material quickly, be careful not to overuse them. A few pertinent numbers are far more effective than a battery of statistics. When you believe you must use many statistics, try preparing a visual aid, perhaps a chart, to help your audience visualize them.

Expert Opinions

Expert opinions are interpretations and judgments made by authorities in a particular subject area. "Watching 28 hours of television a week is far too much for young children," "Having a CD-ROM port on your computer is a necessity," and "The invention of printing from movable type was for all intents and purposes the start of mass communication" are all opinions based on the factual statements cited previously. Whether they are expert opinions or not depends on who made the statements.

How do you tell if a source is an expert? First, the expert must be a master of the specific subject. Second, experts have engaged in long-term study of their subject. Third, an expert is recognized by other people in his or her field as being a knowledgeable and trustworthy authority. For instance, a history professor may be an expert in ancient Greek city-states but know little about Aztec civilization.

When you use expert opinions in your speech, you should identify them as opinions and indicate to your audience the level of confidence that you attach to them. For instance, an informative speaker might say, "Temperatures throughout the 1990s were much higher than average. Paul Jorgenson, a space biologist, believes that these higher-than-average temperatures represent the first stages of the greenhouse effect, but the significance of these temperatures is still being debated."

Although opinions should not take the place of facts, expert opinions can help interpret and give weight to facts that you present.

expert opinions interpretations and judgments made by authorities in a particular subject area

Elaborations

Factual information and expert opinions can be elaborated upon through anecdotes and narratives, comparisons and contrasts, or quotable explanations and opinions.

Marion Wright Edelman

We Can Do Better

> We've lost nearly 90,000 children to guns since 1979. . . . It's safer to be an on-duty police officer or law enforcement officer than a child under ten in America. We can do better.

The idea of "doing better" is what motivates Marion Wright Edelman to speak. "Doing better" pushed young Edelman to defy barriers in the segregated south of the 1940s, and this personal triumph resonates when she speaks. After graduating from Spelman College, Edelman earned a law degree from Yale University and became the first African American woman admitted to the Mississippi Bar. "Doing better" inspired her to work with Martin Luther King, Jr., and in 1974 to found of the Children's Defense Fund, the most successful advocacy and research organization for child heath care, education, and welfare. "Doing better" is a plea she continues to make when she speaks before parents, corporations, politicians, and presidents. Hers is a relentless voice that effectively uses relevant information born of careful research and vast personal experience to speak to diverse audiences about reality.

She is especially effective at using elaborations to dramatize her points:

> This country has had enormous scientific and technological progress. We've sent a man to the moon, we've sent space ships to Mars, we've created a tiny microchip that, you know, has raised billions and trillions of dollars, we have broken the genetic code. Don't tell me we can't figure out and make the commitment to teach every child to read by the third grade, and we just need to make that happen.

Although she has received numerous awards and attained global prominence for her work, Edelman continues to raise her voice to speak, not for her own glory, but on behalf of impoverished children and families.

Quotes: Marion Wright Edelman speaking at the Town Hall Los Angeles luncheon, October 2002.

ANECDOTES AND NARRATIVES

anecdotes brief, often amusing stories

narratives accounts, personal experiences, tales, or lengthier stories

Anecdotes are brief, often amusing stories; **narratives** are accounts, personal experiences, tales, or lengthier stories. Because holding audience interest is important in a speech and because audience attention is likely to be captured by a story, anecdotes and narratives are worth looking for, creating, and using. In a five-minute speech, you have little time to tell a detailed story, so one or two anecdotes or a very short narrative would be preferable.

The key to using stories is to make sure that the point of the story directly states or reinforces the point you are making in your speech. In the following speech excerpt, John Howard makes a point about failure to follow guidelines.

> The knight was returning to the castle after a long, hard day. His face was bruised and badly swollen. His armor was dented. The plume on his helmet was broken, and his steed was limping. He was a sad sight.
>
> The lord of the castle ran out and asked, "What hath befallen you, Sir Timothy?"
>
> "Oh, Sire," he said, "I have been laboring all day in your service, bloodying and pillaging your enemies to the West."
>
> "You've been doing what?" gasped the astonished nobleman. "I haven't any enemies to the West!"
>
> "Oh!" said Timothy. "Well, I think you do now."
>
> There is a moral to this little story. Enthusiasm is not enough. You need to have a sense of direction.[12]

Good stories and narratives may be humorous, sentimental, suspenseful, or dramatic.

COMPARISONS AND CONTRASTS

One of the best ways to give meaning to new ideas is through comparison and contrast. **Comparisons** illuminate a point by showing similarities. Although you can easily create comparisons using information you have found, you should still keep your eyes open for creative comparisons developed by the authors of the books and articles you have found.

comparison illuminating a point by showing similarities

Comparisons may be literal or figurative. Literal comparisons show similarities of real things:

> The walk from the lighthouse back up the hill to the parking lot is equal to walking up the stairs of a 30-story building.

Figurative comparisons express one thing in terms normally denoting another:

> I always envisioned myself as a four-door sedan. I didn't know she was looking for a sports car!

Comparisons make ideas both clearer and more vivid. Notice how Stephen Joel Trachtenberg, in a speech to the Newington High School Scholars' Breakfast, uses a figurative comparison to demonstrate the importance of being willing to take risks even in the face of danger. Although the speech was given years ago, the point is timeless:

> The eagle flying high always risks being shot at by some hare-brained human with a rifle. But eagles and young eagles like you still prefer the view from that risky height to what is available flying with the turkeys far, far below.[13]

Whereas comparisons suggest similarities, **contrasts** highlight differences. Notice how the following humorous contrast dramatizes the difference between "participation" and "commitment."

contrast highlighting differences

> If this morning you had bacon and eggs for breakfast, I think it illustrates the difference. The eggs represented "participation" on the part of the chicken. The bacon represented "total commitment" on the part of the pig![14]

QUOTATIONS

When you find an explanation, an opinion, or a brief anecdote that seems to be exactly what you are looking for, you may quote it directly in your speech. Because audiences want to listen to your ideas and arguments, they do not want to hear a string of long quotations. Nevertheless, a well-selected quotation may be perfect in one or two key places.

Quotations can both explain and vivify. Look for quotations that make a point in a particularly clear or vivid way. For example, in his speech "Enduring Values for a Secular Age," Hans Becherer, Executive Officer at Deere & Company, used this Henry Ford quote to show the importance of enthusiasm to progress:

> Enthusiasm is at the heart of all progress. With it, there is accomplishment. Without it, there are only alibis.[15]

Frequently, historical or literary quotations can reinforce a point vividly. Cynthia Opheim, Chair of the Department of Political Science at Southwest Texas State University, in her speech "Making Democracy Work," used this quote from Mark Twain on the frustration of witnessing legislative decision making:

> There are two things you should never watch being made: sausage and legislation.[16]

Quotations may come from a book of quotations, from an article, or from an interview that you have conducted as part of the speech research process. Regardless of the source, however, when you use a direct quotation you need to

plagiarism the unethical act of representing another person's work as your own

verbally acknowledge the person it came from. Using any quotation or close paraphrase without crediting its source is **plagiarism,** the unethical act of representing another person's work as your own.

Drawing Information from Multiple Cultural Perspectives

How facts are perceived and what opinions are held are often influenced by a person's cultural background. Therefore, it is important to draw your information from culturally diverse perspectives by seeking sources that have differing cultural orientations and by interviewing experts with diverse cultural backgrounds. For example, when Carrie was preparing for her speech on proficiency testing in grade schools, she purposefully searched for articles written by noted Hispanic, Asian, and African American, as well as European American, authors. In addition, she interviewed two local school superintendents—one from an urban district and one from a suburban district. Because she consciously worked to develop diverse sources of information, Carrie felt more confident that her speech would more accurately reflect all sides of the debate on proficiency testing.

REFLECT ON ETHICS

"Dan, I was wondering whether you'd listen to the speech I'm giving in class tomorrow. It will only take about five minutes."

"Sure."

Tom and Dan found an empty classroom and Tom went through his speech.

"What did you think?"

"Sounded pretty good to me. I could follow the speech—I knew what you wanted to do. But I was wondering about that section where you had the statistics. You didn't give any source."

"Well, the fact is I can't remember the source."

"You remember the statistics that specifically, but you don't remember the source?"

"Well, I don't remember the statistics all that well, but I think I've got them about right."

"Well, you can check them, can't you?"

"Check them? Where? That would take me hours. And after all, I told you I think I have them about right."

"But Tom, the accuracy of the statistics seem pretty important to what you said."

"Listen, trust me on this—no one is going to say anything about it. You've already said that my goal was clear, my main points were clear, and I sounded as if I know what I'm talking about. I really think that's all Goodwin is interested in."

"Well, whatever you say, Tom. I just thought I'd ask."

"No problem, thanks for listening. I thought I had it in pretty good shape, but I wanted someone to hear my last practice."

"Well, good luck!"

1. What do you think of Tom's assessment of his use of statistics that "No one is going to say anything about it"?
2. Does Tom have any further ethical obligation? If so, what is it?

Recording Information

As you find the facts, opinions, and elaborations that you want to use in your speech, you need to record the information accurately and keep a careful account of your sources so that they can be cited appropriately.

Preparing Note Cards

How should you keep track of the information you plan to use? Although it may seem easier to record all material from one source on a single sheet of paper (or to photocopy source material), sorting and arranging material is much easier when each item is recorded separately. So it is wise to record information on note cards that allow you to easily find, arrange, and rearrange each item of information as you prepare your speech.

In the note card method, each factual statement, expert opinion, or elaboration, along with the bibliographical information on its source, is recorded on a 4×6 inch or larger index card containing three types of information. First, each card should have a heading or key words that identify the subcategory to which the information belongs. Second, the specific fact, opinion, or elaboration statement should be recorded on the card. Any part of the information item that is quoted directly from the source should be enclosed in quotation marks. Third, the bibliographic publication data related to the source should be recorded.

The bibliographic information you will record depends on whether the source is a book, a periodical, a newspaper, an interview, or a Web site. For a book, include names of authors, title of the book, the place of publication and the publisher, the date of publication, and the page or pages from which the information is taken. For a periodical or newspaper, include the name of the author (if given), the title of the article, the name of the publication, the date, and the page number from which the information is taken. For online sources, include the URL for the Web site, the heading under which you found the information, and the date that you accessed the site. Be sure to record enough source information so that you can relocate the material if you need to. Exhibit 6.3 shows a sample note card.

As your stack of information note cards grows, you can sort the material, placing each item under the heading to which it is related. For instance, for a speech on Ebola you might have note cards related to causes, symptoms, treatment, and means of transmission. The card in Exhibit 6.3 would be indexed under the heading "treatment."

The number of sources you will need depends in part on the type of speech you are giving and your own expertise. For a narrative/personal experience, you obviously will be the main, if not the only, source. For informative reports and persuasive speeches, however, speakers ordinarily draw from multiple sources.

EXHIBIT 6.3   A sample note card

Topic: Ebola

Heading: Treatments

In December 2003, Army scientists reported taking a significant step in developing a possible treatment by successfully treating monkeys that had been deliberately injected with Ebola with an experimental drug.

Lawrence K. Altman and Judith Miller, "Scientists report progress in Ebola treatment," *New York Times,* 12 December 2003, Section A, p. 36, col. 1.

For a five-minute speech on Ebola in which you plan to talk about causes, symptoms, and treatment, you might have two or more note cards under each heading. Moreover, the note cards should come from at least three different sources. Avoid using only one source for your information because this often leads to plagiarism; furthermore, basing your speech on one or two sources suggests that you have not done sufficient research. Selecting and using information from several sources allows you to develop an original approach to your topic, ensures a broader research base, and makes it more likely that you will have uncovered various opinions related to your topic.

SPEECH PLANNING

3 | Research

ACTION STEP 3

ACTIVITY 3B **Preparing Note Cards**

The goal of this activity is to review the source material that you identified in Action Step Activity 3A and to record on note cards specific items of information that you might wish to use in your speech.

1. Carefully read all print and electronic sources (including Web site material) that you have identified and evaluated as appropriate sources for your speech. Review your notes and tapes from all interviews and observations.

2. As you read an item (fact, opinion, example, illustration, statistic, anecdote, narrative, comparison/contrast, quotation, definition, or description) that you think might be useful in your speech, record the item on a note card or on the appropriate electronic note card form available at the Challenge of Effective Speaking Web site. (If you are using an article that appeared in a periodical source that you read online, use the periodical note card form.)

You can complete this activity online and, if requested, e-mail it to your instructor. You can also use online forms to prepare your own note cards and print them out for use in preparing your speech. Use your Challenge of Effective Speaking CD-ROM to access Action Step Activity 3B.

STUDENT RESPONSE

3 | Research

ACTION STEP 3

ACTIVITY 3B Preparing Note Cards

Speech goal: *I would like the audience to understand three tests that can be used to tell if a diamond is real.*

Card 1
Topic: *Testing diamonds*
Heading: *Streak test*

A streak test is conventionally done by scraping the sample across a piece of glazed tile or porcelain and then examining the color of the mark made.

Carla W. Montgomery, Fundamentals of Geology, *3d ed. (Dubuque, IA: Wm C. Brown, 1997), p. 22.*

Card 2

Topic: *Testing diamonds*
Heading: *Streak test*

Malachite leaves a green streak mark; hematite leaves a reddish-brown streak mark.

Cornelius Klein, Manual of Mineralogy, *2d ed. (New York: John Wiley & Sons, 1993), p. 126.*

Card 3

Topic: *Testing diamonds*

A new pocket-sized diamond and gemstone identification device may be available to jewelers soon.

John Gallagher, "Diamond Detector Measures Density," National Jeweler, June 16, 2001, v45, p. 14.

Citing Sources in the Speech

In your speeches, as in any communication in which you use ideas that are not your own, you need to acknowledge the sources of your ideas and statements. Specifically mentioning your sources not only helps the audience evaluate the content but also adds to your credibility. In addition, citing sources will give concrete evidence of the depth of your research. Failure to cite sources, especially when you are presenting information that is meant to substantiate a controversial point, is unethical.

In a written report, ideas taken from other sources are credited in footnotes; in a speech, these notations must be included in your verbal statement of the material. Although you do not want to clutter your speech with long bibliographical citations, be sure to mention the sources of your most important information. Exhibit 6.4 gives several examples of appropriate source citations.

EXHIBIT 6.4   Appropriate speech source citations

"Thomas Friedman, noted international editor for the *New York Times,* stated in his book *The Lexis and the Olive Tree.* . ."

"In an interview with *New Republic* magazine, Governor Arnold Schwarzenegger stated . . ."

"According to an article about the 9/11 Commission Report in last week's *Newsweek* magazine . . ."

"In the latest Gallup poll cited in the February 10 issue of *Newsweek* . . ."

"But to get a complete picture we have to look at the statistics. According to the 2004 *Statistical Abstract,* the level of production for the European Economic Community rose from . . ."

"In a speech on business ethics delivered to the Public Relations Society of America last November, Preston Townly, CEO of the Conference Board, said . . ."

ACTIVITY 3C Citing Sources

On the back of each note card, write a short phrase that you can use in your speech as a verbal citation for the material on this note card.

3 | Research   **STUDENT RESPONSE**   ACTION STEP 3

ACTIVITY 3C Citing Sources

"According to a leading text by Montgomery, the streak test . . ."

"According to the Manual of Mineralogy, . . ."

Summary

Effective speaking requires high-quality information. You need to know where to look for information, what kind of information to look for, how to record it, and how to cite sources in your speeches.

To find material, begin by exploring your personal knowledge, experience, and observations. Then work outward through library and electronic sources, interviewing, and surveying. Look for material in books, articles in periodicals, newspapers, encyclopedias, statistical sources, biographical references, U.S. government publications, and the Internet. You may also want to take surveys and interview people who are knowledgeable on your subject. By skimming material you can quickly evaluate sources to determine whether or not to read them in full. Three criteria for judging sources are authority, objectivity, and currency.

Two major types of material for speeches are factual statements and expert opinions. Factual statements are presented in the form of examples and statistics. Expert opinions are interpretations of facts and judgments made by qualified authorities. Depending on your topic and speech goal, you may use facts and opinions and elaborate them with examples, anecdotes, narratives, comparisons, contrasts, and quotations.

A good method for recording material that you may want to use in your speech is to record each bit of data along with necessary bibliographical documentation on a separate note card. As your stack of information grows, sort the material under common headings. During the speech, cite the sources for the information.

Now that you've read Chapter 6, use your Challenge of Effective Speaking CD-ROM for quick access to the electronic study resources that accompany this text. Your CD-ROM gives you access to InfoTrac College Edition, Speech Builder Express, and the Challenge of Effective Speaking Web site. When you get to the Challenge of Effective Speaking home page, click on "Student Book Companion Site" in the Resource box at the right to access the online study aids for this chapter, including a digital glossary, review quizzes, and the chapter activities.

KEY TERMS

At the Challenge of Effective Speaking Web site, select chapter resources for Chapter 6. Print a copy of the glossary for this chapter, test yourself with the electronic flash cards, or complete the crossword puzzle to help you master the following key terms.

periodicals (87)
Internet (90)
newsgroup (bulletin board) (90)
survey (91)
interviewing (91)
primary questions (92)
follow-up questions (92)
open questions (92)
closed questions (92)
neutral questions (92)
leading questions (92)

skimming (93)
factual statements (97)
examples (97)
hypothetical examples (97)
statistics (98)
expert opinions (99)
anecdotes (100)
narratives (100)
comparison (101)
contrast (101)
plagiarism (102)

WEB RESOURCES

Access the Web resources for this chapter online at the Challenge of Effective Speaking Web site. Select the chapter resources for Chapter 6, then click on "Web Resources."

6.1 Online Encyclopedias (89)
6.2 Statistics Online (89)
6.3 Online Biographical References (89)
6.4 Quotations Online (89)

6.5 Government Publications Online (90)
6.6 Conducting Surveys (91)
6.7 Analyzing Information Sources (96)

Access the Action Step activities for this chapter online at the Challenge of Effective Speaking Web site. Select the chapter resources for Chapter 6, then click on the activity number you want. You may print out your completed activities, and you should save your work so you can use it as needed in later Action Step activities.

3A: Locating and Evaluation Information Sources (96)

3B: Preparing Note Cards (104)

3C: Citing Sources (106)

INFOTRAC COLLEGE EDITION EXERCISE

Use your Challenge of Effective Speaking CD-ROM to access InfoTrac College Edition. Find information on the subject you have selected for the speech you are working on now. Enter your speech subject in the search bar and then press Enter. Look for articles that include information that seems relevant to your speech. Whether you download the article or make note cards, make sure you have the necessary data to cite the source of information if you use it in your speech.

The InfoTrac College Edition database contains hundreds of articles from reliable periodicals and journals. You can use this database to research sources for your speech. Use the password that accompanied a new copy of this text and your Challenge of Effective Speaking CD-ROM to log onto InfoTrac College Edition.

Enter your speech topic into the InfoTrac College Edition keyword search box, as shown here. You can search for keywords in the title, source citation, or abstract of articles, or you can search for a keyword within the content of an article. You can also limit your search to articles published within a certain time frame, to a particular periodical, or to articles that contain certain words. When you've entered your keyword and search criteria, click on "Search."

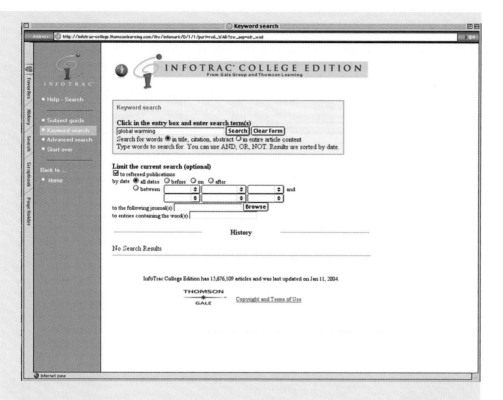

A list of citations containing your keyword appears. Click on a link that interests you to view an article. If you want to narrow your choice of citations to work from, check the "Mark" box, then click "View Mark List" in the menu at the left. A list of only the citations you selected will appear.

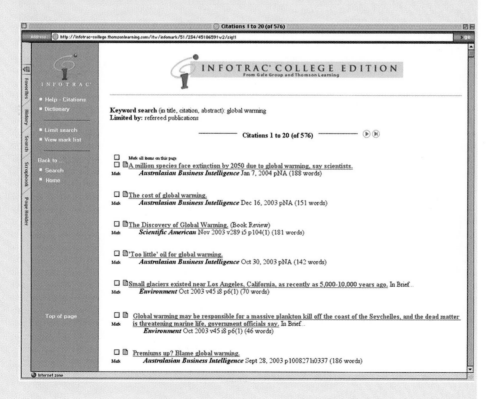

When you click to view an article, you'll see the full text of the article. The menu at the left allows you to print, e-mail, or retrieve an Adobe Acrobat version of the article you selected. When you click on "Links," links to related articles will appear.

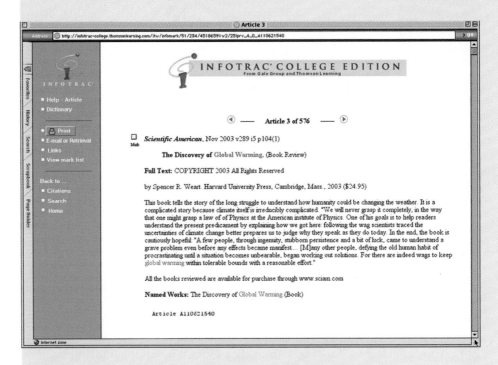

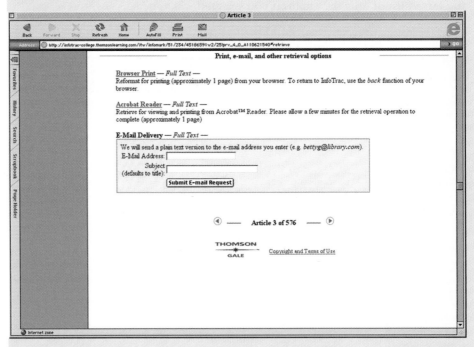

Organizing and Outlining the Speech Body

7

Construct a Thesis Statement
- Identify Main Points
- Write the Thesis Statement

Outline the Body of the Speech
- Outline Main Points
- Identify and Outline Subpoints
- List Supporting Material

Create Section Transitions

Every discourse like a living creature, should be put together
that it has its own body and lacks neither head nor feet,
middle nor extremities, all composed in such a way
that suit both each other and the whole.

Plato, *Phaedrus*

111

Organize Information

A. Identifying main points
B. Writing a thesis statement
C. Developing the main points of your speech
D. Outlining the speech body

"Troy, Mareka gave an awesome speech on recycling paper. I didn't realize the efforts that other universities are making to help the environment, and I haven't heard so many powerful stories in a long time."

"Yeah, Brett, I agree, the stories were interesting. But, you know, I had a hard time following the talk. I couldn't really get ahold of what the main ideas were. Did you?"

"Well, she was talking about recycling and stuff, . . . but now that you mention it, I'm not sure what she really wanted us to think or do about it. I mean, it was really interesting, but kind of confusing too."

Troy and Brett's experience is not that unusual; even well-known speakers can give speeches that aren't as tightly organized as they could or should be. Yet if your speeches are well organized, you are more likely to achieve your speech goal. In the next two chapters, we explain the fourth speech plan action step: Organize your ideas and develop supporting material that achieves your goal and is appropriate for your audience. This chapter describes how to (1) identify main points that are implied in the specific goal statement and write them into a thesis statement for the speech; (2) organize the body of your speech by carefully wording and ordering your main points, and develop each main point with supporting material that is appropriate to the audience; and (3) create transitional statements that move the speech from one main point to the next. In the next chapter we explain how to create introductions and conclusions that pique audience interest and aid audience understanding. Also in that chapter you will learn how working with a complete speech outline enables you to test the structure and development of your ideas before you worry about the specific wording or begin practicing the speech aloud.

Construct a Thesis Statement

Once you have analyzed your audience, created a speech goal, and assembled a body of information on your topic, you are ready to identify the main ideas you wish to present in your speech and to craft them into a well-phrased thesis statement.

Identify Main Points

main points complete-sentence statements of the two to five central ideas that will be used in the thesis statement

The **main points** of a speech are complete-sentence statements of the two to five central ideas that will be used in the thesis statement. The number of main points in a well-organized speech is limited to help audience members keep track of the ideas and to allow each idea to be developed with appropriate supporting material. The difference between a five-minute speech and a twenty-five-minute speech with the same speech goal will be the extent to which each main point is developed.

In some cases, identifying the main points is easy. For Speech Planning Action Step 1, Activity 1E, in Chapter 4, Erin *might* have written "I want the audience to understand the steps in spiking a volleyball." Because she is an excellent volleyball player, however, she doesn't need to do much research in order to identify the steps in this skill, so she is able to write a clear thesis statement: "I want my audience to understand the three major steps in spiking a volleyball—having a proper approach, a powerful swing, and an effective follow-through."

But instead of being in Erin's position, let's say that you are in Emming's. Even though you may have written a goal statement for Activity 1E that is on the right track, you may not be able to turn it into a clearly stated thesis statement at this time. For instance, Emming may have written the specific goal statement "I want the audience to understand the criteria for choosing a credit card." He may even have decided that, because he would probably have time to discuss only a few of these criteria, he would write the specific goal statement "I want the audience to understand three criteria for choosing a credit card." But at this stage he is not yet ready to write a meaningful thesis statement.

If you find yourself in Emming's shoes, you will need to do some further work. How can you proceed? First, begin by listing the ideas you have found that relate to your specific goal. Like Emming, you may be able to list as many as nine or more. Second, eliminate ideas that your audience analysis suggests this audience already understands. Third, check to see if some of the ideas can be grouped together under a broader concept. Fourth, eliminate ideas for which you do not have strong support in the sources you consulted. Fifth, eliminate any ideas that might be too complicated for this audience to comprehend in the time you have to explain them. Finally, from the ideas that remain choose three to five that are the most important for your audience to understand if you are to accomplish your specific speech goal.

Let's look at how Emming used these steps to identify the main points for his speech on criteria for choosing a credit card. To begin with, Emming had a few ideas about what might be the main points for the speech, but it wasn't until he completed most of his research, sorted through what he had collected, and thought about it that he was able to choose his main points. First, he listed ideas (in this case, nine) that were discussed in the information about choosing a credit card that he had discovered.

what is a credit card

interest rates

credit rating

convenience

discounts

annual fee

rebates

institutional reputation

frequent flyer points

Second, Emming eliminated the idea "what is a credit card" because he knew that his audience already understood this. This left him with eight—far too many for his first speech. Third, Emming noticed that several of the ideas seemed to be related. Discounts, rebates, and frequent flyer points are all types of incentives that card companies offer to entice people to choose their card. So Emming grouped these three ideas together under the single heading "incentives." Fourth, Emming noticed that several of the sources had provided considerable information on interest rates, credit ratings, discounts, annual fees, rebates, and frequent flyer points, but had provided very little information on convenience or institutional reputation, so he crossed these ideas out.

Finally, Emming considered each of the remaining ideas in light of the five-minute time requirement he faced. He decided to cross out "credit rating" because, although it influences the types of cards and interest rates for which a person might qualify, Emming believed that he could not adequately explain this idea in the short time available. Explaining to this audience how a credit rating was made might take longer than five minutes by itself and wasn't really as basic as some of the other ideas he had listed. When he was finished with his analysis and synthesis, his list looked like this:

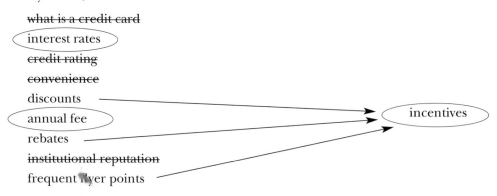

This process left Emming with three broad-based points that he could develop in his speech: interest rates, annual fee, and incentives.

So, if you find that you want to talk about a topic that includes numerous forms, types, or categories, follow Emming's steps to reduce the number of your main points to two to five. To identify the main points of your speeches, you will want to complete Speech Planning Action Step 4, Activity A: Identifying Main Points. Another example of identifying main points is presented in the Student Response to Speech Planning Action Step 4, Activity A.

|  **SPEECH PLANNING** | **ACTION STEP 4** |

4 | Organization

ACTIVITY 4A Identifying Main Points

1. List all of the ideas you have found that relate to the specific purpose of your speech.
2. If you have trouble limiting the number, do the following:
   a. Draw a line through each of the ideas that you believe the audience already understands, or that you have no information to support, or that just seems too complicated.
   b. Combine ideas that can be grouped together under a single heading.
3. From those ideas that remain, choose the two to five you will use as main points in your speech.

You can complete this activity online with Speech Builder Express and, if requested, e-mail your completed activity to your instructor. Use your Challenge of Effective Speaking CD-ROM to access Action Step Activity 4A.

ACTIVITY 4A Identifying Main Points

Specific goal: *I want my audience to understand the disease of leukemia.*

1. List all of the ideas you have found that relate to the specific purpose of your speech.

> *causes of leukemia*
> *chronic mylogeneous leukemia*
> *acute mylogeneous leukemia*
> *bone marrow*
> *bone marrow biopsy*
> *components of blood (red & white cells & platelets)*
> *chronic lymphatic leukemia*
> *acute lymphatic leukemia*
> *lymphoma*
> *prognosis*
> *diagnosis*
> *myloproliferative disorders*
> *types of blood tests*

2. If you have trouble limiting the number, do the following:
  a. Draw a line through each of the ideas that you believe the audience already understands, or that you have no information to support, or that just seems too complicated.
  b. Combine ideas that can be grouped together under a single heading.

3. From those ideas that remain, choose the two to five you will use as main points in your speech.

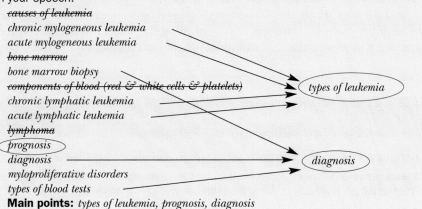

> ~~*causes of leukemia*~~
> *chronic mylogeneous leukemia*
> *acute mylogeneous leukemia*
> ~~*bone marrow*~~
> *bone marrow biopsy*
> ~~*components of blood (red & white cells & platelets)*~~
> *chronic lymphatic leukemia*
> *acute lymphatic leukemia*
> ~~*lymphoma*~~
> *prognosis*
> *diagnosis*
> *myloproliferative disorders*
> *types of blood tests*

> *types of leukemia*
> *diagnosis*

Main points: *types of leukemia, prognosis, diagnosis*

Write the Thesis Statement

A **thesis statement** is a sentence that states the main points of the speech. Not only will you write this sentence on your speech outline, but you will use this sentence as a basis for the transition from the introduction to the body of your speech (see Emming's complete outline in Chapter 8, pages 150–151). Thus, your thesis statement provides a blueprint from which you will organize the body of your speech.

Now let's consider how you arrive at this thesis statement. First, let's look at a situation like Erin's, in which you have enough knowledge to go directly from a specific speech goal to a thesis statement.

thesis statement a sentence that states the main points of the speech

The body of the speech is introduced with a clearly stated thesis statement.

© Keith Dannemiller/Corbis

Recall that Erin might have written her speech goal as "I want the audience to understand the steps in spiking a volleyball." In fact, given her knowledge of volleyball, she was able to write: "I want my audience to understand the three major steps in spiking a volleyball—having a proper approach, a powerful swing, and an effective follow-through." Because she knows what the main points will be, she can write the following thesis statement that she will put on her speech outline: "The three major steps in spiking a volleyball are having a proper approach, a powerful swing, and an effective follow-through."

In order to reach the same level of preparedness as Erin, Emming went through the complete process of determining the ideas for his speech in order to arrive at his three choices: interest rates, annual fee, and incentives. Based on

---

EXHIBIT 7.1   Sample speech goals and thesis statements

Goal: I want my audience to understand how to improve their grades in college.

Thesis statement: Three proven techniques for improving test scores in college are to attend classes regularly, develop a positive attitude, and study efficiently.

Goal: I want the audience to understand the major characteristics of impressionistic painting.

Thesis statement: Impressionistic painting is characterized by unique subject matter, use of color, and technique.

Goal: I want my audience to believe that parents should limit the time their children spend viewing television.

Thesis statement: Parents should limit the time their children spend viewing television because heavy television viewing desensitizes children to violence and increases violent tendencies in children.

Goal: I want my audience to believe that they should learn to speak Spanish.

Thesis statement: You should learn to speak Spanish because it will benefit you personally, economically, and practically.

his specific goal and the main points he had identified, Emming was able to write the following thesis statement: "Three criteria you should use to find the most suitable credit card are level of real interest rate, annual fee, and advertised incentives."

Exhibit 7.1 provides other examples of specific speech goals and thesis statements.

For guidance on writing analytical, expository, and persuasive thesis statements, use your Challenge of Public Speaking CD-ROM to access **Web Resource 7.1: Writing Different Types of Thesis Statements**.

Speech Planning Action Step 4, Activity 4B: Writing a Thesis Statement, directs you in writing a thesis statement for your speech. To see an example of a student's response to this activity, see the Student Response to Activity 4B.

SPEECH PLANNING	ACTION STEP 4

4 | Organization

ACTIVITY 4B **Writing a Thesis Statement**

The goal of this activity is to use your specific goal statement and the main points you have identified to develop a well-worded thesis statement for your speech.
1. Write the specific goal you developed in Activity 4A.
2. List the main points you identified in Activity 4A.
3. Now write a complete sentence that combines your specific goal with your main point ideas.

You can complete this activity online with Speech Builder Express, view a student sample of this activity, and, if requested, e-mail your completed activity to your instructor. Use you Challenge of Effective Speaking CD-ROM to access Action Step Activity 4B.

STUDENT RESPONSE	ACTION STEP 4

4 | Organization

ACTIVITY 4B **Writing a Thesis Statement**

1. Write the specific goal you developed in Activity 4A.
   Specific goal: *I want the audience to be able to find the credit card that is most suitable for them.*
2. List the main points you identified in Activity 4A.
   interest rates
   annual fee
   incentives
3. Now write a complete sentence that combines your specific goal with your main point ideas.
   Three criteria you can use to find a suitable credit card are level of real interest rate, annual fee, and incentives.

Outline the Body of the Speech

An outline of the body of a speech will include three levels of information: (1) main points (I, II, III); (2) a maximum of two sets of subpoints and sub-subpoints (A, B, C; 1, 2, 3) for some or all of your main points; and (3) the elaboration material you choose to develop your main points and subpoints (a, b, c). Why are there two levels of subpoints? In speeches of more than a few minutes, the first level of subpoints (A, B, C) will often require additional explanation, indicated by sub-subpoints (1, 2, 3), before elaboration can begin. Suggested items of relevant elaborations (a, b, c) will then be noted in appropriate places. Exhibit 7.2 shows the general form of how the speech outline system looks.

If you have developed expertise on your topic and done a lot of research, you will have to choose what subpoints and supporting information to present, because the same two to five main points can be developed into a speech that will last for three to five minutes, five to seven minutes, eight to ten minutes, or even become a fifty-minute major presentation! The length of your speech is determined not by the number of main points but by how thoroughly you develop each of them. As you will see, a complex main point may have two, three, or even more subpoints. Each subpoint will be developed through one or more sub-subpoints. And subpoints and/or sub-subpoints may be elaborated with definitions, examples, statistics, personal experiences, stories, quotations, and other items. We want to emphasize that it's often the number and length of elaborations that determine the length of the speech. Whereas in a five-minute speech you may be

---

EXHIBIT 7.2   General form for a speech outline

 I. **Main point one**
    A. Subpoint A for main point one
        1. Sub-subpoint one for subpoint A of main point one
        2. Sub-subpoint two for point A of main point one
    B. Subpoint B of main point one
        1. Sub-subpoint one for subpoint B of main point one
        2. Sub-subpoint two for subpoint B of main point one

 II. **Main point two**
    A. Subpoint one for main point two
        1. Sub-subpoint one for subpoint one of main point two
        2. Sub-subpoint two for subpoint one of main point two
    B. Subpoint two of main point two
        1. Sub-subpoint one for subpoint two of main point two
        2. Sub-subpoint two for subpoint two of main point two
        3. Sub-subpoint three for subpoint two of main point two
    C. Subpoint three of main point two
        1. Sub-subpoint one for subpoint three of main point two
        2. Sub-subpoint two for subpoint three of main point two
        3. Sub-subpoint three for subpoint three of main point two

 III. **Main point three**
    A. Subpoint one of main point three
        1. Sub-subpoint one for subpoint one of main point three
        2. Sub-subpoint two for subpoint one of main point three
    B. Subpoint two of main point three
        . . . etc.

limited to only three elaborations of developmental information of fifteen seconds each, an hour speech may allow six to ten or more elaborations of developmental information of up to several minutes for each.

Now let's look at an example to show how three or four levels of points may be shown on your outline. Notice that all main points, subpoints, and sub-subpoints are written in complete sentences.

   I. One criterion for finding a suitable credit card is to examine the level of real interest rate.

      A. Interest rates are the percentages that a company charges you to carry a balance on your card past the due date.

         1. The average credit card charges 18 percent.

What if you believe that the audience needs to be given additional information to understand what this means? During the speech you may decide to provide an example, present statistics, offer a quotation, tell a story, or provide some other elaboration. But none of these needs to be spelled out in any detail on the outline. The kinds of elaboration you use, length of statements, and the like will be determined during practice sessions. We'll discuss consideration of various points of elaboration further in this section and return to the issue in Chapter 11, Practicing Delivery.

Outline Main Points

Once you have a thesis statement, you can begin outlining the main points that will make up the body of your speech. The main points in your outline are complete-sentence representations of the main ideas that you have identified and specified in your thesis statement. It is important to write main points, subpoints, and sub-subpoints as complete sentences because only sentences can fully express the relationship among the main points and between each main point and the specific goal of the speech. Once you have worded each main point, you will choose an organizing pattern.

WORDING MAIN POINTS

Recall that Emming determined that interest rates, annual fee, and advertised inducements are the three major criteria for finding a suitable credit card and that his thesis statement was "Three criteria that you can use to find a suitable credit card are level of real interest rate, annual fee, and advertised incentives." Suppose he wrote his first draft of main points as follows:

   I. Level of real interest rate

  II. Annual fee

 III. Incentives

From this wording Emming would have some ideas of the main points he was going to talk about, but he wouldn't have specified clearly how each main point was related to his goal. To make the relationships clear, Emming needs to create complete sentences for each. So Emming might write a first draft of the main points of his speech like this:

   I. Examining the level of real interest rate is one criterion that you can use to find a credit card that is suitable for where you are in life.

  II. Another criterion that you can use to make sure that you find a credit card that is suitable for where you are in life is to examine the annual fee.

III. Finding a credit card can also depend on weighing the advertised incentives, which is the third criterion that you will want to use to be sure that it is suitable for where you are in life.

Study these statements. Do they seem a bit vague? Notice that we have emphasized that this is a first draft. Sometimes the first draft of a main point is well expressed and doesn't need additional work. More often, however, we find that our first attempt doesn't quite capture what we want to say. So we need to rework our points to make them clearer. Let's consider Emming's draft statements more carefully. Emming has made a pretty good start. His three main points are complete sentences. Now let's see how Emming might use two test questions to assure himself that he has achieved the best wording for his points.

1. Is the relationship of each main point statement to the goal statement clearly specified? Emming's first main point statement doesn't indicate how we should use interest rates when judging credit cards. So he could improve this statement by stating:

> A low interest rate is one criterion that you can use to select a credit card that is suitable for where you are in life.

Similarly, he can improve the second main point statement by stating:

> Another criterion that you can use to make sure that you find a credit card that is suitable for where you are in life is to look for a card with no annual fee or a very low one.

The third point might be redrafted to state:

> Finding a credit card can also depend on weighing the value of the advertised incentives against the increased annual cost or interest rate, which is the third criterion that you will want to use to be sure that it is suitable for where you are in life.

2. Are the main points parallel in structure? Main points are **parallel** to each other when their wording follows the same structural pattern, often using the same introductory words. Parallel structure helps the audience recognize main points by recalling a pattern in the wording.

Emming notices that each of his main points is worded differently. So he needs to make them parallel:

I. The first criterion for choosing a credit card is to select a card with a lower level of real interest rate.

II. A second criterion for choosing a credit card is to select a card with no or a low annual fee.

III. A third criterion for choosing a credit card is to weigh the value of the advertised incentives against the increased annual cost or interest rate.

Parallelism can be achieved in many ways. Emming used numbering: "first . . . second . . . third." Another way is to start each sentence with an active verb. Suppose Kenneth wants his audience to understand the steps involved in antiquing a table. He might write the following first draft of his main points:

I. Clean the table thoroughly.

II. The base coat can be painted over the old surface.

III. A stiff brush, sponge, or piece of textured material can be used to apply the antique finish.

IV. Then you will want to apply two coats of shellac to harden the finish.

After further consideration, Kenneth might revise his main points to make them parallel in structure by using active verbs (italicized):

I. *Clean* the table thoroughly.

II. *Paint* the base coat over the old surface.

---

parallel when wording of points follows the same structural pattern, often using the same introductory words

III. *Apply* the antique finish with a stiff brush.

IV. *Harden* the surface with two coats of shellac.

Notice how the similarity of structure clarifies and strengthens the message. The audience can immediately identify the key steps in the process.

Well-written main points help you clarify what you will need to present to develop each point.

SELECTING AN ORGANIZATIONAL PATTERN FOR MAIN POINTS

A speech can be organized in many different ways. Your objective is to find or create the structure that will help the audience make the most sense of the material. Although speeches may follow many types of organization, beginning speakers should learn three fundamental patterns: time or sequential order, topic order, and logical reasons order.

1. Time or sequential order. Time order, a frequently used pattern in informational speeches, organizes main points in a chronological sequence or by steps in a process. Thus, time order is appropriate when you are explaining how to do something, how to make something, how something works, or how something happened. Kenneth's speech on the *steps* in antiquing a table (clean, paint, apply, harden) is an example of time order. As the following example illustrates, the order of main points is as important for audiences to remember as the ideas themselves.

time order organizing the main points of the speech in a chronological sequence or by steps in a process

Specific goal: I want the audience to understand the four steps involved in developing a personal network.

Thesis statement: The four steps involved in developing a personal network are to analyze your current networking potential, to position yourself in places for opportunity, to advertise yourself, and to follow up on contacts.

I. First, analyze your current networking potential.

II. Second, position yourself in places for opportunity.

III. Third, advertise yourself.

IV. Fourth, follow up on contacts.

A time order is appropriate when you are showing others how to do or make something or how something works.

Although the use of "first," "second," and so on, is not a requirement when using a time order, their inclusion provides markers that help audience members understand that the *sequence* is important.

2. Topic order. A second often used organization for informative speeches is topic order. **Topic order** organizes the main points of the speech by categories or divisions of a subject. This is a common way of ordering main points because nearly any subject can be subdivided or categorized in many different ways. The order of the topics may go from general to specific, move from least important to most important, or follow some other logical sequence.

In the example that follows, the topics are presented in the order that the speaker believes is most suitable for the audience and speech goal, with the most important point at the end.

Specific goal: I want the audience to understand three proven methods for ridding our bodies of harmful toxins.

Thesis statement: Three proven methods for ridding our bodies of harmful toxins are reducing intake of animal foods, hydrating, and eating natural whole foods.

> **I.** One proven method for ridding our bodies of harmful toxins is reducing our intake of animal products.
>
> **II.** A second proven method for ridding our bodies of harmful toxins is keeping well hydrated.
>
> **III.** A third proven method for ridding our bodies of harmful toxins is eating more natural whole foods.

Whereas time order suggests a sequence that must be followed, topic order suggests that of any possible ideas or methods, these two to five are particularly important, valuable, or necessary. Emming's speech on the three criteria that will enable audience members to find the credit card that is most suitable is another example of a speech using topic order.

3. Logical reasons order. Logical reasons order organizes the main points of a persuasive speech by the reasons that support the speech goal. It emphasizes why the audience should believe something or behave in a particular way. The logical reasons order is most appropriate for a persuasive speech.

Specific goal: I want the audience to donate money to the United Way.

Thesis statement: Donating to the United Way is appropriate because your one donation covers many charities, you can stipulate which specific charities you wish to support, and a high percentage of your donation goes to charities.

> **I.** When you donate to the United Way, your one donation covers many charities.
>
> **II.** When you donate to the United Way, you can stipulate which charities you wish to support.
>
> **III.** When you donate to the United Way, you know that a high percentage of your donation will go directly to the charities you've selected.

As we mentioned earlier, these three organizational patterns are the most common. As you develop your public speaking skill, you may find that you will need to revise one of these patterns or create a totally different one to meet the needs of your particular subject matter or audience. In Chapter 13, Persuasive Speaking: Reasoning with Your Audience, we describe four organizational patterns that are commonly used in persuasive speeches, including the logical reasons pattern.

In summary, then, to organize the body of your speech, (1) turn your speech goal into a thesis statement that forecasts main points; (2) state the main points in complete sentences that are clear, parallel, meaningful, and limited to a max-

topic order organizing the main points of the speech by categories or divisions of a subject

logical reasons order organizing the main points of a persuasive speech by the reasons that support the speech goal

imum of five in number; and (3) organize the main points in the pattern best suited to your material and the needs of your specific audience.

At this point, you have the structure for your complete outline: a speech goal, a thesis statement, and an outline of the main points of the speech.

Figure 7.1 shows what Emming's outline would look like at this stage of preparation. Notice that his specific speech goal is written at the top of the page. His thesis statement comes right after the goal because later it is likely to become part of his introduction.

Use Speech Planning Action Step 4, Activity 4C: Developing the Main Points of Your Speech, to develop well-written main points for your speech. The Student Response to Activity 4C gives an example of this activity completed by a student in this course.

 SPEECH PLANNING   ACTION STEP 4

4 | Organization

ACTIVITY 4C Developing the Main Points of Your Speech

The goal of this activity is to help you phrase and order your main points.
1. Write your thesis statement.
2. Underline the two to five main points identified in your thesis statement.
3. For each underlined item, write one sentence that summarizes what you want your audience to know about that idea.
4. Review the main points as a group.
   a. Is the relationship of each main point statement to the goal statement clearly specified? If not, revise.
   b. Are the main points parallel in structure? If not, consider why and revise.
5. Choose an organizational pattern for your main points.
6. Identify the pattern you have used.

You can complete this activity online with Speech Builder Express, view a student sample of this activity, and, if requested, e-mail your completed activity to your instructor. Use your Challenge of Effective Speaking CD-ROM to access Activity 4C.

 STUDENT RESPONSE   ACTION STEP 4

4 | Organization

ACTIVITY 4C Developing the Main Points of Your Speech

1. Write your thesis statement.

   The three tests that you can use to determine whether a diamond is real are the acid test, the streak test, *and* the hardness test.

   (continued)

2. Underline the two to five main points identified in your thesis statement.
3. For each underlined item, write one sentence that summarizes what you want your audience to know about that idea.

   I. *One way to identify a diamond is by using the acid test.*
   II. *You can also identify a diamond by using the streak test.*
   III. *You can also identify a diamond by using the hardness test.*

4. Review the main points as a group.

   a. Is the relationship of each main point statement to the goal statement clearly specified? If not, revise.

   No. Purpose of test is to identify whether the diamond is real by using a test. The following revision puts emphasis in the right place.

   Revision:

   I. *One way to identify whether a diamond is real is by using the acid test.*
   II. *You can also identify whether a diamond is real by using the streak test.*
   III. *You can also identify whether a diamond is real by using the hardness test.*

   b. Are the main points parallel in structure? If not, consider why and revise.

   Revision:

   I. *One way to determine whether a diamond is real is to use the acid test.*
   II. *A second way to determine whether a diamond is real is to use the hardness test.*
   III. *A third way to determine whether a diamond is real is to use the streak test.*

5. Choose an organizational pattern for your main points.

   I. *One way to determine whether a diamond is real is to use the acid test.*
   II. *A second way to determine whether a diamond is real is to use the streak test.*
   III. *A third way to determine whether a diamond is real is to use the hardness test.*

6. Identify the type of order you have used.

   Topic

Identify and Outline Subpoints

Just as we must identify the main points of our speech, we must also identify the subpoints of the speech. As we said earlier, your outline will include complete-sentence statements of each of your subpoints. A main point may have two, three, or even more subpoints depending on the complexity of the main point.

IDENTIFYING SUBPOINTS

We can identify subpoints by sorting the note cards we prepared while conducting research into piles that correspond to each of our main points. The goal at this point is to see what information we have that supports each of our main points. For example, at the end of sorting his note cards Emming might find that he has the following items of information that support the first main point:

Main point: The first criterion for choosing a credit card is to select a card with a lower interest rate.

Most credit cards carry an average of 8 percent after specified 0 interest period.

Some cards carry as much as 21 percent after the first year.

Some cards offer a grace period.

Department store rates are often higher than bank rates.

Variable rate means that the rate can change from month to month.

Fixed rate means that the rate will stay the same.

Many companies offer 0 percent interest for up to 12 months.

Many companies offer 0 interest for a few months.

Once you have listed the items of information that make the point, look for relationships between and among ideas. As you analyze, you can draw lines connecting items of information that fit together logically, cross out information that seems irrelevant or doesn't really fit, and combine similar ideas using different language. Exhibit 7.3 depicts Emming's analysis of the information listed under his first main point.

In most cases, similar items that you have linked can be grouped under broader headings. For instance, Emming has four statements related to specific percentages and two statements related to types of interest rates. For the four statements related to specific percentages, he might create the following heading:

Interest rates are the percentages that a company charges you to carry a balance on your card past the due date.

Then under that heading, he can list the four statements:

Most credit cards carry an average of 8 percent.

Some cards carry as much as 21 percent.

Many companies offer 0 percent interest for up to 12 months.

Other companies offer 0 interest for a few months.

For the two statements related to types of interest rates, he might create the following heading:

Interest rates can be variable or fixed.

Under that heading, he can list the two statements:

Variable rate means that the rate can change from month to month.

Fixed rate means that the rate will stay the same.

You are also likely to have listed information that you decide not to include in the outline. Emming decided to cut the department store point because his emphasis was not on who was offering the rates, but on what percentages were being

---

EXHIBIT 7.3   Editing material supporting the main point

I. The first criterion for choosing a credit card is to select a card with a lower interest rate.

→ Most credit cards carry an average of 8 percent after specified 0 interest period.

→ Some cards carry as much as 21 percent after the first year.

~~Some cards offer a grace period.~~

~~Department store rates are often higher than bank rates.~~

→ Variable rate means that the rate can change from month to month.

→ Fixed rate means that the rate will stay the same.

→ Many companies offer 0 percent interest for up to 12 months.

→ Many companies offer 0 interest for a few months.

charged. Likewise, he thought that the grace period point wasn't directly related to either of the main subpoints he wanted to emphasize.

Sometimes you'll find you have stated the same point two different ways:

Many companies offer 0 interest for the first year.

Some companies offer 0 interest for a few months.

Emming might combine the two to read:

Many companies are now offering 0 interest rates for anywhere from a few months to a full year.

OUTLINING SUBPOINTS

Subpoints should also be represented on the outline in full sentences. As with main points, they should be revised until they are clearly stated. The items of information listed for Emming's first main point might be grouped and subordinated as follows:

I. The first criterion for choosing a credit card is to select a card with a lower interest rate.

    A. Interest rates are the percentages that a company charges you to carry a balance on your card past the due date.

        1. Most credit cards carry an average of 8 percent.

        2. Some cards carry as much as 21 percent.

        3. Many companies quote very low rates (0 to 3 percent) for specific periods.

    B. Interest rates can be variable or fixed.

        1. A variable rate means that the rate can change from month to month.

        2. A fixed rate means that the rate will stay the same.

List Supporting Material

supporting material developmental material that will be used in the speech, including personal experiences, examples, illustrations, anecdotes, statistics, and quotations

A good outline will also include short outline statements of **supporting material**—developmental material that will be used in the speech, including personal experiences, examples, illustrations, anecdotes, statistics, quotations, and other forms of supporting material. You will choose these items to meet the needs of your specific audience.

As we have mentioned, it is the supporting material that elaborates the main points and subpoints of the speech. Although it is theoretically possible to deliver a speech by merely presenting the outlined main points and subpoints, these points can ordinarily be stated in only a couple of minutes. Thus, if the time limit for your speech is three to five minutes, counting the addition of an introduction and conclusion, you will still have a minute or so for elaboration. The point is that whether a speech is three to five minutes, five to seven minutes, or ten or more minutes may not affect the statement of your main points and subpoints. Making the speech longer will involve your developing (elaborating) your main points and subpoints with various supporting materials.

How to build developmental materials during practice sessions will be discussed at length in Chapter 11, Practicing Delivery.

Create Section Transitions

Once you have outlined your main points, subpoints, and potential supporting material, you will want to consider how you will move smoothly from one main point to another. **Transitions** are words, phrases, or sentences that show the relationship between, or bridge, two ideas. Transitions act like tour guides leading the audience from point to point through the speech. **Section transitions** are complete sentences that show the relationship between, or bridge, major parts of the speech. They may summarize what has just been said or preview the next main idea.

For example, suppose Kenneth has just finished the introduction of his speech on antiquing tables and is now ready to launch into his main points. Before stating his first main point, he might say, "Antiquing a table is a process that has four steps. Now let's consider the first one." When his listeners hear this transition, they are signaled to mentally prepare to listen to and remember the first main point. When he finishes his first main point, he will use another section transition to signal that he is done speaking about step one and is moving on to discuss step two: "Now that we see what is involved in cleaning the table, we can move on to the second step."

You might be thinking that this sounds repetitive or patronizing, but section transitions are important for two reasons. First, they help the audience to follow the organization of ideas in the speech. If every member of the audience were able to pay complete attention to every word, then perhaps section transitions would not be needed. But as people's attention rises and falls during a speech, they often find themselves wondering where they are. Section transitions give us a mental jolt and say "Pay attention."

Second, section transitions are important in helping us retain information. We may well remember something that was said once in a speech, but our retention is likely to increase markedly if we hear something more than once. Good transitions are important in writing, but they are even more important in speaking. If listeners get lost or think they have missed something, they cannot check back as they can when reading.

transitions words, phrases, or sentences that show a relationship between, or bridge, two ideas

section transitions complete sentences that show the relationship between, or bridge, major parts of a speech

© Michael Newman./PhotoEdit

Section transitions mentally prepare the audience to move to the next main point.

In a speech, if we forecast main points, then state each main point, and also provide transitions between points, audiences are more likely to follow and remember the organization.

On your speech outline, section transitions are written in parentheses at the junctures of the speech.

Complete the outline for the body of your speech by doing Speech Planning Action Step 4, Activity 4D: Outlining the Speech Body. The Student Response to Activity 4D shows Emming's response to this activity.

SPEECH PLANNING   ACTION STEP 4

4 | Organization

ACTIVITY 4D Outlining the Speech Body

The goal of this exercise is to help you get started on the outline for the body of your first speech. Using complete sentences, write the following:
1. The specific speech goal you developed in Activity 1E.
2. The thesis statement you developed in Activity 4A.
3. A transition to the first main point.
4. The first main point you developed in Activity 4B.
5. The outline of the subpoints and support for your first main point that you developed in Activity 4C.
6. A transition from your first main point to your second.
7. The other points, subpoints, support, and transition statements. Use the format for numeration, spacing, and so on, shown in the Student Response to Activity 4D. (Note that the labels Introduction, Conclusion, and Sources are included just to help you understand the requirements for your final outline.) For a sample of a completed outline, see pages 150–151 of Chapter 8.

You can complete this activity online with Speech Builder Express and, if requested, e-mail your completed activity to your instructor. Use your Challenge of Effective Speaking CD-ROM to access Activity 4D.

STUDENT RESPONSE   ACTION STEP 4

4 | Organization

ACTIVITY 4D Outlining the Speech Body

Emming's outline, including his goal, thesis statement, speech body (complete development of one main point and subpoints), and transitions.

Specific speech goal: *I would like the audience to understand the major criteria for finding a suitable credit card.*

Thesis statement: *Three criteria that will enable the audience to find the credit card most suitable for them are level of real interest rate, annual fee, and advertised incentives.*

Introduction

(Transition: Let's consider the first criterion.)

Body

    I. *The first criterion for choosing a credit card is to select a card with a lower interest rate.*

        A. *Interest rates are the percentages that a company charges you to carry a balance on your card past the due date.*

[Then under that heading, he can list the relevant subpoints.]

            1. *Most credit cards carry an average of 8 percent.*

            2. *Some cards carry as much as 21 percent.*

            3. *Many companies offer 0 interest rates anywhere from a few months to a full year.*

        B. *Interest rates can be variable or fixed.*

            1. *Variable rates mean that the rate can change from month to month.*

            2. *Fixed rates mean that the rate will stay the same.*

(Transition: Now that we've considered interest rates, let's look at the next criterion.)

    II. *A second criterion for choosing a credit card is to select a card with no or a low annual fee.*

(Transition: After considering interest rates and annual fee, you can consider the final criterion.)

    III. *A third criterion for choosing a credit card is to weigh the value of the advertised incentives against the increased annual cost or interest rate.*

Conclusion

Sources

REFLECT ON ETHICS

Carson had done a variety of computer searches for his speech on cloning and had come up with more than seven major articles, but time was getting short. He had had three tests the week before his assigned speech, and even though he had taken the time to get an excellent list of sources, the speech itself was due the next morning.

As Carson thought about his problem, it occurred to him that the one magazine article he had read really "said it all." In fact, as far as he could see, most of the key ideas he had noticed in scanning the other articles were included in this one source. Suddenly a "plan" for his speech organization hit him. He would use the organization of this article for his speech and adapt the thesis statement from the article as his own. He would list the other articles in his bibliography. Moreover, because the article actually referenced three of the sources his search had uncovered, his bibliography really did reflect what he had found and what was in the speech.

Quickly then, Carson took the three key paragraphs from the article and outlined them for his speech. He used a story related in the article as his introduction and wrote a short summary of the three main points for the conclusion. "Great," he thought, "in just about fifteen minutes I've got a great speech for tomorrow." He even had time to read through the three paragraphs about four times before he went to bed—he knew he was in great shape for the speech.

1. Was Carson's method of organizing his speech ethical? Why do you reach this conclusion?
2. How should material from a key article be used?

Summary

A speech that is well organized is likely to achieve its goal. Speech organization begins by writing a thesis statement that articulates your goal to inform, persuade, or entertain and is based on the main points suggested in your specific speech goal. The thesis statement identifies the key ideas that you will present in the speech.

The body of the speech includes main points and subpoints that should be written in complete sentences and checked to make sure that they are clear, parallel in structure, meaningful, and limited in number to five or less.

The order in which you present your main points depends on the type of speech you are giving and on the specific nature of the material you want to present. Three fundamental organizational patterns are time, topic, and logical reasons. You will want to choose an organizational pattern that best helps your audience understand and remember your main points.

The next step in organizing your speech is to choose and order material that you will use to explain each main point. To begin this process, create lists of the information you have that relates to each of your main points. Then review each list, grouping similar information under larger headings and identifying the information that is most important for helping the audience understand and remember the main point. These subpoints should be written in complete sentences and entered on your outline below the main point to which they belong. As a speaker, you will also want to consider such elements as definitions, examples, statistics, personal experiences, stories, and quotations that you can use to elaborate your key subpoints.

Sectional transitions bridge major parts of the speech and occur between the introduction and the body, between main points within the body, and between the body and the conclusion. Sectional conclusions should be preplanned and place in the outline as parenthetical statements where they are to occur.

topic order (122)
logical reasons order (122)
supporting material (126)

transitions (127)
section transitions (127)

INFOTRAC COLLEGE EDITION EXERCISE

Use your Challenge of Effective Speaking CD-ROM to access InfoTrac College Edition. Click on PowerTrac, then click on Keyword and find Journal Name in the drag-down menu. Enter the journal name "Vital Speeches." Find the speech "Service: Life beyond Self" by Geneva B. Johnson, "The Great Equalizers: Six Secrets to Success for All Entrepreneurs" by Katherine K. Clark, or a similar speech.

1. For the speech you chose, what is the speech goal?
2. Outline the main points of the speech. Were they clearly stated? If not, how might the speaker have increased their clarity? If so, what led to their clarity?
3. Identify any transitions between main points. Which transition(s) seemed particularly informative or useful? Why?

WEB RESOURCE

Access the Web resource for this chapter online at the Challenge of Effective Speaking Web site. Select the chapter resources for Chapter 7, then click on "Web Resources."

7.1 Writing Different Types of Thesis Statements (117)

SPEECH PLANNING ACTION STEPS

Access the Action Step activities for this chapter online at the Challenge of Effective Speaking Web site. Select the chapter resources for Chapter 7, then click on the activity number you want. You may print out your completed activities, and you should save your work so you can use it as needed in later Action Step activities.

4A: Identifying Main Points (114)
4B: Writing a Thesis Statement (117)
4C: Developing the Main Points of Your Speech (123)

4D: Outlining the Speech Body (128)

Completing the Outline: Creating the Introduction and the Conclusion

© Phil Boorman/Taxi/Getty Images

To lose our fluency of speech, has nowhere a worse effect than at the commencement . . . that pilot is surely one of the worst who runs his vessel aground as it is leaving the harbor.

Quintilian, *Institutes of Oratory*, IV, 1, 61

Margot had asked Donna to listen to her rehearse her speech. As she stood in front of the classroom where she was practicing, she began, "Today I want to tell you some things about diamonds. There are several criteria you can use in evaluating a diamond."

"Whoa, Margot," Donna said. "That's your introduction?"

"Yes," Margot replied. "People know what diamonds are. Why shouldn't I just get on with the speech?"

○ ○ ○
△ △ △
□ □ □

ACTION STEP 4

4 | Organization

Organizing Information

E. Creating speech introductions
F. Creating speech conclusions
G. Compiling a list of sources
H. Completing the speech outline

Margot's question sounds reasonable—most people know what diamonds are. But this doesn't mean that everyone in the audience is ready to listen to a speech about evaluating diamonds. People might think the topic is boring, irrelevant to them, or for some other reason not worth their time. For most speeches, how well you start the speech may determine whether most members of the audience even listen, and how well you start and how well you finish your speech can play a major role in the speech's overall success.

In the previous chapter we described the first few tasks involved in organizing your speech. These resulted in a complete-sentence outline of the body. In this chapter we describe how you complete your organizational process by creating an introduction that both gets attention and leads into the body of the speech; creating a conclusion that both summarizes the material and leaves the speech on a high note; writing a title; and completing a list of sources used to develop the speech.

Creating the Introduction

Now that the body of the speech has been developed, you can decide how to begin your speech. Because the introduction establishes your relationship with your audience, you will want to develop two or three different introductions and then select the one that seems best for this particular audience. Although your introduction may be very short, it should gain audience attention and motivate them to listen to all that you have to say. An introduction is generally about 10 percent of the length of the entire speech, so for a five-minute speech (approximately 750 words), an introduction of 60 to 85 words is appropriate.

Goals of the Introduction

An effective introduction is designed to get audience attention and introduce the thesis. In addition, effective introductions may also begin to establish speaker credibility, set the tone for the speech, and create a bond of goodwill between the speaker and the audience.

GETTING ATTENTION

An audience's physical presence does not guarantee that people will actually listen to your speech. Your first goal, then, is to create an opening that will win your listeners' attention by arousing their curiosity and motivating them to

An effective speech introduction will not only get attention and lead into the body of the speech, but will also build goodwill and set the tone for the speech.

© Charles Gupton /corbisstockmarket.com

continue listening. In this chapter we discuss six types of attention-getting devices you can use not only to get attention but also to stimulate audience excitement for finding out what you have to say.

STATING THE THESIS

Because audiences want to know what the speech is going to be about, it's important to introduce the two, three, or (occasionally) four or five points of your speech by stating your thesis. Thus, for his speech about romantic love, after Miguel gains attention, he might draw from his thesis statement and say, "In the next five minutes, I'd like to explain to you that romantic love is comprised of three elements: passion, intimacy, and commitment." Stating main points in the introduction is necessary unless you have some special reason for not revealing the details of the thesis. For instance, after getting the attention of his audience Miguel might say, "In the next five minutes, I'd like to explain the three aspects of romantic love," a statement that specifies the number of main points, but leaves stating specifics for transition statements immediately preceding main points.

Now let's consider three additional goals that may be achieved during the opening—especially for speeches that are ten to fifteen minutes or more.

ESTABLISHING YOUR CREDIBILITY

If someone hasn't formally introduced you before you speak, audience members are going to wonder who you are and why they should pay attention to what you have to say. So, another goal of the introduction may be to begin to build your credibility. For instance, if the audience is likely to question Miguel's qualifications for speaking on the topic of romantic love, after his attention-getting statement he might say, "Last semester I took an interdisciplinary seminar on romantic love, and now I'm doing an independent research project on commitment in relationships, so I feel comfortable talking with you about this topic."

SETTING A TONE

The introductory remarks may also reflect the emotional tone that is appropriate for the topic. A humorous opening will signal a lighthearted tone; a serious opening signals a more thoughtful or somber tone. For instance, a speaker who starts with a rib-tickling ribald story is putting the audience in a lighthearted, devil-may-care mood. If that speaker then says, "Now let's turn to the subject of abortion (or nuclear war, or drug abuse)," the audience will be confused by the preliminary introduction that signaled a far different type of subject.

CREATING A BOND OF GOODWILL

In your first few words, you may also establish how an audience will feel about you as a person. If you're enthusiastic, warm, and friendly and give a sense that what you're going to talk about is in the audience's best interest, it will make them feel more comfortable with spending time listening to you.

For longer speeches you may be able to accomplish all five goals in the introduction. But for shorter speeches, such as those you are likely to be giving in class, you will focus on getting attention and stating the thesis and will try to build your credibility, establish an appropriate tone, and develop goodwill as the speech moves along.

Types of Introductions

The ways to begin a speech are limited only by your imagination. Here we describe six types of introductions that can get attention and excite curiosity and interest in the topic: startling statements, rhetorical questions, stories, personal references, quotations, and suspense.

STARTLING STATEMENT

A startling statement is a sentence or two that grabs your listeners' attention by shocking them in some way. Because of the shock of what has been said, audience members stop what they were doing or thinking and focus on the speaker. The following example illustrates the attention-getting effect of a startling statement:

> Suppose that as I walked to the front of this room I had pulled a gun and pointed it at you. Would you be scared? Now suppose I said, "Oh, don't worry, this gun is registered." Would you feel relieved? Today I want to explain three reasons why gun registration is an ineffective means of gun control.

In less than thirty seconds of speaking time for most speakers, this 58-word introduction grabs attention and leads into the speech.

RHETORICAL QUESTION

Asking a **rhetorical question**—a question seeking a mental rather than a vocal response—is another appropriate opening for a short speech. Notice how a student began her speech on counterfeiting with these three short rhetorical questions:

rhetorical question a question seeking a mental rather than a vocal response

> What would you do with this twenty-dollar bill if I gave it to you? Take your friend to a movie? Treat yourself to a pizza and drinks? Well, if you did either of these things, you could get in big trouble—this bill is counterfeit!
>
> Today I want to explain the extent of counterfeiting in America and what our government is doing to curb it.

Again, another short opening that can be stated in less than thirty seconds gets attention and leads into the speech.

Using rhetorical questions can also lay the groundwork for a speech of thirty minutes or more. Notice how Wendy Liebermann, President of WSL Strategic Retail, got the attention of her audience—members of the Non-Prescription Drug

Manufacturers Association—with a series of questions. Then notice how she continues her opening that sets a tone:

> Have you wondered of late what's going on with consumers? Why they are so full of contradictions when it comes to spending money? Why they will buy a $500 leather jacket at full price but wait for a $50 sweater to go on sale? Will buy a top-of-the-line sports utility vehicle then go to Costco to buy new tires? Will eagerly pay $3.50 for a cup of coffee but think $1.29 is too expensive for a hamburger? Will spend $2.00 for a strawberry-smelling bath soap but wait for a coupon to buy a $0.99 twin pack of toilet soap?
>
> The economy is booming. Unemployment is at a 25-year low. Real income has increased. Why isn't everyone out spending like they did in the 1980s—shopping everywhere, buying everything? Why are so many companies struggling? What is this paradox? Is there a paradox?
>
> Well, that's what we are going to talk about today. This apparent consumer paradox: what it is, what it means and how to make sense out of it. Because if we don't understand it and respond to it, there's a very good chance we won't attract the consumers we want, and a very, very good chance we won't build long-term profitable sales, and a very, very, very good chance we won't all be sitting here this time next year.[1]

This 221-word opening (two minutes or less) would work for a speech of ten to fifteen minutes or longer. Notice that the series of questions in the first paragraph touches the behavior of many of us and even introduces some light humor. Right away, the speaker is not only getting attention but gaining goodwill. Moreover, the lighthearted approach also sets the tone for her speech. Then notice that her second series of questions starts to really get the audience to think with her. Finally, notice that in the third paragraph she concludes her introduction by telling the audience exactly what she will be looking at in reference to these questions.

STORY

A story is an account of something that has happened. Because most people enjoy a well-told story, you may want to consider using one for your introduction.

Unfortunately, many stories are lengthy and can take more time to tell than is appropriate for the length of your speech, so only use such a story if you can abbreviate it so that it is just right for your speech length. Notice how the following story, appropriate for a longer speech, captures attention and leads into the topic of the speech, balancing stakeholder interests.

> A tightrope walker announced that he was going to walk across Niagara Falls. To everyone's amazement, he made it safely across, and everybody cheered. "Who believes I can ride a bicycle across?" And they all said, "Don't do it, you'll fall!" But he got on his bicycle and made it safely across. "Who believes I can push a full wheelbarrow across?" Well, by this time the crowd had seen enough to make real believers of them, and they all shouted, "We do! We do!" At that he said, "OK . . . Who wants to be the first to get in?" And they all remained silent.
>
> Well, that's how many investors feel about companies who have adopted the philosophy that balancing the interests of all stakeholders is the true route to maximum value. They go from skeptics to believers, but are very reluctant to get in that wheelbarrow.
>
> What I would like to do this afternoon is share with you Eastman's philosophy of stakeholder balance, give you some specific examples of how we're putting this philosophy into practice, and then I'll give you some results.[2]

PERSONAL REFERENCE

Introductions that personalize the topic for audience members quickly establish how the topic is in the individual's self-interest. In addition to getting attention, a personal reference can be especially effective at engaging listeners as active participants in a speech. A personal reference opening like this one on exercise may be suitable for a speech of any length:

> Say, were you panting when you got to the top of those four flights of stairs this morning? I'll bet there were a few of you who vowed you're never going to take a class on the top floor of this building again. But did you ever stop to think that maybe the problem isn't that this class is on the top floor? It just might be that you are not getting enough exercise.
>
> Today I want to talk with you about how you can build an exercise program that will get you and keep you in shape, yet will only cost you three hours a week, and not one red cent!

This 112-word opening, which can be presented in less than a minute, not only gets attention but also personalizes the topic in a way that helps motivate listeners to pay attention.

For longer speeches, you can build personal references that tie together the speaker, the audience, and the setting. Let's see how Dana Mead, Chairman and Chief Executive Officer of Tenneco, used a personal reference in the opening to his speech to the Executives' Club of Chicago:

> Thank you and good afternoon. It's great to be back in Chicago, the city of new beginnings. In 1893, Chicago hosted the world's fair—the Columbian Exposition—commemorating one of the world's greatest beginnings, the 400th anniversary of Columbus' voyage to America. (Actually, it took 401 years before Chicago completed the exhibition—but it was so grand no one was nitpicking!)
>
> The fair had a real second purpose—to demonstrate to the world what progress Chicago had made since the fire of 1871—and of course it succeeded in truly impressing the world.
>
> Chicago continues to impress the world. As one of the global economy's industrial titans, your hosting of the Transatlantic Business Dialogue, in my recent experience, was the catalyst for the impressive progress which that meeting produced. So, when I talk about the new American economy, my remarks should be familiar—you are already part of it.[3]

Although this personal reference was only the first part of Mead's speech introduction, it gives you a good idea of the kinds of information you can use to relate to your audience.

QUOTATION

A particularly vivid or thought-provoking quotation makes an excellent introduction to a speech of any length, especially if you can use your imagination to relate the quotation to your topic. For instance, in the beginning of her introduction, notice how Susan Morse, Director of the Pew Partnership for Civic Change, uses a quotation to get the attention of her audience:

> A few years ago one of America's foremost philosophers, Yogi Berra, remarked to his wife on a trip to the Baseball Hall of Fame in Cooperstown, New York, "We are completely lost but we are making good time." I am afraid Yogi's observation may be true for more than just his navigational skills. For Americans, our direction on the important social issues of the day finds us lost but still driving.
>
> As we think about strategies for change needed for America's third century, we must go in new directions.[4]

As the introduction progresses, she introduces the topic of her speech, liberty versus power.

In the following excerpt from her speech to the annual meeting of the American Medical Association, AMA President Nancy Dickey exemplifies the way a clever speaker can use a quotation in the opening to serve as the theme for the entire speech:

> A wise person once said, "Always have your bags packed, you never know where life's journey is going to take you." I couldn't agree more. In fact, as you can see, I have my

bag with me tonight [she holds up her standard medical bag for the audience to see]. I've chosen to bring that traditional black bag that physicians have carried with them for generations. And I'm here to tell you—my bag is packed and ready to go as I prepare for this year-long journey of my AMA presidency.

Of course, having your bag packed isn't really about having a change of clothes ready. It's about being prepared to take advantage of the opportunities that come your way in life. And I am prepared. . . .

I've also packed some more tangible items in my bag tonight. Symbolic items, really, which represent my presidential priorities for the year ahead. And tonight I want to share these items and priorities with you—and ask for your help in making them a reality during the next 12 months.[5]

I think you would agree that if you were a physician in her audience, you would be intrigued by what she had to say about her priorities for the year.

SUSPENSE

An introduction that is worded so that what is described remains uncertain or mysterious during the first few sentences will excite the audience. When you begin your speech in a way that gets the audience to ask "What is she leading up to?" you may well get them hooked for the entire speech. The suspense opening is especially valuable when the topic is one that an audience does not already have an interest in hearing. Consider the attention-getting value of this introduction:

> It costs the United States more than $116 billion per year. It has cost the loss of more jobs than a recession. It accounts for nearly 100,000 deaths a year. I'm not talking about cocaine abuse—the problem is alcoholism. Today I want to show you how we can avoid this inhumane killer by abstaining from it.

Notice that by putting the problem "alcoholism" at the end, the speaker encourages the audience to try to anticipate the answer. And since the audience may well be thinking "narcotics," the revelation that the answer is alcoholism is likely to be that much more effective.

 For further discussion of these and other types of introductions, use your Challenge of Effective Speaking CD-ROM to access Web Resource 8.1: Strategies for Introducing Speeches.

Selecting and Outlining an Introduction

Because the introduction is critical in establishing your relationship with your audience, it's worth investing the time to compare different openings. Try working on two or three different introductions; then pick the one you believe will work best for your specific audience and speech goal.

For instance, Emming created the following three introductions for his speech on evaluating credit cards:

> Have you seen the number of agencies that have showered the campus with credit card applications? Sounds good, doesn't it? Take just a few minutes to fill out a statement, and you'll be in control of your economic destiny. But wait a minute. The road down consumer credit lane is not as smooth as the companies would have you believe. Today I'm going to share with you the criteria gained from my reading and personal experience that you'll want to consider for selecting a credit card. (86 words)

> How many of you have been hounded by credit card vendors outside the Student Union? They make a credit card sound like the answer to all your dreams, don't they? Today I'm going to share with you the three criteria gained from my reading and personal experience that you'll want to consider for selecting a credit card. (57 words)

> Banks and credit unions are willing to shower us with incentives in order to get us to sign up for our own credit card. But we'd be wise to look before we leap. P. T. Bar-

num said, "There's a sucker born every minute." Today I'm going to share with you the criteria that you'll want to consider for selecting a credit card so that you won't end up being one of those "suckers." (72 words)

Each of these is an appropriate length for a short speech. Which one do you prefer?

Whether or not your speech introduction meets all five of the goals directly, it should be long enough to put listeners in a frame of mind that will encourage them to hear you out, without being so long that it leaves too little time to develop the substance of your speech. Of course, the shorter the speech, the shorter the introduction.

The introduction will not make your speech an instant success, but it can get an audience to look at and listen to you and to choose to focus on your topic. That is about as much as a speaker can ask of an audience during the first minute or two of a speech.

By completing Speech Planning Action Step 4, Activity 4E: Writing Speech Introductions, you will develop three choices for your speech introduction. The Student Response to Activity 4E provides an example of a student response to this activity.

| SPEECH PLANNING | ACTION STEP 4 |

4 | Organization

ACTIVITY 4E Creating Speech Introductions

The goal of this activity is to create choices for how you will begin your speech.
1. For the speech body you outlined earlier, write three different introductions—using a startling statement, a rhetorical question, a story, a personal reference, a quotation, or suspense—that you believe meet the goals of effective introductions and would be appropriate for your speech goal and audience.
2. Of the three introductions you drafted, which do you believe is the best? Why?
3. Write that introduction in outline form.

You can complete this activity online with Speech Builder Express, view a student sample of this activity, and, if requested, e-mail your completed activity to your instructor. Use your Challenge of Effective Speaking CD-ROM to access Activity 4E.

| STUDENT RESPONSE | ACTION STEP 4 |

4 | Organization

ACTIVITY 4E Creating Speech Introductions

1. For the speech body you outlined earlier, write three different introductions—using a startling statement, a rhetorical question, a story, a personal reference, a quotation, or suspense—that you believe meet the goals of effective introductions and would be appropriate for your speech goal and audience.
   Specific goal: *I would like the audience to understand the three ways to tell if a diamond is real.*

(continued)

(1) *As Dr. Verderber mentioned earlier in the course, we are in the age group where buying or receiving diamonds might be on our minds. I would like to tell you how you can know for sure if your diamond is real.*

(2) *Men, have you ever wondered if you would know if the diamond that the jeweler is trying to sell you is real? Ladies, have you ever wondered how you would be able to tell if your engagement ring is fake? Today, I am going to share some information that can help you answer these questions.*

(3) *Calcite, quartz, cubic zirconia, diamond. How can you tell these minerals apart? They are all colorless and can sometimes look alike. But, let me tell you three ways that you can tell if you are holding a diamond.*

2. Of the three introductions you drafted, which do you believe is the best? Why?

I believe the second one is the best, because the rhetorical questions are likely to motivate the audience to listen and it leads into the body of the speech.

3. Write that introduction in outline form.

    I. *Men, have you ever wondered if you would know if the diamond that the jeweler is trying to sell you is real?*

    II. *Ladies, have you ever wondered how you would be able to tell if your engagement ring is fake?*

    III. *Today, I am going to tell you three ways to identify a real diamond.*

REFLECT ON ETHICS

As Marna and Gloria were eating lunch together, Marna happened to ask Gloria, "How are you doing in Woodward's speech class?"

"Not bad," Gloria replied. "I'm working on this speech about product development. I think it will be really informative, but I'm having a little trouble with the opening. I just can't seem to get a good idea for getting started."

"Why not start with a story—that always worked for me in class."

"Thanks, Marna, I'll think on it."

The next day when Marna ran into Gloria again, she asked, "How's that introduction going?"

"Great. I've prepared a great story about Mary Kay—you know, the cosmetics woman? I'm going to tell about how she was terrible in school and no one thought she'd amount to anything. But she loved dabbling with cosmetics so much that she decided to start her own business—and the rest is history."

"That's a great story. I really like that part about being terrible in school. Was she really that bad?"

"I really don't know—the material I read didn't really focus on that part of her life. But I thought that angle would get people listening right away. And after all, I did it that way because you suggested starting with a story."

"Yes, but . . ."

"Listen, she did start the business. So what if the story isn't quite right? It makes the point I want to make—if people are creative and have a strong work ethic, they can make it big."

1. What are the ethical issues here?

2. Is anyone really hurt by Gloria's opening the speech with this story?

3. What are the speaker's ethical responsibilities?

Creating the Conclusion

Shakespeare said, "All's well that ends well." A strong conclusion can heighten the impact of a good speech. Even though the conclusion will be a relatively short part of the speech—seldom more than 5 percent (35 to 45 words for a five-minute speech)—it is important that your conclusion be carefully planned.

Goals of the Conclusion

The conclusion of a speech has two major goals. The first is to review the key ideas in the speech so that the audience remembers what you have said; the second is to leave the audience members with a vivid impression so that they will understand the importance of what you have said or be persuaded by your arguments.

Types of Conclusions

Just as with your speech introduction, you should prepare two or three conclusions and then choose the one you believe will be the most effective with your audience. Each of your choices should include a summary. Persuasive speeches are likely to also include an appeal to action or a statement of emotional impact. And any speech might also incorporate a story or anecdotal material to help drive home the point that is being made.

SUMMARY

Any effective speech conclusion is likely to include a summary of the main points. In very short speeches a summary may be the only conclusion that is necessary. Thus, a short appropriate ending for an informative speech on how to improve your grades might be, "So I hope that you now understand that three techniques for helping you improve your grades are to attend classes regularly, to develop a positive attitude toward the course, and to study systematically." Likewise a short ending for a persuasive speech on why you should lift weights might be, "So remember that three major reasons why you should consider lifting

The conclusion offers you one last chance to hit home with your point. Supplementing a summary with a quote or a short anecdote is often a good way of emphasizing what you want the audience to get from the speech.

weights are to improve your appearance, to improve your health, and to accomplish both with a minimum of effort."

Although summaries achieve the first goal of an effective conclusion, a speaker may need to develop additional material designed to achieve the second goal: leaving the audience with a vivid impression. The following represent three ways to supplement the summary.

APPEAL TO ACTION

The appeal to action is a common way to end a persuasive speech. The **appeal** describes the behavior that you want your listeners to follow after they have heard your arguments. Notice how Heather Ettinger concludes her speech on "Shattering the Glass Floor" with a strong appeal to action:

> We have to stop thinking someone else will change the world. We've got to get it that we're the ones.
>
> As you drive home tonight, remember to lift while you climb and outstretch that hand to help another woman, another girl. Let's shatter the glass floor. Let's be women donors who are leaders of fundamental change.[6]

By their nature, appeals are most relevant for persuasive speeches, especially when the goal is to motivate an audience to act.

EMOTIONAL IMPACT

Some conclusions are designed to drive home the most important points with real emotional impact. An emotional conclusion can be used in informative speeches but is more likely to be used for a persuasive speech whose goal is to reinforce belief, change belief, or motivate an audience to act. Consider the way Chester Burger, retired communications management consultant, ends his speech on how technology is changing the world:

> And in the earliest days of the automobile, Mercedes Benz asked its experts to analyze and forecast the future demand for cars. Their answer was, the total market for automobiles would be less than one million, because it would be impossible to find or train more than one million chauffeurs. And you'd need a chauffeur, because to drive a horseless carriage would require as much expertise and strength as driving horses.
>
> The same resistance to change, and the same narrowness of vision, is present today in most countries of the world, and in most peoples and most cultures. Never mind: fundamental changes will come, faster than we think, more profound than we can imagine, more unpredictable than were the effects of the railroad, the telephone, or electricity. In 1943, Thomas Watson, the chairman of IBM, said, "I think there is a world market for maybe five computers." Even a great visionary such as Mr. Watson couldn't foresee what would happen.
>
> We won't have to wait very long to see a different world. Technology is changing the world, the results showing sooner than we can conceive, pulling the whole world together, closer than Cyrus Field could ever have dreamed when the famous steamship *Great Eastern* dropped his little copper thread underneath the North Atlantic all the way from Newfoundland to Ireland. It's a new world.[7]

Like the appeal, the emotional conclusion is likely to be used for a persuasive speech whose goal is to reinforce belief, change belief, or motivate an audience to act.

STORY

For longer informative or persuasive speeches, speakers may also look for stories or other types of material that can further reinforce the message of the speech. Here we will give you one example of such a story. In his speech on corporate responsibility in the Hispanic business community, Solomon D. Trujillo ends with a story that dramatizes the importance of acting now:

In closing, there's an old tale called "The Four Elements" from the Hispanic Southwest by my friend Rudolfo Anaya that captures my message.

In the beginning, there were four elements on this earth, as well as in man. These basic elements in man and earth were Water, Fire, Wind and Honor. When the work of the creation was completed, the elements decided to separate, with each one seeking its own way. Water spoke first and said: "If you should ever need me, look for me under the earth and in the oceans." Fire then said: "If you should need me you will find me in steel and in the power of the sun." Wind whispered: "If you should need me, I will be in the heavens among the clouds." Honor, the bond of life, said: "If you lose me, don't look for me again—you will not find me."

So it is for corporate responsibility. Once lost, honor cannot be replaced. It is the right thing to do . . . it is right for business . . . it is inseparable in our interdependent world. Let's act now to bring Hispanic issues to the forefront of America's agenda.[8]

Selecting and Outlining a Conclusion

To determine how you will conclude your speech, create two or three conclusions, then choose the one that you believe will best reinforce your speech goal with your audience.

For his short speech on evaluating credit cards, Emming created the following three variations of summaries for consideration. Which do you like best?

Having a credit card gives you power—but only if you make a good choice. If you decide to apply for a credit card, you'll now be able to make an evaluation based upon sound criteria: interest rates, annual fee, and incentives.

So don't play Russian roulette when choosing a card; instead examine interest rates, annual fee, and incentives. That way you'll know that the odds are in your favor.

Now you see the importance of making sure that you have examined interest rates, annual fee, and incentives before you select a credit card. And you can rest with the knowledge that card you selected is the best one for you.

Because this first speech is relatively short, Emming decided to end his speech with just a couple of sentences. For speeches that are no longer than five minutes, a one- to two-sentence conclusion is often appropriate. You're likely to need as much of your time as possible to do a good job of presenting the main points. But as speech assignments get longer, you'll want to consider supplementing the summary to give the conclusion more impact. See the InfoTrac College Edition exercise at the end of this chapter for tips on how to supplement your summary.

By completing Speech Planning Action Step 4, Activity 4F: Creating Speech Conclusions, you will develop choices for your speech conclusion. The Student Response to Activity 4F provides an example of one student's response to this activity.

SPEECH PLANNING   ACTION STEP 4

4 | Organization

ACTIVITY 4F Creating Speech Conclusions

The goal of this activity is to help you create choices for how you will conclude your speech.

1. For the speech body you outlined earlier, write three different conclusions—summary, story, appeal to action, or emotional impact—that review important points you want the audience to remember and leave the audience with vivid imagery or an emotional appeal.

(continued)

2. Which do you believe is the best? Why?

3. Write that conclusion in outline form.

You can complete this activity online with Speech Builder Express, view a student sample of this activity, and, if requested, e-mail your completed activity to your instructor. Use your Challenge of Effective Speaking CD-ROM to access Activity 4F.

STUDENT RESPONSE   **ACTION STEP 4**

4 | Organization

ACTIVITY 4F Creating Speech Conclusions

1. For the speech body you outlined earlier, write three different conclusions—summary, story, appeal to action, or emotional impact—that review important points you want the audience to remember and leave the audience with vivid imagery or an emotional appeal.

Specific goal: *I would like the audience to understand the three ways to tell if a diamond is real.*

(1) *So, the next time you buy or receive a diamond, you will know how to do the acid, streak, and hardness tests to make sure the diamond is real.*

(2) *Before making your final diamond selection, make sure it can pass the acid test, streak test, and hardness test. Remember, you want to make sure you're buying a diamond— not paste!*

(3) *You now know how to tell if your diamond is real. So, folks, if you discover that the gem you're considering effervesces in acid, has a streak that is not clear, or can be scratched, you will know that the person who tried to sell it to you is a crook!*

2. Which do you believe is the best? Why?

The third one, because it restates the characteristics.

3. Write that conclusion in outline form.

I. *You now know how to tell if your diamond is real.*

II. *If it effervesces, streaks, or scratches, the seller is a crook.*

Completing the Outline

At this point you have a draft outline of your speech. To complete the outline, you will want to compile a list of the source material you will be drawing from in the speech, create a title (if required), and review your draft to make sure that the outline conforms to a logical structure.

Listing Sources

Regardless of the type of speech or how long or how short it will be, you'll want to prepare a list of the sources you are going to use in the speech. Although you may be required to prepare this list for the course you are taking, in real settings this list will enable you to direct audience members to the specific source of the information you have used and will allow you to quickly find the information at a later date. The two standard methods of organizing source lists are alphabetically by author's last name or by content category, with items listed alphabetically by author within each category. For speeches with a short list, the first method is efficient. But for long speeches with a lengthy source list, it is helpful to group sources by content categories.

Many formal bibliographic styles can be used in citing sources (for example, MLA, APA, Chicago, CBE); the "correct" form differs by professional or academic discipline. Check to see if your instructor has a preference about which style you use in class.

Regardless of the particular style, the specific information you need to record differs depending on whether the source is a book, a periodical, a newspaper, or an Internet source or Web site. The elements that are essential to all are author, title of article, title of publication, date of publication, and page numbers. Exhibit 8.1 gives examples of Modern Language Association (MLA) citations for the most commonly used types of sources. To view examples of common citations using the APA (American Psychological Association), *Chicago Manual of Style,* and AMA (American Medical Association) styles, use your Challenge of Effective Speaking CD-ROM to access **Web Resource 8.2: Citation Styles.**

EXHIBIT 8.1   Examples of the MLA citation form for speech sources

Book
Miller, Robert B. *The Five Paths to Persuasion: The Art of Selling Your Message.* New York: Warner Business Books, 2004.

Edited Book
Janzen, Rod. "Five Paradigms of Ethnic Relations." *Intercultural Communication 10th ed.* Eds. Larry Samovar and Richard Porter. Belmont, CA: Wadsworth, 2003. 36–42.

Magazine
Krauthammer, Charles. "What Makes the Bush Haters So Mad?" *Time* 22 Sept. 2003: 84.

Academic Journal
Barge, J. Kevin. "Reflexivity and Managerial Practice." *Communication Monographs* 71:1 (Mar. 2004): 70–96.

Newspaper
Cohen, Richard. "Wall Street Scandal: Whatever the Market Will Bear." *The Cincinnati Enquirer* 17 Sept. 2003: C6.

Electronic Article
Friedman, Thomas L. "Connect the Dots." 25 Sept. 2003. *New York Times.* 20 Aug. 2004 <http://www.nytimes.com/2003/09/25/opinion/25FRIED.html>.

Electronic Site
Osterweil, Neil and Michael Smith. "Does Stress Cause Breast Cancer?" *Web M.D. Health.* 24 Sept. 2003. WebMD Inc. 20 Aug. 2004. <http://my.webmd.com/contents/article/74/89170.htm?z=3734_00000_1000_ts_01>.

Experience
Fegel's Jewelry, senior year of high school, 2003–2004.

Observation
Schoenling Brewery, April 22, 2004. Spent an hour on the floor observing the use of various machines in the total process and employees' responsibilities at each stage.

Interviews
Mueller, Bruno. Diamond cutter at Fegel's Jewelry. Personal Interview. 19 March 2004.

Speech Planning Action Step 4, Activity 4G: Compiling a List of Sources, helps you compile a list of sources used in your speech. The Student Response to Activity 4G provides an example of a student's response to this activity.

| | SPEECH PLANNING | ACTION STEP 4 |

4 | Organization

ACTIVITY 4G Compiling a List of Sources

The goal of this activity is to help you record the list of sources you used in your speech.

1. Review your note cards, separating those whose information you have used in your speech from those whose information you have not used.
2. List the sources whose information was used in the speech by copying the bibliographic information recorded on the note card.
3. For short lists, organize your list alphabetically by the last name of the first author. Be sure to follow the form given in the text. If you did not record some of the bibliographic information on your note card, you will need to revisit the library, database, or other source to find it.

You can complete this activity online with Speech Builder Express, view a student sample of this activity, and, if requested, e-mail your completed activity to your instructor. Use your Challenge of Effective Speaking CD-ROM to access Activity 4G.

| | STUDENT RESPONSE | ACTION STEP 4 |

4 | Organization

ACTIVITY 4G Compiling a List of Sources

1. Review your note cards, separating those whose information you have used in your speech from those whose information you have not used.
2. List the sources whose information was used in the speech by copying the bibliographic information recorded on the note card.
3. For short lists, organize your list alphabetically by the last name of the first author. Be sure to follow the form given in the text. If you did not record some of the bibliographic information on your note card, you will need to revisit the library, database, or other source to find it.

Sources

Dixon, Dougal, The Practical Geologist *(New York: Simon & Schuster, 1992).*
Farver, John, Professor of Geology, Personal Interview, June 23, 2004.
Klein, Cornelius, Manual of Mineralogy, 2nd ed. *(New York: John Wiley & Sons, 1993).*
Montgomery, Carla W., Fundamentals of Geology, 3rd ed. *(Dubuque, IA: Wm. C. Brown, 1997).*

Writing a Title

In many classroom situations, speeches are not required to have titles. But in most speech situations outside the classroom, it helps to have a title that lets the audience know what to expect. A title is probably necessary when you will be formally introduced, when the speech is publicized, or when the speech will be published. A good title helps to attract an audience and build interest in what you will say. Titles should be brief, descriptive of the content, and if possible, creative. Most speakers don't settle on a title until the rest of the speech preparation is complete.

Three kinds of titles can be created: a simple statement of subject, a question, or a creative title.

1. Simple statement of subject. This straightforward title captures the subject of the speech in a few words.

> Courage to Grow
>
> Selling Safety
>
> The Dignity of Work
>
> America's Destiny

2. Question. To spark greater interest, you can create a title by phrasing your speech goal as a question. A prospective listener may then be motivated to attend the speech to find out the answer.

> Do We Need a Department of Play?
>
> Are Farmers on the Way Out?
>
> What Is the Impact of Computers on Our Behavior?
>
> Are We Living in a Moral Stone Age?

3. Creative title. A more creative approach is to combine a familiar saying or metaphor with the simple statement of subject.

> Teaching Old Dogs New Tricks: The Need for Adult Computer Literacy
>
> Promises to Keep: Broadcasting and the Public Interest
>
> The Tangled Web: How Environmental Climate Has Changed
>
> Freeze or Freedom: On the Limits of Morals and Worth of Politics

A creative title helps attract audience interest even before you begin to talk.

The simple statement of subject gives a clear idea of the topic but is not especially eye- or ear-catching. Questions and creative titles capture interest but may not give a clear idea of content unless they include subtitles.

Once you are comfortable with your goal, you can begin thinking about a title. When you are trying to be creative, you may find a title right away or not until the last minute.

Reviewing the Outline

Now that you have created all of the parts of the outline, it is time to put them together in complete outline form and edit them to make sure the outline is well organized and well worded. Use this checklist to complete the final review of the outline before you move into adaptation and rehearsal.

1. Have I used a standard set of symbols to indicate structure? Main points are indicated by Roman numerals, major subdivisions by capital letters, minor subheadings by Arabic numerals, and further subdivisions by lowercase letters.

2. Have I written main points and major subdivisions as complete sentences? Complete sentences help you to see (1) whether each main point actually develops your speech goal and (2) whether the wording makes your intended point. Unless the key ideas are written out in full, it will be difficult to follow the next guidelines.

3. Do main points and major subdivisions each contain a single idea? This guideline ensures that the development of each part of the speech will be relevant to the point. Thus, if your outline contains a point like this:

    I. The park is beautiful and easy to get to.

Divide the sentence so that the two parts are separate:

    I. The park is beautiful.

    II. The park is easy to get to.

Sort out distinct ideas so that when you line up supporting material you can have confidence that the audience will see and understand its relationship to the main points.

4. Does each major subdivision relate to or support its major point? This principle, called subordination, ensures that you don't wander off point and confuse your audience. For example:

    I. Proper equipment is necessary for successful play.

        A. Good gym shoes are needed for maneuverability.

        B. Padded gloves will help protect your hands.

        C. A lively ball provides sufficient bounce.

        D. And a good attitude doesn't hurt.

Notice that the main point deals with equipment. A, B, and C (shoes, gloves, and ball) all relate to the main point. But D, attitude, is not equipment and should appear somewhere else, if at all.

5. Are potential subdivision elaborations indicated? Recall that it is the subdivision elaborations that help to build the speech. Because you don't know how long it might take you to discuss these elaborations, it is a good idea to include more than you are likely to use. During rehearsals you may discuss each a different way.

6. Does the outline include no more than one-third to a little more than one-half the total number of words anticipated in the speech? An outline is only a skeleton of the speech—not a complete manuscript with letters and numbers attached. The outline should be short enough to allow you to experiment with different methods of development during practice periods and to adapt to audience reaction during the speech itself. An easy way to judge whether your outline is about the right length is to estimate the number of words that you are likely to be able to speak during the actual speech and compare this to the number of words in the outline (counting only the words in the outline minus speech goal, thesis statement, headings, and list of sources). Because approximate figures are all you need, start by assuming an average speaking rate of 160 words per minute. (Last term, the speaking rate for the majority of speakers in my class was 140 to 180 words per minute.) Thus, a three- to five-minute speech would contain roughly 480 to 800 words, and the outline should be 160 to 300 words. An eight- to ten-minute speech, roughly 1,300 to 1,600 words, should have an outline of approximately 430 to 530 words.

Now that we have considered the various parts of an outline, let us put them together for a final look. The outline in Exhibit 8.2 illustrates the principles in practice. The commentary in the margin relates each part of the outline to the guidelines we have discussed.

SPEECH PLANNING   ACTION STEP 4

4 | Organization

ACTIVITY 4H Completing the Speech Outline

Write and review a complete-sentence outline of your speech, using material you've developed so far with the Action Steps in Chapters 4–8. You can complete this activity online with Speech Builder Express, view a student sample of this activity, and, if requested, e-mail your completed activity to your instructor. Use your Challenge of Effective Speaking CD-ROM to access Activity 4H. For this activity, Emming's complete outline (Exhibit 8.2) will serve as the student response.

Summary

The organization process is completed by creating an introduction and a conclusion, listing the sources you used in the speech, writing a title (if required), and reviewing the draft outline. An effective speech introduction gets audience attention and introduces the thesis; it may also establish credibility, set the tone for the speech, and create goodwill. Types of speech introductions include startling statements, rhetorical questions, stories, personal references, quotations, and statements that create suspense.

A well-designed informative speech conclusion almost always summarizes the main points. Persuasive speech conclusions not only summarize but also include material that appeals to action and provides emotional impact. Longer informative and persuasive speeches may also include stories that help reinforce major ideas.

A good outline also includes a list of sources compiled from the bibliographic information recorded on research note cards. Short lists are alphabetized by first authors' last names. Longer source lists group sources by content category before alphabetizing by author.

Although most classroom speeches may not require a title, in most speech situations outside the classroom it helps to have an informative and appealing title. Three kinds of titles are the simple statement of subject, the question, and the creative title.

The complete draft outline should be reviewed and revised to make sure that you have used a standard set of symbols, used complete sentences for main points and major subdivisions, limited each point to a single idea, related minor points to major points, and limited the outline length to no more than one-third the number of words of the final speech.

EXHIBIT 8.2 **Sample complete outline**

Write your specific goal at the top of the page. Refer to the goal to test whether everything in the outline is relevant.

Specific goal: I would like the audience to understand the major criteria for finding a suitable credit card.

The heading *Introduction* sets the section apart as a separate unit. The introduction attempts to (1) get attention and (2) lead into the body of the speech as well as establish credibility, set a tone, and gain goodwill.

Introduction
I. How many of you have been hounded by credit card vendors outside the Student Union?
II. They make a credit card sound like the answer to all of your dreams, don't they?
III. Today I want to share with you three criteria you need to consider carefully before deciding on a particular credit card.

The thesis statement states the elements that are suggested in the specific goal. In the speech, the thesis serves as a forecast of the main points.

Thesis statement: Three criteria that will enable audience members to find the credit card that is most suitable for them are level of real interest rate, annual fee, and advertised incentives.

The heading Body sets this section apart as a separate unit. In this example, main point I begins a topical pattern of main points. It is stated as a complete sentence.

Body
I. The first criterion for choosing a credit card is to select a card with a lower interest rate.

The two main subdivisions designated by A and B indicate the equal weight of these points. The second-level subdivisions—designated by 1, 2, and 3 for major subpoint A, and 1 and 2 for major subpoint B—give the necessary information for understanding the subpoints.

A. Interest rates are the percentages that a company charges you to carry a balance on your card past the due date.
  1. Most credit cards carry an average of 8 percent.
  2. Some cards carry as much as 21 percent.
  3. Many companies offer 0 interest rates for up to 12 months.

The number of major and second-level subpoints is at the discretion of the speaker. After the first two levels of subordination, words and phrases may be used in place of complete sentences for elaboration.

B. Interest rates can be variable or fixed.
  1. Variable rates mean that the rate can change from month to month.
  2. Fixed rates mean that the rate will stay the same.

This transition reminds listeners of the first main point and forecasts the second.

(Now that we have considered interest rates, let's look at the next criterion.)

EXHIBIT 8.2 **Sample complete outline (*continued*)**

II. A second criterion for choosing a suitable credit card is to select a card with no or a low annual fee.
   A. The annual fee is the cost the company charges you for extending you credit.
   B. The charges vary widely.
      1. Some cards advertise no annual fee.
      2. Most companies charge fees that average around 25 dollars.

(After you have considered interest and fees, you can weigh the incentives that the company promises you.)

III. A third criterion for choosing a credit card is to weigh the incentives.
   A. Incentives are extras that you get for using a particular card.

      1. Some companies promise rebates.
      2. Some companies promise frequent flyer miles.
      3. Some companies promise discounts on "a wide variety of items."
   B. Incentives don't outweigh other criteria.

Conclusion
   I. So, getting the credit card that's right for you may be the answer to your dreams.
   II. But only if you exercise care in examining interest rates, annual fee, and incentives.

Sources
Bankrate Monitor, http://www.Bankrate.com.
"Congratulations, Grads—You're Bankrupt: Marketing Blitz Buries Kids in Plastic Debt," *Business Week,* May 21, 2001, p. 48.
Hennefriend, Bill, *Office Pro,* October 2004, Vol. 64, pp. 17–20.
"Protect Your Credit Card," *Kiplinger's,* December 2004, p. 88.
Rose, Sarah, "Prepping for College Credit," *Money,* September 1998, pp. 156–157.
Speer, Tibbett L., "College Come-ons," *American Demographics,* March 1998, pp. 40–45.

Main point II, continuing the topical pattern, is a complete sentence that parallels the wording of main point I. Notice that each main point considers only one major idea.

This transition summarizes the first two criteria and forecasts the third.

Main point III, continuing the topical pattern, is a complete sentence paralleling the wording of main points I and II.

Throughout the outline, notice that main points and subpoints are factual statements. The speaker adds examples, experiences, and other developmental material during practice sessions.

The heading *Conclusion* sets this section apart as a separate unit.

The content of the conclusion is intended to summarize the main ideas and leave the speech on a high note.

A list of sources should always be a part of the speech outline. The sources should show where the factual material of the speech came from. The list of sources is not a total of all sources available—only those that were used, directly or indirectly. Each of the sources is shown in proper form.

Now that you've read Chapter 8, use your Challenge of Effective Speaking CD-ROM for quick access to the electronic study resources that accompany this text. Your CD-ROM gives you access to InfoTrac College Edition, Speech Builder Express, and the Challenge of Effective Speaking Web site. When you get to the Challenge of Effective Speaking home page, click on "Student Book Companion Site" in the Resource box at the right to access the online study aids for this chapter, including a digital glossary, review quizzes, and the chapter activities.

KEY TERMS

At the Challenge of Effective Speaking Web site, select chapter resources for Chapter 8. Print a copy of the glossary for this chapter, test yourself with the electronic flash cards, or complete the crossword puzzle to help you master the following key terms.

rhetorical question (135)   **appeal** (142)

INFOTRAC COLLEGE EDITION EXERCISE

In an InfoTrac College Edition article titled "Happy Endings," a prizewinning journal writer is quoted as saying that a "story with a strong lead and a strong conclusion is 'like some kind of basket where you've got to have a handle at both ends.'" Indeed, many speakers forget that people tend to remember what they heard first and what they heard last.

Use your Challenge of Effective Speaking CD-ROM to access InfoTrac College Edition. Conduct a search using the keywords "introductions, conclusions." What points does the quote above make that are applicable to speech preparation? Use the Link button to discover references to Closure. What will you do to ensure that your speeches begin and end with a bang?

WEB RESOURCES

Access the Web resources for this chapter online at the Challenge of Effective Speaking Web site. Select the chapter resources for Chapter 8, then click on "Web Resources."

8.1 Strategies for Introducing   8.2 Citation Style (145)
Speeches (138)

Access the Action Step activities for this chapter online at the Challenge of Effective Speaking Web site. Select the chapter resources for Chapter 8, then click on the activity number you want. You may print out your completed activities, and you should save your work so you can use it as needed in later Action Step activities.

4E: Writing Speech Introductions (139)

4F: Creating Speech Conclusions (143)

4G: Compiling a List of Sources (146)

4H: Completing the Speech Outline (149)

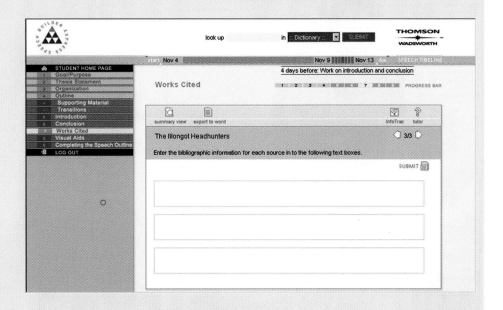

Constructing and Using Visual Aids

A picture is worth a thousand words.

"How's it going with the speech, Jeremy?"

"I'm frustrated."

"Why's that?"

"Well, I know we're supposed to think about using visual aids with this speech. But I can't think of what I could depict that would be useful."

"What's your topic?"

"Effects of media violence, but I don't see any sense in showing any act of violence."

"Right, but there are lots of other visuals you could show that would be helpful."

"Like what?"

"Well, I'll bet that you're using some statistics about the amount of violence."

"Sure."

"Well, couldn't you show statistics while you talked about them?"

"But wouldn't showing statistics be just as boring as giving them?"

In the chapter opening dialog, Jeremy makes a good point. It is probable that just showing some statistics would be boring. But the question he needs to answer is what he could do to show the statistics in an interesting, meaningful way. In this chapter the focus is on developing a strategy for adapting to your audience visually. Although there are times when visual aids may not be necessary, having them will help capture your audience's attention and make your speech more interesting.

A **visual aid** is a form of speech development that allows the audience to see as well as hear information. You'll want to consider using visual aids because they enable you to adapt to an audience's level of knowledge by clarifying and dramatizing your verbal message. Visual aids also help audiences retain the information they hear. Research has shown that people are likely to remember features of visual aids even over long periods[1] and that people are likely to learn considerably more when ideas appeal to both eye and ear than when they appeal to the ear alone.[2] In our classes, students report that they enjoy the speeches more and remember more information during the round of speeches in which we require the use of visual aids than in any other round. In addition, speakers report that when they use visual aids, they tend to be less anxious and have more confidence.[3]

In this chapter we describe the types of visual aids you might use, the criteria for making choices about which and how many visual aids to use, ways of designing visual aids to best adapt to your audience's needs, and guidelines for using them in your speech.

visual aid a form of speech development that allows the audience to see as well as hear information

Types of Visual Aids

Before you can choose what visual aids you might want to use for a specific speech, you need to recognize the various types of visual aids that you can choose from. Visual aids range from those that are simple to use and readily available from some existing source, to those that require practice to use effectively and must be custom produced for your specific speech. In this section we describe the types of visual aids that you can consider using as you prepare your speech.

OBJECTS

Objects are three-dimensional representations of the idea that you are communicating. Objects make good visual aids if (1) they are large enough to be seen by all audience members and (2) they are small enough to carry to the site of the speech. A volleyball or a braided rug would be appropriate in size for most classroom-size audiences. A cell phone might be OK if the goal was simply to show a phone, but might be too small if the speaker wanted to demonstrate how to key in certain specialized functions.

On occasion, *you* can be an effective object visual aid. For instance, through descriptive gestures you can show the height of a tennis net; through your posture and movement you can show the motions involved in the butterfly swimming stroke; and through your own attire you can illustrate the native dress of a different country.

Viewing a model can help the audience understand your topic. In this photo, architecture students at the University of Southwestern Louisiana gather around their instructor to view a novel design.

© Philip Gould/Corbis

MODELS

When an object is too large to bring to the speech site or too small to be seen (like the cell phone), a three-dimensional model is appropriate. In a speech on the physics of bridge construction, a scale model of a suspension bridge would be an effective visual aid. Likewise, in a speech on genetic engineering, a model of the DNA double helix might help the audience to understand what happens during these microscopic procedures.

PHOTOGRAPHS

If an exact reproduction of material is needed, enlarged still photographs are excellent visual aids. In a speech on "smart weapons," enlarged before and after photos of target sites would be effective in helping the audience to understand the pinpoint accuracy of these weapons.

SLIDES

Like photographs, slides allow you to present an exact visual image to the audience. The advantage of slides over photographs is that the size of the image can be manipulated onsite so that it is easy for all audience members to see. In addition, if more than one image is to be shown, slides eliminate the awkwardness associated with manually changing photographs. The remote control device allows you to move smoothly from one image to the next and to talk about each image as long as you like. One drawback to using slides, however, is that in most cases the room must be darkened for the slides to be viewed. In this situation, it is easy for the slides to become the focal point for the audience. Moreover, many novice speakers are tempted to look and talk to the slides rather than to the audience. Finally, to use slides you must bring a projector to class with you.

FILM AND VIDEO CLIPS

You can use short clips from films and videos to demonstrate processes or to expose audiences to important people. But because effective clips generally run one to three minutes, they are ineffective and inappropriate for most classroom speeches because they dominate the speech and speaker. When clips are used in longer speeches, speakers must ensure that the equipment needed is available and operational. This means performing a dry run onsite with the equipment before beginning the speech.

SIMPLE DRAWINGS

Simple drawings are easy to prepare. If you can use a compass, a straightedge, and a measure, you can draw well enough for most speech purposes. For instance, if you are making the point that water skiers must hold their arms straight, with the back straight and knees bent slightly, a stick figure (see Exhibit 9.1) will illustrate the point. Stick figures may not be as aesthetically pleasing as professional drawings or photographs, but to demonstrate a certain concept they can be quite effective. In fact, elaborate, detailed drawings may not be worth the time and effort, and actual photographs may be so detailed that they obscure the point you wish to make.

Once a drawing is prepared, it can be scanned and used as part of a Power-Point presentation or as an overhead, or the drawing can be used freestanding if it is enlarged and prepared on poster board or foam core. Obviously you will want to prepare drawings that are easily seen by all audience members. Drawings

EXHIBIT 9.1   Sample drawing

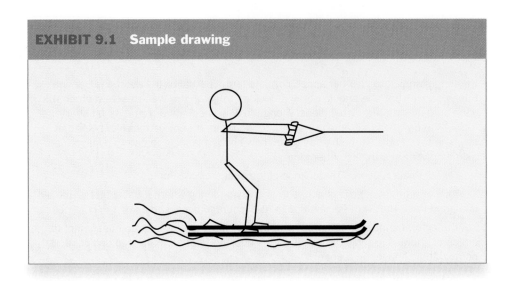

should be prepared on poster board (or foam core) so that they remain rigid and are easy to display.

MAPS

Like drawings, maps are relatively easy to prepare. Simple maps allow you to orient audiences to landmarks (mountains, rivers, and lakes), states, cities, land routes, weather systems, and so on. Commercial maps are available, but simple maps are relatively easy to prepare and can be customized so that audience members are not confused by visual information that is irrelevant to your purpose. Like drawings, maps can be used as part of a PowerPoint presentation, as overheads, or as freestanding items. Exhibit 9.2 is a good example of a map that focuses on weather systems.

EXHIBIT 9.2   Sample map

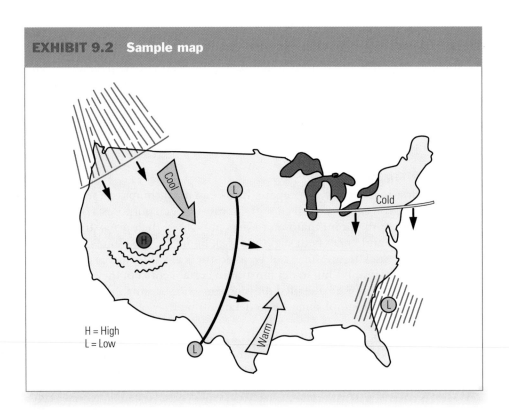

CHARTS

A **chart** is a graphic representation that distills a lot of information and presents it to an audience in an easily interpreted visual format. Word charts and flowcharts are the most common.

A **word chart** is used to preview, review, or highlight important ideas covered in a speech. In a speech on Islam, a speaker might make a word chart that lists the five pillars of Islam, as shown in Exhibit 9.3. An outline of speech main points can become a word chart.

A **flowchart** uses symbols and connecting lines to diagram the progressions through a complicated process. An organizational chart is a common type of flowchart that shows the flow of authority and chain of command in an organization. The chart in Exhibit 9.4 illustrates the organization of a student union board.

In a PowerPoint presentation, you can design the chart so that each part is displayed as you talk about it. If overheads are used, multiple overheads can be "stacked" so that each overhead adds information that appears on the screen. You can create the same effect by using a large newsprint pad if you make a series of charts in which you add more information on each succeeding page. Then mount the pad on an easel and, as you are talking, flip the pages to reveal more information as you discuss it.

GRAPHS

A **graph** is a diagram that presents numerical comparisons. Bar graphs, line graphs, and pie graphs are the most common forms of graphs.

chart a graphic representation that distills a lot of information and presents it to an audience in an easily interpreted visual format

word chart a chart used to preview, review, or highlight important ideas covered in a speech

flowchart a chart that uses symbols and connecting lines to diagram the progressions through a complicated process

graph a diagram that presents numerical comparisons

EXHIBIT 9.3 Word chart

Five Pillars of Islam

1. Shahadah: Witness to Faith
2. Salat: Prayer
3. Sawm: Fasting
4. Zakat: Almsgiving
5. Hajj: Pilgrimage

EXHIBIT 9.4 Organizational chart

Chairperson   Financial Advisor

Executive Council

Space Utilization Committee   Cultural Events Committee   Recreation Committee

---

bar graph a diagram that uses vertical or horizontal bars to show relationships between two or more variables at the same time or at various times on one or more dimensions

line graph a diagram that indicates changes in one or more variables over time

pie graph a diagram that shows the relationships among parts of a single unit

A **bar graph** is a diagram that uses vertical or horizontal bars to show relationships between two or more variables at the same time or at various times on one or more dimensions. For instance, in a speech on fluctuations in the economy, the bar graph in Exhibit 9.5 shows the actual (and estimated) increases in clothing exports from China from 1998 to 2005.

A **line graph** is a diagram that indicates changes in one or more variables over time. In a speech on the population of the United States, for example, the line graph in Exhibit 9.6 helps by showing the population increase, in millions, from 1810 to 2000.

A **pie graph** is a diagram that shows the relationships among parts of a single unit. In a speech on comparative family net worth, a pie graph such as the one in

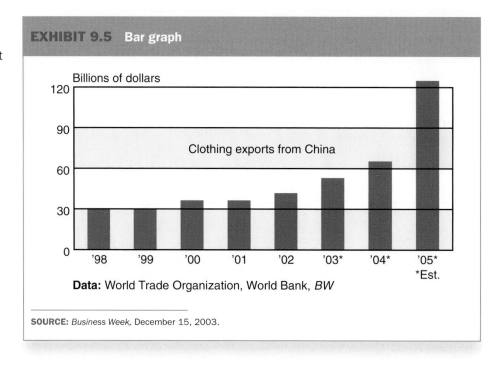

EXHIBIT 9.5   Bar graph

Billions of dollars

Clothing exports from China

'98 '99 '00 '01 '02 '03* '04* '05*
*Est.

Data: World Trade Organization, World Bank, *BW*

SOURCE: *Business Week,* December 15, 2003.

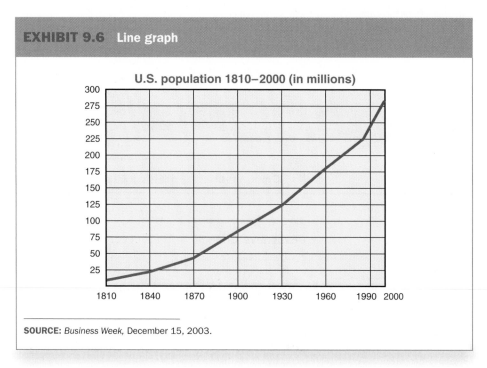

EXHIBIT 9.6   Line graph

U.S. population 1810–2000 (in millions)

1810   1840   1870   1900   1930   1960   1990 2000

SOURCE: *Business Week,* December 15, 2003.

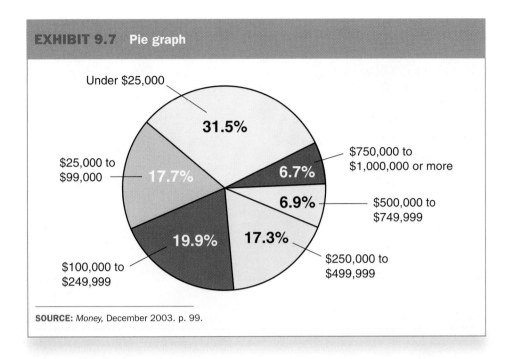

EXHIBIT 9.7 Pie graph

Under $25,000 — 31.5%

$25,000 to $99,000 — 17.7%

$100,000 to $249,999 — 19.9%

$250,000 to $499,999 — 17.3%

$500,000 to $749,999 — 6.9%

$750,000 to $1,000,000 or more — 6.7%

SOURCE: *Money*, December 2003. p. 99.

Exhibit 9.7 could be used to show the percentage of U.S. households that have achieved various levels of net worth.

Most spreadsheet computer programs allow you to prepare colorful graphs easily and to compare the data arrayed as a bar, line, or pie graph. This allows you to choose which display you think will be most effective for your presentation. If you prepare your graphs on the computer, you will be able to insert them into a PowerPoint slide or print them onto an overhead.

When choosing or preparing graphs, make sure that labels are large enough to be read easily by audience members.

To see a video clip of a student speaker's use of visual aids, use your Challenge of Effective Speaking CD-ROM to access the chapter resources for Chapter 9 at the Challenge Web site. Click on "Eye Chip" in the left-hand menu.

Methods for Displaying Visual Aids

Once you have decided on the specific visual aids for your speech, you will need to choose the method you will use to display them. There are trade-offs to be considered when choosing a method. Methods for displaying visual aids vary in the type of preparation they require, the amount of specialized training needed to use them effectively, and the professionalism they convey. Some methods, such as writing on a chalkboard, require little advance preparation. Other methods, such as computer-generated presentations, can require extensive preparation. Similarly, it's easy to use an object or a flipchart, but you will need training to properly set up and run a slide or PowerPoint presentation. Finally, the quality of your visual presentation will affect your perceived credibility. A well-run computer-generated presentation is impressive, but technical difficulties can make you look ill prepared. Hand-prepared charts and graphs that are hastily or sloppily developed mark you as an amateur, whereas professional-looking visual aids enhance your credibility. Speakers can choose from the following methods.

COMPUTER-MEDIATED PRESENTATIONS

Today, in many professional settings audiences expect speakers to use computer-mediated visual aids. PowerPoint, Adobe Persuasion, and Lotus

If you have access to an LCD (liquid crystal display) panel that allows you to project your visual aid directly from your computer, make sure that the lighting in the room isn't so bright that it competes with your presentation.

Courtesy of InFocus Systems, Inc.

Freelance are popular presentation software programs. Using these programs, you can create your visual aids on your computer, download them to a disk or CD-ROM, and then use them on a computer/projector or monitor system at your speech site. Additionally, through the Internet you can find, download, and store your own "library" of images. Most presentation software allows you to insert an image from your "library" into your presentation. Using a computer scanner, you can also digitize a photograph from a book or magazine and transfer it to your computer library.

Not only can the visuals you create be displayed directly on a screen or TV monitor as a computer "slide show," but they can be used to create slides, overhead transparencies, or handouts. Visual aids developed with presentation software give a very polished look to your speech and allow you to develop complex multimedia presentations.

Today, most colleges and universities offer classes in developing and using presentation software and have dedicated classrooms or portable roll-around carts that house the equipment needed to present computer-mediated visuals.

Preparing visual aids with presentation software is time-consuming. Smoothly presenting a computerized visual presentation takes practice. But if you start simply, over time you will become more adept at creating professional-quality visuals. Well-developed and well-presented computer-mediated visual aids greatly enhance audience perceptions of speaker credibility. *Caution:* Computer-mediated presentations can be addicting. Many novices overuse them, so instead of having visual aids (visuals that "aid" speaker's ideas), the visuals become the show and the speaker is relegated to the role of projectionist.[4]

OVERHEAD TRANSPARENCIES

An easy way to display drawings, charts, and graphs is to transfer them to an acetate film and project them onto a screen via an overhead projector. With a master copy of the visual, you can make an overhead transparency using a copy machine, thermograph, color lift, or if the master is a computer document, with a computer printer. Overheads are easy and inexpensive to make, and the equipment needed to project overheads is easy to operate and likely to be available at most speech sites. Overheads work well in nearly any setting, and unlike other kinds of projections, they don't require dimming the lights in the room. Moreover, overheads can be useful for demonstrating a process because it is possible to write, trace, or draw on the transparency while you are talking. The size at which an overhead is projected can also be adjusted to the size of the room so that all audience members can see the image.

FLIPCHARTS

A **flipchart,** a large pad of paper mounted on an easel, can be an effective method for presenting visual aids. Flipcharts (and easels) are available in many sizes. For a presentation to four or five people, a small tabletop version works well; for a larger audience, a larger-size pad (30″ × 40″) is needed.

flipchart a large pad of paper mounted on an easel

Flipcharts are prepared before the speech using colorful markers to record the information. At times, a speaker may record some of the information before the speech begins and then add information while speaking.

When preparing flipcharts, leave several pages between each visual on the pad. If you discover a mistake or decide to revise, you can tear out that sheet without disturbing the order of other visuals you may have prepared. After you have the visuals, tear out all but one sheet between each chart. This blank sheet serves as both a transition page and a cover sheet. Because you want your audience to focus on your words and not on visual material that is no longer being discussed, you can flip to the empty page while you are talking about material not covered by charts. Also, the empty page between charts ensures that heavy lines or colors from the next chart will not show through.

For flipcharts to be effective, the information that is handwritten or drawn must be neat and appropriately sized. Flipchart visuals that are not neatly done detract from speaker credibility. Flipcharts can be comfortably used with smaller audiences (less than one hundred people) but are not appropriate for larger settings. It is especially important when creating flipcharts to make sure that the information is written large enough to be easily seen by all audience members.

POSTER BOARDS

The easiest method for displaying simple drawings, charts, maps, and graphs is by preparing them on stiff cardboard or (foam core). Then the visual can be placed on an easel or in a chalk tray when it is referred to during the speech. Like flipcharts, poster boards must be neat and appropriately sized. They are also limited in their use to smaller audiences.

CHALKBOARD

Because the chalkboard is a staple in every college classroom, many novice (and ill-prepared) speakers rely on this method for displaying their visual aids. Unfortunately, the chalkboard is easy to misuse and to overuse. Moreover, chalkboards are not suitable for depicting complex material. Writing on a chalkboard is appropriate to use for very short items of information that can be written in a few seconds. Nevertheless, being able to use a chalkboard effectively should be a part of any speaker's repertoire.

Chalkboards should be written on prior to speaking or during a break in speaking. Otherwise, the visual is likely to be either illegible or partly obscured by your body as you write. Or you may end up talking to the board instead of to the audience. Should you need to draw or write on the board while you are talking, you should practice doing it. If you are right-handed, stand to the right of what you are drawing. Try to face at least part of the audience while you work. Although it may seem awkward at first, your effort will allow you to maintain contact with your audience and will allow the audience to see what you are doing while you are doing it.

"Chalk talks" are easiest to prepare, but they are the most likely to result in damage to speaker credibility. It is the rare individual who can develop well-crafted visual aids on a chalkboard. More often, chalkboard visuals signal a lack of preparation.

HANDOUTS

At times it may be useful for each member of the audience to have a personal copy of the visual aid. In these situations you can prepare a handout. On the plus side, you can prepare handouts (material printed or drawn on sheets of paper) quickly, and all the people in the audience can have their own professional-quality material to refer to and take with them from the speech. On the minus side is the distraction of distributing handouts and the potential for losing audience members' attention when you want them to be looking at you. Before you decide to use handouts, carefully consider why a handout is superior to other methods. If you do decide on handouts, you may want to distribute them at the end of the speech.

Criteria for Choosing Visual Aids

Now that you understand the various types of visual aids and the methods you can use to display them, you have to decide what content needs to be depicted and the best way to do this. In this section we focus on some of the key questions you need to answer to help you make visual aid choices.

1. What are the most important ideas the audience needs to understand and remember? These ideas are ones you may want to enhance with visual aids. Visual aids are likely to be remembered. So, you will want to make sure that what you present visually is what you want your audience to remember.

2. Are there ideas that are complex or difficult to explain verbally but would be easy for members to understand visually? The old saying "One picture is worth a thousand words" is true. At times we can help our audience by providing a visual explanation. Demonstrating the correct way to hold a golf club is much easier and clearer than simply describing the positioning of each hand and finger.

3. How many visual aids should I consider? Unless you are doing a slide show in which the total focus of the speech is on visual images, the number of visual aids you use should be limited. For the most part, you want the focus of the audience to be on you, the speaker. You want to use visual aids when their use will hold attention, exemplify an idea, or help the audience remember. For each of these goals, the more visual aids used, the less value they will contribute. In a five-minute speech, using three visual aids at crucial times will get attention, exemplify, and stimulate recall far better than using six or eight.

There is another reason for keeping the visual aids to a small number. A couple of really well crafted visual aids may well maximize the power of your statements, whereas several poorly executed or poorly used visual aids may actually detract from the power of your words.

4. How large is the audience? The kinds of visual aids that will work for a small group of fifteen or twenty differ from the kinds that will work for an audience of a hundred or more. For an audience of fewer than twenty, as in most of your classroom speeches, you can show relatively small objects and use relatively small models and everyone will be able to see. For larger audiences, you'll want projections that can be seen with ease from 100 or 200 feet away.

5. Is necessary equipment readily available? At times, you may be speaking in an environment that is not equipped for certain visual displays. At many colleges and universities, most rooms are equipped with only a chalkboard, an overhead projector, and electrical outlets. Anything else you want to use you will have to bring yourself or schedule through the appropriate university media office. Be prepared! In any situation in which you have scheduled equipment from an outside source, you need to prepare yourself for the possibility that the equipment may not arrive on time or may not work the way you thought it did. Call ahead, get to your speaking location early, and have an alternative visual aid to use, just in case.

6. Is the time involved in making or getting the visual aid and/or equipment cost-effective? Visual aids are supplements. Their goal is to accent what you are doing verbally. If you believe that a particular visual aid will help you better achieve your goal, then the time spent is well worth it.

You'll notice that most of the visual aids we've discussed can be obtained or prepared relatively easily. But because some procedures are "so easy," we find ourselves getting lost in making some of them. Visual aids definitely make a speech more interesting and engaging. However, I've found that the best advice is to "keep it simple."

Use the following guidelines when choosing visual aids:

◆ Take a few minutes to consider your visual aid strategy. Where would some kind of visual aid make the most sense? What kind of visual aid is most appropriate?

◆ Adapt your visuals to your situation, speech topic, and audience needs.

◆ Choose visuals with which you are both comfortable and competent.

◆ Check out the audiovisual resources of the speaking site before you start preparing your visual aids.

◆ Be discriminate in the number of visual aids you use and the key points that they support.

For a thorough discussion of the methods and guidelines for using visual aids, use your Challenge of Effective Speaking CD-ROM to access **Web Resource 9.1: Visual Aids**.

Speech Planning Action Step 5, Activity 5A: Choosing and Preparing Visual Aids, helps you choose and prepare visual aids. The Student Response to Activity 5A provides an example of one student's response to this activity.

SPEECH PLANNING   ACTION STEP 5

5 | Visual Aids

ACTIVITY 5A Choosing and Preparing Visual Aids

The goal of this activity is to identify information whose visual presentation would increase audience interest, understanding, and retention.

1. Identify the key ideas in your speech for which you believe a visual presentation would increase audience interest, facilitate understanding, or increase retention.
2. For each idea you have identified, list the type of visual aid you think would be most appropriate to develop and use.
3. For each visual you have identified, decide on the method you will use to present it.

You can complete this activity online with Speech Builder Express, download a Visual Aids Planning Chart to help you organize your visual aids, and, if requested, e-mail your completed activity to your instructor. Use your Challenge of Effective Speaking CD-ROM to access Activity 5A.

ACTIVITY 5A Choosing and Preparing Visual Aids

Speech goal: I would like my audience to learn the skills necessary to play the game of lacrosse.

1. Identify the key ideas in your speech for which you believe a visual presentation would increase audience interest, facilitate understanding, or increase retention.

   Catching, throwing, and cradling.

2. For each idea you have identified, list the type of visual aid you think would be most appropriate to develop and use.

   I will use a lacrosse stick and a ball.

3. For each visual you have identified, decide on the method you will use to present it.

   I will use myself to demonstrate catching, throwing, and cradling with the lacrosse stick and ball.

Principles for Designing Effective Visual Aids

However simple you think your visual aids will be, you still have to design them carefully. The visual aids that you are most likely to design for a classroom presentation are charts, graphs, diagrams, and drawings written on poster board or flipcharts or projected on screens using overheads or slides.

In this section we will suggest eight principles for designing effective visual aids. Then, we'll look at several examples that illustrate these principles.

1. Use a print or type size that can be seen easily by your entire audience. If you're designing a hand-drawn poster board, check your lettering for size by moving as far away from the visual aid you've created as the farthest person in your audience will be sitting. If you can read the lettering and see the details from that distance, then both are large enough; if not, draw another sample and check it for size.

When you project a typeface from an overhead onto a screen, the lettering on the screen will be much larger than the lettering on the overhead itself. So, what's a good rule of thumb for overhead lettering? Try 36-point type for major headings, 24-point for subheadings, and 18-point for text. Exhibit 9.8 shows how these sizes look on paper. The 36-point type will project to about two to three inches on the screen; 24-point will project to about one to two inches; 18-point will project to about one inch. Most presentational software will prompt you if you have chosen a font size that is too small.

2. Use a typeface that is easy to read and pleasing to the eye. Modern software packages, such as Microsoft Word, come with a variety of typefaces (fonts). Yet only a few of them will work well in projections. In general, avoid fonts that have heavy serifs or curlicues. Exhibit 9.9 shows a sample of four standard typefaces in regular and boldface 18-point size. Most other typefaces are designed for special situations.

EXHIBIT 9.8 Visual aid print sizes

36 Major Headings

24 Subheads

18 Text material

EXHIBIT 9.9 Typefaces in 18-point regular and boldface

Helvetica	Selecting Typefaces **Selecting Typefaces**
Times	Selecting Typefaces **Selecting Typefaces**
Frutiger	Selecting Typefaces **Selecting Typefaces**
Palatino	Selecting Typefaces **Selecting Typefaces**

Which of these typefaces seem easiest to read and most pleasing to your eye? Perhaps you'll decide that you'd like to use one typeface for the heading and another for the text. In general, you will not want to use more than two typefaces—headings in one, text in another. You want the typefaces to call attention to the material, not to themselves.

3. Use upper- and lowercase type. The combination of upper- and lowercase is easier to read than uppercase only. Some people think that printing in all capital letters creates emphasis. Although that may be true in some

EXHIBIT 9.10   All capitals versus upper- and lowercase letters

CARAT: THE WEIGHT OF A DIAMOND
Carat: The Weight of a Diamond

instances, ideas printed in all capital letters are more difficult to read—even when the ideas are written in short phrases (see Exhibit 9.10).

4. Limit the lines of type to fewer than seven. You don't want the audience to spend a long time reading your visual aid; you want them listening to you. Limit the total number of lines to six or fewer, and write points as phrases rather than complete sentences. The visual aid is a reinforcement and summary of what you say, not the exact words you say. You don't want the audience to have to spend more than six or eight seconds "getting" your visual aid.

5. Include only items of information that you will emphasize in your speech. We often get ideas for visual aids from other sources, and the tendency is to include all the material that was in the original. But for speech purposes, keep the aid as simple as possible. Include only the key information, and eliminate anything that distracts or takes emphasis away from the point you want to make.

Because the tendency to clutter is likely to present a special problem on graphs, let's consider two graphs that show college enrollment by age of students (Exhibit 9.11), based on figures reported in the *Chronicle of Higher Education*. The graph on the left shows all eleven age categories mentioned; the graph on the right simplifies this information by combining age ranges with small percentages. The graph on the right is not only easier to read, but it also emphasizes the highest percentage classifications.

6. Make sure information is laid out on the aid in a way that is aesthetically pleasing. Layout involves leaving white space around the whole message, indenting subordinate ideas, and using different type sizes as well as different treatments, such as bolding and underlining.

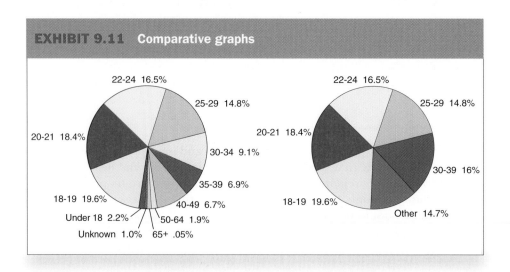

EXHIBIT 9.11   Comparative graphs

7. Add pictures or clip art where appropriate to add interest. If you are working with computer graphics, consider adding clip art. Most computer graphics packages have a wide variety of clip art that you can import to your document. You can also buy relatively inexpensive software packages that contain thousands of clip art images. A relevant piece of clip art can make the image look both more professional and more dramatic. Be careful, though; clip art can be overdone. Don't let your message be overpowered by unnecessary pictures.

8. Use color strategically. Although black and white can work well for your visual aids, you should consider using color. Color can be used strategically to emphasize points. Here are some suggestions for incorporating color in your graphics:

   ✦ Use color to show similarities and differences between ideas.

   ✦ Use the same color background for each visual. Avoid dark backgrounds.

   ✦ Use bright colors, such as red, to highlight important information.

   ✦ Use black or deep blue for lettering, especially on flipcharts.

   ✦ When using yellow or orange for lettering, outline the letters with a darker color; unless outlined, they can't be seen well from a distance.

   ✦ Use no more than four colors; two or three are even better.

   ✦ When you want to get into more complex color usage, use a color wheel to select harmonizing colors.

   ✦ Don't crowd. Let the background color separate lettering and clip art.

   ✦ Always make a quick template before you prepare your visual aids.

   ✦ Pretend you are your audience. Sit as far away as they will be sitting, and evaluate the colors you have chosen for their readability and appeal.

Let's see if we can put all of these principles to work. Exhibit 9.12 contains a lot of important information that the speaker has presented, but notice how unpleasant it is to the eye. As you can see, this visual aid ignores all principles. However, with some thoughtful simplification, this speaker could produce the visual aid shown in Exhibit 9.13, which sharpens the focus by emphasizing the key words (reduce, reuse, recycle), highlighting the major details, and adding clip art for a professional touch.

Guidelines for Presenting Visual Aids

Many speakers think that once they have prepared good visual aids, they will have no trouble using them in the speech. However, many speeches with good visual aids have become shambles because the speaker neglected to practice with them. As a general rule of thumb, you will want to make sure that you practice using visual aids in your rehearsals. During practice sessions, indicate on your notes exactly when you will use each visual aid (and when you will remove it). Work on statements for introducing the visual aids, and practice different ways of showing the visual aids until you are comfortable using them and satisfied that everyone in the audience will be able to see them. Following are several guidelines for using visual aids effectively in your speech.

1. Plan carefully when to use visual aids. As you practice your speech, indicate on your outline when and how you will use each visual aid. Avoid displaying visual aids before you begin talking about the specific information to which

EXHIBIT 9.12 A cluttered and cumbersome visual aid

I WANT YOU TO REMEMBER THE THREE R'S OF RECYCLING

Reduce the amount of waste people produce, like overpacking or using material that won't recycle.

Reuse by relying on cloth towels rather than paper towels, earthenware dishes rather than paper or plastic plates, and glass bottles rather than aluminum cans.

Recycle by collecting recyclable products, sorting them appropriately, and getting them to the appropriate recycling agency.

EXHIBIT 9.13 A simple but effective visual aid

Remember the Three R's of Recycling

Reduce waste

Reuse
   cloth towels
   dishes
   glass bottles

Recycle
   collect
   sort
   deliver

they relate, as they may distract your audience's attention from important information that precedes the visual. Likewise, if you find that a visual aid does not contribute directly to the audience's attention to, understanding of, or retention of information on your topic, then reconsider its use.

2. Show visual aids only when talking about them. Visual aids will draw audience attention. The basic rule of thumb is: When the visual aid is no longer the focus of attention, remove it, turn it off, or get rid of it.

If you use an overhead projector, it may come with a lid or cover on the light. If yours doesn't, then either turn the machine off or cover your transparency with a blank sheet of paper. If you are using an LCD and a computer, show your visual and then advance to a blank screen. You can insert blank pages in areas where you know you will need them.

Often a single visual aid contains several bits of information. In order to keep audience attention where you want it, you can prepare the visual aid with cover-ups. Then, as you move from one portion of the visual aid to another, you can remove covers to expose the portion of the visual aid that you are discussing.

3. Talk about the visual aid while showing it. Since you know what you want your audience to see in the visual aid, tell your audience what to look for, explain the various parts, and interpret figures, symbols, and percentages.

When you show your visual—for example, a transparency projected onto a screen in front of the class—use the following "turn-touch-talk" technique.

Don't display visual aids when you're not referring to them.

✦ When you display the visual, walk to the screen—that's where everyone will look anyway. Slightly turn to the visual and touch it—that is, point to it with your arm or a pointer (use carefully). Then, with your back to the screen and your body still at a slight 45-degree angle to the group, talk to your audience about the visual.

✦ When you finish making your comments, return to the podium or your speaking position, and turn off the projector or otherwise put the visual away.

4. Display visual aids so that everyone in the audience can see them. If you hold the visual aid, position it away from your body and point it toward the various parts of the audience. If you place your visual aid on a chalkboard or easel or mount it in some way, stand to one side and point with the arm nearest the visual aid. If it is necessary to roll or fold the visual aid, bring some transparent tape to mount it to the chalkboard or wall so that it does not roll or wrinkle.

5. Talk to your audience, not to the visual aid. You may need to look at the visual aid occasionally, but it is important to maintain eye contact with your audience as much as possible—in part so that you can gauge how they are reacting to your visual material. When speakers become too engrossed in their visual aids, looking at them instead of the audience, they tend to lose contact with the audience entirely.

6. Avoid passing objects around the audience. People look at, read, handle, and think about whatever they hold in their hands. While they are so occupied, they are not likely to be listening to you.

To see a video clip of a student speaker presenting visual aids effectively, use your Challenge of Effective Speaking CD-ROM to access the chapter resources for Chapter 9 at the Challenge Web site. Click on "Electoral College" in the left-hand menu.

Summary

Visual aids allow an audience to see as well as hear information. They are useful when they help audience members understand or remember important information. The most common types of visual aids are objects, models, photographs, slides, film and video clips, simple drawings, maps, charts, and graphs. Methods that speakers can use to present visual aids include computer-mediated presentations, overhead transparencies, flipcharts, poster boards, a chalkboard, and handouts. Advancements in computer graphics give the speaker a wide range of flexibility in creating professional-quality visual materials.

Before you start collecting or creating the visual aids you plan to use, you need to consider a number of questions. What are the most important ideas in helping me achieve my speech goal? Are there ideas that are complex or difficult to explain verbally but would be easy for members to understand visually? How many visual aids should I consider? How large is the audience? Is necessary equipment readily available? Is the time involved in making or getting the visual aid and/or equipment cost-effective?

Take time to design your visual aids with the following principles in mind: Use a print or type size that can be seen easily by your entire audience. Use a typeface that is easy to read and pleasing to the eye. Use upper- and lowercase type. Try to limit the lines of type to six or fewer. Include only items of information that you will emphasize in your speech. Make sure information is laid out in a way that is aesthetically pleasing. Add clip art where appropriate. Use color strategically.

When you plan to use visual aids in a speech, make sure that you practice using them in rehearsal. Keep the following suggestions in mind: Plan carefully when you will use each visual aid. Show visual aids only when talking about them. Talk about the visual aid while showing it. Display visual aids so that everyone in the audience can see them. Talk to your audience, not to the visual aid. Avoid passing objects around the audience.

CHALLENGE ONLINE

Now that you've read Chapter 9, use your Challenge of Effective Speaking CD-ROM for quick access to the electronic study resources that accompany this text. Your CD-ROM gives you access to InfoTrac College Edition, Speech Builder Express, and the Challenge of Effective Speaking Web site. When you get to the Challenge of Effective Speaking home page, click on "Student Book Companion Site" in the Resource box at the right to access the online study aids for this chapter, including the video clips described on pages 161 and 171, a digital glossary, review quizzes, and the chapter activities.

KEY TERMS

At the Challenge of Effective Speaking Web site, select chapter resources for Chapter 9. Print a copy of the glossary for this chapter, test yourself with the electronic flash cards, or complete the crossword puzzle to help you master the following key terms.

visual aid (155)　　　　　　　bar graph (160)
chart (159)　　　　　　　　　line graph (160)
word chart (159)　　　　　　pie graph (161)
flowchart (159)　　　　　　　flipchart (163)
graph (159)

INFOTRAC COLLEGE EDITION EXERCISE

This chapter on visual aids barely scratches the surface in explaining all of the technology that is available to make the presentation portion of your speech interesting and engaging. Use your Challenge of Effective Speaking CD-ROM to access InfoTrac College Edition. Conduct a search using "presentation" as your Search Guide word. Take a look at all the article citations under Business Presentations. It seems that technology is now an important component of success in presenting ideas and speeches in the business world.

WEB RESOURCE

Access the Web resources for this chapter online at the Challenge of Effective Speaking Web site. Select the chapter resources for Chapter 9, then click on "Web Resources."

9.1 Visual Aids (165)

SPEECH PLANNING ACTION STEP

Access the Action Step activity for this chapter online at the Challenge of Effective Speaking Web site. Select the chapter resources for Chapter 9, then click on the activity number you want. You may print out your completed activity, and you should save your work so you can use it as needed in later Action Step activities.

5A: Choosing and Preparing Visual Aids (165)

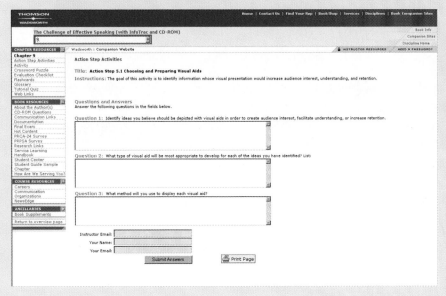

10

Practicing Speech Wording

© William Thomas Cain/Getty Images

A speech reminds us that words, like children, have the power to make dance the dullest beanbag of a heart.

Peggy Noonan, *What I Saw at the Revolution*, 1990

As Rhonda replayed the recording she had made of her first speech practice session, she listened carefully to the section on the effects of Rohypnol. She stopped the tape after she heard herself saying, "Rohypnol leaves many bad effects on people. And a lot of these are really, really terrible. I mean, you can be totally out of it for a long time."

"Yuck," thought Rhonda, "sounds so vague. I say, 'leaves bad effects,' but I don't specifically state any of the effects. And calling the effects 'really, really terrible' isn't very descriptive. Let's see, what could I say instead. . . ?"

6 | Delivery   **ACTION STEP 6**

Practice Speech Wording and Delivery

A. Practice until the wording is clear, vivid, emphatic, and appropriate

With an outline in hand and your visual aids prepared, you are ready to practice your speech, switching your focus from the structure of what you plan to say to how you will say it. In the chapter opening, Rhonda is working on developing clear, vivid, emphatic, and appropriate wording for her ideas. Once she does this, she will continue to rehearse until she is fluent, enthusiastic, and expressive in her delivery. In this chapter we explain how you can conduct rehearsal sessions that help you achieve effective wording and delivery in your speech.

In a written communication, effective wording evolves through editing and finally appears on the printed page. In a speech, however, effective wording develops through oral practice. The outline of your speech is a skeleton that includes from 35 percent to more than 50 percent of the words that you may use in the speech. During each rehearsal, you fill out the outline to the appropriate speech length. As you continue to rehearse, you will change your wording so that the ideas are presented in language that is clear, vivid, emphatic, and appropriate for the audience.

In this chapter you will learn to use the kind of language that is instantly intelligible to the *ear,* so that the audience receives the same meanings as you intend. When a written sentence is unclear, the reader can reread it and puzzle out its meaning, but when a sentence in a speech is unclear, the listener cannot go back, and the meaning may be misunderstood or lost. So, as a speaker you must focus on how to help the specific audience understand the meaning *as the speech is given.*

Let's begin our discussion by briefly examining the complex relationship between language and meaning that makes language choices so important in speech making. Then we will describe the specific tactics you can use to increase the clarity, vividness, emphasis, and appropriateness of the words you use.

Language and Meaning

On the surface, the relationship between language and meaning seems perfectly clear: You select a word to represent your meaning, and audience members will interpret your words and understand the meaning you wished to convey. In fact, the relationship between language and meaning is not so simple for three reasons.

First, we are not born knowing a language—we must learn it. Moreover, each generation within a language community learns the language anew. Much of our language we learn early in life from our families; we learn more in school; and we continue to learn more throughout our lives. But we do not all learn to use the same words in the same way.

Second, although each language has a system of syntax and grammar, each utterance is a creative act. When we speak, we use language to create new sentences that represent our meaning. Although on occasion we repeat other people's sentence constructions to represent what we are thinking or feeling, most of our talk is unique.

Third, even though two people may know the same word, they may interpret the meaning of the word differently. Words have two kinds of meaning: denotative and connotative. Thus, when Melissa tells Trish that her dog died, what Trish understands Melissa to mean depends on both word denotation and connotation.

DENOTATION

The direct, explicit meaning a language community formally gives a word is its **denotation.** Word denotation is the meaning found in a dictionary. So denotatively when Melissa said her dog died, she meant that her domesticated canine no longer demonstrates physical life. In some situations the denotative meaning of a word may not be clear. Why? First, dictionary definitions reflect current and past practice in the language community; and second, the dictionary uses words to define words. The end result is that words are defined differently in various dictionaries and may include multiple meanings that change over time.

Moreover, meaning may vary depending on the context in which the word used. For example, the dictionary definition of *gay* includes both (1) having or showing a merry, lively mood and (2) homosexual. Thus, **context**—the position of a word in a sentence and its relationship to the other words around it— has an important effect on correctly interpreting which denotation of a word is meant. Not only will the other words, the syntax, and the grammar of a verbal message help us to understand the denotative meaning of certain words, but so will the situation in which they are spoken. Whether the comment, "He's really gay," is understood to be a comment on someone's sexual orientation or on his merry mood may depend on the age of the speaker or the circumstances in which it is said.

CONNOTATION

The feelings or evaluations we associate with a word, its **connotation,** color the meaning we give it. Thus, our perception of a word's connotation may be even more important than its denotation in how we interpret the meaning of the word.

C. K. Ogden and I. A. Richards were among the first scholars to consider the misunderstandings resulting from the failure of communicators to realize that their subjective reactions to words will be a product of their life experiences.[1] For instance, when Melissa tells Trish that her dog died, Trish's understanding of the message depends on the extent to which her feelings about pets and death—her connotations of the words—correspond to the feelings that Melissa has about pets and death. Whereas Melissa, who sees dogs as truly indispensable friends, may be intending to communicate her overwhelming grief, Trish, who has never had a pet and doesn't particularly care for pets in general or dogs in particular, may miss the emotional meaning of Melissa's statement.

Being aware of and sensitive to word denotation and connotation are important because regardless of what a speaker says, the only message meaning that counts is the message meaning that is understood by audience members.

denotation the explicit meaning a language community formally gives a word

context the position of a word in a sentence and its relationship to other words around it

connotation the feelings or evaluations we associate with a word

Speaking Clearly

Speaking clearly results from reducing your use of ambiguous and confusing language. Compare the clarity of the following two descriptions of the same incident:

> Some nut almost ran into me a while ago.

> Last Saturday afternoon an older man in a banged-up Honda Civic ran through the red light at Calhoun and Clifton and came within inches of hitting my car while I was waiting to turn left.

Using specific, concrete, precise, and familiar words decreases ambiguity and audience confusion when we speak.

Using Specific Language

Specific language clarifies meaning by narrowing what is understood from a general category to a particular item or group within that category. Often, as we try to express our thoughts, the first words that come to mind are general, abstract, and imprecise. The ambiguity of these words makes the listener choose from many possible images rather than picturing the single, focused image we have in mind. The more listeners are called on to provide their own images, the more likely they are to see meanings different from what we intend.

© Pablo Corral V/Corbis

To differentiate among individuals in this picture, you would have to be precise, specific, and concrete in your description.

specific language words that clarify meaning by narrowing what is understood from a general category to a particular item or group within that category

concrete words words that appeal to the senses or conjure up a picture

precise words words that narrow a larger category

Specific words are more concrete and precise than are general words. Saying "a banged-up Honda Civic" is more specific than saying "a car." **Concrete words** appeal to the senses. In effect, we can see, hear, smell, taste, or touch what they describe. Thus we can picture that banged-up Civic. Abstract ideas, such as justice, equality, or fairness, can be made concrete through examples or metaphors. **Precise words** are words that narrow a larger category. For instance, if in her speech Nevah refers to a "blue-collar worker," you might picture any number of occupations that fall within this broad category. If, instead, she is more precise and says he's a "construction worker," the number of possible images you can picture is reduced. Now you select your image from the subcategory of construction worker, and your meaning is likely to be closer to the one she intended. If she is even more precise, she may say "bulldozer operator." Now you are even clearer on the specific occupation.

In the preceding example, the continuum of specificity goes from blue-collar worker to construction worker to bulldozer operator. Exhibit 10.1 provides another illustration of increasing precision. To see a video clip of a student speaker using specific, concrete, and precise language, use your Challenge of Effective Speaking CD-ROM to access the chapter resources for Chapter 10 at the Challenge Web site. Click on "Shakespeare" in the left-hand menu.

Choosing specific language is easier when you have a large working vocabulary. As a speaker, the larger your vocabulary, the more choices you have from

EXHIBIT 10.1   Levels of precision

Gambling games
Games of skill
Card games
Poker
Seven-card stud

which to select the word you want. As a listener, the larger your vocabulary, the more likely you are to understand the words used by others.

One way to increase your vocabulary is to study one of the many vocabulary-building books on the shelves of most any bookstore, such as *Word Smart: Building an Educated Vocabulary*.[2] You might also study magazine features such as "Word Power" in the *Reader's Digest*. By completing this monthly quiz and learning the words with which you are not familiar, you could increase your vocabulary by as many as twenty words per month. To take a vocabulary test online, use your Challenge of Effective Speaking CD-ROM to access **Web Resource 10.1: WordsmartChallenge.**

A second way to increase your vocabulary is to take note of words that you read or that people use in their conversations with you that you don't know and look them up. For instance, suppose you read or hear, "I was inundated with phone calls today!" If you wrote down *inundated* and looked it up in a dictionary later, you would find that it means "overwhelmed" or "flooded." If you then say to yourself, "She was inundated—overwhelmed or flooded—with phone calls today," you are likely to remember that meaning and apply it the next time you hear the word. If you follow this practice, you will soon notice the increase in your vocabulary.

A third way to increase your vocabulary is to use a thesaurus (a list of words and their synonyms) to identify synonyms that are more concrete and precise than the word you may have chosen. An easy way to consult a thesaurus is to access Merriam-Webster's online *Collegiate Thesaurus*. For instance, when you type "difficult" into the search box, you'll find such synonyms as "hard," "laborious," "arduous," and "strenuous." Use your Challenge of Effective Speaking CD-ROM to access **Web Resource 10.2: Merriam-Webster Online.**

Having a larger vocabulary won't help your speaking if you don't have a procedure for accessing it when you speak. So, during practice sessions you will want to consciously experiment using specific words that precisely reflect your ideas. Suppose you were practicing a speech on registering for classes and said "Preregistration is awful." If this word isn't quite right, you can quickly brainstorm better words, such as *frustrating, demeaning, cumbersome,* and *annoying*. Then, as you continue to practice, you might say, "Preregistration is a cumbersome process."

Some speakers think that to be effective they must impress their audience with their extensive vocabularies. As a result, instead of looking for common or simple words, they use words that appear pompous, affected, or stilted to the listener. Speaking precisely and specifically does not mean speaking obscurely. So when you have a choice, select the simplest, most familiar words that convey your specific meaning. The following story illustrates the problem with pretentious, unfamiliar words:

> A plumber wrote to a government agency, saying that he found that hydrochloric acid quickly opened drain pipes but that he wasn't sure whether it was a good thing to use. A scientist at the agency replied, "The efficacy of hydrochloric acid is indisputable, but the corrosive residue is incompatible with metallic permanence."
>
> The plumber wrote back thanking him for the assurance that hydrochloric acid was all right. Disturbed by this turn of affairs, the scientist showed the letter to his boss, another scientist, who then wrote to the plumber: "We cannot assume responsibility for the production of toxic and noxious residue with hydrochloric acid and suggest you use an alternative procedure."
>
> The plumber wrote back that he agreed, hydrochloric acid worked fine. Greatly disturbed by this misunderstanding, the scientists took their problem to the top boss. She wrote to the plumber: "Don't use hydrochloric acid. It eats the hell out of pipes."

The decision rule is to use a more difficult word *only* when you believe that it is the very best word for a specific context. Suppose you wanted to use a more precise or specific word for *building*. Using the guideline of familiarity, you might select *house, apartment, high-rise*, or *skyscraper*, but you would avoid *edifice*. Each of the other choices is more precise or more specific, but *edifice* is neither more precise nor more specific, and in addition to being less well understood, it will be perceived as affected or stilted. Likewise, you would choose *clothing* instead of *apparel, bury* instead of *inter, avoid* instead of *eschew, predict* instead of *presage*, and *beauty* instead of *pulchritude*.

You will know that you have really made strides in improving specificity, precision, and concreteness when you find that you can form clear messages even under pressure of presenting your speeches.

The larger your vocabulary, the more chance you have of communicating effectively. One way to enrich your vocabulary is through study of basic vocabulary books and books of synonyms.

Providing Details and Examples

Sometimes the word we use may not have a concrete or precise synonym. In these situations, clarity can be achieved by adding details or examples. For instance, Linda says, "Rashad is very loyal." The meaning of *loyal* (faithful to an idea, person, company, or other entity) is abstract, so to avoid ambiguity and confusion, Linda might add, "He defended Gerry when Sara was gossiping about her." By following up her use of the abstract concept of loyalty with a concrete example, Linda makes it easier for her listeners to "ground" their idea of this personal quality in a concrete or "real" experience.

Likewise, providing details can clarify our messages. Saying "He lives in a really big house" can be clarified by adding "He lives in a fourteen-room Tudor mansion on a six-acre estate."

Being Sensitive to Cultural Differences

Verbal communication rules and expectations about clarity of language vary from culture to culture. One major dimension that is used by theorists to explain similarities and differences in language and behavior is individualism versus collectivism.[3] In general, individualistic cultures emphasize individual goals more than group goals because these cultures value uniqueness. Many individualistic cultures are found in western Europe and North America. In contrast, collectivistic cultures emphasize group goals more than individual goals because these cultures value harmony and solidarity. Many collectivistic cultures are found in Asia, Africa, and Latin America.[4]

Individualistic cultures tend to use low-context communication, in which information is (1) embedded mainly in the messages transmitted and (2) presented directly. Collectivistic cultures tend to use high-context communication, in which people (1) expect others to know how they're thinking and feeling and (2) present some messages indirectly to avoid embarrassing the other person. Thus, speakers from low-context cultures such as the United States operate on the principle of saying what they mean and getting to the point. They prize clear and direct messages that do not depend on an interpretation of the context to be understood. Their approach may be characterized by such expressions as "Say what you mean" and "Don't beat around the bush."[5] In contrast, speakers from high-context cultures such as China form messages with language that is intentionally ambiguous and indirect; to interpret these messages correctly, listeners need to understand not only the message but the context in which it is uttered.

What does this mean to you as a student of public speaking? When you are a member of a cultural group that operates differently from that of the majority of your audience members, you need to adapt your language so that it is clear and appropriate for your audience. If you are uncertain, then during your rehearsals ask someone from the same cultural group as the majority of your audience to listen to the parts of your speech in which your wording is raising questions and to suggest ways in which your wording can be adapted to the audience. For speaking to low-context audiences, this may mean using more concrete examples so that your audience members will be more likely to get the same meanings that you intended. For high-context audiences, it may mean stating certain parts of your message indirectly and trusting that the context will enable them to understand your meaning.

 To read more about how to adapt to audiences from other cultures, use your Challenge of Effective Speaking CD-ROM to access Web Resource 10.3: Speaking to International Audiences.

Speaking Vividly and Emphatically

Listeners cannot "reread" what you have said. To be an effective speaker, it is important to speak clearly, but you will also want to speak vividly and emphasize key words and ideas.

Using Vivid Language

vivid language language that is full of life—vigorous, bright, and intense

Vivid language is full of life—vigorous, bright, and intense. For example, a mediocre baseball announcer might say "Jackson made a great catch," but a better commentator's vivid account might be "Jackson leaped and made a spectacular one-handed catch just as he crashed into the center field wall." The words *leaped, spectacular, one-handed catch,* and *crashed* paint an intense verbal picture of the action. Vivid language begins with vivid thought. You are much more likely to express yourself vividly if you can physically or psychologically sense the meanings you are trying to convey. If you feel the "bite of the wind" or "the sting of freezing rain," if you hear and smell "the thick, juicy sirloin steaks sizzling on the grill," you will be able to describe these sensations. Does the cake "taste good"? Or do your taste buds "quiver with the sweet double-chocolate icing and velvety feel of the rich, moist cake"?

You can make your ideas vivid by using similes and metaphors. A **simile** is a direct comparison of dissimilar things using the word *like* or *as.* Clichés such as "She walks like a duck" and "She sings like a nightingale" are similes. A more vivid simile is one used by an elementary school teacher who said that being back at school after a long absence "was like trying to hold 35 corks under water at the same time."[6] This is a fresh, imaginative simile for a public school teacher's job.

A **metaphor** is a comparison that establishes a figurative identity between objects being compared. Instead of saying that one thing is like another, a metaphor says that one thing is another. Thus, problem cars are "lemons" and the leaky roof is a "sieve." Notice how one speaker used a metaphor effectively to conclude a speech: "It is imperative that we weave our fabric of the future with durable thread."[7]

As you think about and develop similes and metaphors, try to avoid clichés. Instead, use your creativity and develop original metaphors for your speech. As you rehearse, try out different metaphors and similes as a way to create vividness in your language.

simile a direct comparison of dissimilar things using *like* or *as*

metaphor a comparison that establishes a figurative identity between objects being compared

Emphasizing Key Words and Ideas

Emphasis is the weight or importance given to certain words or ideas. Emphasis tells the audience what it should seriously pay attention to. Key words and ideas are emphasized through proportion, sequential position, repetition, and use of transitions.

emphasis the weight or importance given to certain words or ideas

PROPORTION

You emphasize an idea by the amount of time you spend discussing it. Ideas to which you devote more time are perceived by listeners to be more important, whereas ideas that are mentioned quickly are perceived to be less important. So as you practice, you will want to monitor the amount of time you devote to each idea you discuss to be sure you are emphasizing the material that is most crucial.

SEQUENTIAL POSITION

The order in which you present your ideas should reflect their importance. Generally, ideas that are presented in the middle of a sequence are not remembered as well as those that come first or last. So, you will want to build idea sequences in such a way that the ideas you are trying to emphasize are either first or last in the series. For example, if Emming believes that the most important criterion for choosing a credit card is its interest rate, he will want to use it as either the first or the last main point.

REPETITION

Emphasizing by repeating means saying important words or ideas more than once. You can either repeat the exact words, "A ring-shaped coral island almost or completely surrounding a lagoon is called an atoll—the word is atoll," or you can restate the idea in different language, "The test will consist of four essay questions; that is, all the questions on the test will be the kind that require you to dis-

Benazir Bhutto

I Dream of a Pakistan

In 1988, Benazir Bhutto made history when she became the first female prime minister of Pakistan, a country whose Muslim religious tradition is unaccustomed to female leadership. Yet Bhutto argued against the "preconceptions about the role of women in our society." Putting this belief into action, Bhutto served two terms as prime minister, but her journey was not without turmoil and controversy.

Unconstitutionally ousted only twenty months into her first term as prime minister, Bhutto did not give up. Her message of equality and rights for all people in a culturally splintered nation won her reelection in 1993. She governed for three more years before again being dismissed from office. The platform from which she moved her country forward (or backward, as some of her critics would charge) is echoed in this excerpt from her speech "Male Domination of Women," presented at the United Nations Fourth World Conference on Women in Beijing in 1995. Notice how effectively Bhutto uses repetition to emphasize her ideas about social justice.

> Equal rights are not defined only by political values.
>
> Social justice is a triad of freedom, an equation of liberty:
>
> Justice is political liberty.
>
> Justice is economic independence.
>
> Justice is social equality.
>
> Delegates, sisters, the child who is starving has no human rights.
>
> The girl who is illiterate has no future.
>
> The woman who cannot plan her life, plan her family, plan a career, is fundamentally not free. . . .
>
> I am determined to change the plight of women in my country. More than sixty million of our women are largely sidelined.
>
> It is a personal tragedy for them. It is a national catastrophe for my nation. I am determined to harness their potential to the gigantic task of nation building. . . .
>
> I dream of a Pakistan in which women contribute to their full potential. I am conscious of the struggle that lies ahead. But, with your help, we shall persevere. Allah willing, we shall succeed.

cuss material in some detail." As you practice, try repeating or restating your main ideas or important supporting points.

INTERNAL TRANSITIONS

In Chapter 7, we talked about using section transitions to summarize, clarify, and forecast between main points. **Internal transitions** are words and phrases that emphasize the relationships between ideas within a main point. For example, notice how the emphasis changes when we add internal transition words to the following:

internal transitions words and phrases that emphasize the relationships between ideas within a main point

a. Miami gets a lot of rain. Phoenix does not.

b. Miami gets a lot of rain, *but* Phoenix does not.
   or
   Although Miami gets a lot of rain, Phoenix does not.

a. You should become an organ donor. It saves lives.

b. You should become an organ donor *because* organ donation saves lives.

Many words can be used to show idea relationships and signal that an idea is important. These words have several functions:

Adding material: *also, and, likewise, again, in addition, moreover, similarly, further*

Summarizing or showing results: *therefore, and so, so, finally, all in all, on the whole, in short, thus, as a result*

Indicating changes in direction or contrasts: *but, however, yet, on the other hand, still, although, while, no doubt*

Indicating reasons: *because, for*

Showing causal or time relationships: *then, since, as*

Explaining, exemplifying, or limiting: *in other words, in fact, for example, that is to say, more specifically*

In addition, you can add emphasis with straightforward transitional statements:

"Now we come to the most damaging statistic . . ."

"Listen carefully here because this is important . . ."

"Of the three examples we've discussed, this one is the saddest . . ."

To see a video clip of a student speaker using vivid and emphatic language, use your Challenge of Effective Speaking CD-ROM to access the chapter resources for Chapter 10 at the Challenge Web site. Click on "Gut Instincts" in the left-hand menu.

Speaking Appropriately

During the past several years, we have seen much controversy over "political correctness," especially on college campuses. Although many issues germane to the debate on political correctness go beyond the scope of this chapter, at the heart of this controversy is the question of what language behaviors are appropriate—and what language behaviors are inappropriate.

Speaking appropriately means using language that adapts to the needs, interests, knowledge, and attitudes of the listener and avoiding language that alienates audience members. Through appropriate language, we communicate our respect for and acceptance of those who differ from us. In this section we discuss specific strategies that will help you craft appropriate verbal messages.

As you begin rehearsing your speech, you may inadvertently use language that jolts audience members in such a way that they stop listening or shift their focus to you as a person rather than the content you are presenting. So, as you consider various ways of communicating a point, beware of common pitfalls that may be distracting or detrimental to achieving your goal.

Let's consider a few important guidelines that you will want to follow as you choose ways of expressing your ideas.

speaking appropriately using language that adapts to the needs, interests, knowledge, and attitudes of the listener and avoiding language that alienates audience members

Adapting Formality of Language to the Occasion

Language should be appropriately formal for the occasion. Your goal is to adapt your language to the occasion and the specific audience to which you are speaking. Thus, we are likely to use more informal language when speaking to a small audience of colleagues at a department meeting and more formal language when

Not only is the formality of your language suggested by the occasion and audience, but so is the way you present yourself through your attire. We expect Lance Armstrong to adapt his speaking to the formality of the occasion.

speaking with large audiences or with people whom we know less well or who have great power and authority.

Some people mistakenly believe that it is appropriate to use the language in a way the speaker believes the members of the audience speak. Rather than being appropriate, however, this is likely to be counterproductive. For instance, when a middle-class adult gives a speech to young teenagers and tries to use teen slang or street talk, he or she may come off to the teens as a patronizing phony. Appropriately formal language, then, reflects the audience and the occasion but does not call for the speaker to adopt language patterns that are uncharacteristic of the speaker's usual style.

Limiting the Use of Jargon and Slang

jargon technical terminology; meaningless talk, gibberish

slang informal, nonstandard vocabulary

Appropriate language makes limited use of **jargon** (technical terminology; meaningless talk, gibberish) and **slang** (informal, nonstandard vocabulary). We form language communities as a result of the work we do, our ethnic group, our hobbies, and the subcultures with which we identify. Slang and jargon are so pervasive that there are special dictionaries devoted to the specialized vocabulary of different communities. You can even find slang dictionaries online. To access one maintained by California State University at Pomona, use your Challenge of Effective Speaking CD-ROM to access Web Resource 10.4: Slang Dictionary.

We can forget that people who are not in our same line of work or who do not have the same hobbies or are not from our group may not understand the jargon and slang that seem to be such a part of our daily communication. For instance, when Jenny, who is sophisticated in the use of cyber language, starts talking with her computer-illiterate friend Sarah about "social MUDs based on fictional universes," Sarah is likely to be totally lost. If, however, Jenny recognizes Sarah's lack of sophistication in cyber language, she can work to make her language appropriate by discussing the concepts in words that her friend understands. In short, when talking with people outside your language community, you are speaking appropriately when you limit your use of jargon or slang or when you explain in-group terms to your listener.

Showing Sensitivity

Language is appropriate when it is sensitive to usages that others perceive as offensive. Some of the mistakes in language that we make result from using expressions that others perceive as sexist, racist, or otherwise biased—that is, any language that is perceived as belittling any person or group of people by virtue of their sex, race, age, disability, or other identifying characteristic. Four of the most prevalent linguistic uses that communicate insensitivity are profanity and vulgarity, generic language, nonparallel language, and stereotyping.

Avoiding Profanity and Vulgarity

Appropriate language avoids profanity and vulgar expressions. Fifty years ago a child was punished for using "hell" or "damn" and adults used profanity and vulgarity only in rare situations as an expression of strong emotions. Today "casual swearing"—profanity injected into regular conversation—is epidemic in some language communities, including college campuses.[8] In some settings, even the crudest and most offensive terms are so commonly used that speakers and (as a result) listeners alike have become desensitized and the words have lost their ability to shock and offend.

Despite the growing, mindless use of crude speech, many people are still shocked and offended by swearing. And people who casually pepper their speech with profanity and vulgar expressions are often perceived as abrasive and lacking in character, maturity, intelligence, manners, and emotional control.[9]

Unfortunately, profanity and vulgarity are habits that are easily acquired and hard to extinguish. If you have acquired a "potty mouth," you're going to have to work very hard to clean up your act because verbal habits are hard to break. For tips on how to "tame your tongue," use your Challenge of Effective Speaking CD-ROM to access Web Resource 10.5: Cuss Control Academy.

Using Inclusive Language

Language is appropriate when you avoid usages that others perceive as derogatory and exclusionary. Language that our receivers perceive as sexist, racist, or otherwise biased is inappropriate. Two common types of exclusionary language are generic and nonparallel language.

Generic language uses words that may apply only to one sex, race, or other group as though they represent everyone. This language is a problem because, in essence, it excludes a portion of the population. Let's consider some examples.

Traditionally, English speakers have used the masculine pronoun *he* to stand for all humans regardless of gender. For example, "When a person shops, he

generic language using words that may apply only to one sex, race, or other group as though they represent everyone

should have a clear idea of what he wants to buy." Now when you read that sentence, what did you picture? Did you picture a woman shopping? Probably not. Despite traditional usage, it is hard to picture people of both sexes when we hear the masculine pronoun *he*.

Inclusive language avoids using male pronouns when no specific gender reference is intended. You can avoid this in one of two ways. First, you can use plurals: "When people shop, they should have a clear idea of what they want to buy." Alternatively, you can use both male and female pronouns: "When a person shops, he or she should have a clear idea of what he or she wants to buy." Stewart, Cooper, Stewart, and Friedley cite research to show that using "he or she," and to a lesser extent "they," gives rise to listeners' including women in their mental images, thus increasing gender balance in their perceptions.[10] These changes are small, but the resulting language is more accurate and demonstrates inclusiveness. To read an interesting article about masculine and feminine pronouns and think about how this topic might apply to your speeches, complete the Info-Trac College Edition Exercise at the end of this chapter.

A second problem of noninclusive language results from the traditional use of *man*. Consider the term *man-made*. What this really means is that a product was produced by human beings, but its underlying connotation is that a male human being made the item. Some people try to argue that just because a word has "man" within it does not really affect people's understanding of meaning. But as in the case of masculine pronouns, research has demonstrated that people usually visualize men (not women) when they read or hear these words. Moreover, when job titles end in "man," those holding the job are assumed to have stereotypically masculine personality traits.[11]

For most noninclusive expressions, suitable inclusive alternatives are available—for instance, *police officer* instead of *policeman*, *synthetic* instead of *man-made*, and *humankind* instead of *mankind*. Not only is inclusive language more appropriate, it is also more accurate.

Nonparallel language is language in which terms are changed because of the sex, race, or other group characteristics of the individual. Because it treats groups of people differently, nonparallel language is also belittling. Two common forms of nonparallelism are marking and unnecessary association.

Marking is the addition of sex, race, age, or other group designations to a description. For instance, a doctor is a person with a medical degree who is licensed to practice medicine. Notice the difference between the following two sentences:

Jones is a good doctor.

Jones is a good black doctor.

In the second sentence, use of the marker "black" is offensive. It has nothing to do with doctoring. Marking is inappropriate because you trivialize the person's role by introducing an irrelevant characteristic. The speaker may be intending to praise Jones, but listeners may interpret the sentence as saying that Jones is a good doctor for a black person (or a woman, or an old person) but not that Jones is as good as a good white doctor (or a male doctor, or a young doctor).

A second form of nonparallelism is emphasizing one person's relationship to another when that relationship is irrelevant. Introducing a speaker as "Gladys Thompson, whose husband is CEO of Acme Inc., is the chairperson for this year's United Way campaign," for example, is inappropriate. Using her husband's status implies that Gladys Thompson is chairperson because of her husband's accomplishments, not her own.

SHUNNING HATE SPEECH

You've heard the old child's saying, "Sticks and stones will break my bones, but words will never hurt me." As children we all knew that this statement was a lie.

---

nonparallel language language in which terms are changed because of the sex, race, or other group characteristics of the individual

marking the addition of sex, race, age, or other group designations to a description

Heather had agreed to listen to a portion of Terry's speech on nutrition. Terry said to her, "I think you'll love this opening—it's a little risky, but I think it will really get people's attention.

"'It's obvious that several of you are getting pretty fat—and I know that you'd like to be looking more like normal people. Well, today I'm going to talk about nutrition and how even those of you who aren't as overweight as some others in class can still profit from the following advice that I've got to offer.'"

"Whoa, Terry—are you listening to what you're saying?"

"Come on, I'm just trying to get people to take a good look at themselves. My startling statement is designed to give people a jolt. And anyway, they know me and know that I don't mean anything by it."

"Terry, saying 'It's obvious that several of you are getting pretty fat—and I know that you'd like to be looking more like normal people' isn't funny. It's flat-out offensive, and you know it!"

"I still don't think most people would take it wrong. But OK, I'll be more politically correct. How about this: 'It's obvious that a lot of you are overweight—in fact, I'm sure that you'd like to get rid of some of that fat. Well, today I'm going to talk about nutrition and how even those of you who aren't so overweight can still profit from following the advice that I've got to offer.' There, that's better, isn't it?"

1. Is it better? Has Terry made sufficient changes in the opening?
2. If not, how can Terry revise further to get people to think about themselves but not be offended by his wording?

Still it gave us psychological comfort in the face of cruel name-calling. Unfortunately, name-calling can take on even uglier forms in adult speech. Think of the damage caused by the use of words such as "nigger," "cracker," "kike," or "fag."

Hate speech is the use of words and phrases to demean another person or group and to express the speaker's hatred and prejudice toward that person or group. Under the Constitution of the United States people are generally afforded free speech protection. From a communication perspective, however, hate speech is always unethical and should be shunned.

By monitoring yourself, you can become more sensitive in your language choices. How can you speak more appropriately? (1) Use language geared to the formality of the relationship and setting; (2) limit your use of jargon and slang; and (3) show sensitivity by avoiding profanity and vulgarity, using inclusive language, and shunning hate speech.

hate speech the use of words and phrases to demean another person or group and to express the speaker's hatred and prejudice toward that person or group

Summary

Your overall language goal is to develop a "personal" oral style that captures your uniqueness. Language usage should be guided by the knowledge that words are only representations of ideas, objects, and feelings. Meaning is often a product of both word denotation, or dictionary meaning, and word connotation, or the thoughts and feelings that words evoke.

Specific goals of language use are to state ideas clearly, vividly, emphatically, and appropriately.

Ideas are clarified through specific, concrete, precise language. Specific language clarifies meaning. Concrete language appeals to the senses. Precise words are those that narrow a larger category. The larger your vocabulary, the more choices you have to select a word you want. Ways to increase your vocabulary are to study vocabulary-building books, to look up meanings of words you don't understand, and to use a thesaurus to identify synonyms. Clarity can also be achieved by providing details and examples. A speaker must also take into account how audience members might mistake meaning if they represent a culture different from that of the speaker.

Vividness means full of life, vigorous, bright, and intense. Increase the vividness of your language by using active rather than passive voice; using specific, active verbs that form sharp mental pictures; and using figurative language, especially similes and metaphors.

Emphasis means giving certain words and ideas more importance than others. One way to emphasize is through proportion, or spending more time on one point than another. A second way is through repetition. A third way is through transitions, or words and phrases that show relationships between ideas.

Appropriateness means using language that adapts to the audience's needs, interests, knowledge, and attitudes and that avoids alienating listeners. Language in a speech will be appropriate if it is suited to the audience and occasion, if slang and jargon are avoided or defined, and if the language is sensitive and avoids profanity and vulgarity while using inclusive terms and shunning hate speech.

CHALLENGE ONLINE

Now that you've read Chapter 10, use your Challenge of Effective Speaking CD-ROM for quick access to the electronic study resources that accompany this text. Your CD-ROM gives you access to InfoTrac College Edition, Speech Builder Express, and the Challenge of Effective Speaking Web site. When you get to the Challenge of Effective Speaking home page, click on "Student Book Companion Site" in the Resource box at the right to access the online study aids for this chapter, including the video clips described on pages 177 and 183, a digital glossary, review quizzes, and the chapter activities.

KEY TERMS

At the Challenge of Effective Speaking Web site, select chapter resources for Chapter 10. Print a copy of the glossary for this chapter, test yourself with the electronic flash cards, or complete the crossword puzzle to help you master the following key terms.

denotation (176)	**emphasis** (181)
context (176)	**internal transitions** (182)
connotation (176)	**speaking appropriately** (183)
specific language (177)	**jargon** (184)
concrete words (177)	**slang** (184)
precise words (177)	**generic language** (185)
vivid language (180)	**nonparallel language** (186)
simile (181)	**marking** (186)
metaphor (181)	**hate speech** (187)

Use your Challenge of Effective Speaking CD-ROM to access InfoTrac College Edition. Using the Subject Guide, enter the search term "sexism in language" and select "periodical references." Locate the article titled "Does Alternating between Masculine and Feminine Pronouns Eliminate Perceived Gender Bias in Text?" by Laura Madson and Robert M. Hessling in *Sex Roles: A Journal of Research*, October 1999. Read the opening section and the "Discussion" section, which presents the analysis of answers to the question. The article reports a study of printed material, but what can you as a speaker learn from this study? How will you use pronouns in your speech? Why will you make this choice? Would your choice change if you spoke on a different topic? If you were a member of the opposite sex?

WEB RESOURCES

Access the Web resources for this chapter online at the Challenge of Effective Speaking Web site. Select the chapter resources for Chapter 10, then click on "Web Resources."

10.1 WordsmartChallenge (178)

10.2 Merriam-Webster Online (178)

10.3 Speaking to International
      Audiences (180)

10.4 Slang Dictionary (184)

10.5 Cuss Control Academy (185)

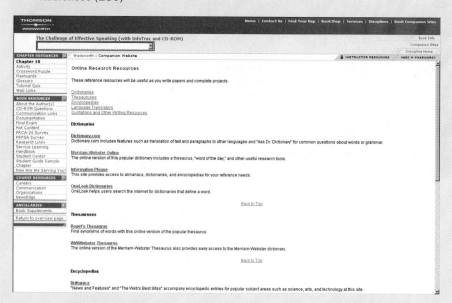

11 Practicing Delivery

© Anne Dowie

Delivery I say has the sole and supreme power of oratory.

Cicero

When Nadia finished speaking, everyone in the audience burst into spontaneous applause and whistles.

"I just don't get it, Maurice. My speech was every bit as good as Nadia's, but when I got done all I got was the ordinary polite applause that everyone gets regardless of what they've done. Of course, I'm not as hot as Nadia."

"Come on, Sylvia, get off it. Yeah, Nadia's pretty, but that's not why the audience loved her. Your speech was good. You had an interesting topic, good information, and it was well organized. But when it comes to delivery, Nadia has it all over most of us, including you."

6 | Delivery

ACTION STEP 6

Practice Speech Wording and Delivery

B. Practice until the delivery is enthusiastic, vocally expressive, fluent, spontaneous, and direct.
C. Continue practicing until you can deliver your speech extemporaneously within the time limit.

In leveling with Sylvia, Maurice recognized what has been well known through the ages: Dynamic delivery can make a mediocre speech appear good and a good speech great. Why? Because how well the ideas are spoken can have a major impact on the audience's interest, understanding, and memory. A speaker's delivery alone cannot compensate for a poorly researched, organized, or developed speech, but a well-delivered speech can rise above the ordinary and capture an audience. Some people, like former Presidents Clinton and Reagan, seem to be naturally gifted in delivering speeches. Other speakers, like George W. Bush and John Kerry, must spend time practicing the speeches they give in order to be dynamic. And most of us will need to practice our speeches if we are to capture and hold the attention of our audience.

In this chapter we will describe the physical elements of effective delivery. We will also explain the characteristics that are the hallmarks of a conversational delivery style. Next we discuss the three types of speech delivery. Then we suggest how you can conduct rehearsal sessions in which you can practice wording until it is clear, vivid, emphatic, and appropriate and practice delivery until it is enthusiastic, vocally expressive, spontaneous, and direct. Finally, we explain criteria you can use for evaluating your speech and others you might hear. At the end of this chapter are the outline and text of a first speech given by a student in a beginning speaking course. In the margins of the speech text you can read our comments and critique.

Elements of Delivery

The physical elements that affect delivery are voice, articulation, and bodily action.

Voice

Your voice is the vehicle that communicates the words of your speech to the audience. How you sound to your audience emphasizes, supplements, and at times even contradicts the meaning of the words you speak. As a result, the sound of your voice affects how successful you are in getting your ideas across. To use it well, it helps to understand how your voice works.

The four major characteristics of voice are pitch, volume, rate, and quality. You can control these characteristics to create vocal variety and emphasis that will help communicate your meaning effectively.

pitch the scaled highness or lowness of the sound a voice makes

Pitch refers to scaled highness or lowness of the sound a voice makes. Your voice is produced in the larynx by the vibration of your vocal folds. To feel this vibration, put your hand on your throat at the top of the Adam's apple and say "ah." Now, just as the pitch of a guitar string is changed by making it tighter or looser, so the pitch of your voice is changed by tightening and loosening the vocal folds. Natural pitch varies from person to person, but adult men generally have voices pitched lower than those of children and adult women. On average, people have a comfortable pitch range of more than an octave—eight full notes of a musical scale.

Most of us speak at a pitch range that is appropriate for us. Some people, however, have pitch difficulties—that is, they have become accustomed to talking in tones that are either above or below their natural pitch. If you suspect that you have developed pitch difficulty, your instructor can refer you to a speech therapist who can help you readjust to your normal pitch. For most of us, the question is not whether we have a satisfactory pitch range but whether we are using our pitch range when we speak to help us communicate our thoughts.

volume the degree of loudness of the tone you make

Volume is the degree of loudness of the tone you make. As you normally exhale, your diaphragm relaxes, and air is expelled through the trachea. When you speak, you can increase the force of the expelled air on the vibrating vocal folds by contracting your abdominal muscles. This greater force behind the air you expel increases the volume of your tone.

To feel how these muscles work, place your hands on your sides with your fingers extended over the stomach. Say "ah" in a normal voice. Now say "ah" as loudly as you can. If you are making proper use of your muscles, you should feel an increase in stomach contractions as you increase volume. If you feel little or no stomach muscle contraction, you are probably trying to gain volume from the wrong source. This can result in tiredness, harshness, and lack of sufficient volume to be heard in a large room.

Regardless of your size, you can speak louder. If you are normally soft-spoken and have trouble talking loudly enough to be heard by an audience, you will need to increase pressure from your abdominal area while you are talking.

rate the speed at which you talk

Rate is the speed at which you talk. In normal conversations most people speak between 130 and 180 words per minute, but the rate that is best in a speech is determined by whether listeners can understand what you are saying. Usually, even a very fast rate of talking is acceptable if the ideas are not new and complex and if words are well articulated with sufficient vocal variety and emphasis.

If you are told you speak too rapidly or too slowly, you may need to change your speaking rate. To do this, start by computing your speaking rate when reading written passages. First, read aloud for exactly 3 minutes. When you have finished, count the number of words you have read and divide by 3 to compute the number of words you read per minute. If you find that your reading rate varies significantly from the 130–180 words per minute range, then reread the same passage for another 3-minute period, consciously decreasing or increasing the number of words you read. Again, count the words and divide by 3.

At first, it may be difficult to change speed significantly, but with practice you will see that you can read much faster or much slower when you want to. You may find that a different rate, whether faster or slower, will sound strange to you. To show improvement in your normal speaking, you have to learn to adjust your ear to a more appropriate rate of speed. If you practice daily, within a few weeks you should be able to accustom your ear to changes so that you can vary your rate with the type of material you read. As you gain confidence in your ability to alter your rate, you can practice with portions of speeches. You will talk faster when material is easy or when you are trying to create a mood of excitement; you will talk more slowly when the material is difficult or when you are trying to create a somber mood.

Quality is the tone, timbre, or sound of your voice. The best vocal quality is a clear and pleasant tone. Difficulties with quality include nasality ("talking through your nose" on vowel sounds), breathiness (too much escaping air during phonation), harshness (too much tension in the throat and chest), and hoarseness (a raspy sound). If you think your voice has one of these undesirable qualities, ask your instructor. If your instructor believes you need help, ask for a referral to a speech therapist with extensive knowledge of vocal anatomy and physiology who can pinpoint your problem and help you correct it. Many colleges have speech therapists on staff to work with students.

quality the tone, timbre, or sound of your voice

Articulation

Articulation is using the tongue, palate, teeth, jaw movement, and lips to shape vocalized sounds that combine to produce a word. Articulation should not be confused with **pronunciation**—the form and accent of various syllables of a word. In the word "statistics," for instance, articulation refers to the shaping of the ten sounds (s-t-a-t-i-s-t-i-k-s); pronunciation refers to the grouping and accenting of the sounds (sta-tis'-tiks).

Many speakers suffer from minor articulation problems such as adding a sound where none appears ("athalete" for *athlete*), leaving out a sound where one occurs ("libary" for *library*), transposing sounds ("revalent" for *relevant*), and distorting sounds ("truf" for *truth*). Although some people have consistent articulation problems that require speech therapy (such as substituting *th* for *s* consistently in speech), most of us are guilty of habitual carelessness that is easily corrected.

articulation using the tongue, palate, teeth, jaw movement, and lips to shape vocalized sounds that combine to produce a word

pronunciation the form and accent of various syllables of a word

Two of the most troublesome articulation problems for public speakers are slurring sounds (running sounds and words together) and leaving off word endings. Most spoken English contains some slurring of sounds. For instance, most English speakers are likely to say "tha-table" because it is simply too difficult to make two *t* sounds in a row. But some people slur sounds and drop word endings to excess, making it difficult for listeners to understand. "Who ya gonna see?" for "Who are you going to see?" illustrates both of these errors.

If you have a mild case of "sluritis" caused by not taking time to form sounds clearly, you can make considerable improvement in articulation by taking ten to fifteen minutes three days a week to read passages aloud, trying to overaccentuate each sound. Some teachers advocate "chewing" your words—that is, making sure that lips, jaw, and tongue move carefully for each sound you make. As with most other problems of delivery, to improve, speakers must work conscientiously for days, weeks, or months depending on the severity of the problem.

Constant mispronunciation can give the impression that a speaker is unintelligent, so it is important to learn to articulate clearly. Exhibit 11.1 lists many common words that people are likely to mispronounce or misarticulate.

A major concern of speakers from different cultures and different parts of the country is their **accent**—the articulation, inflection, tone, and speech habits typical of the natives of a country, a region, or even a state or city. Everyone speaks with some kind of an accent, since "accent" means any tone or inflection that differs from the way others speak. Natives of a particular city or region in the United States will speak with inflections and tones that they believe are "normal" North American speech—for instance, people from the Northeast who drop the *r* sound (saying "cah" for *car*) or people from the South who "drawl." But when they visit a different city or region, they will be accused of having an "accent," because

accent the inflection, tone, and speech habits typical of the natives of a country, a region, or even a state or city

EXHIBIT 11.1 Problem words

Word	Incorrect	Correct
arctic	ar'-tic	arc'-tic
athlete	ath'a-lete	ath'lete
family	fam'-ly	fam'-a-ly
February	Feb'-yu-ary	Feb'-ru-ary
get	git	get
larynx	lar'-nix	ler'-inks
library	ly'-ber-y	ly'brer-y
nuclear	nu'-kyu-ler	nu'-klee-er
particular	par-tik'-ler	par-tik'-yu-ler
picture	pitch'-er	pic'-ture
recognize	rek'-a-nize	rek'-ig-nize
relevant	rev'-e-lant	rel'-e-vant
theater	thee-ay'-ter	thee'-a-ter
truth	truf	truth
with	wit or wid	with

the people living in the city or region they visit hear inflections and tones that they perceive as *different* from their own speech.

When should people work to lessen or eliminate an accent? Only when the accent is so "heavy" or different from audience members' expectations that they have difficulty in communicating effectively, or if they expect to go into teaching, broadcasting, or other professions in which an accent may have an adverse effect on their performance.

Bodily Action

When you deliver a speech, your meaning also depends on how your nonverbal bodily actions supplement the message of your voice. The nonverbal characteristics that affect your delivery are your facial expressions, gestures, movement, posture, and poise.

FACIAL EXPRESSIONS

facial expression eye and mouth movement

Your **facial expressions,** eye and mouth movements, convey your personableness. Audiences expect them to vary and to be appropriate to what you are saying. Speakers who do not vary their facial expressions during their speech but who wear deadpan expressions, perpetual grins, or permanent scowls will be perceived by their audience as boring, insincere, or stern. Audiences respond positively to natural facial expressions that reflect what you're saying and how you feel about it.

GESTURES

gestures movements of hands, arms, and fingers

Your **gestures**—movements of your hands, arms, and fingers—describe and emphasize what you are saying. Some of us gesture a lot in our casual conversations; others do not. If gesturing does not come easily to you, don't force yourself to gesture in a speech. Some people who normally use gestures find that when giving a speech they aren't able to gesture because their hands are clasped behind their backs, buried in their pockets, or gripping the speaker's stand. Unable to pry them free gracefully, they wiggle their elbows weirdly or appear stiff. To avoid this problem, when you practice and speak, leave your hands free so that they will be available to gesture as you normally do.

MOVEMENT

Movement refers to motion of the entire body. Some speakers stand perfectly still throughout an entire speech. Others are constantly on the move. In general, it is probably best to remain in one place unless you have some reason for moving. A little movement, however, adds action to a speech, so it may help hold attention. Ideally, movement should help to focus on a transition, emphasize an idea, or call attention to a particular aspect of a speech. Avoid such unmotivated movement as bobbing, weaving, shifting from foot to foot, or pacing from one side of the room to the other. At the beginning of your speech, stand up straight on both feet. If you find yourself in some peculiar posture during the course of the speech, return to the upright position with your weight equally distributed on both feet.

POSTURE

Your **posture** refers to the position or bearing of the body. In speeches, an upright stance and squared shoulders communicate a sense of poise to an audience. Speakers who slouch may give an unfavorable impression of themselves, including the impression of limited self-confidence and an uncaring attitude. As you practice, be aware of your posture and adjust it so that you remain upright with your weight equally distributed on both feet. To read a thought-provoking discussion of how various body motions, including posture, affect audience attention during a speech, use your Challenge of Effective Speaking CD-ROM to access Web Resource 11.1 Body Motions and Audience Attention.

POISE

Poise refers to assurance of manner. A poised speaker is able to avoid mannerisms that distract the audience, such as taking off or putting on glasses, jiggling pocket change, smacking the tongue, licking the lips, or scratching the nose, hand, or arm. As a general rule, anything that calls attention to itself is negative, and anything that helps reinforce an important idea is positive. Likewise, a poised speaker is able to control behaviors that accompany speech nervousness. All speakers show some amount of nervousness, but poised speakers have learned to control nervous behaviors by concentrating on communicating with the audience rather than focusing on themselves.

Bodily action is a natural part of effective speaking. If you are relaxed and focused on what you are saying, your bodily action will probably be appropriate. If you tend to use either too much or too little bodily action, your instructor will notice and can give you pointers for limiting or accenting your normal behavior. Even though you discover minor problems, do not be concerned unless your bodily action takes away from your speaking effectiveness.

During speech practice sessions, try various methods to monitor or alter your bodily action. Videotape provides an excellent means of monitoring your bodily action. You may want to practice before a mirror to see how you look to others

© Bill Aron/PhotoEdit

When a person speaks, we expect appropriate facial expression, gesture, and movement.

movement the motion of the entire body

posture the position or bearing of the body

poise assurance of manner

when you speak. (Although some speakers swear by this method, others find it a traumatic experience.) Perhaps the best method is to get a willing listener to critique your bodily action and help you improve. Once you have identified the behavior you want to change, tell your helper what to look for. For instance, you might say, "Raise your hand every time I begin to rock back and forth." By getting specific feedback when the behavior occurs, you can make immediate adjustments.

To see a video clip of a student speaker using effective bodily action, use your Challenge of Effective Speaking CD-ROM to access the chapter resources for Chapter 11 at the Challenge Web site. Click on "No More Sugar" in the left-hand menu.

conversational style an informal way of presenting a speech so that your listeners feel that you are talking with them

enthusiasm excitement or passion about your speech

Conversational Style

In your speech practice, as well as in the speech itself, the final measure of your presentation is how well you use your vocal and nonverbal components to develop a **conversational style**—an informal style of presenting a speech so that your listeners feel that you are talking with them, not at them. Five hallmarks of a conversational style are enthusiasm, vocal expressiveness, spontaneity, fluency, and eye contact.

Enthusiasm

Enthusiasm is excitement or passion about your speech. If sounding enthusiastic does not come naturally to you, it will help if you have a topic that really excites you. Even normally enthusiastic people can have trouble sounding enthusiastic when they choose an uninspiring topic. Then focus on how your listeners will benefit from what you have to say. If you are convinced that you have something worthwhile to communicate, you are likely to feel and show more enthusiasm.

To validate the importance of enthusiasm, think of how your attitude toward a class differs depending on whether the professor's presentation says "I'm really excited to be talking with you about geology (history, English lit)" or "I'd rather be anywhere than talking to you about this subject." A speaker who looks and sounds enthusiastic will be listened to, and that speaker's ideas will be remembered.

To see a video clip of a student speaker exhibiting a lot of enthusiasm for her topic, use your Challenge of Effective Speaking CD-ROM to access the chapter resources for Chapter 11 at the Challenge Web site. Click on "Why Pi?" in the left-hand menu.

Vocal Expressiveness

vocal expressiveness vocal contrasts in pitch, volume, rate, and quality that affect the meaning audiences get from the sentences you speak

emphasize give different shades of expressiveness to

Vocal expressiveness is the vocal contrasts in pitch, volume, rate, and quality that affect the meaning audiences get from the sentences you speak. Read the following sentence:

We need to prosecute abusers.

What did the writer intend the focus of that sentence to be? Without hearing it spoken, it is difficult to say. Why? Because it is vocal expressiveness that helps us understand meaning. Read the sentence aloud four times. Each time **emphasize** (give a different shade of expressiveness to) a different word, and listen to how it changes the meaning. The first time, try to emphasize *We;* the second time, emphasize *need;* the third time, emphasize *prosecute;* and the fourth time, emphasize *abusers* (see Exhibit 11.2).

EXHIBIT 11.2	A speaker's vocal variety and emphasis help to control the meaning listeners receive

We need to prosecute abusers. (*we:* we personally)

We *need* to prosecute abusers. (*need:* no choice)

We need to *prosecute* abusers. (*prosecute:* not let them go)

We need to prosecute *abusers.* (*abusers:* people who hurt other folks)

When you emphasize *We,* it answers the question "Who will do it?" When you emphasize *need,* it answers the question "How important is it?" When you emphasize *prosecute,* it answers "What are we going to do?" When you emphasize *abusers,* it answers the question "Who will be prosecuted?" Thus, to ensure audience understanding, your voice must be expressive enough to delineate shades of meaning.

A total lack of vocal expressiveness produces a **monotone**—a voice in which the pitch, volume, and rate remain constant, with no word, idea, or sentence differing significantly from any other. Although few people speak in a true monotone, many severely limit themselves by using only two or three pitch levels and relatively unchanging volume and rate. An actual or near monotone not only lulls an audience to sleep but, more important, diminishes the chances of audience understanding. For instance, if the sentence "Congress should pass laws limiting the sale of pornography" is presented in a monotone, listeners will be uncertain whether the speaker is concerned with who should be responsible for the laws, what Congress should do with the laws, or what the subject of the laws should be.

monotone a voice in which the pitch, volume, and rate remain constant, with no word, idea, or sentence differing significantly from any other

Spontaneity

Spontaneity is a naturalness that does not seem rehearsed or memorized. In a spontaneous speech, the delivery is fresh; it sounds as if the speaker is really thinking about both the ideas and the audience as he or she speaks. In contrast, labored speech sounds like a rote recitation and decreases the audience's attention to both the speaker and the speech.

spontaneity a naturalness that does not seem rehearsed or memorized

Audiences often perceive a lack of spontaneity when speakers have memorized their speeches, because people who try to memorize often have to struggle so hard to remember the words. As a result, their delivery tends to become laborious. Although talented actors can make lines that they have spoken literally hundreds of times sound spontaneous and vocally expressive, most novice public speakers cannot.

How can you make your outlined and practiced speech still sound spontaneous? Learn the *ideas* of the speech rather than trying to memorize its *words.* Suppose someone asks you about the route you take on your drive to work. Because you are familiar with the route, you can present it spontaneously. You have never written out the route, nor have you memorized it—you "know" it. You develop spontaneity in public speaking by getting to know the ideas in your speech as well as you know the route you take to work. Study your outline, absorb the material you are going to present, and then enjoy talking with the audience about it.

Fluency

Effective delivery is also **fluent**—speech that flows easily without hesitations and vocal interferences. Most of us are occasionally guilty of using some vocal interferences such as "er," "uh," "well," "ok," "you know," and "like." These interferences become a problem when they are perceived by others as excessive, and

fluent speech that flows easily without hesitations and vocal interferences when they begin to call attention to themselves and so prevent listeners from concentrating on meaning.

Vocal interferences may initially be used as "place markers" designed to fill in momentary gaps in speech that would otherwise be silence. Although the chance of being interrupted in a conversation may be real (some people will seek to interrupt at any pause), the use of fillers in speech making creates the impression that you are not well prepared or that you have forgotten what you intended to say.

Equally prevalent, and perhaps even more disruptive to fluent speech making than filler sounds, is the incessant use of "you know" and "like." The "you know" habit may begin as a way to find out whether what we are saying is already known by others, or as an attempt at identification, or a way to establish common ground. But flooding sentence after sentence with "you knows" is a bad habit that distracts from the speech and can be eliminated with practice.

Similarly, the overuse of "like" may start from making legitimate comparisons, as in "He's hot, he looks like Denzel Washington." Soon the comparisons become shortcut, as in "He's like really hot!" Finally, the use of "like" becomes pure filler: "Like, he's really cool, like I can't really explain it, but I'll tell you he's like hot!" Although most of us tolerate these fillers in daily conversation, their use by speakers becomes annoying and detracts from the message.

Curiously, audience members are unlikely to acknowledge their irritation with a speaker's use of "you know" or "like," even when the use affects their attention to the ideas. So, if you want to know whether your use of these interferences is excessive, you need to be proactive. The following steps can help you decrease your use of interferences.

1. Train yourself to hear your interferences. Even people with a major problem can be unaware of the interferences they use. You can train your ear in at least two ways:

a. Tape-record yourself talking for several minutes about any subject—the game you saw yesterday, the course you plan to take next term, or anything else that comes to mind. Before you play it back, estimate the number of times you think you peppered your speech with "uh," "you know," and "like." Then compare the actual number with your estimate. As your ear becomes trained, your estimates will be closer to the actual number.

b. Have a close friend listen to you and raise a hand every time you use a filler such as "uh" or "you know." The experience may be traumatic or nerve-wracking, but your own ear will soon start to pick up the vocal interferences as fast as the listener's.

2. Practice seeing how long you can talk without using a vocal interference. Begin by talking for fifteen seconds. Gradually increase the time until you can talk for two minutes without a single interference. Meaning may suffer, and you may spend a disproportionate amount of time avoiding interferences. Still, it is good practice.

3. Mentally note your interferences in conversation and in speech making. You will make real headway when you can recognize your own interferences in real communication settings. When you reach this stage, you will find yourself avoiding and limiting interferences.

Eye Contact

eye contact looking directly at the people to whom you are speaking

Eye contact is looking directly at the people to whom you are speaking. In speech making it involves looking at people in all parts of an audience throughout a speech. As long as you are looking at someone (those in front of you, in the left rear of the room, in the right center of the room, and so on) and not at your notes or the ceiling, floor, or window, everyone in the audience will perceive you as having good eye contact with them.

Maintaining eye contact is important for several reasons.

1. Maintaining eye contact helps audiences concentrate on the speech. If speakers do not look at us while they talk, we are unlikely to maintain eye contact with them. This break in mutual eye contact often decreases concentration on the speaker's message.

2. Maintaining eye contact increases the audience's confidence in you, the speaker. Just as you are likely to be skeptical of people who do not look you in the eye as they converse, so too audiences will be skeptical of speakers who do not look at them. Eye contact is perceived as a sign of sincerity. Speakers who fail to maintain eye contact with audiences are perceived almost always as ill at ease and often as insincere or dishonest.[1]

3. Maintaining eye contact helps you gain insight into the audience's reaction to the speech. Because communication is two-way, your audience is speaking to you at the same time you are speaking to it. In conversation, the audience's response is likely to be both verbal and nonverbal; in public speaking, the audience's response is more likely to be shown by nonverbal cues alone. Audiences that pay attention are likely to look at you with varying amounts of intensity. Listeners who are bored yawn, look out the window, slouch in their chairs, and may even sleep. If audience members are confused, they will look puzzled; if they agree with what you say or understand it, they will nod their heads. By monitoring your audience's behavior, you can adjust by becoming more animated, offering additional examples, or moving more quickly through a point. If you are well prepared, you will be better equipped to make the adjustments and adapt to the needs of your audience.

One way of ensuring eye contact during your speech is to gaze at various groups of people in all parts of the audience throughout the speech. To establish effective eye contact, mentally divide your audience into small groups scattered around the room. Then, at random, talk for four to six seconds with each group. Perhaps start with a Z pattern. Talk with the group in the back left for a few seconds, then glance at people in the far right for a few seconds, and then move to

The better you are able to maintain eye contact with all parts of the audience during your speech, the more confident they will be that you are a sincere speaker.

a group in the middle, a group in the front left, and then a group in the front right, and so forth. Then perhaps reverse the order, starting in the back right. Eventually you will find yourself going in a random pattern in which you look at all groups over a period of a few minutes. Using such a pattern helps you avoid spending a disproportionate amount of your time talking with those in front of you or in the center of the room.

Types of Delivery

Speeches vary in the amount of content preparation and the amount of practice that the speaker does ahead of time. Each of these factors influences how a speech can be delivered. The three most common types of delivery are impromptu, scripted, and extemporaneous.

Impromptu Speeches

impromptu speech a speech that is delivered with only seconds or minutes of advance notice for preparation and is usually presented without referring to notes of any kind

At times you may be called on to speak on the spot. At a business meeting or in a class, you may be asked to speak with little advance warning. An **impromptu speech** is one that is delivered with only seconds or minutes of advance notice for preparation and is usually presented without referring to notes of any kind. You may have already been called on in this class to give an impromptu speech, so you know the kind of pressures and problems that this type of speaking creates.

Because impromptu speakers gather their thoughts as they speak, it is difficult for them to carefully organize their ideas and develop what they are saying. As a result, they may leave out important information or confuse audience members. Delivery can suffer as speakers use "ahs," "ums," "like," and "you know" to buy time as they scramble to collect their thoughts.

You can improve your impromptu performances by practicing "mock" impromptu speeches. For example, if you are taking a class in which the professor calls on students to answer questions, you can prepare by anticipating the questions that might be asked and by practicing giving your answers out loud. Over time you will become more adept at quickly organizing your ideas and "thinking on your feet."

Scripted Speeches

scripted speech a speech that is prepared by creating a complete written manuscript and delivered by reading a written copy

At the other extreme, there are situations in which a speaker carefully prepares a complete written manuscript of the entire speech text and delivers it either word-for-word from memory or by reading the manuscript from a printed document or a teleprompter. A **scripted speech** is one that is prepared by creating a complete written manuscript and delivered by reading a written copy.

Obviously, effective scripted speeches take a great deal of time to prepare and practice. Not only must you prepare an outline, but you must also write out the entire speech, carefully choosing language and sentence structures that sound natural when they are spoken. Once the manuscript is prepared, you either memorize the script and then begin to rehearse orally, or you rehearse with the written manuscript. When scripted speeches are memorized, you face the increased anxiety caused by fear of forgetting your lines. When scripted speeches are read from a printed manuscript or from a teleprompter, you must become adept at looking at the script with your peripheral vision so that you can maintain eye contact with your audience.

Scripted speeches take the most time to prepare and to rehearse if they are to be done well. So, when people are called on to give important speeches that have grave consequences, they will take the time and make the effort to prepare a scripted speech. Political "stump" speeches, keynote addresses at conventions, commencement addresses, and CEO remarks at annual stockholder meetings are examples of occasions when a scripted speech might be appropriate.

Extemporaneous Speeches

In this book our emphasis is on the third type of delivery, because in most situations, whether at work or in the community, speeches are delivered extemporaneously. An **extemporaneous speech** is researched and planned ahead of time, but the exact wording is not scripted and will vary from presentation to presentation. When speaking extemporaneously, you may refer to simple notes you have prepared to remind you of the ideas you want to present and the order in which you want to present them.

Extemporaneous speeches are the easiest to give effectively. Unlike impromptu speeches, when speaking extemporaneously, you are able to prepare your thoughts ahead of time and to have notes to prompt you. Yet unlike scripted speeches, extemporaneous speeches do not require as lengthy a preparation and practice process in order to be effective. In the next section of this chapter we describe how to rehearse successfully for an extemporaneous speech.

extemporaneous speech a speech that is researched and planned ahead of time but whose exact wording is not scripted and will vary from presentation to presentation

Rehearsal

Rehearsing is practicing the presentation of your speech aloud. In this section we describe how to schedule your preparation and practice, how to prepare and use notes, how to handle your visual aids, and guidelines for effective rehearsal.

rehearsing practicing the presentation of your speech aloud

Scheduling and Conducting Rehearsal Sessions

Inexperienced speakers often believe they are ready to present the speech once they have finished their outline. But a speech that is not practiced is likely to be far less effective than it would have been had you given yourself sufficient practice time. In general, if you are not an experienced speaker, try to complete the outline at least two days before the speech is to be presented so that you have sufficient practice time to revise, evaluate, and mull over all aspects of the speech. Exhibit 11.3 provides a useful timetable for preparing a classroom speech.

Is it really necessary to practice a speech out loud? A study by Menzel and Carrell supports this notion and concludes that "The significance of rehearsing out loud probably reflects the fact that verbalization clarifies thought. As a result, oral rehearsal helps lead to success in the actual delivery of a speech."[2]

Preparing Speaking Notes

Prior to your first rehearsal session, prepare a draft of your speech notes. **Speech notes** are a word or phrase outline of your speech, including hard-to-remember information such as quotations and statistics, designed to help trigger memory. The best notes contain the fewest words possible written in lettering large enough to be seen instantly at a distance.

speech notes a word or phrase outline of your speech, plus hard-to-remember information such as quotations and statistics, designed to trigger memory

EXHIBIT 11.3   Timetable for preparing a speech

7 days before	Select topic; begin research
6 days before	Continue research
5 days before	Outline body of speech
4 days before	Work on introduction and conclusion
3 days before	Finish outline; find additional material if needed; have all visual aids completed
2 days before	First rehearsal session
1 day before	Second rehearsal session
Due date	Give speech

Effective speakers relate better to their audience using a few note cards rather than a complete outline or manuscript.

© Michael Newman/PhotoEdit

To develop your notes, begin by reducing your speech outline to an abbreviated outline of key phrases and words. Then, if you have details in the speech for which you must have a perfectly accurate representation—such as a specific example, a quotation, or a set of statistics—add these in the appropriate places. Finally, indicate exactly where you plan to show visual aids.

Making speaking notes not only provides you with prompts when you are speaking, but also helps in two other ways. First, the act of compiling the speaking notes helps to cement the flow of the speech's ideas in your mind. Second, as you prepare your notes, think about key ideas and phrasings. Notes don't include all the developmental material.

For a three- to five-minute speech, you will need only one or two 3 × 5 inch note cards to record your speaking notes. For longer speeches you might need one card for the introduction, one for each main point, and one for the conclusion. If your speech contains a particularly important and long quotation or a complicated set of statistics, you can record this information in detail on separate cards. Exhibit 11.4 shows how Emming could represent his complete outline, shown on pages 150–151 of Chapter 8 on two 3 × 5 inch note cards.

During practice sessions, use the notes as you would in the speech. If you will use a podium, set the notes on the speaker's stand or, alternatively, hold them in one hand and refer to them only when needed. How important is it to construct good note cards? Speakers often find that the act of making a note card is so effective in helping cement ideas in the mind that during practice, or later during the speech itself, they do not need to use the notes at all.

EXHIBIT 11.4 Two note cards

Note Card 1

Intro

How many hounded by vendors?

Three criteria: 1 IR, 2 Fee, 3 Inducements

Body

1st C: Examine interest rates

IR's are % that a company charges to carry balance

- Average of 8%
- As much as 21%
- Start as low as 0 to 8%—but contain restrictions

IR's variable or fixed

- Variable—change month to month
- Fixed—stay same

(Considered IR's: look at next criterion)

Note Card 2

2d C: Examine the annual fee

AF charges vary

- Some, no annual fee
- Most companies average around $25

(After considered interest and fees, weigh benefits)

3d C: Weigh incentives

- Rebates
- Freq flyer miles
- Discounts

Incentives not outweigh other factors

Conclusion

So, 3 criteria: IRs, annual fees, inducements

Using Visual Aids during the Speech

Many speakers think that once they have prepared good visual aids, they will have no trouble using them in the speech. However, many speeches with good visual aids have become shambles because the aids were not well handled. You can avoid problems by following these guidelines.

　　1. Carefully plan when to use visual aids. Indicate on your outline (and mark on your speaking notes) exactly when you will display each visual aid and when you will remove it. Practice introducing visual aids, handling them until you can use them comfortably and smoothly.

　　2. Consider audience needs carefully. As you practice, consider eliminating any visual aid that does not contribute substantially and directly to the audience's attention to, understanding of, or retention of the key ideas in the speech.

3. Show a visual aid only when talking about it. Because visual aids will draw audience attention, practice displaying them only when you are talking about them, then removing them from sight when they are no longer the focus of attention.

A single visual aid may contain several bits of information. In order to keep audience attention where you want it, you can prepare the visual aid so that you only expose the portion of the visual aid that you are currently discussing.

4. Describe specific aspects of the visual aid while showing it. Practice helping your audience understand the visual aid by verbally telling your audience what to look for, describing various parts, and interpreting figures, symbols, and percentages.

5. Display visual aids so that everyone in the audience can see them. It's frustrating not to be able to see a visual aid. So, if you hold the visual aid, practice positioning it away from your body and pointing it toward all parts of the audience. If you place your visual aid on a chalkboard or easel or mount it in some way, practice standing to one side and pointing with the arm nearest the visual aid. If it is necessary to roll or fold the visual aid, bring some transparent tape to mount it to the chalkboard or wall so that it does not roll or wrinkle. If you are projecting your visual aid, try to practice in the space where you will give your speech so that you know how to position the equipment so that the image is the appropriate size and in focus. If you cannot practice ahead of the date, be sure to arrive early enough on the day of the presentation to practice quickly with the equipment you will use.

6. Talk to your audience, not to the visual aid. Although you will want to acknowledge the visual aid by looking at it occasionally, it is important to keep your eye contact focused on your audience. When speakers become too engrossed in their visual aids, looking at the aid instead of at the audience, audience members can become bored. So, as you practice, resist the urge to stare at your visual aid.

7. Carefully consider the disadvantages of passing objects through the audience. People look at, read, handle, and think about whatever they hold in their hands. While they are so occupied, they are not likely to be listening to you. So if you have a powerful and essential visual aid that must be passed, consider what you will do to maintain audience focus on what you are saying.

Rehearsing the Speech

Just as with any other activity, effective speech making requires practice, and the more you practice the better your speech will be. During practice sessions you have three goals. First, you will practice wording your ideas so they are vivid and emphatic. Second, you will practice "doing" your speech—working with your voice and body so that your ideas are delivered with enthusiasm, appropriate emphasis, and spontaneity. Third, you will practice using visual aids. As part of each practice, you will want to analyze how well it went and set goals for the next practice session. Let's look at how you can proceed through several practice rounds.

FIRST REHEARSAL
Your initial rehearsal should include the following steps:

1. Audiotape your practice session. If you do not own a recorder, try to borrow one. You may also want to have a friend sit in on your practice.

2. Read through your complete sentence outline once or twice to refresh memory. Then put the outline out of sight and practice the speech using only the note cards you have prepared.

3. Make the practice as similar to the speech situation as possible, including using the visual aids you've prepared. Stand up and face your imaginary audience. Pretend that the chairs, lamps, books, and other objects in your practice room are people.

4. Write down the time that you begin.

5. Begin speaking. Regardless of what happens, keep going until you have presented your entire speech. If you goof, make a repair as you would have to if you were actually delivering the speech to an audience.

6. Write down the time you finish. Compute the length of the speech for this first rehearsal.

ANALYSIS

Listen to the tape and look at your complete outline. How did it go? Did you leave out any key ideas? Did you talk too long on any one point and not long enough on another? Did you clarify each of your points? Did you adapt to your anticipated audience? (If you had a friend or relative listen to your practices, have him or her help with your analysis.) Were your note cards effective? How well did you do with your visual aids? Make any necessary changes before your second rehearsal.

SECOND REHEARSAL

Repeat the six steps listed for the first rehearsal. By practicing a second time right after your analysis, you are more likely to make the kind of adjustments that begin to improve the speech.

ADDITIONAL REHEARSALS

After you have completed one full rehearsal session, consisting of two practices and analysis, put the speech away until that night or the next day. Although you should rehearse the speech at least one more time, you will not benefit if you cram all the practices into one long rehearsal time. You may find that a final practice right before you go to bed will be very helpful; while you are sleeping, your subconscious will continue to work on the speech. As a result, you are likely to find significant improvement in your mastery of the speech when you practice again the next day.

How many times you practice depends on many variables, including your experience, your familiarity with the subject, and the length of your speech.

SPEAKING EXTEMPORANEOUSLY

When practicing, try to learn the speech ideas, but do not memorize specific phrasings. Recall that memorizing the speech involves saying the speech the same way each time until you can give it word for word without notes. Learning the speech involves understanding the ideas of the speech, but having the freedom to present the ideas differently during each practice.

To illustrate how extemporaneous presentations change from one time to the next, let's see how a short portion of the speech outline for the credit card criteria speech might be modified from one practice to the next. That portion of the outline reads as follows:

A. Interest rates are the percentages that a company charges you to carry a balance on your card past the due date.

   1. Most credit cards carry an average of 8 percent.

Now let's consider three practices that focus on this small portion of the outline.

First practice: "Interest rates are the percentages that a company charges you to carry a balance on your card past the due date. Most credit cards carry an average of 8 percent. Did you hear that? 8 percent."

Second practice: "Interest rates are the percentages that a company charges you when you don't pay the balance in full and thus still owe the company money. Most credit cards carry an average of 8 percent—think of that, 8 percent. So, if you leave a balance every month, before you know it you're going to be paying a lot more money than you thought you would."

Third practice: "Interest rates are the percentages that a company charges you when you don't pay the balance in full—you can rack up a lot of debt by not paying on time. Most credit cards carry an average of 8 percent. Did you hear that? A whopping 8 percent, at a time when you can get about any kind of a loan for less than 6."

Notice that points A and 1 of the outline are in all three versions. As this illustrates, the essence of the outline will be part of all versions. But because you make slight variations using different words each time, when you finally give the speech, the extemporaneous delivery will ensure spontaneity.

SPEECH PLANNING

6 | Delivery

ACTION STEP 6

ACTIVITY 6B Rehearsing Your Speech

The goal of this activity is to rehearse your speech, analyze it, and rehearse it again. One complete rehearsal includes (1) a practice, (2) an analysis, and (3) a second practice.

1. Find a place where you can be alone to practice your speech. Follow the six points of the First Rehearsal as listed on pages 204–205.
2. Listen to the tape. Review your outline as you listen and then answer the following questions.

   Are you satisfied with how well:

   The introduction got attention and led into the speech? ___

   The main points were clearly stated? ___ well developed? ___

   The material was adapted to the audience? ___

   The section transitions were present? ___ clear? ___

   The conclusion summarized the main points? ___ left the speech on a high note? ___

   Visual aids were used? ___

   The ideas were expressed clearly? ___ vividly? ___ emphatically? ___

   You maintained a conversational tone throughout? ___

   You had good eye contact? ___

   You sounded enthusiastic? ___ spontaneous? ___

   You spoke fluently? ___

List three specific changes you will make in your next practice session.

One: _____

Two: _____

Three:_____

3. Go through the six steps outlined for the first practice again. Then assess: Did you achieve the goals you set for the second practice? ____

    Reevaluate the speech using the checklist and continue to practice until you are satisfied with all of your presentation.

You can complete this activity online, print out copies of this rehearsal analysis sheet, see a student sample of a practice round, and if requested, e-mail your work to your instructor. Use your Challenge of Effective Speaking CD-ROM to access Activity 6B.

6 | Delivery **STUDENT RESPONSE** **ACTION STEP 6**

ACTIVITY 6B Rehearsing Your Speech

First Practice
1. Find a place where you can be alone to practice your speech. Follow the six points of the First Rehearsal as listed on pages 204–205.
2. Listen to the tape. Review your outline as you listen and then answer the following questions.

    Are you satisfied with how well:

    The introduction got attention and led into the speech? *Yes*
    The main points were clearly stated? *Yes* well developed? *OK*
    The material was adapted to the audience? *Need more*
    The section transitions were present? *Yes* clear? *Yes*
    The conclusion summarized the main points? *Yes* left the speech on a high note? *No*
    Visual aids were used? *OK*
    The ideas were expressed clearly? *OK* vividly? *need more* emphatically? *OK*
    You maintained a conversational tone throughout? *Pretty well*
    You had good eye contact? *Need more*
    You sounded enthusiastic? *Need more* spontaneous? *Too close to notes*
    You spoke fluently? *Too much "uh"*

    List three specific changes you will make in your next practice session.

    One: *Need more complete development of second point.*
    Two: *Need to use more personalization for adaptation.*
    Three: *Biggest weakness was in delivery, especially eye contact, enthusiasm, spontaneity, and reliance on notes.*

3. Go through the six steps outlined for the first practice again. Then assess: Did you achieve the goals you set for the second practice? *For the most part*

    Reevaluate the speech using the checklist and continue to practice until you are satisfied with all of your presentation. *Delivery was a lot better. Doing the speech twice in a row really helped—I was able to show more enthusiasm. My eye contact was better because I didn't look at notes as much. Content was also better. I had a better grasp of the information. I still need more work on audience adaptation.*

General Criteria for Evaluating Speeches

As we said in Chapter 3, in addition to learning to prepare and present speeches, you are learning to evaluate the speeches you hear. From a pedagogical standpoint, critical analysis of speeches not only provides the speaker with an analysis of where the speech went right and where it went wrong but also gives you, the critic, insight into the methods that you want to incorporate, or perhaps avoid, in presenting your own speeches.

In the past several chapters, as you have been learning the steps involved in speech preparation, you have also learned the general criteria by which all speeches are measured. If a speech has good content, is well organized, is adapted to the audience, and is delivered well, it is more likely to achieve its goal. Thus, regardless of the type of speech, the necessary conditions for judging it relate to the basics of content, organization, and delivery.

You can use the Speech Evaluation Checklist below to analyze your first graded speech as you practice and then to critique other speeches. As you will see later in this text, in addition to these major criteria, each type of speech (informative and persuasive) also has specific criteria that you will want to meet.

SPEECH ASSIGNMENT

Presenting Your First Speech

1. Based on the specific assignment of your instructor, prepare a three- to five-minute informative or persuasive speech by completing the Speech Plan Action Step Activities.
2. The primary criteria for evaluating this speech are clarity of goal, clarity and appropriateness of main points, and delivery (items that are in boldface on the checklist). An example of one student's outline and speech follows.

SPEECH EVALUATION CHECKLIST

Please note that although all major criteria for evaluating any speech are included, emphasis for this first speech is placed on items in boldface (speech goal, all items of speech organization, and several items of speech presentation).

Check items that were accomplished effectively.

Content

_____ 1. **Did the speaker seem to have expertise in the subject area?**

_____ 2. **Was the goal of the speech clear?**

_____ 3. Did the speaker have high-quality information?

_____ 4. Did the speaker use a variety of kinds of developmental material?

_____ 5. Were visual aids appropriate and well used?

_____ 6. Did the speaker establish common ground and adapt the content to the audience's interests, knowledge, and attitudes?

Organization

_____ 7. **Did the introduction gain attention, gain goodwill for the speaker, and lead into the speech?**

_____ 8. **Were the main points clear, parallel, and meaningful complete sentences?**

_____ 9. **Did transitions lead smoothly from one point to another?**

_____ 10. **Did the conclusion tie the speech together?**

Presentation

_____ 11. Was the language clear?

_____ 12. Was the language vivid?

_____ 13. Was the language emphatic?

_____ 14. **Did the speaker sound enthusiastic?**

_____ 15. **Did the speaker show sufficient vocal expressiveness?**

_____ 16. **Was the presentation spontaneous?**

_____ 17. **Was the presentation fluent?**

_____ 18. **Did the speaker look at the audience?**

_____ 19. Were the pronunciation and articulation acceptable?

_____ 20. Did the speaker have good posture?

_____ 21. Was speaker movement appropriate?

_____ 22. Did the speaker have sufficient poise?

Based on these criteria, evaluate the speech as (check one):

_____ excellent _____ good _____ satisfactory _____ fair _____ poor

You can use your Challenge of Effective Speaking CD-ROM to access this checklist online under student resources for Chapter 11 at the Challenge of Effective Speaking Web site.

REFLECT ON ETHICS

For the first graded assignment, Professor Graves required that students prepare an extemporaneous speech—that is, a speech that is outlined but delivered from note cards, not a complete manuscript. Any student who was guilty of reading the entire speech from a manuscript (or from several note cards) would be given a failing grade regardless of how well organized the speech was.

Tina was scared. But because she was majoring in Theater, she knew she could "perform" if she had a script. So she outlined the speech, then wrote it out word for word and memorized it.

While presenting the speech in class, she glanced at her "preps"—note cards that included key phrases from her speech outline—and for the most part she appeared to be talking spontaneously with the audience, adapting well to their needs, and delivering the speech with great enthusiasm that engaged audience interest.

After all the students had spoken, during the evaluation portion of class, her professor praised her content, organization, adaptation, and delivery as he announced that she had given the best speech of the day.

1. Was Tina's behavior ethical?
2. Explain.

This section presents the adaptation plan, outline, and transcript of a speech given by a student in an introductory speaking course as her first major speech.

The Buckeye Tree

by Rebecca Jackson[3]

Adaptation Plan

1. **Speaking directly:** I will ask questions to bring the audience into the topic. I will talk directly to them.
2. **Building credibility:** I will use real samples from a tree to show the description of the tree.
3. **Getting and maintaining interest:** I will use vocal changes to show my interest in the tree.
4. **Facilitating understanding:** I will increase understanding by repeating the main points and using rhetorical questions to stimulate the audience.
5. **Increasing retention:** By asking and repeating main points, I will engage the audience as well as reinforce the main points. I will also show my enthusiasm about the topic.

Outline

SPECIFIC GOAL: I would like my audience to be familiar with the buckeye tree.

INTRODUCTION

I. On a beautiful summer day, how many of you used to play in trees? Or build tree houses? Or just sit or lie under a big shade tree enjoying a summer day?

II. Did you ever think about that tree?

III. For us who live in Ohio, a tree that is of particular significance to us—yet one that we may not know a great deal about—is the buckeye tree.

THESIS STATEMENT: I'd like my audience to understand the identifying characteristics, uses, and story behind why the buckeye is the Ohio state tree.

Body

I. First, several characteristics can be used to identify the buckeye tree.

A. A mature tree will be from thirty to fifty feet in height and two to three feet in diameter.

B. Each leaf has five different petals—like the fingers of your hand—that comprise this single leaf.

C. It produces round, smooth, dark brown nuts with a lighter brown "eye."

TRANSITION: Now we've learned what it looks like, let's consider how it has been used.

II. Second, buckeye trees have had many uses over the years.

A. In the early days native Americans used the buckeye for food.
   1. Native Americans roasted the nut for three days to leach out the poisons to make it edible.

B. The nub of the nut was carried by early European settlers for relief of pain from arthritis and rheumatism.

C. The early European settlers also used the tree wood for utensils, furniture, and to make artificial limbs.

D. Today almost all of the wood from buckeye trees is turned to pulp, to make paper.

TRANSITION: But it wasn't its usefulness that led it to become the state tree of Ohio.

III. Third, there is an interesting story that explains why the buckeye became Ohio's tree.

  A. In the 1800s William Henry Harrison, who was born in Ohio, ran for president.

  B. During the campaign an opposition newspaper made a cartoon depicting Harrison sitting on the porch of a log cabin with a string of buckeyes on it.

  C. This cartoon associating Harrison with buckeyes became so famous that the citizens of Ohio began to be called "Buckeyes."

  D. As a result, in 1953 Ohio officially adopted the buckeye as the state tree.

CONCLUSION

So, here in the state of Ohio, as you rest in the shade of a beautiful green mid-sized tree with palm-sized leaves of five petals and smooth deer-eyed nuts, a tree whose pulp is used to make paper, you can gaze up and say "Hey, this is Ohio's tree."

SOURCES: Little, Elbert L. *The Audubon Society Field Guide to North American Trees—Eastern Region.* Alfred A. Knopf, 1987. http://www.dnr.state.oh.us/forestry/Education/buckeyetrees.htm

---

Speech

Part of the joy of my life is to walk in the midst of a forest and play among the trees. I'll bet there have been times when you relaxed under a big shade tree enjoying a summer day. If you did, you might well have thought about some aspect of that tree. For those of us who live in Ohio, a tree that is of particular significance to us—yet one that we may not know a great deal about—is the buckeye tree. Today I'd like to describe the characteristics and the uses of the buckeye tree, and tell you the story of how the buckeye became Ohio's tree.

Let's begin by describing the major characteristics of the buckeye—how you can identify it. Like many trees, the buckeye tree can grow anywhere from thirty to fifty feet in height and two to three feet in diameter. A major characteristic that makes it unique is that each buckeye leaf has five different petals—like the fingers of your hand—that comprise this single leaf [holds leaf in her hand]. This configuration is known as compound palming.

A second major characteristic is that the buckeye tree produces nuts. The Native Americans in Ohio first noted that the round, smooth, dark brown nuts with light brown centers looked like the eyes of a male deer—a buck. So they called it the buckeye. There is one problem with the buckeye nut—it's poisonous.

Now that we can identify it, let's consider some of the uses for this tree. In the early days Native Americans used the buckeye for food. Even though it is poisonous, the Native Americans learned how to roast the nut, leaching out the poison. It took nearly three days to make the nut edible. The nub of the nut was also carried by early settlers who believed that it relieved their pain from arthritis and rheumatism. The early settlers also used the tree to make utensils, furniture, and to make artificial limbs because of the light weight and the nature of the wood. It is actually twenty-eight pounds per cubic foot versus seventy-five pounds per cubic foot for an oak tree—a lot lighter than most of the trees around. They also used the wood to make thin strips for bundling. But today, almost all of the wood is used for wood pulp. And we know what pulp is used for: [holds up a blank sheet of paper] paper.

Now that you know its characteristics, you might wonder how it became Ohio's tree. Some of you may remember that President William Henry Harrison was born in Ohio. Although his presidency gives us little to remember in general, his behavior during his campaign inadvertently gave the buckeye tree significance. When he was running for office, an opposition newspaper made a cartoon with a photograph depicting Harrison sitting on the porch of a log cabin with a string of buckeyes hung on the rungs of the fence. What the photographer hoped to achieve with the cartoon

Analysis

These first sentences are designed to get the audience into a comfortable mood.

She then begins to focus on a particular tree: the buckeye.

She concludes her introduction with a clear thesis statement.

Her first main point focuses on (1) structure—the size of the tree and its leaves—and (2) the nuts it produces.

In her discussion of the nuts the tree produces, she tells how the tree received its name: the buckeye tree.

After her transition (now that we can identify it), she moves on to her second main point, the uses of the tree.

She now begins a detailed description of those uses.

Here she shows specifically how much lighter in weight the tree is than most.

Here she uses a visual aid to help emphasize what is now the most important use of the tree.

With this transition she moves the emphasis from discussion of the tree itself to how the tree became Ohio's tree.

This is a vivid explanation of the particular event that spurred tremendous interest in the tree.

In her conclusion she prompts us to remember the characteristics of the tree and its uses as well as emphasizing the significance of the tree to Ohio.

The speech has a good introduction, good transitions, clearly stated and developed main points, and a good conclusion. In general, this is a good example of a three- to five-minute speech. ■

picture is insignificant. But the showing of Harrison being associated with buckeyes became so famous that all citizens of Ohio began to be called "Buckeyes." So, even though the tree grows in several other states, it became Ohio's tree. In fact, in 1953 Ohio officially adopted the buckeye as the state tree.

So, here in the state of Ohio, as you rest under the shade of a beautiful green mid-sized tree with palm leaves of five petals and smooth deer-eyed nuts, a tree whose pulp is used to make paper, you can gaze up and say, "Hey, this is Ohio's tree!" And if you're with someone you want to impress, you can tell them what else you know about the buckeye tree. ■

Summary

Delivery refers to the use of voice and body to communicate the message of the speech; it is what the audience sees and hears.

The physical elements of delivery include voice, articulation, and bodily action. The four major characteristics of voice are pitch, volume, rate, and quality. Pitch refers to the highness or lowness of a voice. Volume is the loudness of tone. Rate is the speed at which a speaker talks. Quality is the tone, timbre, or sound of a voice.

Effective speakers are also careful with their articulation (the shaping of speech sounds) and their pronunciation (the form and accent of various syllables).

Nonverbal bodily actions affect a speaker's meaning. Facial expression, gestures, movement, posture, and poise all work together in effective speaking.

Effective speeches achieve a conversational quality, including enthusiasm, vocal expressiveness (variety, emphasis, and freedom from monotonous tone), spontaneity (sounding fresh, not memorized), fluency (freedom from such vocal interferences as "uh," "um," "well," "you know," and "like"), and eye contact.

Speeches vary in the amount of content preparation and the amount of practice that the speaker does ahead of time. Although speeches may be delivered impromptu (with little advanced preparation) or scripted (delivered from a written manuscript), in this course we focus on speeches that are presented extemporaneously—researched and planned ahead of time, but with the exact wording varying from presentation to presentation.

Between the time the outline is completed and the speech is given, it is important to engage in rehearsal sessions consisting of a rehearsal, an analysis, and a second rehearsal. During these rehearsal sessions, you will work on presenting ideas spontaneously and using notes effectively.

CHALLENGE ONLINE

Now that you've read Chapter 11, use your Challenge of Effective Speaking CD-ROM for quick access to the electronic study resources that accompany this text. Your CD-ROM gives you access to the evaluation checklist shown on pages 208–209, InfoTrac College Edition, Speech Builder Express, and the Challenge of Effective Speaking Web site. When you get to the Challenge of Effective Speaking home page, click on "Student Book Companion Site" in the Resource box at the right to access the online study aids for this chapter, including the video clips described on page 196, a digital glossary, review quizzes, and the chapter activities.

KEY TERMS

At the Challenge of Effective Speaking Web site, select chapter resources for Chapter 11. Print a copy of the glossary for this chapter, test yourself with the electronic flash cards, or complete the crossword puzzle to help you master the following key terms.

pitch (192)

volume (192)

rate (192)

quality (193)

articulation (193)

pronunciation (193)

accent (193)

facial expression (194)

gestures (194)

movement (195)

posture (195)

poise (195)

conversational style (196)

enthusiasm (196)

vocal expressiveness (196)

emphasize (196)

monotone (197)

spontaneity (197)

fluent (197)

eye contact (198)

impromptu speech (200)

scripted speech (200)

extemporaneous speech (201)

rehearsing (201)

speech notes (201)

INFOTRAC COLLEGE EDITION EXERCISE

Good delivery depends not only on excellent verbal skills, but also on excellent nonverbal communication. Use your Challenge of Effective Speaking CD-ROM to access InfoTrac College Edition. Conduct a search using the words "nonverbal communication" for the Subject Guide. Locate three articles that would be helpful in preparing you to develop your nonverbal behavior in your next speech.

WEB RESOURCE

Access the Web resources for this chapter online at the Challenge of Effective Speaking Web site. Select the chapter resources for Chapter 11, then click on "Web Resources."

11.1 Body Motions and Audience Attention (195)

Access the Action Step activity for this chapter online at the Challenge of Effective Speaking Web site. Select the chapter resources for Chapter 11, then click on the activity number you want. You may print out your completed activity, and you should save your work so you can use it as needed in later Action Step activities.

6B: Rehearsing Your Speech (206)

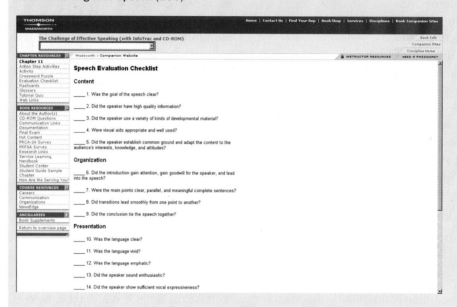

Informative Speaking

Any piece of knowledge that I acquire today has a value at this moment exactly proportioned to my skill to deal with it.

Ralph Waldo Emerson, "Natural History of Intellect," 1871

© Jose Luis Pelaez, Inc./Corbis

For several months, a major architectural firm had been working on designs for the arts center to be built in the middle of downtown. Members of the city council and guests from various constituencies in the city, as well as a number of concerned citizens, were taking seats, as the long anticipated presentation was about to begin. As Linda Garner, mayor and presiding officer of the city council, finished her introduction, Donald Harper, the principal architect of the project, walked to the microphone to begin his speech explaining the proposed design.

This is but one of many scenes played out every day when experts deliver speeches to help others understand complex information. In the previous chapters we described the basic Speech Plan Action Steps that you will use to prepare any kind of speech. In this chapter we go beyond the basics and focus on the characteristics of good informative speaking and the methods that you can use to develop an effective informative speech.

informative speech a speech whose goal is to explain or describe facts, truths, and principles in a way that stimulates interest, facilitates understanding, and increases the likelihood of remembering

An **informative speech** is one whose goal is to explain or describe facts, truths, and principles in a way that stimulates interest, facilitates understanding, and increases the likelihood of remembering. In short, informative speeches are designed to educate an audience. Thus, most lectures that your instructors present in class are classified as informative speeches (although, as you are aware, they may range from excellent to poor in quality). In the first section we will focus on three distinguishing characteristics of informing. In the second section we discuss five methods of informing. And finally, we discuss two common types of informative speeches and provide examples of each.

Characteristics of Effective Informative Speaking

Effective informative speeches are intellectually stimulating, creative, and use emphasis to aid memory.

Intellectual Stimulation

Information will be perceived by your audience to be **intellectually stimulating** when it is new to them and when it is explained in a way that piques audience curiosity and excites their interest. When we say "new" information, we mean either that most of your audience is unfamiliar with what you present or that the way you present the information provides your audience with new insights into a topic with which they are already familiar.

intellectually stimulating information that is new to audience members and is explained in a way that piques their curiosity and excites their interest

If your audience is unfamiliar with your topic, you should consider how you might tap the audience's natural curiosity. Imagine that you are an anthropology major who is interested in early human forms, not an interest that is widely shared by most members of your audience. You know that in 1991 a 5300-year-old man, Ötzi, as he has become known, was found perfectly preserved in an ice field in the mountains between Austria and Italy. Even though it was big news at the time, it is unlikely that most of your audience knows much about this. You can draw on their natural curiosity, however, as you present "Unraveling the Mystery of the Iceman," in which you describe scientists' efforts to understand who Ötzi was and what happened to him.[1]

If your audience is familiar with your topic, you will need to identify information that is new to them. Suppose you are a car buff and want to give a speech on SUVs. Since most of your audience is familiar with these cars and their drawbacks, what can you talk about that is likely to be intellectually stimulating to the audience? Well, you know that SUVs are prone to flip over, and so do most folks in the audience, but with a little research you can discover why this happens. So, explaining the physics behind this problem would make an interesting informative speech. Or, since you and your audience are aware that SUVs are gas hogs, you might find out the challenges manufacturers face when they try to make them more fuel efficient. As you can see, when your topic is one that the audience is familiar with, you will need to find a new angle if you are going to intellectually stimulate them.

So whether your topic is familiar or unfamiliar to the audience, your special burden is to choose a goal and develop your speech so that your audience will feel informed rather than bored.

Creativity

Creativity is the ability to produce new or original ideas and insights. You may never have considered yourself to be creative, but that may be because you have never worked to develop innovative ideas. Contrary to what you may think, creative inspiration is the product of perspiration. Creativity takes raw informational material, time, and productive thinking.

creativity a person's ability to produce new or original ideas and insights

Creative informative speeches begin with lots of research. The more you learn about the topic, the more you will have to think about, and creative ideas come from having things to think about. If all you know about your topic is enough information to fill the time you are allotted, how can you think creatively about it? If I have only read one story, located one set of statistics, or consulted one expert, how can I do much more than present this material? Speakers who present information creatively do so because they have given themselves lots of material to work with.

For the creative process to work, you have to give yourself time. If you finish your outline an hour before you are to speak, you are unlikely to come up with creative ideas for maintaining audience interest. Rarely do creative ideas come when we are in a time crunch. Instead they are likely to come when we least expect it—when we're driving our car, preparing for bed, or daydreaming. So, a simple way to increase the likelihood that you will develop creative ideas is to give yourself time by completing your outline several days before you are to speak. Then you will have time to consider how to present your ideas creatively.

productive thinking working to think about something from a variety of perspectives

Productive thinking occurs when we work to think about something from a variety of perspectives. Then, with numerous ideas to choose from, the productive thinker selects the ones that are best suited to a particular audience. In an article "Thinking Like a Genius," available through InfoTrac College Edition, author Michael Michalko describes eight specific tactics that can be used to become a productive thinker. To read this article, use your Challenge of Effective Speaking CD-ROM to access **Web Resource 12.1: Thinking Like a Genius.**

Let's look at how productive thought can help to identify different approaches to a topic. Suppose you want to give a speech on climatic variation in the United States, and in your research you run across the data shown in Exhibit 12.1.

EXHIBIT 12.1	Temperature and precipitation highs and lows in selected U.S. cities			
	Yearly Temperature (in degrees Fahrenheit)		Precipitation (in inches)	
City	High	Low	July	Annual
Chicago	95	−21	3.7	35
Cincinnati	98	−7	3.3	39
Denver	104	−3	1.9	15
Los Angeles	104	40	trace	15
Miami	96	50	5.7	56
Minneapolis	95	−27	3.5	28
New Orleans	95	26	6.1	62
New York	98	−2	4.4	42
Phoenix	117	35	0.8	7
Portland, ME	94	−18	3.1	44
St. Louis	97	−9	3.9	37
San Francisco	94	35	trace	19
Seattle	94	23	0.9	38

With productive thinking, you can identify several lines of development for your speech. For instance, notice that the yearly high temperatures vary less than the yearly low temperatures. Most people wouldn't understand why this is so and would be curious about it. Looking at the data from another perspective, you might notice that it hardly ever rains on the west coast in the summer. In fact, Seattle, a city that most of us consider to be rainy, is shown as receiving less than an inch of rain in July, which is three inches less than any eastern city and five inches less than Miami. Again, an explanation of this anomaly would interest most audience members. Looking at these data yet another way reveals that although most of us might think of July as a month that is relatively dry, cities in the Midwest and on the east coast get more than the one-twelfth of average annual rainfall we would expect in July. Again, an interesting speech could be given to explain this.

Productive thought can also help us find alternative ways to make the same point. Again, using the information in Exhibit 12.1, we can quickly create two ways to support the point "Yearly high temperatures in U.S. cities vary far less than yearly low temperatures."

Alternative A: Of the thirteen cities in this table, ten cities, or 77 percent, had yearly highs between 90 and 100 degrees. Four cities, or 30 percent, had yearly lows above freezing; two cities, or 15 percent, had yearly lows between 0 and 32 degrees; and seven cities, or 54 percent, had low temperatures below zero.

Alternative B: Cincinnati, Miami, Minneapolis, New York, and St. Louis—cities at different latitudes—all had yearly high temperatures of 95 to 98 degrees. In contrast, the lowest temperature for Miami was 50 degrees, whereas the lowest temperatures for Cincinnati, Minneapolis, New York, and St. Louis were −7, −27, −2, and −9 degrees, respectively.

Emphasis to Aid Memory

If your speech is really informative, your audience will hear a lot of new information. But the audience is likely to remember only a small part of what they hear. So, it is your responsibility to decide what the audience should remember and then to use various techniques to highlight information. Effective informative speeches emphasize the specific goal, main ideas, and key facts so that audience members remember them. You can use several techniques to emphasize the material you want your audience to remember.

VISUAL AIDS

When we see and hear, we remember more than when we only hear. As a result, in an informative speech audiences are more likely to remember things that are presented with visual aids. Thus, visually representing your key ideas can help your audience remember them. Likewise, if you use an interesting visual aid for a minor point, your audience may mistakenly believe that it is important to remember.

REPETITION

We remember those things that are repeated. Think about it. In class, when you are taking notes, aren't you more likely to write down something that your instructor repeats? An easy way to help the audience remember something is to repeat it. You can repeat the idea word for word ("The first dimension of romantic love is passion—passion"), or you can paraphrase the idea ("The first dimension of romantic love is passion; that is, it can't really be romantic love if there is no sexual attraction"). So, it is a good idea to use repetition to highlight your main ideas and the key facts that you want the audience to remember.

TRANSITIONS

Effective transitions can help your audience members identify your organization pattern and differentiate between main ideas and subpoints. In your introduction you can preview the structure so that audience members will know what to listen for. For example, toward the end of the introduction to a speech on romantic love, the speaker might preview what will be discussed:

> Today, I'm going to explain the three characteristics of romantic love, and five ways you can keep romantic love alive.

Then, as the speaker moves from describing the characteristics to discussing the how-tos, the speaker might use a transition to summarize and orient the audience:

> So, there are three characteristics of romantic love: passion, intimacy, and commitment. Now let's see how people keep love alive.

Again, as the speaker moves into the conclusion, a good transition will remind the audience of the main ideas and signal that the speech is coming to a close:

> Today, I've told you that romantic love is comprised of passion, intimacy, and commitment. You've also learned how small talk, being supportive, openly sharing ideas and feelings, self-development, and relationship rituals can keep the romantic flame burning. . . .

Effective transitions emphasize your main ideas and help the audience to remember them.

HUMOR

We remember things that are funny. So, effective speakers use humor to emphasize important ideas. For example, in a speech on reducing stress, one of the main points was "Keep things in perspective." So the speaker told the following story to emphasize the point:

> A problem that seems enormous at the moment can be perceived as less stressful when put in perspective. For instance, there was a man who went to the racetrack and in the first race bet two dollars on a horse that had the same name as the elementary school he had attended. The horse won and the man won $10. In each of

Audiences are more likely to remember ideas that have been presented humorously.

© Jeff Greenberg/PhotoEdit

the next several races he continued with his "system," betting on "Apple Pie," his favorite dessert, and "Kathie's Prize," his wife's name. And he kept on winning, each time betting all that he had made on the subsequent race. By the end of the sixth race, he had won $700. He was about to leave when he noticed that in the seventh race, "Seventh Veil" was scheduled to race from the number 7 position, and was currently going off at odds of seven to one. Well, he couldn't resist. So he took the entire $700 and bet it on the horse . . . who sure enough, came in seventh. When he got home his wife asked, "How did you do at the track today?" to which he calmly replied, "Not too bad, I lost two dollars." Now that's perspective!

Memory Aids

You can emphasize ideas and help your audience remember them by creating memory aids such as mnemonics and acronyms. For example, if you can word your main points so that a key word in each point starts with the same letter, then you can point out this mnemonic to your audience. Thus, in an informative speech on diamonds, the four criteria for evaluating a diamond of weight, clarity, tint, and shape might be recast into "the four Cs": Carat, Clarity, Color, and Cut. Similarly, you might develop an acronym—a word formed from the key word in each main point—to emphasize the ideas. In a speech on effective goal setting, a speaker might say, "Useful goals are SMART: Specific, Measurable, Action-oriented, Reasonable, and Time-bound."

 To see a video clip of a good start to a student informative speech, use your Challenge of Effective Speaking CD-ROM to access the chapter resources for Chapter 12 at the Challenge Web site. Click on "Gut Instincts" in the left-hand menu.

Now that you understand the characteristics of effective informative speeches, let's look at the different methods you can use to inform your audience about your topic.

Methods of Informing

Once you have decided that the general goal of your speech will be to inform, you must decide what methods you will use to educate your audience about your topic. We can inform by describing, by defining, by comparing and contrasting, by narrating or reporting, and by showing or demonstrating. For example, you might describe the surface of the moon, define neo-conservatism, compare and contrast community colleges with liberal arts colleges and universities, narrate the myth of Pandora and her box, or demonstrate how to prepare a canvas for painting. In some cases you might choose one method of informing as the basis for organizing your entire speech. For example, when an architect presents the plans for a new building, we expect the speech to describe what the building will look like. But in most cases you will use different methods of informing as you develop each main point.

In this section of the chapter we are going to explain each method of informing that you might use in developing your speeches. Later in the chapter we will describe two of the most common types of informative speeches: process (or demonstration) speeches and expository speeches.

Description

Description is the informative method used to create an accurate, vivid, verbal picture of an object, geographic feature, setting, or image. If the thing that is to be described is simple and familiar (like a light bulb or a river), the description may not need to be detailed. But if the thing to be described is complex and unfamiliar (like a sextant or holograph), the description will be more exhaustive. Descriptions are of course easier if you have a visual aid, but verbal descriptions that are clear and vivid can create mental pictures that are equally informative. To describe something effectively, you will want to consider explaining its size, shape, weight, color, composition, age, condition, and spatial organization. Although your description may focus on only a few of these, each is helpful to consider as you create your description.

You can describe size subjectively as large or small and objectively by noting the specific numerical measures. For example, you can describe a book subjectively as large, and specifically by pointing out that it is nine by six inches with 369 pages. Likewise you can describe Cincinnati as a medium-size city, or you can provide its actual population statistics or the square miles within the city limits.

You can describe shape by reference to common geometric forms, such as round, triangular, oblong, spherical, conical, cylindrical, or rectangular, or by reference to common objects such as a book, a milk carton, or a pitcher. Your audience will understand that most things that are described by shape do not conform perfectly, but using shapes will help them to get a clearer picture of what you are describing. For example, DNA is described as a double helix, and the lower peninsula of Michigan can be described as a left-handed mitten. Shape is made more vivid by using adjectives such as smooth or jagged.

You can describe weight subjectively as heavy or light and objectively by pounds and ounces or kilograms, grams, and milligrams. As with size, descriptions of weight are clarified by comparison. So, you can describe a Humvee as weighing about 7600 pounds, or about as much as three Honda Civics together.

You can describe color as black, white, red, yellow, orange, blue, green, and brown. Since these eight basic colors will not always describe accurately, a safe way to describe color is to couple a basic color with a common familiar object. For instance, instead of describing something as puce or ocher, you might do better by describing the object as "eggplant purple" or "clay pot red."

You can describe composition as brick, concrete, wood, aluminum, steel, or plastic. Thus, if you say that a building is brick or aluminum-sided, the audience will have a reasonably clear picture. At times you can create the most vivid image of something by describing what it seems like, rather than what it is. For example, an object may appear and best be described as "metallic" even if it is made of plastic, not metal.

description the informative method used to create an accurate, vivid, verbal picture of an object, geographic feature, setting, or image

You can describe something by age as old or new and by condition as worn or pristine, either of which helps the audience to visualize what is being described more clearly. Together, descriptions of age and condition can give the audience cues about the worth or value of what is being described. For example, describing a coin as old but in mint condition indicates that it may be worth far more than its face value. Similarly, describing a city as ancient and well-kept gives rise to different mental pictures than does describing a city as old and decrepit.

Finally, you can describe by spatial organization, going from top to bottom, left to right, or outer to inner. A description of the Sistine Chapel might go from the floor to the ceiling; a description of a painting might proceed from foreground to background, left to right, or top to bottom; and a description of the heart might begin by explaining how the outside appears before discussing the chambers of the interior. However the description proceeds, it is important that your description is orderly and does not jump around, thus helping the audience to systematically "see" the thing you are describing.

Definition

definition a method of informing that explains something by identifying its meaning

Definition is a method of informing that explains something by identifying its meaning. There are four ways that you can use to explain what something means.

First, you can define a word or idea by classifying it and differentiating it from similar ideas. For example, in a speech on vegetarianism, you might use information from the Vegan Society's Web site (http://www.vegansociety.com) to develop the following definition of a vegan: "A vegan is a vegetarian who is seeking a lifestyle free from animal products for the benefit of people, animals, and the environment. Vegans eat a plant-based diet free from all animal products, including milk, eggs, and honey. Vegans also don't wear leather, wool, or silk and avoid other animal-based products."

Second, you can define a word by explaining its derivation or history. For instance, a vegan is a form of vegetarian, one who omits all animal products from his or her diet. So where did that come from? At the Vegan Society Web site we learn that "the word vegan is made up from the beginning and end of the word VEGetariAN and was coined in the UK in 1944 when the Vegan Society was founded. The derivation of the word symbolizes that veganism is at the heart of vegetarianism and the logical conclusion of the vegetarian journey in pursuit of good health without the suffering or death of any animal."[2] Offering this etymology will help your audience remember the meaning of vegan.

Third, you can define a word by explaining its use or function. When you say "a plane is a hand-powered tool that is used to smooth the edges of a wooden board," you are defining this tool by indicating its use. Not all terms can be defined by their use or function, but for those that can, it is an excellent means of definition.

synonym a word that has the same or a similar meaning

antonym a word that is directly opposite in meaning

The fourth, and perhaps the quickest way you can define something is by using a familiar synonym or antonym. A **synonym** is a word that has the same or a similar meaning; an **antonym** is a word that is directly opposite in meaning. Synonyms for *glad* are *eager, elated, joyful, pleased,* and *delighted.* Antonyms for *fast* are *slow* and *poky.* Of course using synonyms and antonyms will only be effective if the audience is familiar with the ones we use. So if you wanted to give a quick definition of a vegan, you could use the word *vegetarian.*

comparison and contrast a method of informing that explains something by focusing on how it is similar to and different from other things

Comparison and Contrast

Comparison and contrast is a method of informing that explains something by focusing on how it is similar to and different from other things. For example, in a speech on vegans, you might want to tell your audience how vegans are similar to and different from other types of vegetarians. You can point out that like all vegetarians, vegans don't eat meat, but that unlike semi-vegetarians, they also do not eat fish or poultry. Like lacto-vegetarians, they don't eat eggs, but unlike this group and the lacto-ovo vegetarians, vegans also don't use dairy products. So of all vegetarians, vegans have the most restrictive diets.

As you will remember, comparisons and contrasts can be figurative or literal. So you can use metaphors and analogies in explaining your ideas, as well as making actual comparisons.

Narration

Narration is a method of informing that explains something by recounting events. Narration of autobiographical or biographical events, myths, stories, and other accounts can be effective ways to explain an idea. Narrations usually have four parts. First, the narration orients the listener to the event to be recounted by describing when and where the event took place and by introducing the important people or characters. Second, once listeners are oriented, the narration explains the sequence of events that led to a complication or problem, including details that enhance the development. Third, the narration discusses how the complication or problem affected the key people in the narrative. Finally, the narration recounts how the complication or problem was solved. The characteristics of a good narration include a strong story line; use of descriptive language and detail that enhances the plot, people, setting, and events; effective use of dialogue; pacing that builds suspense; and a strong voice.[3]

Narrations can be presented in a first, second, or third person voice. When you use first person, you report what you have personally experienced or observed, using the pronouns "I," "me," and "my" as you recount the events. Your narration will be effective if your audience can identify and empathize with you and the situation and events you describe. "Let me tell you about the first time I tried to become a vegetarian . . ." might be the opening for a narrative story told in first person. When you use second person, you place your audience "at the scene" and use the pronouns "you" and "your." Second person narration can be effective because it asks the audience to recall an event that has happened to them or to become an "actor" in the story being told. "Imagine that you have just gotten off the plane in Pakistan. You look at the signs, but can't read a thing. Which way is the terminal? . . ." When you use third person, you describe to your audience what has happened, is happening, or will happen to other people. Third person narration uses pronouns like "he," "her," and "they." The effectiveness of third person narration will depend on how much your audience can identify with the key people in the story.

Demonstration

Demonstration is a method of informing that explains something by showing how something is done, by displaying the stages of a process, or by depicting how something works. Demonstrations range from very simple with a few easy-to-follow steps (such as how to iron a shirt) to very complex (such as demonstrating how a nuclear reactor works). Regardless of whether the topic is simple or complex, effective demonstrations require expertise, developing a hierarchy of steps, and using visual language and aids.

In a demonstration, your experience with what you are demonstrating is critical. Expertise gives you the necessary background to supplement bare-bones instructions with personally lived experience. During a demonstration you speak from that experience as you guide your audience through. Why are TV cooking shows so popular? Because the chef doesn't just read the recipe and do what it

narration a method of informing that explains something by recounting events

demonstration a method of informing that explains something by showing how something is done, by displaying the stages of a process, or by depicting how something works

Demonstrations of products are frequently presented at trade shows.

© Reuters/Corbis

says. Rather, while performing each step, the chef shares tips about what to do that won't be mentioned in any cookbook. It is personal experience that allows the chef to say that one egg will work as well as two, or that you can't substitute margarine for butter, or how to tell if the cake is really done.

In a demonstration, you organize the steps into a time-ordered hierarchy so that your audience will be able remember the sequence of actions accurately. Suppose that you want to demonstrate the steps in using a touch-screen voting machine. If, rather than presenting fourteen separate points, you group them under four headings—(1) get ready to vote; (2) vote; (3) review your choices; (4) cast your ballot—chances are much higher that the audience will be able to remember most if not all the items in each of the four groups.

Although you could explain how to do something using only words, most demonstrations involve actually showing the audience how to do something. If what you are demonstrating is relatively simple, you can demonstrate the entire process from start to finish. However, if the process to be demonstrated is lengthy or complex, you may choose to modify the demonstration and pre-prepare material so that although all stages in the process are shown, not every step is completed as the audience watches.

Whether you actually demonstrate a complete process or modify your demonstration to include pre-prepared visual aids for some steps, you will need to practice the demonstration many times so that you can do it smoothly and easily. Remember, under the pressure of speaking to an audience even the simplest task can become difficult (did you ever try to thread a needle with twenty-five people watching you?). As you practice, you will want to consider the size of your audience and the configuration of the room. Be sure that all of your audience can actually see what you are doing. You may find that your demonstration takes longer than the time limit you have been given. In that case, you may want to pre-prepare a step or two. We will discuss more about how to organize lengthy demonstrations in the next section.

 To see a video clip of an effective demonstration from a student informative speech, use your Challenge of Effective Speaking CD-ROM to access the chapter resources for Chapter 12 at the Challenge Web site. Click on "Flag Etiquette" in the left-hand menu.

After class, as Gina and Paul were discussing what they intended to talk about in their process speeches, Paul said, "I think I'm going to talk about how to make a synthetic diamond."

"That sounds interesting, Paul, but I didn't know that you had any expertise with that."

"I don't. But Gina, the way I see it, Professor Henderson will really be impressed with my speech because my topic will be so novel."

"That may be," Gina replied, "but didn't he stress that for this speech we should choose a topic that was important to us and that we knew a lot about?"

"Sure," Paul said sarcastically, "he's going to be impressed if I talk about how to hold a golf club? Not on your life. Trust me, everyone's going to think I make diamonds in my basement and I'm going to get a good grade, just watch."

1. Is Paul's plan unethical? Why?

2. What should Gina say to challenge Paul's last statement?

Now that you understand the methods you can use when your general goal is to inform, we want to explain two speech frameworks that commonly use informative speaking: process explanation and exposition.

Common Informative Frameworks

Process explanations and expositions are the most common types of informative speeches. In this section we describe each framework and then provide a sample speech given by a student as part of a basic speech course.

Process Speeches

One of the most common informative speeches is a process explanation that shows how something is done, is made, or works. For instance, a loan officer might explain the steps in applying for a mortgage, an engineer might explain the newest design for a turbojet engine, or an author might discuss the process of writing a book. Effective process explanations require that you first carefully delineate the steps and the order in which they occur. Then you need to develop concrete explanations of each step.

A process explanation may verbally describe steps with the help of visual aids, and it may also involve a full or partial demonstration. If the process is a simple one, such as how to get more power on a forehand table-tennis shot, you may want to try a complete demonstration, going through the complete process in front of the audience. But for relatively complicated processes, you will want to present a modified demonstration in which you exhibit completed stages of the process and only physically demonstrate small parts of each step or one or two complete steps.

For example, Allie works in a florist shop and has been asked by her former art teacher to speak on the basics of floral arrangement to a high school art class. The teacher has given her five minutes for her presentation. In preparing for the speech, Allie recognized that in five minutes she could not complete arranging one floral display of any size let alone help students understand how to create various effects. So she opted to physically demonstrate only parts of the process and bring, as additional visual aids, arrangements in various stages of completion. For example, the first step in floral arranging is to choose the right vase and frog. So she brought in vases and frogs of various sizes and shapes to show as she explained how to choose a vase and frog based on the types of flowers to be used and the visual effect that is desired. The second step is to prepare the basic triangle of blooms, so she began to demonstrate how to place the flowers she had brought to form one triangle. Rather than hurrying and trying to get everything perfect in the few seconds she had, however, she also brought out several other partially finished arrangements that were behind a draped table. These showed other, carefully completed triangles that used other types of flowers. The third step is placing additional flowers and greenery to complete an arrangement and achieve various artistic effects. Again, Allie actually demonstrated how to place several blooms, and then, as she described them, she brought out several completed arrangements that illustrated various artistic effects. Even though Allie did not physically perform all of each step, her visual presentation was an excellent demonstration of floral arranging.

Although some process speeches require you to demonstrate, others are not suited to demonstrations; instead, you can use visual aids to help the audience "see" the steps in the process. In a speech on making iron, it would not be practical to demonstrate the process; however, a speaker would be able to greatly enhance the verbal description by showing pictures or drawings of each stage.

In process speeches, the steps are the main points, and the speech is organized in time order so that earlier steps are discussed before later ones. Just as in a demonstration, speaker expertise is essential to the effectiveness of a process speech, and vivid language accompanied by well-prepared visual aids ensure that the speech will be effective.

SPEECH ASSIGNMENT

Process Speech

Prepare a three- to six-minute speech in which you explain how something is made, how something is done, or how something works. An adaptation plan and a complete outline are required. To help you prepare your speech and your outline, use your Challenge of Effective Speaking CD-ROM to access Speech Builder Express and complete the Speech Planning Action Step Activities.

Notice that the sample Process Speech Evaluation Form on page 227 includes both primary criteria related to process and demonstration speeches and general criteria items that are common to all speeches.

The following topics are examples of ones that would be appropriate for a process explanation speech:

How to Do It	How to Make It	How It Works
hang wallboard	fishing flies	helicopter
grade meat	origami birds	ice cream maker
apply for a loan	plastic	asexual reproduction
organize a golf outing	spinach soufflé	cell phone

Process Speech Evaluation Form

You can use this form to critique a process speech that you hear in class. As you listen to the speaker, outline the speech. Then answer the questions below.

Primary Criteria

____ **1.** Was the specific goal appropriate for a process explanation speech?

____ **2.** Did the speaker show personal expertise with the process?

____ **3.** Did the speaker emphasize the process steps?

____ **4.** Did the speaker have good visual aids that helped explain the process?

____ **5.** If the speaker demonstrated the process, or parts of the process, was the demonstration fluid and skillful?

____ **6.** Could the audience easily see the visual aids or demonstration?

____ **7.** Were the speaker's demonstration or visual aids important to understanding the main ideas?

General Criteria

____ **1.** Was the specific goal clear?

____ **2.** Was the introduction effective in creating interest and introducing the process to be explained?

____ **3.** Was the speech organized using time order?

____ **4.** Was the language clear, vivid, emphatic, and appropriate?

____ **5.** Was the conclusion effective in summarizing the steps?

____ **6.** Was the speech delivered enthusiastically, with vocal expressiveness, fluency, spontaneity, and directness?

Based on these criteria, evaluate the speech as (check one):

____ excellent   ____ good   ____satisfactory   ____ fair   ____ poor

You can use your Challenge of Effective Speaking CD-ROM to access this checklist online under student resources for Chapter 12 at the Challenge of Effective Speaking Web site.

Sample Process Speech

Tablature

by John Mullhauser[4]

Read the speech adaptation plan, outline, and a transcript of the speech on guitar tablature given by John Mullhauser in an introductory speaking course. Use your Challenge of Effective Speaking CD-ROM to watch a video clip of John presenting his speech in class. Click on the Speech Interactive icon in the menu at left, then click on Speech Menu in the menu bar at the top of the screen. Select "Process Speech: Tablature" to watch the video (it takes a minute for the video to load).

(continued)

You can identify some of the strengths of John's speech by using your CD-ROM to prepare an evaluation checklist and an analysis. You can then compare your answers to those of the authors. To complete the checklist electronically, click on Evaluation in the menu bar at the top of the screen. To prepare your feedback electronically, click on Analysis in the menu bar. To compare your answers to those provided by the authors, click the "Done" button.

Adaptation Plan

Speaking directly to the audience: Throughout the speech I will talk directly to the audience. I will use personal pronouns, and I will go slowly so that they will be able to follow my directions.

Building credibility: From the start I will show how I have mastered tablature. Then by explaining tablature carefully the audience will see that I know what I'm talking about.

Getting and maintaining interest: I'll start the speech with a startling statement and then show that everyone in class can learn to do what I can do. I believe that as the class starts to understand, they will become even more interested.

Facilitating understanding: I will take the class through each step slowly and carefully. By using visual aids (the guitar itself and an example of tablature) to show the class the notes on paper and then to show where to pluck the strings, class members should be able to see themselves playing along with me. Although they may be doubtful at first, as we go along, they will come to understand how simple the process is.

Increasing retention: Again, use of visual aids should help retention. And I will also use repetition to make sure that they can follow.

Speech Outline

SPECIFIC SPEECH GOAL: I want my audience to understand how to use the tablature notation to play guitar chords.

INTRODUCTION

I. If someone asked me to play a song on the guitar by almost any artist, I could.

II. I'm not a prodigy, but I do have a trick that allows me to play guitar music.

III. Today I want to share with you this trick called tablature.

THESIS STATEMENT: The three steps that will enable audience members to utilize tablature are getting a basic understanding of the guitar, learning tablature notation, and applying notation to the playing.

BODY

I. The first step for utilizing tablature is holding the guitar.

    A. Hold the guitar on your right quad while in a sitting position.

    B. Use your hands correctly.

        1. Your right hand holds the pick between your thumb and index finger.

        2. Your left hand lies along the neck of the guitar.

    C. Each of the metal bars on the neck divides the guitar into frets.

    D. The strings are plucked to play the guitar.

        1. There are six strings on a standard guitar.

        2. The notes of each string from lowest to highest are E, A, D, G, B, E.

(Now that you have a basic understanding of holding the guitar, let's move on to the next step.)

II. The second step for utilizing tablature is to grasp tablature notation.

    A. Tablature is just a picture of the guitar from the player's viewpoint.

    B. Each line represents a string on the guitar verbatim.

        1. The first line represents the high E, the highest string on the guitar.

        2. The last line represents the low E, the lowest string on the guitar.

C. The numbers on the lines of the tablature represent which string and which fret are to be played.

D. Groups of notes are separated.

   1. A line separates the notes to be played into groups.

   2. This enables you to learn one part at a time.

(Now that you understand the basics of the guitar and tablature, it is time to move to the third step.)

III. The third step for utilizing tablature is to apply tablature to playing the guitar by playing notes.

   A. To demonstrate how tablature works, I will play this guitar.

   B. As I play, notice how each tablature notation identifies a note on the guitar.

CONCLUSION

Now that you know the basics of the guitar, understand the nature of tablature, and know how to use tablature to play the notes, you are ready to play nearly any song you choose.

SOURCES: Dowland, John. *Lute Songs of John Dowland*. Mineola, NY: Dover, 1997. Vogler, Leonard. *The Encyclopedia of Picture Chords*. Amsco Publishing, 1990. P. 6.

Speech and Analysis

Read the following aloud at least once. Then analyze it on the basis of the primary criteria in the checklist on page 227: Process Speech Evaluation Form. Although John used himself, his guitar, and a visual aid of tablature throughout the speech, you will see only a few snapshots in this written version.

Speech

If someone asked me to play nearly any song on the guitar I could. I could play songs by almost any artist—I could play Dave Matthews band, Phish, Metallica, Slayer, Negata, Spoon, Rick James, you name it, I could probably play it. I'm not a prodigy on the guitar, I'm not some kind of an evil genius or something, I just know the special trick that allows me to play nearly any tune. Um, today I'm going to share this trick with you, called tablature. There are three steps that can enable you to understand and utilize tablature.

The first step is a basic understanding of a guitar. The second step that will help you understand and use tablature is learning tablature notation. And the third step that will help you utilize tablature is applying tablature back to the guitar.

The first step that I want to look at is learning the basics of playing the guitar. This is a guitar. To properly hold the guitar, you place it on your right knee where it's ergonomically designed to fit. You place the pick in your right hand in between your thumb and your index finger. Your left hand placement will vary on the neck as to what you are playing. Each of these metal bars divides the guitar up into what are called frets. And on your standard guitar you're going to have six strings, which the notes, respectively, are E, A, D, G, B, and E. Now that you have a basic understanding of a guitar, let's take a look at tablature notation.

The second step for understanding tablature is learning the notation. This is what tablature would look like. All it is is an exact copy of the guitar strings onto a piece of paper from a player's viewpoint. The first line on the tablature represents the highest string on the guitar—or the E string, the high E string. The last line on the guitar represents the lowest string on the guitar, or the low E string, and all the other ones, respectively. The numbers 7 5 3 represent to play seventh fret, the fifth fret, and the third fret. And they also signify which string you're going to play on. For example, these are all on the D strings so you know to play on the D string. This one right here, these two 5s, mean you play the fifth fret on the G string, or the third highest string. The lines which break the tablature up have nothing to do with the song. All it does is

(continued)

Analysis

John begins with a startling statement. Then he mentions the trick that allows a person to play nearly any tune—tablature.

He finishes his introduction with a preview of the three steps—a preview that serves as a transition to the body of the speech.

Here John states the first step. Throughout the remainder of the speech he demonstrates the various steps. During the first step he sits on the edge of the desk and shows the audience how to hold a guitar. Then he identifies the frets and the string. Here he uses a transition to lead into the second step.

John presents his second main point clearly.

In this section, in addition to using his guitar, he uses a piece of paper with numbers that represent the frets and lines that represent the strings.

Here again John uses a transition to lead into the third step.

John presents a clear statement of the third step.

In this section he goes slowly through the start of a song, clearly showing how anyone would know which string to pluck and where to pluck it by applying the tablature notations.

This section of the speech represents a true demonstration of tablature application.

As he goes along, everyone in class quickly recognizes the song he is playing.

In the conclusion, John summarizes the steps and assures us that we too can play the guitar by using tablature. ■

break the song down so that it is easier to learn—into smaller chunks. Now that you have a basic understanding of the guitar and you know something about tablature notation, let's take a look at applying tablature to playing the guitar.

The third step for utilizing tablature is applying your knowledge of tablature notation. To effectively show this, I'm going to take you through a song piece by piece and show you exactly how to do so. Right here it says to play 7 5 3, and again it's on the third lowest string here—so you want to find the third lowest string, which is the D string right here.

Then you want to look for the first note is the 7th fret so [counting up] 1, 2, 3, 4, 5, 6, 7, so there's your note 7 5 3. Next it says play 5 7 7, again all on the D string. So, 1, 2, 3, 4, 5, 5 7 7. Then it says 5 5 5 again on the D string. Then this is where it changes. You have a 7 on the D string. Then you go up higher one note, one string, to the G string and you play 5 5 5. So you start at the 7 and go up a string to the—and play the 5, so it's 7 5 5. So I'll play this all over again—I'm sure you know what song this is: 7 5 3 5 7 7 7 5 5 5 7 5 5 as easy as that and I'm sure everyone knows what song that was.

In conclusion, now that you know some basics of guitar, and you know how to read basic tablature notation, and you can apply it all back to the guitar, you guys are ready to go out and play nearly any song of your choosing. ■

Expository Speeches

expository speech an informative presentation that provides carefully researched in-depth knowledge about a complex topic

An **expository speech** is an informative presentation that provides carefully researched in-depth knowledge about a complex topic. For example, "Understanding the Health Care Debate," "The Origins and Classification of Nursery Rhymes," "The Sociobiological Theory of Child Abuse," and "Viewing Gangsta Rap as Poetry" are all topics on which you could give an interesting expository speech. Lengthy expository speeches are known as lectures. In this section we describe four kinds of expository speeches.

All expository speeches require that the speaker use an extensive research base for preparing the presentation, choose an organizational pattern that helps the audience understand the material being discussed, and use a variety of informative methods to sustain the audience's attention and comprehension of the material presented.

Even college professors who are experts in their fields draw from a variety of source material when they prepare their lectures. So you will want to acquire your information from reputable sources. Then, as you are speaking, you will want to cite the sources for the information you present. In this way you can establish the trustworthiness of the information you present as well as strengthen your own credibility.

Expository speakers also must choose an organizational pattern that is best suited to the material they will present. Different types of expository speeches are suited to different organizational patterns. It is up to the speaker to arrange the main points of the speech thoughtfully so that they flow in a manner that aids audience understanding and memory.

Finally, a hallmark of effective expository speaking is that it uses various methods of informing for developing material. Within one speech, you may hear the

An expository speech, like a classroom lecture, is an informative presentation that provides in-depth knowledge of a subject.

speaker use descriptions, definitions, comparisons and contrasts, narration, and short demonstrations to develop the main points.

Expository speeches include those that explain a political, economic, social, religious, or ethical issue; those that explain events or forces of history; those that explain a theory, principle, or law; and those that explain a creative work.

EXPOSITION OF POLITICAL, ECONOMIC, SOCIAL, RELIGIOUS, OR ETHICAL ISSUES

Before we can solve a problem, we must understand it. So there is a need for someone to explain issues to us. In an expository speech you have the opportunity to help the audience understand the background or context of an issue, including the forces that gave rise to the issue and are continuing to affect it. You may also present the various positions that are held about the issue and the reasoning behind these positions. Finally, you may discuss various ways that have been presented for the issue to be resolved.

The general goal of your speech is to inform, not to persuade. Therefore, you will want to present all sides of controversial issues without advocating which side is better. You will also want to make sure that the sources you are drawing from are respected experts and are objective in what they report. Finally, you will want to present complex issues in a straightforward manner that helps your audience to understand while not oversimplifying knotty issues.

For example, Mahalia has decided to give a speech on the issue of drilling for oil and natural gas in the Arctic National Wildlife Refuge. In doing her research, Mahalia needs to be careful that she consults articles and experts on all sides of this controversial issue and fairly incorporates their views in her outline. Because this is a very complex issue, if she has time, she will want to discuss all important aspects of the controversy, including the ecological, economic, political (national, state, and local), and technological aspects. If time is limited, she may limit her discussion to just one or two of these aspects, but she should at least inform her audience of the other considerations that affect the issue.

You can identify an issue that you could use for an expository speech by reviewing the list of topics that you brainstormed earlier in this course. The following list of topic ideas might stimulate your thinking as you work with your own list.

the Bush doctrine of preemption	stem cell research
gay marriage	partial birth abortion
affirmative action	universal health care
hate speech	school vouchers
media bias	teen curfews
school uniforms	home schooling
immigration	acid rain
tort reform	downloading music

EXPOSITION OF HISTORICAL EVENTS AND FORCES

It has been said that those who don't understand history may be forced to repeat it, so an important type of expository speech is one that explains historical events or forces. History can be fascinating for its own sake, but when history is explained, we can see its relevance for what is happening today. Unfortunately, there are people who think history is boring; we believe that is because many people have learned history from sources that are boring. As an expository speaker, you have a special obligation during your research to seek out stories and narratives that can enliven your speech. And you will want to consult sources that analyze the events you describe so that you can discuss what impact they had at the time they occurred and what meaning they have today. Although many of us are familiar with the historical fact that the United States developed the atomic bomb during World War II, an expository speech on the Manhattan Project (as it was known) that dramatized the race to produce the bomb and told the stories of the main players would not only add to our understanding of the inner workings of "secret" government-funded research projects but might also place modern arms races and the fear of nuclear proliferation in their proper historical context. The following list of topic ideas might stimulate your thinking about historical topics you might be interested in speaking about.

slavery	Gandhi's movement
the Papacy	the colonization of Africa
Irish immigration	building the Great Pyramids
the suffrage movement	the Industrial Revolution
the Olympics	the Ming dynasty of China
conquering Mt. Everest	the Vietnam War
the Balfour Declaration (which laid the groundwork for creating the state of Israel)	the Crusades

EXPOSITION OF A THEORY, PRINCIPLE, OR LAW

The way we live is affected by natural and human laws and principles, and explained by various theories. Yet there are many theories, principles, and laws that we do not completely understand, or don't understand how they affect us. An expository speech can inform us by explaining these important phenomena. As an expository speaker, you will be challenged to find material that explains the theory, law, or principle in language that is understandable to the audience. You will want to search for or create examples and illustrations that demystify esoteric or complicated terminology. Using effective examples and comparing unfamiliar ideas with those that the audience already knows can help you explain the law. For example, in a speech on the psychological principles of operant conditioning, a speaker could help the audience understand the difference between continuous reinforcement and intermittent reinforcement with the following explanation:

When a behavior is reinforced continuously, each time people perform the behavior they get the reward, but when the behavior is reinforced intermittently, the reward is not always given when the behavior is displayed. Behavior that is learned by continuous reinforcement disappears quickly when the reward is no longer provided, but behavior that is learned by intermittent reinforcement continues for long periods of time, even when not reinforced. You can see examples of how behavior was conditioned in everyday encounters. For example, take the behavior of putting a coin in the slot of a machine. If the machine is a vending machine, you expect to be rewarded every time you "play." And if the machine doesn't eject the item, you might wonder if the machine is out of order and "play" just one more coin, or you might bang on the machine. In any case, you are unlikely to put in more than one more coin. But suppose the machine is a slot machine, or a machine that dispenses instant winner lottery tickets. Now how many coins will you "play" before you stop and conclude that the machine is "out of order"? Why the difference? Because you have been conditioned to a vending machine on a continuous schedule, but a slot machine or automatic lottery ticket dispenser "teaches" you on an intermittent schedule.

The following list of topic ideas might stimulate your thinking about topics for an expository speech on a theory, principle, or law.

natural selection	diminishing returns
gravity	Boyle's law
number theory	psychoanalytic theory
global warming	intelligent design
feminist theory	Maslow's hierarchy of needs
the normal distribution	color theory: complements and contrasts

EXPOSITION OF A CREATIVE WORK

Probably every university in the country offers courses in art, theater, music, literature, and film appreciation. The purpose of these courses is to explain the nature of the creative work and to give the student tools by which to recognize the style, historical period, and quality of a particular piece or group of pieces. Yet most of us know very little about how to understand a creative work, so presentations designed to explain creative works such as poems, novels, songs, or even famous speeches can be very instructive for audience members.

When developing a speech that explains a creative work or body of work, you will not only want to find information on the work and the artist who created it, but you will also want to find sources that help you understand the period in which this work was created and learn about the criteria that critics use to evaluate works of this type. So, for example, if you wanted to give an expository speech on Fredrick Douglass's Fourth of July Oration given in Rochester, New York, in 1852, you might need to orient your audience by first reminding them of who Douglass was. Then you would want to explain the traditional expectation that was set for Fourth of July speakers at this point in history. After this, you might want to summarize the speech and perhaps share a few memorable quotes. Finally, you would want to discuss how speech critics view the speech and why the speech is considered to be "great."

The following list of topic ideas might stimulate your thinking about topics for an expository speech on a creative work.

jazz	the films of Alfred Hitchcock
Impressionist painting	the love sonnets of Shakespeare
salsa dancing	Kabuki theater
inaugural addresses	iconography
a postmodern critique of *A Farewell to Arms*	*Catcher in the Rye:* a coming-of-age novel
Van Gogh's *Starry Night*	Spike Lee's *Mo' Better Blues*

Expository Speech

Prepare a five- to eight-minute informative speech in which you present carefully re-searched in-depth information about a complex topic. To help you prepare your speech and your outline, use your Challenge of Effective Speaking CD-ROM to access Speech Builder Express and complete the Speech Planning Action Step Activities.

Notice that the sample Expository Speech Evaluation Form that follows includes both primary criteria related to expository speeches and general criteria items that are common to all speeches.

To see sample topics that would be appropriate for this speech assignment, review the topic lists provided earlier with the descriptions of types of expository speeches.

Expository Speech Evaluation Form

You can use this form to critique an expository speech that you hear in class. As you listen, outline the speech and identify which expository speech type it is. Then an-swer the questions below.

Type of expository speech

____ Exposition of political, economic, social, religious, or ethical issues

____ Exposition of historical events or forces

____ Exposition of a theory, principle, or law

____ Exposition of a creative work

Primary Criteria

____ **1.** Was the specific goal of the speech to provide well-researched information on a complex topic?

____ **2.** Did the speaker effectively use a variety of methods to convey the information?

____ **3.** Did the speaker emphasize the main ideas and important supporting material?

____ **4.** Did the speaker use high-quality sources for the information presented?

____ **5.** Was the speech well organized with clearly identifiable main points?

____ **6.** Did the speaker present in-depth high-quality information?

General Criteria

____ **1.** Was the specific goal clear?

____ **2.** Was the introduction effective in creating interest and introducing the pro-cess to be explained?

____ **3.** Was the speech organized using time order?

____ **4.** Was the language clear, vivid, emphatic, and appropriate?

____ **5.** Was the conclusion effective in summarizing the steps?

6. Was the speech delivered enthusiastically, with vocal expressiveness, fluency, spontaneity, and directness?

Based on these criteria, evaluate the speech as (check one):

____ excellent ____ good ____satisfactory ____ fair ____ poor

You can use your Challenge of Effective Speaking CD-ROM to access this checklist online under student resources for Chapter 12 at the Challenge of Effective Speaking Web site.

SAMPLE SPEECH

Sample Expository Speech

This section presents a sample expository speech given by a student in an introductory speaking course, including adaptation plan, outline, and transcript.

Women in World War II

by Lindsey Degenhardt[5]

You can access a video clip of Lindsey presenting her speech in class by using your Challenge of Effective Speaking CD-ROM. Click on the Speech Interactive Icon, then click on Speech Menu and select "World War II." You can also prepare an evaluation checklist and an analysis of her speech, and then compare your answers to those of the authors'.

Adaptation Plan

1. **Speaking directly to members of the audience:** I will use rhetorical questions and personal pronouns to show audience I am talking to them directly.
2. **Building credibility:** I will use documented sources to show that I have good information, and I will use an example of my grandmother's experience to show that I have personal knowledge of events.
3. **Getting and maintaining interest:** Since the audience interest level will not be high, I will compare the 1940s to now and show that some of the fads now are the same as the fads then. I will try to show that although World War II happened a long time ago, the results have affected our current culture. I will also try to make my delivery enthusiastic.
4. **Facilitating understanding:** I will present the information clearly. I will use repetition and transitions to make my points clearer. I will also use examples and show visual aids.
5. **Increasing retention:** I will repeat my main points three times throughout the speech—in the introduction, in the body, and in the conclusion. I will use sectional transitions to reinforce retention of main points. I will tell stories and use visual aids to help the audience retain the information. I will also tell how the 1940s have had an impact on our culture today.

Speech Outline

SPECIFIC GOAL: I would like the audience to understand the three ways that women helped the war effort during World War II.

INTRODUCTION

I. Do you think that World War II happened so long ago that it has no effect on us now?

(continued)

II. Some of our music is based on 1940s swing, and several recent movies are based on 1940s events.

III. Today I am going to share with you the roles that women played during World War II.

THESIS STATEMENT: Three ways in which women helped the war effort during World War II were by working at home, working outside of the home, and enlisting in the military.

BODY

I. One way in which women helped the war effort was by working at home.

  A. Women rationed food and supplies.
    1. They cut back on their use of sugar, canned goods, silk, and gasoline.
    2. They donated their pots and pans.
  B. Women planted "Victory gardens."

(Now that we have seen how women helped from their homes, let's see how they helped outside of their homes.)

II. A second way in which women helped the war effort was by working outside of the home.

  A. During the war, the number of women working increased from 14 to 19 million.
  B. By the end of the war, women had taken jobs in occupations that had been held primarily by men.

(We have now seen how women helped the war effort by getting jobs. Let me tell you the third way in which women helped.)

III. A third way in which women helped the war effort was by enlisting in the military.

  A. The Army and Navy Nurse Corps were started in the early 1900s.
    1. During World War II, 31.3% of all active nurses were women.
  B. By January 1943, all of the branches of the United States military included women.
    1. There were three positions that women could be trained in: radio operators, storekeepers, and secretaries.
    2. To be in the WAVES, women had to meet higher standards and be older than males to enlist.
    3. My grandmother was in the WAVES, the women's branch of the Navy.

CONCLUSION

I. Women helped at home, at work, and in the military.

II. If women had just gone back to their positions as homemakers, there might not be so many women enrolled in college right now.

SOURCES: Creedy, Brooks Spive. *Women Behind the Lines*. New York: The Women's Press, 1949.
Hartmann, Susan M. *Home Front and Beyond*. Boston: Twain Publishers, 1982.
O'Neill, William L. *A Democracy at War*. New York: The Free Press, 1993.
Stein, Conrad R. *World at the Home Front*. Chicago: Children's Press, 1986.
U.S. Bureau of the Census. *Historical Statistics of the United States: Colonial Times to 1957*. Washington, DC: 1960.
U.S. Bureau of the Census. *Statistical Abstract of the United States*. Washington, DC: 2000.
Weatherford, Doris. *American Women and World War II*. New York: Facts on File, 1990.

Speech and Analysis

Read the following aloud at least once. Then analyze it on the basis of the primary criteria in the checklist on page 234.

Speech

When someone mentions World War II, do you groan and think, "I don't want to hear about World War II, that happened such a long time ago and it doesn't have anything to do with me"? Did you know that swing dancing and swing music similar to that played by Big Daddy Little Daddy was popular in the 1940s? Even some recent movies such as *Pearl Harbor* are based on 1940s events. Since so many more movies are portraying the roles that men played during the war, I'm going to share with you the roles women played during World War II. There are three ways in which women helped the war effort during World War II. They worked at home, worked outside of the home, and enlisted in the military.

One way in which women helped the war effort was by working at home. To help the soldiers, women rationed food and supplies. They cut back on their use of sugar, canned goods, soap, and gasoline. The canned goods and sugar went to feed the soldiers. The soap was used to make parachutes. And the gasoline was used to fuel tanks and airplanes. When the military had a shortage of aluminum, women donated pots and pans so that the military could make tanks, planes, and artillery.

Another way in which women helped at home was—they grew Victory gardens. Victory gardens are just normal vegetable gardens, um carrots, beans, cucumbers— that sort of thing. But the reason that women planted these was they thought that if they grew their own food, they wouldn't buy so much food from the store, and the surplus could be used to feed the soldiers. Now that we've seen how women helped from their homes, let's see how they helped outside of their homes.

A second way in which women helped the war effort was working outside of their homes. Before the war started, not very many women were employed. According to the New York Census, less than 14 million women were employed in 1940, compared to 42 million men. When women worked during this time, they were usually teachers, secretaries, or librarians. But during the war a lot of men were either drafted or enlisted, so a lot of the factory jobs opened up and no one but women were there to work. So women became crane operators, hydraulic press operators, tractor drivers, and miners. According to Conrad Stein, author of *World at the Home Front,* by 1944, 40% of the workforce in aircraft assembly was made up of women and 12% in shipyards. In 1945, 19 million women worked, compared to 46 million men.

So now the ratio is getting a little closer. And compare that to today when 65 million women worked in 1999, compared to 75 million men. Now we have seen how women helped on the home front by getting jobs, let me tell you about another way women helped.

A third way that women helped the war effort was by enlisting in the military. In the early 1900s the Army/Navy Nurse Corps was started. And according to Susan Hartmann, author of *Home Front and Beyond,* during World War II, 31.3% of all active nurses were women. And Doris Weatherford, author of *American Women and World War II,* stated in her book that by January 1943 all of the branches of the United States military included women. Now not only could they be nurses, they could also be radio operators, secretaries, and storekeepers. But although women were now allowed in the military, they had to be of higher standards and also had to be older to enlist. And they couldn't actually use guns and fight in other countries. For instance, my grandmother was in the WAVES and she was positioned in Texas. But she couldn't be, even though she went to two years of college, she couldn't be a commissioned officer. She had to have a degree to be a commissioned officer—but she was a noncommissioned officer.

In summer of 1945, Japan surrendered. This defeat might not have been possible without the help of women at home, at work, and in the military. Not only did women have an effect on the outcome of the war, women also, the women of the '40s also had an effect on our culture today. Because if women had just gone back to their housewife positions after working in factories there might not be so many women with college degrees today. ▪

Analysis

Lindsey begins her speech with rhetorical questions.

Her goal in this part of the introduction is to get the class to wonder what she is going to talk about. After stating her goal, Lindsey clearly previews the three ways women helped the war effort.

Here Lindsey states her first subpoint, that women rationed food and supplies. She then supports this point with specific examples.

Now she introduces her second subpoint, that another way women helped at home was to grow Victory gardens. After defining "Victory gardens," she shows how this effort helped the war effort. She finishes the subpoint with a good transition to the second main point. Here Lindsey clearly states the second way women helped.

In this section she documents the statistics she uses to develop her main point.

Here is another good transition.

Now, Lindsey clearly states her third main point.

In this section she gives specific examples of the kinds of roles women filled in the military. She concludes her speech by pointing out the many occupational possibilities for women from then on.

This is a very good expository speech, with a good introduction that captures attention and leads into the speech, three clearly stated and well-developed main points using high-quality information, and a good conclusion that not only summarizes the main points but also shows the effects of their efforts on our culture today. ▪

Summary

An informative speech is one whose goal is to explain or describe facts, truths, and principles in a way that stimulates interest, facilitates understanding, and increases the likelihood that audiences will remember. In short, informative speeches are designed to educate an audience.

Effective informative speeches are intellectually stimulating, creative, and use emphasis to aid memory. Informative speeches will be perceived as intellectually stimulating when the information presented is new and when it is explained in a way that excites interest. Informative speeches are creative when they produce new or original ideas or insights. Informative speeches use emphasis to stimulate audience memory.

We can inform by describing something, defining it, comparing and contrasting it with other things, narrating stories about it, or demonstrating it.

Two common forms of informative speeches are process speeches, in which the steps of making or doing something are shown, and expository speeches, which are well-researched explanations of complex ideas. Types of expository speeches include those that explain political, economic, social, religious, or ethical issues; those that explain events or forces of history; those that explain a theory, principle, or law; and those that explain a creative work.

CHALLENGE ONLINE

Now that you've read Chapter 12, use your Challenge of Effective Speaking CD-ROM for quick access to the electronic study resources that accompany this text. Your CD-ROM gives you access to the evaluation checklists shown on pages 227 and 234, the videos of John's and Lindsey's speeches on pages 227–230 and 235–237, InfoTrac College Edition, Speech Builder Express, and the Challenge of Effective Speaking Web site. When you get to the Challenge of Effective Speaking home page, click on "Student Book Companion Site" in the Resource box at the right to access the online study aids for this chapter, including the video clips described on pages 227 and 235, a digital glossary, review quizzes, and the chapter activities.

KEY TERMS

At the Challenge of Effective Speaking Web site, select chapter resources for Chapter 12. Print a copy of the glossary for this chapter, test yourself with the electronic flash cards, or complete the crossword puzzle to help you master the following key terms.

informative speech (216)	**synonym** (222)
intellectually stimulating (216)	**antonym** (222)
creativity (217)	**comparison and contrast** (222)
productive thinking (217)	**narration** (223)
description (221)	**demonstration** (223)
definition (222)	**expository speech** (230)

Use your Challenge of Effective Speaking CD-ROM to access InfoTrac College Edition. Under the subject of "learning," click on "Learning, Psychology of." Look for articles that discuss "how people learn" and "how people think" in order to gain additional information that is relevant to informative speaking. Read one or more articles to help you better understand how to prepare your informative speech.

WEB RESOURCE

Access the Web resource for this chapter online at the Challenge of Effective Speaking Web site. Select the chapter resources for Chapter 12, then click on "Web Resources."

12.1: Thinking Like a Genius (217)

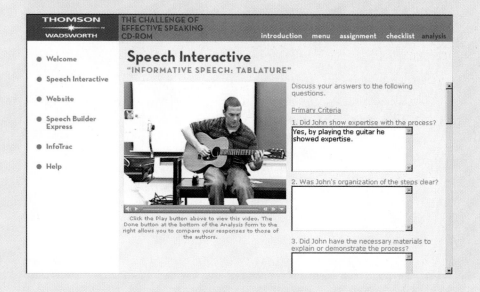

13 Persuasive Speaking: Reasoning with Your Audience

© PhotoDisc

Speech is power: speech is to persuade, to convert, to compel.

Ralph Waldo Emerson, "Social Aims," 1875

As members of the zoning commission walked out of the auditorium, Dan remarked, "Wow, after an hour and a half of dull speeches most of us were about to go to sleep, but two minutes into Commissioner Kate Tucker's speech you could tell it was a whole new ball game!"

"You said it," Lydia replied. "I mean, with each main point she gave you could see that more and more people were on her bandwagon."

"Well," said Stan, "when you've got the supporting reasons she presented, how could you not believe what she had to say? I mean, I was nodding so vigorously at the way she presented her arguments that I thought I was going to break my neck."

Although it is easy to get excited about a really powerful speech, real-life attempts to persuade others require the speaker to be knowledgeable about forming arguments and really adapt them to the needs of the audience. A **persuasive speech** is one whose goal is to influence the beliefs and/or behavior of audience members. It is the most demanding speech challenge, because it not only requires the skills you've studied so far, but also means that you must understand how to convince audience members to alter their attitudes and behavior. In these two chapters we will explore what it takes to be effective in persuasive speaking.

> **persuasive speech** a speech whose goal is to influence the beliefs and/or behavior of audience members

This chapter focuses on reasoning with the audience. We begin by discussing how the audience's initial attitude toward your topic affects the specific goal that you select. Then we explain how to select the arguments or reasons that you will use to convince your audience as well as the evidence you will want to present in support of those reasons. Next we describe how you can test the logic of your argument. After that we present methods for organizing your material. Finally, we will look at one framework used in persuasive speaking—the speech to convince—and we will present the criteria that can be used to evaluate speeches of this type. The next chapter will explore the role of emotion in persuasive speaking.

Constructing a Persuasive Speech Goal

The first step in preparing your persuasive speech is constructing a persuasive speech goal. In this section we consider using audience attitude toward your topic to help you in the phrasing of your speech goal.

Adapting Your Persuasive Goal to Initial Audience Attitude

As you begin considering your speech goal, you'll want to understand the current direction and strength of audience members' attitudes about your topic.

An **attitude** is "a general or enduring positive or negative feeling about some person, object, or issue."[1] People express their attitudes about something when

> **attitude** a general or enduring positive or negative feeling about some person, object, or issue

EXHIBIT 13.1   Sample opinion continuum

Highly opposed	Opposed	Mildly opposed	Neither in favor nor opposed	Mildly in favor	In favor	Highly in favor
2	2	11	1	2	2	0

they give their opinions. So, someone who states "I think physical fitness is important" is expressing an opinion that reflects a favorable attitude about physical fitness.

In Chapter 4 you learned that you can assess your audience's attitudes by actually surveying the audience or by referring to published surveys and extrapolating these polls to the members of your audience. So, you will want to begin your persuasive speech preparation by understanding the attitudes that your audience is likely to have about your topic. Your knowledge of the audience attitude will help you phrase your goal and choose your arguments.

Audience member attitudes (expressed by their opinions) about your speech topic can range from highly favorable to strongly opposed and can be visualized as lying on a continuum like the one pictured in Exhibit 13.1.

Even though an audience will include individuals whose opinions fall at nearly every point along the distribution, generally audience members' opinions tend to cluster in one area of the continuum. For instance, the opinions of the audience represented in Exhibit 13.1 cluster around "mildly opposed," even though a few people are more hostile and a few have favorable opinions. That cluster point represents the general audience attitude for that topic. Based on the cluster point, you can classify your audience's initial attitude toward your topic as "in favor" (already supportive of a particular belief), "no opinion" (uninformed, neutral, or apathetic), or "opposed" (opposed to a particular belief or holding an opposite point of view). Given that initial attitude, you can develop a speech goal and arguments designed to influence your audience's attitudes in the way you would like.

OPPOSED

If your audience is very much opposed to your goal, it is unrealistic to believe that you will be able to change their attitude from "opposed" to "in favor" in only one short speech. Instead, you should consider changing the wording of your goal in order to have a better chance to change their attitude. For example, if you determine that your audience is likely to be totally opposed to the goal "I want to convince my audience that gay marriage should be legalized," you might rephrase your goal as "I want to convince my audience that committed gay couples should be able to have the same legal protection that is afforded to committed heterosexual couples through state-recognized marriage."

If you believe your listeners are only mildly opposed to your topic, you will need to understand their resistance and present arguments to overcome it. Your goal should be to provide them with strong reasons that support your position, including evidence that would counter other attitudes. Your goal might be phrased "I want to convince my audience that gay marriage will benefit society."

NEUTRAL

If you perceive that your audience is neutral, you can be straightforward with the reasons in support of your goal. Still, it might be wise for you to consider whether they are uninformed, impartial, or apathetic about your topic. If they are **uninformed**—that is, they do not know enough about the topic to have formed an opinion—you will need to provide the basic arguments and information that they need to become informed. Make sure that each of your reasons is really well supported with good information. You may find that your audience is **impartial;** that is, the audience has no opinion. In this case, they are likely to listen objectively and accept sound reasoning. So, as with the uninformed audience, you can keep your focus on sound reasons and evidence. Finally, you may find that your audience members have no opinion because they are **apathetic.** An apathetic audience has no opinion because it is uninterested, unconcerned, or indifferent to your topic. In order to convince this audience type, you will need to find ways to arouse them. Look for materials that seem to relate to audience needs.

uninformed not knowing enough about a topic to have formed an opinion

impartial having no opinion

apathetic uninterested, unconcerned, or indifferent to your topic

IN FAVOR

If your audience is only mildly in favor of your proposal, your task is to reinforce and strengthen their beliefs. An audience whose beliefs favor your topic will still benefit from a logical explanation of the reasons for holding these beliefs. The audience may also become further committed to a belief by hearing additional or new reasons and more recent evidence that support it.

If your audience analysis reveals that your listeners strongly agree with your topic, then you can consider a speech goal that builds on that belief and moves the audience to act on it. So, for example, if the topic is gay marriage and your audience poll shows that most audience members strongly favor the idea, then your goal might be "I want my audience to write their state legislators to express their support for gay marriage." We will discuss speeches that call to action in the next chapter.

© Jose Carrillo/PhotoEdit, Inc.

When you know that your audience is already leaning in your favor, you can focus your speech on a specific course of action.

Phrasing Persuasive Speech Goals as Propositions

proposition a declarative sentence that clearly indicates the position that the speaker will advocate in a persuasive speech

In a persuasive speech, the specific goal is stated as a proposition. A **proposition** is a declarative sentence that clearly indicates the position on the topic that the speaker will advocate. For example, "I want to convince my audience that smoking causes cancer" is a proposition. From it we know that the speaker will present arguments, reasons, and evidence to prove the validity of the proposition.

Notice how a persuasive proposition differs from an informative speech goal on the same subject: "I want to inform my audience of the research about smoking and cancer." In the informative speech, the goal is met if the audience understands and remembers what the speaker has said. In the persuasive situation, however, the audience must not only understand what has been said, but accept it as true and believe it.

The three major types of persuasive goals are stated as propositions of fact, value, or policy.

proposition of fact a statement designed to convince your audience that something is or is not true, exists, or happens

A **proposition of fact** is a statement designed to convince your audience that something is or is not true, exists, or happens. "I want to persuade the audience that there is a God," "I want to convince the audience that smoking causes cancer," and "I want the audience to believe that large numbers of elementary school children are illiterate" are all propositions of fact.

proposition of value a statement designed to convince your audience that something is good, bad, desirable, undesirable, sound, beneficial, important, or unimportant

A **proposition of value** is a statement designed to convince your audience that something is good, bad, desirable, undesirable, sound, beneficial, important, or unimportant.[2] You can persuade your audience that something has more value than something else, or you can persuade your audience that something meets valued standards. For instance, "I want to convince my audience that Suleman is more qualified for office than O'Neil" is a proposition that will require you to prove that Suleman has more of the traits that we value in our elected leaders

SPOTLIGHT ON SPEAKERS

Susan B. Anthony

Under Arrest

In 1872, Susan B. Anthony was arrested. Her crime? She voted in a presidential election.

Today, it's hard for us to imagine a United States where people are denied the right to vote because of their sex. But imagine you were in Anthony's shoes. If you were denied the right to vote because of *your* sex, what strategy would you use to change the system? Would you file a lawsuit? Foment a rebellion? Advocate a hunger strike? Or take to the talk show circuit? And what would your goal be? Shut out of making headway in the courts, Anthony hit the talk show circuit of her time, presenting public lectures in fifty-four counties in New York following her arrest. Anthony believed that mustering support for suffrage and women's rights required not only making appeals to the male voters, but also encouraging other women to risk arrest by exercising their right to vote. In this excerpt from her speech "Is It a Crime for a Citizen to Vote?" we see Anthony arguing that change to the franchise policy of the United States would come only as the result of massive civil disobedience.

> We no longer petition Legislature or Congress to give us the right to vote. We appeal to the women everywhere to exercise their too long neglected "citizen's right to vote." We appeal to the inspectors of election everywhere to receive the votes of all United States citizens as it is their duty to do. We appeal to United States commissioners and marshals to arrest the inspectors who reject the names and votes of United States citizens.

A powerful advocate for woman's suffrage, Susan B. Anthony died fourteen years before an amendment to the U.S. Constitution guaranteed women the right to vote.

EXHIBIT 13.2 Examples of persuasive speech propositions

Propositions of Fact	Propositions of Value	Propositions of Policy
Mahatma Gandhi was the father of passive resistance.	Mahatma Gandhi was a moral leader.	Mahatma Gandhi should be given a special award for his views on passive resistance.
Pharmaceutical advertising to consumers increases prescription drug prices.	Pharmaceutical advertising of new prescription drugs on TV is better than marketing new drugs directly to doctors.	Pharmaceutical companies should be required to refrain from advertising prescription drugs on TV.
Using paper ballots is a popular method for voting in U.S. elections.	Using paper ballots is better than using electronic voting machines.	Using paper ballots should be required for U.S. elections.

than does O'Neil. Similarly, the proposition "I want my audience to believe that multilingual education is beneficial to children" requires you to prove that children who receive multilingual education receive specific educational rewards that we, as a society, value.

A **proposition of policy** is a statement designed to convince your audience that they should take a specific course of action. "I want my audience to believe that a public speaking course should be required for all students at this university," "I want to persuade the audience that the United States should restore normal diplomatic relations with Cuba," and "I want to convince the audience that to receive a high school diploma all home-schooled children should be required to take and pass the same tests as public school children" are all propositions that advocate a specific policy.

Exhibit 13.2 provides several examples of how propositions of fact, value, and policy can be developed from the same topic idea.

As you begin work on your persuasive speeches, you can use the Speech Planning Action Steps and Speech Builder Express to help you organize and develop them, although some of the steps will be modified to provide you with guidance that is particular to persuasive speeches. You can use Activity 7A and the sample student response to help you develop a specific goal for a persuasive speech that is stated as a proposition.

proposition of policy a statement designed to convince your audience that they should take a specific course of action

SPEECH PLANNING   ACTION STEP 1

1 | Goals

ACTIVITY 7A Speech Planning Action Step for Persuasive Speeches

Writing a Specific Goal as a Persuasive Proposition

1. Tentatively phrase your goal as a proposition.
2. Check whether you believe that your audience is ___ opposed, ___ neutral, or ___ in favor of your proposition. Why?
3. Check whether you believe that ___ the degree of your audience attitude makes your goal too difficult to meet or ___ your audience is already convinced of your

(continued)

goal. If you've checked either of these, then rephrase your goal to adapt to that audience attitude.

4. Check whether your proposition, as stated or revised, is one of ___ fact, ___ value, or ___ policy.

You can complete this activity online with Speech Builder Express. Use your Challenge of Effective Speaking CD-ROM to access Activity 7A.

| | STUDENT RESPONSE | ACTION STEP 1 |

1 | Goals

ACTIVITY 7A Student Response Action Step for Persuasive Speeches

Writing a Specific Goal as a Persuasive Proposition

1. Tentatively phrase your goal as a proposition.

   I want to convince members of the audience that they should not download music from the Internet.

2. Check whether you believe that your audience is ___ opposed, ✓ neutral, or ___ in favor of your proposition. Why?

   Although some students may be opposed or in favor of this proposition, I judge that the majority of the students in class are undecided.

3. Check whether you believe that ___ the degree of your audience attitude makes your goal too difficult to meet or ___ your audience is already convinced of your goal. If you've checked either of these, then rephrase your goal to adapt to that audience attitude.

4. Check whether your proposition, as stated or revised, is one of ___ fact, ___ value, or ✓ policy.

Identifying Good Reasons and Sound Evidence

Once you have identified a specific goal, you will use the research you have acquired to help you choose the main points of the speech. In a persuasive speech, the main points are reasons that support the goal, and the supporting material is evidence that buttresses the reasons.

Finding Reasons to Use as Main Points

reasons main point statements that summarize several related pieces of evidence and show *why* you should believe or do something

Reasons are main point statements that summarize several related pieces of evidence and show *why* you should believe or do something. For example, suppose you have decided to give a speech whose value proposition is "I want the audience to believe that homeownership is good for a society." After you have researched this, you might conclude that everything you have discovered can be grouped under one of six summary statements:

I. Homeownership builds strong communities.

II. Homeownership reduces crime.

III. Homeownership increases individual wealth.

IV. Homeownership increases individual self-esteem.

V. Homeownership improves the value of a neighborhood.

VI. Homeownership is growing in the suburbs.

Once you have identified reasons, you can weigh and evaluate each of them in order to select the three or four that are of the highest quality. You can judge the quality of each reason by asking the following questions.

1. Is the reason directly related to proving the proposition? Sometimes, we find information that can be summarized into a reason, but that reason doesn't directly argue the proposition. For instance, you may have uncovered a lot of research that supports the notion that "Homeownership is growing in the suburbs." Unfortunately, it isn't clear how the growth of homeownership in the suburbs benefits society as a whole. So, in choosing the reasons you will present, eliminate those that are not obviously related to your proposition.

2. Do I have strong evidence to support a reason? Some reasons sound impressive but cannot be supported with solid evidence. For example, the second

Audiences believe reasons when there is strong evidence to support them.

reason, "Homeownership reduces crime," sounds like a good one; but can you support it? Sometimes you may discover that the only proof you have for a reason is an opinion expressed by one person, or that you haven't uncovered any widespread or systematic confirmation of this claim. In fact, in your research you may discover that although crime is lower in areas with high homeownership, there is little evidence to suggest a cause-and-effect relationship. Because the audience will assess whether they accept your reason based on the evidence you present, eliminate reasons for which you do not have strong support.

3. Will this reason be persuasive for this audience? Suppose that you have a great deal of factual evidence to support the reason "Homeownership increases individual self-esteem." This reason might be very persuasive to an audience of social workers, psychologists, and teachers, but less important to an audience of financial planners, bankers, and economists. So, once you are convinced that your reasons are related to the proposition and have strong evidence to support them, choose to use as main points of your speech the three or four that you believe will be most persuasive for your particular audience. You can use Activity 7B and the sample student response to help you select reasons to support your goals.

© IPA/The Image Works

SPEECH PLANNING

ACTION STEP 2

2 | Audience

ACTIVITY 7B Speech Planning Action Step for Persuasive Speeches

Selecting Reasons
1. Write the proposition that is the specific goal for this speech.
2. Try to list at least as many as six reasons that support your specific goal, then put asterisks (*) beside the three or four reasons that your audience analysis suggests will be most persuasive for this particular audience.
3. Write a thesis statement incorporating these reasons.

You can complete this activity online with Speech Builder Express. Use your Challenge of Effective Speaking CD-ROM to access Activity 7B.

STUDENT RESPONSE

ACTION STEP 2

2 | Audience

ACTIVITY 7B Student Response Action Step for Persuasive Speeches

Selecting Reasons
1. Write the proposition that is the specific goal for this speech.

   I want to convince members of the audience that they should not download music from the Internet.

2. Try to list at least as many as six reasons that support your specific goal, then put asterisks (*) beside the three or four reasons that your audience analysis suggests will be most persuasive for this particular audience.

   Downloading music is unethical.

   * *Downloading music is extremely harmful to recording companies.*

   Downloading music is extremely harmful to artists.

   * *Downloading music is extremely harmful to your computer.*

   * *Downloading music is illegal.*

   Downloading music might result in penalties.

3. Write a thesis statement incorporating these reasons.

   Three good reasons for not downloading music off the Internet are that it's extremely harmful to recording companies and artists, it's harmful to your computer, and it's illegal.

Selecting Evidence to Support Reasons

Although a reason may seem self-explanatory, before most audience members will believe it, they want to hear information that backs it up. As you did your research, you may have discovered more evidence to support a reason than you will be able to use in the time allotted to your speech. So, you will have to choose what evidence you will present.

As we learned in Chapter 6, verifiable factual statements are a strong type of supporting material. Suppose that in a speech whose goal is to convince people that Alzheimer's research should be better funded, you give the reason "Alzheimer's disease is an increasing health problem in the United States." The following would be a factual statement that supported this reason: "According to a 2003 article in the *Archives of Neurology*, the number of Americans with Alzheimer's has more than doubled since 1980 and is expected to continue to grow, affecting between 11.3 and 16 million Americans by the year 2050."

Statements from people who are experts on a subject can also be used as evidence to support a reason. For example, the statement "According to the surgeon general, 'By 2050 Alzheimer's disease may afflict 14 million people a year'" is an expert opinion.

Let's look at an example of how both fact and opinion evidence can be used in combination to support a proposition.

> **Proposition:** I want the audience to believe that television violence has a harmful effect on children.
> **Reason:** Television violence desensitizes children to violence.
> **Support:** In Los Angeles, California, a survey of fifty children between the ages of five and ten who had just watched an episode of *Teenage Mutant Ninja Turtles* asked the children whether or not violence was acceptable. Thirty-nine of the fifty, about 80% of them, responded "Yes, because it helps you to win fights" (fact). Regardless of the rationale children express, the fact remains that viewing violence desensitizes children and this can lead to real violence. According to Kirsten Houston, a well-regarded scholar writing in the July 1997 *Journal of Psychology*, "Repeated exposure to media violence is a major factor in the gradual desensitization of individuals to such scenes. This desensitization, in turn, weakens some viewers' psychological restraints on violent behavior" (expert opinion).

Regardless of whether the evidence is fact based or opinion based, you will want to choose to use the best evidence you have found to support your point. You can use the answers to the following questions to help you select evidence that is likely to persuade your audience.

1. Does the evidence come from a well-respected source? This question involves both the people who offered the opinions or compiled the facts and the book, journal, or Internet source where they were reported. Just as some people's opinions are more reliable than others, so are some printed and Internet sources more reliable than others. As we stated in Chapter 6, Researching Information for Your Speech, be especially careful of undocumented information. Eliminate evidence that comes from a questionable, unreliable, or biased source.

2. Is the evidence recent and if not, is it still valid? Things change, so information that was accurate for a particular time period may or may not be valid today. As you look at your evi-

Use evidence from a well-respected expert. Quotes from Madeleine Albright about foreign policy will be more likely to persuade than those from less reliable sources.

© Reuters/Corbis

dence, consider when the evidence was gathered. Something that was true five years ago may not be true today. A trend that was forecast a year ago may have been revised since then. And a statistic that was reported last week may be based on data that was collected three years ago. So, whether it is a fact or an opinion, you want to choose evidence that is valid today.

For example, the evidence "The total cost of caring for individuals with Alzheimer's is at least $100 billion, according to the Alzheimer's Association and the National Institute on Aging" was cited in a 2003 National Institutes of Health publication. But it is based on information from a study conducted using 1991 data, updated to 1994 data before being published. As a result, we can expect that today annual costs would be higher. If you choose to use this evidence, you should disclose the age of the data used in the study and indicate that today the costs would be higher.

3. Does the evidence really support the reason? Just as reasons need to be relevant to the proposition, so does evidence need to be relevant to the reason. Some of the evidence you have found may be only indirectly related to the reason and should be eliminated in favor of evidence that provides more central support.

4. Will this evidence be persuasive for this audience? Finally, just as when you select your reasons, you will want to choose evidence that your particular audience is likely to find persuasive. So, if you have a choice of two quotations from experts, you will want to use the one from the person your audience is likely to find more credible.

REFLECT ON ETHICS

Sara, a social worker in a homeless shelter, received a call from the president of the Lions Club asking her if she would like to speak to the group tomorrow. He was sorry for the late call, but the speaker they had scheduled had canceled. Sara was eager to do this because she wanted to ask the club to contribute "last dollars," about $10,000, to a new family shelter that was being built. This shelter would allow the community to house homeless families as a unit rather than making them break up and go to single-sex shelters.

Her problem was that the research she had gathered and used in speeches four years ago as part of the original fund drive seemed to be dated. But since she was a last-minute fill-in speaker, she didn't have time to do additional research. Sara pondered her dilemma. She figured that one thing she could do would be to use the old information but obscure the actual dates. That way the audience wouldn't really know that the evidence was old. Besides, she reasoned, it's not as though we've solved the homeless problem.

1. Is Sara's plan ethical?
2. How else might she solve her problem?

Reasoning with Audiences

In a persuasive speech, the goal is met by arguing for your point of view using reasons that you support with evidence. In this section of the chapter, we describe how you can build, and test the logic of, the most common types of arguments used in presenting persuasive speeches.

Essentials of Reasoning

When you are **reasoning** with an audience, you are using the mental process of drawing inferences from factual information, providing arguments for your audience to consider. **Arguments** involve proving conclusions you have drawn from reasons and evidence. Thus, when you show your friend that the engine of his or her car is "missing" at slow speeds and stalling at stoplights, you can reason (draw the conclusion/inference) that the car needs a tune-up. To put this in speech order, you say "Jim/Sally, your car needs a tune-up. Why? Because the car is missing at slow speeds and stalling at stoplights."

As you prepare your speeches, you need a method for analyzing the soundness of the reasons or arguments that you are planning to make. Stephen Toulmin,[3] a philosopher/rhetorician, developed a system you can use for analyzing your arguments. The basic elements of an argument are the claim, the support, and the reasoning process, called the warrant.

CLAIM

A **claim** is a conclusion to be proven. In our simple example, one claim is "Your car needs a tune-up," which is supported by the evidence statements "It is missing at slow speeds" and "It is stalling at stoplights." But each of these statements is also a claim that must be supported by evidence if it is to be accepted and be valid as support for the larger claim "Your car needs a tune-up."

SUPPORT

You can support a claim with reasons or evidence, including facts, opinions, experiences, and observations that support the reasons. In the car example, the support for our argument includes two reasons, "missing at slow speeds" and "stalling at lights," and the evidence that supports each of these reasons.

In outline form, our example looks like this:

Specific goal: I want the audience to believe that the car needs a tune-up. (claim)

I. The car misses at slow speeds. (reason and claim)

    A. On Tuesday it was missing when driven below 20 mph. (evidence)

    B. On Wednesday it did the same thing. (evidence)

II. The car stalls at stoplights. (reason and claim)

    A. It stalled three times at lights on Monday. (evidence)

    B. It stalled each time I stopped at a light yesterday. (evidence)

WARRANT

The **warrant** is the logical statement that connects the support to the claim.[4] Sometimes the warrant of an argument is actually verbalized, but other times it is simply implied. For instance, a person who claims that "the car needs a tune-up" on the basis of "missing" and "stalling at stoplights" may verbalize the reasoning process with the warrant "Missing at slow speeds and stalling at lights *are common indications or signs* that the car needs a tune-up." Or the speaker may just assume that you understand that these are signs of a car that needs a tune-up.

Although you may not actually state your warrants during the speech itself, identifying the type of warrants you are planning to use will allow you to build arguments that are persuasive.

Using **C** for claim (propositions or reason), **S** for support (reasons and evidence), and **W** for warrant or explanation of the reasoning process, we

---

reasoning the mental process of drawing inferences (conclusions) from factual information

arguments the process of proving conclusions you have drawn from reasons and evidence

claim the proposition or conclusion to be proven

warrant the logical statement that connects the support to the claim

can write the reasoning for the proposition in our example in outline form as follows:

C I want the owner to believe that the car needs a tune-up. (specific goal)

S I. The engine misses at slow speeds. (plus evidence in support)

S II. The car stalls at lights. (plus evidence in support)

W (I believe this reasoning is sound because missing and stalling are *major indicators—signs—*of the need for a tune-up.) (The warrant is written in parentheses because it may not be verbalized when the speech is given.)

Types and Tests of Arguments

Although an argument *always* includes a claim and support, different logical relationships can exist between the claim and the support on which it is based. Four types of arguments commonly used in persuasive speeches are example, analogy, causation, and sign.

ARGUING FROM EXAMPLE

argue from example to support your claim by providing one or more individual examples

You **argue from example** when the support statements you use are examples of the claim you are making. For almost any topic, it is easy to find examples. So you are likely to use arguing from example quite frequently. The warrant for an argument from example—its underlying logic—is "What is true in the examples provided is (or will be) true in general or in other instances."

Suppose you are supporting Juanita Martinez for president of the local neighborhood council. One of the reasons you present is the claim that "Juanita is electable." In examining her resume to find support for this claim, you find several examples of her previous victories. She was elected treasurer of her high school junior class, chairperson of her church youth group, and president of her college sorority. Each of these is an example that gives support to the claim. What would the warrant statement for this argument look like? You could say, "What was true in several instances (Juanita has been elected in four previous races) is true or will be true in general or in other instances (she will be electable in this situation)."

Let's look at this argument in speech analysis form:

C Juanita Martinez is electable.

S Juanita has won previous elections.

    A. Juanita won the election for treasurer of her high school junior class.

    B. Juanita won the election for chairperson of her church youth group.

    C. Juanita won the election for president of her sorority.

W (Because Juanita Martinez was elected to previous offices, she is electable for this office.)

When arguing from example, you can make sure that your argument is valid by answering the following questions.

1. Are enough examples cited? Are three elections (junior class treasurer, youth group chairperson, and sorority president) enough examples to make your audience believe that your claim is true? Because the instances cited should represent most or all possibilities, enough must be cited to satisfy the listeners that the instances are not isolated or hand-picked.

2. Are the examples typical? Are the three examples typical of all of Martinez's campaigns for office? Typical means that the examples cited must be similar to or representative of most or all within the category. If examples are not typical, they do not support the argument. For instance, because all three of these successes came in youth organizations, they may not be typical of election dynamics in community organizations. If the three examples are not typical, then the logic of the argument can be questioned. As a speaker you might search for additional examples that are typical.

3. Are negative examples accounted for? In searching for supporting material, we may find one or more examples that are exceptions to the argument we wish to make. If the exceptions are minor or infrequent, then they won't invalidate the argument. For instance, in college Juanita may have run for chairperson of the Sociology Club and lost. That one failure does not necessarily invalidate the argument. If, however, negative examples prove to be more than rare or isolated instances, the validity of the argument is open to serious question. For instance, if you found that Juanita had run for office twelve times and was successful on only the three occasions cited, then the argument would be invalid.

If you believe that there are not enough examples, that the examples you have found are not typical, or that negative examples are common, then you will have only weak support for the claim and should consider making a different type of argument.

ARGUING FROM ANALOGY

You **argue from analogy** when you support a claim with a single comparable example that is so significantly similar to the subject of the claim as to be strong proof. The general statement of a warrant for an argument from analogy is "What is true for situation A will also be true in situation B, which is similar to situation A" or "What is true for situation A will be true in all similar situations."

Suppose that you wanted to argue that the Cherry Fork volunteer fire department should conduct a raffle to raise money for three portable defibrillator units. You could support the claim by analogy with a single example: Mack Fire Department conducted a raffle and raised enough money to purchase four units. The form for this argument from analogy looks like this:

C Cherry Fork Fire Department should conduct a raffle to raise money for three portable defibrillator units.

S Mack Fire Department, which is very similar to Cherry Fork, raised enough money through a raffle to purchase four units.

W (What worked at a very similar volunteer fire department, Mack, will work at Cherry Fork.)

Let us return to the claim that Juanita is electable for president of the senior class to see how arguing from analogy works in a more complex situation. If you discover that Juanita has essentially the same characteristics as Paula Jefferson, who was elected president two years ago (both are very bright, both have a great deal of drive, and both have track records of successful campaigns), then you can use the single example of Paula to form a reason "Juanita has the same characteristics as Paula Jefferson, who was elected two years ago." This is analogical reasoning.

Let's look at how the Martinez argument would look in outline form:

C Juanita Martinez is electable.

S Juanita has the same characteristics as Paula Jefferson, who was elected two years ago. (This is also a claim, for which A, B, and C below are support.)

argue from analogy to support a claim with a single comparable example that is significantly similar to the subject of the claim

A. Juanita and Paula are both very bright.

B. Juanita and Paula both have a great deal of drive.

C. Juanita and Paula both have won other campaigns.

W (What was true for Paula will be true for Juanita, who is similar on the important characteristics.)

So, the claim is supported through an analogy; then additional support is offered to validate the analogy.

When arguing from analogy you can make sure that your argument is valid by answering the following questions.

1. Are the subjects being compared similar in every important way? Are intelligence, drive, and track records the most important characteristics on which to determine electability? If criteria on which the subjects are being compared are not the most important ones, or if they really don't compare well, then you can question the reasoning on that basis.

2. Is any of the ways in which the subjects are dissimilar important to the outcome? If Paula is a native of the community whereas Juanita has only been in the area for a year, is this dissimilarity important? When the dissimilarities outweigh the subjects' similarities, then conclusions drawn from the comparisons may be invalid.

ARGUING FROM CAUSATION

argue from causation to cite events that have occurred that result in the claim

You **argue from causation** when you support a claim by citing events that have occurred that result in the claim. Reasoning from causation says that one or more of the events cited always (or almost always) brings about, leads to, or creates or prevents a predictable effect or set of effects.

The general warrant for arguments from cause can be stated as follows: If an event comes before another event and is associated with that event, then we can say that it is the cause of the event. "If A, which is known to bring about B, has been observed, then we can expect B to occur." For instance, you could develop a causal argument based on the relationship between mortgage interest rates and

How would you evaluate the causal claim made on this billboard?

home sales: "Home sales are bound to increase during the next three months (claim), because mortgage interest rates have recently dropped markedly (causal event as support)."

Let's look at this type of argument in outline form:

C Home sales will increase.

S Mortgage interest rates have dropped.

W (Lower interest rates generally lead to higher home sales.)

In researching Juanita's election campaign, you might discover that (1) she has campaigned intelligently and (2) she has won the endorsement of key community leaders. If these two events are usually associated with victory, then you can form the argument that Juanita has engaged in behavior that leads to campaign victories, thus supporting the claim that she is electable. The argument would look like this:

C Juanita Martinez will be elected.

S A. Juanita has campaigned intelligently.

S B. Juanita has key endorsements.

W (Intelligent campaigning and getting key endorsements lead to (cause) electoral victory.)

When arguing from causation you can make sure that your argument is valid by answering the following questions.

1. Are the events alone sufficient to cause the stated effect? Are intelligent campaigning and key endorsements important enough by themselves to result in winning elections? If the events are truly causes, it means that if these events were eliminated, then the effect would be eliminated as well. If the effect can occur without these events occurring, then you can question the causal relationship.

2. Do other events accompanying the cited events actually cause the effect? Are other factors (such as luck, drive, friends) more important in determining whether a person wins an election? If the other events appear equally or more important in bringing about the effect, then you can question the causal relationship between the data cited and the conclusion. If you believe that other data caused the effect, then you can question the reasoning on that basis.

3. Is the relationship between the causal events and the effect consistent? Do intelligent campaigning and key endorsements always (or usually) yield electoral victories? If there are times when the effect has not followed the cause, then you can question whether a causal relationship exists. If you believe that the relationship between the cause and effect is not consistent, then you can question the reasoning on that basis.

ARGUING FROM SIGN

If certain events, characteristics, or situations always or usually accompany something, those events, characteristics, or situations are signs. You **argue from sign** when you support a claim by providing evidence that the events that signal the claim have occurred. For instance, your doctor may claim that you have had an allergic reaction because you have hives and a runny nose.

The general warrant for reasoning from sign can be stated as follows: When phenomena that usually or always accompany a specific situation occur, then we can expect that specific situation is occurring (or will occur). So, the warrant for the allergy argument can be stated as follows: "Hives and a slight fever are indicators (signs) of an allergic reaction."

argue from sign to cite information that signals the claim

Let's look at this argument in outline form:

C You have had an allergic reaction.

S A. You have hives.

    B. You have a slight fever.

W (Hives and a slight fever are signs of an allergic reaction.)

Signs should not be confused with causes; signs accompany a phenomenon but do not bring about, lead to, or create the claim. In fact, signs may actually be the effects of the phenomena. A rash and fever don't cause an allergic reaction; they are indications, or effects, of a reaction.

If in analyzing Juanita's campaign, you notice that Juanita has more campaign workers than all other candidates combined and that a greater number of people from all segments of the community are wearing "Juanita for President" buttons, you may reason "Juanita's campaign has the key signs of an election victory."

A speech outline using this sign argument would look like this:

C Juanita Martinez will be elected.

S A. Juanita has more campaign workers than all other candidates combined.

    B. A greater number of community members are wearing her campaign buttons.

W (The presence of a greater number of campaign posters and buttons than the opponents have is a sign/indicator of victory.)

When arguing from sign you can make sure that your argument is valid by answering the following questions.

1. Do the signs cited always or usually indicate the conclusion drawn? Do large numbers of campaign workers and campaign buttons always (or usually) indicate election victory? If the data can occur independently of the conclusion, then they are not necessarily indicators. If the signs cited do not usually indicate the conclusion, then you can question the reasoning on that basis.

2. Are a sufficient number of signs present? Are campaign workers and buttons enough to indicate a victory? Several signs often indicate events or situations. If enough signs are not present, then the conclusion may not follow. If there are insufficient signs, then you can question the reasoning on that basis.

3. Are contradictory signs in evidence? Are campaign buttons thrown away in great numbers? If signs usually indicating different conclusions are present, then the stated conclusion may not be valid. If you believe that contradictory signs are evident, then you can question the reasoning on that basis.

COMBINING ARGUMENTS IN A SPEECH

An effective speech usually contains several reasons that are based on various types of arguments. For a speech with the goal "I want my audience to believe that Juanita is electable," you might choose to present three of the reasons we've been working with. Suppose you selected the following:

    I. Juanita has run successful campaigns in the past. (argued by example)

        A. Juanita was successful in her campaign for treasurer of her high school class.

        B. Juanita was successful in her campaign for chairperson of her church youth group.

        C. Juanita was successful in her campaign for president of her sorority.

II. Juanita has engaged in procedures that result in campaign victory. (argued by cause)

    A. Juanita has campaigned intelligently.

    B. Juanita has key endorsements.

III. Juanita is a strong leader. (argued by sign)

    A. Juanita has more campaign workers than all other candidates combined.

    B. Juanita has a greater number of community members wearing her campaign buttons.

Just as each of our reasons is presented as an argument, so too is the overall speech. So, we need to determine what type of argument we are making. What relationship do all three of these reasons have with the overall claim? That is, how do running successful campaigns in the past, being engaged in procedures that result in victory, and being a strong leader relate to whether Juanita is electable? Are they examples of being electable? Do they cause one to be elected? Are they signs that usually accompany election? Do they distinguish a person who is electable from one who is not? As you study this you will recognize that the warrant is best stated: "Running successful campaigns in the past, being engaged in procedures that result in victory, and being a strong leader are all signs of electability." Now you can test the soundness of the overall argument by using the tests of sign argument listed earlier.

Avoiding Fallacies of Reasoning

As you are developing your reasons and the arguments you will make, you should check to make sure that your reasoning is appropriate for the particular situation. This will allow you to avoid fallacies, or errors in reasoning. Three common fallacies to avoid are hasty generalization, false cause, and ad hominem arguments.

Hasty Generalization

A **hasty generalization** is a fallacy that presents a generalization that is either not supported with evidence or is supported with only one weak example. Because the supporting material that is cited should be representative of all the supporting material that could be cited, enough supporting material must be presented to satisfy the audience that the instances are not isolated or hand-picked. Avoiding hasty generalizations requires you to be confident that the instances you cite as support are typical and representative of your claim. For example, someone who argued "All Akitas are vicious dogs," whose sole piece of evidence was "My neighbor had an Akita and it bit my best friend's sister," would be guilty of a hasty generalization. It is hasty to generalize about the temperament of a whole breed of dogs based on a single action of one dog.

hasty generalization a fallacy that presents a generalization that is either not supported with evidence or is supported with only one weak example

False Cause

A **false cause** fallacy occurs when the alleged cause fails to be related to, or to produce, the effect. Just because two things happen one after the other does not mean that the first necessarily caused the second. Unlike people who blame monetary setbacks or illness on black cats or broken mirrors, you need to be careful that you don't take coincidental events or signal events and present them as a false cause.

false cause a fallacy that occurs when the alleged cause fails to be related to, or to produce, the effect

Ad hominem arguments attack a person rather than present an argument.

© Paul Hawthorne/Getty Images

AD HOMINEM ARGUMENT

ad hominem argument attacking or praising the person making the argument, rather than addressing the argument itself

An **ad hominem argument** attacks or praises the person making the argument, rather than addressing the argument itself. *Ad hominem* literally means "to the man." For example, if Jamal's support for his claim that his audience should buy an Apple computer is that Steve Jobs, the founder and current president of Apple Computer, is a genius, he is making an ad hominem argument. Jobs's intelligence isn't really a reason to buy a particular brand of computer. TV commercials that feature celebrities using the product are often guilty of ad hominem reasoning.

Organizational Patterns for Persuasive Speeches

Once you have identified and tested the logic of your reasons, you are ready to organize the main points into a pattern that will enable your audience to follow your argument. The most common patterns for organizing persuasive speeches are statement of reasons, comparative advantages, criteria satisfaction, problem solution, and motivated sequence. In this section we describe and illustrate each of the first four persuasive organizational patterns and identify the type of proposition for which they are most commonly used. The fifth pattern, motivated sequence, will be described in the next chapter. So that you can contrast the patterns and better understand their use, we will illustrate each pattern using the same topic with different propositions that use the same (or similar) reasons.

Statement of Reasons Pattern

The **statement of reasons** is a form of persuasive organization used for proving propositions of fact in which you present your best-supported reasons in a meaningful order. For a speech with three reasons or more, place the strongest reason last, because this is the reason you believe the audience will find most persuasive. Place the second strongest reason first, because you want to start with a significant point. Place the other reasons in between.

statement of reasons a straightforward organization in which you present your best-supported reasons in a meaningful order

> **Proposition:** I want my audience to believe that passing the proposed school tax levy is necessary.
>
> I. The income will enable the schools to restore vital programs. (second strongest)
>
> II. The income will enable the schools to give teachers the raises they need to keep up with the cost of living.
>
> III. The income will allow the community to maintain local control and will save the district from state intervention. (strongest)

Comparative Advantages Pattern

The **comparative advantages** organizational pattern shows that a proposed change has more value than the status quo. Each reason is shown as an improvement over the current system. A comparative advantages approach to a school tax proposition would look like this:

comparative advantages an organization that shows that a proposed change has more value than the status quo

> **Proposition:** I want my audience to believe that passing the school tax levy is better than not passing it. (compares the value of change to the status quo)
>
> I. Income from a tax levy will enable schools to reintroduce important programs that had to be cut. (advantage 1)
>
> II. Income from a tax levy will enable schools to avoid a tentative strike by teachers who are underpaid. (advantage 2)
>
> III. Income from a tax levy will enable us to retain local control of our schools, which will be lost to the state if additional local funding is not provided. (advantage 3)

Criteria Satisfaction Pattern

The **criteria satisfaction** pattern is an indirect organization that seeks audience agreement on criteria that should be considered when evaluating a particular proposition and then shows how the proposition satisfies those criteria. A criteria satisfaction pattern is especially useful when your audience is opposed to your proposition, because it approaches the proposition indirectly by first focusing on criteria, which the audience may agree with, before introducing the specific

criteria satisfaction an indirect organization that seeks audience agreement on criteria that should be considered when evaluating a particular proposition and then shows how the proposition satisfies those criteria

proposition. A criteria satisfaction organization for the school tax proposition would look like this:

> **Proposition:** I want my audience to believe that passing a school levy is a good way to fund our schools.
>
> **I.** We all can agree that a good school funding method must meet three criteria:
>
> **A.** A good funding method results in the reestablishment of programs that have been dropped for monetary reasons.
>
> **B.** A good funding method results in fair pay for teachers.
>
> **C.** A good funding method generates enough income to maintain local control, avoiding state intervention.
>
> **II.** Passage of a local school tax levy is a good way to fund our schools.
>
> **A.** A local levy will allow us to re-fund important programs.
>
> **B.** A local levy will allow us to give teachers a raise.
>
> **C.** A local levy will generate enough income to maintain local control and avoid state intervention.

Problem Solution Pattern

problem solution an organizational pattern that provides a framework for clarifying the nature of some problem and for illustrating why a given proposal is the best solution

The **problem solution** pattern is an organizational pattern that provides a framework for clarifying the nature of some problem and for illustrating why a given proposal is the best solution. This organization works well when the audience is neutral or only agrees that there is a problem but has no opinion about a particular solution. In a problem solution speech, the claim ("There is a problem that can be solved by X") is supported by three reasons that take this general form: (1) There is a problem that requires action. (2) Proposal X will solve the problem. (3) Proposal X is the best solution to the problem, because it will lead to positive consequences and minimize or avoid negative ones. A problem solution organization for the school tax proposition might look like this:

> **Proposition:** The current fiscal crisis in the school district can be solved through a local tax levy.
>
> **I.** The current funding is insufficient and has resulted in program cuts, labor problems resulting from stagnant wages, and a threatened state takeover of local schools. (statement of problem)
>
> **II.** The proposed local tax levy is large enough to solve these problems. (solution)
>
> **III.** The proposed local tax levy is the best means of solving the funding crisis.

 To see video clips of a student speaker's use of reasons in an introduction and solutions in a conclusion, use your Challenge of Effective Speaking CD-ROM to access the chapter resources for Chapter 13 at the Challenge Web site. Click on "Online Pharmacies (1)" and "Online Pharmacies (2)" in the left-hand menu.

SPEECH ASSIGNMENT

Persuasive Speaking

1. Prepare a four- to seven-minute speech in which you change audience belief.
2. Write a persuasive plan for adapting to your specific audience that includes:

a. How your goal adapts to whether your prevailing audience attitude is in favor, no opinion, or opposed.

b. What reasons you will use and how the organizational pattern you selected is fitting for your topic and audience.

c. How you will organize those reasons.

3. Write a complete speech outline.

To help you prepare your outline, use your Challenge of Effective Speaking CD-ROM to access Speech Builder Express.

SPEECH EVALUATION CHECKLIST

Speech to Convince

You can use this checklist to critique a persuasive speech that you hear in class. As you listen to the speaker, outline the speech. Pay close attention to the reasoning process that the speaker uses. You will want to note the claims and support used in the arguments, and you will want to identify the types of warrants being used. Then answer the questions below.

Primary Criteria

_____ 1. Did the specific goal appear to be adapted to the initial attitude of most members of the audience?

_____ 2. Was the specific goal phrased as a proposition (were you clear what position on the issue the speaker was taking)?

_____ 3. Was the proposition one of: ___ fact ___ value ___ policy?

_____ 4. Were the reasons (claims) used in the speech:

___ Directly related to the proposition?

___ Supported by strong evidence?

___ Persuasive for the particular audience?

_____ 5. Was the evidence (support) used to back the reasons (claims):

___ From well-respected sources?

___ Recent and/or still valid?

___ Persuasive for this audience?

___ Typical of all evidence that might have been used?

___ Sufficient (enough evidence was cited)?

_____ 6. Could you identify the types of warrants that were used?

___ Did the speaker argue from example? ___ If so, was it valid?

___ Did the speaker argue from analogy? ___ If so, was it valid?

___ Did the speaker argue from causation? ___ If so, was it valid?

___ Did the speaker argue from sign? ___ If so, was it valid?

_____ 7. Did the speaker engage in any fallacies of reasoning?

___ Hasty generalizations

___ Arguing from false cause

___ Ad hominem attacks

(continued)

____ **8.** Did the speaker use an appropriate persuasive speech organizational pattern?

  ___ Statement of reasons

  ___ Comparative advantages

  ___ Criteria satisfaction

  ___ Problem solution

General Criteria

____ **1.** Was the specific goal clear?

____ **2.** Was the introduction effective in creating interest and involving the audience in the speech?

____ **3.** Was the speech organized using an appropriate persuasive pattern?

____ **4.** Was the language clear, vivid, emphatic, and appropriate?

____ **5.** Was the conclusion effective in summarizing what had been said and mobilizing the audience to act?

____ **6.** Was the speech delivered enthusiastically, with vocal expressiveness, fluency, spontaneity, and directness?

Overall evaluation of the speech (check one):

____ excellent ____ good ____ average ____ fair ____ poor

Use the information from this checklist to support your evaluation.

You can use your Challenge of Effective Speaking CD-ROM to access this checklist online under student resources for Chapter 13 at the Challenge of Effective Speaking Web site.

SAMPLE SPEECH

Sample Speech to Convince

This section presents a sample speech to convince given by a student, including adaptation plan, outline, and transcript.

Downloading Music

by Tobias Varland[5]

You can also use your Challenge of Effective Speaking CD-ROM to watch a video clip of another student, Eric Wais, presenting the persuasive speech "Capital Punishment." Click on the Speech Interactive icon and then on Speech Menu. Select "Capital Punishment" to watch the video.

Audience Adaptation Plan

AUDIENCE ATTITUDE: When I asked people about their feelings about downloading, I found that most realized that it was easy to do and that it saved them time and money. There was a general belief that downloading didn't really hurt companies that much. But most also mentioned that they realized that it was not the right thing to do, but with so many doing it, chances of being caught were pretty low. As I put these data together, I determined that although the audience was not set against downloading, they were not totally in favor of doing it either. So I put the majority in the group of undecided, or not that worried about the consequences.

REASONS: I believe that the three reasons that are most likely to convince the audience are that downloading is really harmful to companies, that downloading is harmful to the computer (few people even mention this as a possible downside), and that downloading is not only illegal, but can be costly.

SELECTING AN ORGANIZATION TO MEET AUDIENCE NEEDS: Given that the majority of the class seemed indifferent or unworried about the consequences, I determined that a logical reasons approach was appropriate. I have organized my speech in such a way that it will gain momentum throughout the speech, and by the end of the speech the audience will have no choice but to consider my suggestions.

Outline

SPEECH GOAL: I want to convince members of the audience that they should not download music from the Internet.

INTRODUCTION

I. Over the past few weeks I've discovered that large numbers of people are doing something that in my mind is unbelievably stupid.

II. They're saving approximately 99 cents for doing something that could cost them as much as $150,000.

III. They're downloading copyrighted music off the Internet.

THESIS STATEMENT: There are three good reasons for not downloading music off the Internet: it's extremely harmful to recording companies and artists, it's harmful to computers, and it's illegal.

BODY

I. Downloading music is extremely harmful to recording companies and artists.

    A. Record sales have declined radically in the last five years.

        1. About 41 percent of people are downloading music for free rather than buying records, according to *Fortune* magazine.

        2. Since 1993 average annual profit has dropped from 20 percent to less than 5 percent.

    B. People are losing jobs.

        1. This year three major recording companies, BMG, EMI, and Sony Music, fired 4,200 people as a result.

II. The second reason that you should not be downloading music from the Internet is that it is harmful to your computer.

    A. In order to download music from the Internet people must use some sort of spot check program.

        1. Just one such program, His Eye, has 65 million users.

    B. According to *PC Magazine,* by installing such a program you also install several others, such as spyware.

        1. These programs monitor who you send e-mails to, copy your e-mail messages, and store them on your server.

        2. They send out spam directories that take control of your computer, lock you out of your own computer, use your computer for illegal practices, and say you are responsible.

            a. For instance, a graduate student who is writing a thesis could have it stolen and published before he or she gets a chance to print it.

        3. Saving a few dollars instead of buying CDs or buying individual songs off the Internet can put people at such huge risk that it's unbelievable that they continue to do it.

III. The third and most important reason for not downloading music is that it's illegal.

    A. Music in the United States is protected by copyright law.

        1. When you download music off the Internet, you are committing theft.

    B. Recording studios have filed numerous lawsuits.

        1. According to CBC News, one company just filed a lawsuit against four college students from New England who had all downloaded 1,500 songs apiece.

(continued)

2. They sought fines of $150,000 per song that these students had downloaded, according to the CBC News.

3. Although the company didn't get the $150,000 per song, each student was forced to pay somewhere between $12,500 and $17,500 and was kicked out of school.

C. All of this happened because they wanted to save themselves 15 bucks per CD.

CONCLUSION

I. So, think about it: downloading is harmful to the recording industry, it is likely to be harmful to your computer, and most of all, it could result in tremendous financial loss to you because it is illegal.

II. I would encourage you to consider these things before you download anything else. Consider whether or not it's really worth it.

SOURCES: CBC News (Web Site), http://www.cbc.ca/stories/2003/05/02/Consumers/record/lawsuit 03052.
Seith, Robert CWK Senior Producer, "Downloading Copyrighted Music," http://www.connecting withkids.com/tipsheet/2003/115_mar12/music.html.
"Songs in the Key of Steve," *Fortune Magazine,* May 19, 2003.
"Spyware: It's Lurking on Your Machine," *PC Magazine,* April 22, 2003.
"Study Links Burning and Downloading to Falling Music Sales," *The Write News,* June 20, 2003, www.writenews.com.
Sweeting, Paul "Avast ye pirates! The copyright industries, particularly the record companies, are entering dangerous new waters." *Video Business,* June 30, 2003 v23 i26 p10(1)

Analysis

Tobias begins indirectly by sharing his opinions about a behavior that has become very popular. This indirect method is designed to get people interested in determining what he is going to talk about.

Here, he states his goal and mentions that he will focus on three reasons.

His first reason is designed to focus on one important harm that results from downloading.

Notice the presentation of information used to support his point. Throughout this section he cites sources and gives a variety of statistics.

Here he tries to get his audience to think about what he has said. He makes a good case showing that downloading has in fact a major effect on companies and artists.

In this second reason Tobias looks at material with which the audience may be totally unfamiliar.

Here he is talking about side effects that result from downloading

Speech

As I was talking with a lot of my friends and acquaintances, I discovered a pretty amazing phenomenon. I discovered that almost every person I talked to does something that in my mind is unbelievably stupid. Anyone know what I'm talking about? It's a behavior that has become extremely popular: illegally downloading copyrighted music off the Internet. Today I'd like to convince you that you should not download music on your computer. Why? For at least three reasons.

The first reason is that it's extremely harmful to recording companies and recording artists. I'm going to discuss some numbers with you—and I want you to think about them. The first number is 61. According to *The Write News,* CD record sales in the United States have dropped 61 percent in just the last year. The second number is 41. Downloading has become extremely popular, according to *Fortune* magazine. Today, about 41 percent of people who love music are downloading it for free rather than buying records. Third is a set of numbers: 20/5. Obviously downloading is very harmful to recording companies. In 1993 recording companies made an average annual profit of just over 20 percent. Now they're making less than 5 percent profit. That's 20 to 5! The last number is 4,200. During this last year, three major recording companies, BMG, EMI, and Sony Music, have fired 4,200 people because they could not gainfully employ these people. As much as you would like to think that music is for the sake of art and people do it because they love doing it, music is a business. To get their money out of it, recording companies can't continue to produce music, the artists have no ambition in producing music, and therefore by downloading music most people would say, I'm trying to support this music, I want to listen to it, I want to hear it—what they're really doing is destroying an industry and insuring that there will not be as much music produced in the future.

The second reason that you should not be downloading music from the Internet is that it is extremely harmful to your computer. In order to download this music from the Internet, almost everybody uses some sort of spot check program. The most popular program right now is called His Eye, a program that has as many as 65 million users. The problem is that when you install His Eye on your computer, you install numerous other programs like spyware. This spyware does things to your computer such as monitors who you send e-mails to, copies your e-mail messages and stores them on your server, copies your editors' books, sends those addresses out to spam directories that can actually take control of your computer, locking you out of your own computer, use your computer for illegal practices and saying you are responsible for it since it is your computer. Let's look at a potential consequence. Suppose you're a graduate student and you're writing a thesis paper. It could be stolen and published before you get a chance to print it. It seems that people are doing this to save themselves a few dollars from buying CDs or buying individual songs off the Internet and putting themselves in such huge risk that it's unbelievable that they continue to do it.

methods. Some of these side effects don't seem to be that important, but in fact are. He shows that allowing access enables others to take advantage of your machine.

In short, he's focusing on unnecessary risks that may result from your use of various downloading programs.

Notice how he keeps coming back to his key point: for relatively small savings, you are taking tremendous risks—and you might not even be aware of the potential harms.

The third one, and the most important reason why this should not be done is, it's illegal. Music in the United States is protected by copyright law. When you download this music off the Internet, you are committing theft. Recording companies recently have been on a kind of a rampage in catching people who've been doing this. They want to be very aggressive about it. And they just filed a lawsuit against four college students from New England who had all downloaded 1,500 songs apiece. The recording industry sought a fine of 150,000 dollars per song that these students had downloaded. This is according to the CBC News. The recording industry didn't get the 150,000 dollars per song, there's no way that these students could ever pay that much money to the recording companies. Each student was forced to pay somewhere between 12,500 and 17,500 dollars along with being kicked out of school and they were very lucky apparently to avoid at least a six-month jail sentence. All to save themselves 15 bucks per CD. I know that as a college student if somebody told me that I was responsible all of a sudden for paying a 15,000 dollar fine, I'm kind of out of luck—I can't pay a 15,000 dollar fine.

Since the audience may not totally accept the importance of these first two reasons, Tobias closes with his third, and most important reason—that some or much of what you're doing is not only illegal, but also could be tremendously detrimental to you.

The point is that the industry is making examples of some individuals by seeing to it that they pay fines. So the costs are not $150,000, but would you be able to afford the 12,500 to 17,500 dollars that some have been required to pay? And, can you afford to be "kicked out of school?"

Again he comes back to the relatively small amount of money that people save in comparison to what can be monumental risks.

So, thinking about it, there are these three very obvious reasons that by downloading off the Internet you are costing people dollars, you're destroying some people's careers, sound engineers, that's all they know, they can't be employed anymore, because their companies are undermined by people trying to save a few dollars. You're putting your privacy and your computer at risk and making yourself further liable for damages done with your computer by other people. And you're breaking the law. In a society where people—if people don't obey the law, in one instance, what's to keep them from not obeying in another instance. How can you break this law and condemn somebody else for breaking another law? It doesn't make sense, the whole package of downloading copyrighted music off the Internet doesn't make sense, and most people just don't think about that. So I would encourage you to consider these things before you download anything else. ■

Here he does a good job of reinforcing and reemphasizing the nature of the problems that are being created as a result of downloading.

He finishes with a strong appeal to the lack of sense of continuing such behavior.

A very good speech of reasons. Notice how he put a strong reason first, a reason that might be important second, and the strongest reason third.

Most of his information was well documented. And the way he presented the information really gets us to think. ■

Summary

Persuasive speeches are designed to influence the beliefs and/or the behavior of audience members. The first step in preparing a persuasive speech is to construct a speech goal. These goals are chosen based on the audience's initial attitude. An audience may be opposed to the proposition, neutral (because they are un-informed, impartial, or apathetic), or in favor. Persuasive speech goals are phrased as propositions in which the position advocated by the speaker is clearly indicated.

The second step is to choose good reasons and sound evidence. Reasons are main point statements that support the proposition. Evidence is information (in-cluding facts and expert opinions) selected to support reasons.

The third step is to evaluate the quality of your reasons. As you reason with your audience, you will make claims that you support with evidence. The logic that links your claim and your support is called the warrant. The warrant may be voiced or just implied. Different types of warrants can be used to link claims and support. Four of the most common are arguing from example, analogy, cause, and sign. As you prepare your speech, you will want to decide which types of war-rants you will use and test them to ensure that they are valid. You will also want to make sure that you avoid three common fallacies that occur in reasoning: hasty generalizations, false cause, and ad hominem arguments.

Finally, once you have selected your reasons and evidence and tested the logic of your warrants, you can choose from among five patterns of persuasive organi-zation: statement of reasons, comparative advantages, criteria satisfaction, prob-lem solution, and motivated sequence (to be discussed in the next chapter).

CHALLENGE ONLINE

Now that you've read Chapter 13, use your Challenge of Effective Speaking CD-ROM for quick access to the electronic study resources that accompany this text. Your CD-ROM gives you access to the evaluation checklist shown on pages 261–262, the video of Eric's speech described on page 262, InfoTrac College Edition, Speech Builder Express, and the Challenge of Effective Speaking Web site. When you get to the Challenge of Effective Speaking home page, click on "Student Book Companion Site" in the Resource box at the right to access the online study aids for this chapter, including the video clips described on pages 260 and 262, a digital glossary, review quizzes, and the chapter activities.

KEY TERMS

At the Challenge of Effective Speaking Web site, select chapter resources for Chapter 13. Print a copy of the glossary for this chapter, test yourself with the electronic flash cards, or complete the crossword puzzle to help you master the following key terms.

persuasive speech (241)　　　　　　**apathetic** (243)

attitude (241)　　　　　　　　　　　**proposition** (244)

uninformed (243)　　　　　　　　　**proposition of fact** (244)

impartial (243)　　　　　　　　　　**proposition of value** (244)

proposition of policy (245)

reasons (246)

reasoning (251)

arguments (251)

claim (251)

warrant (251)

argue from example (252)

argue from analogy (253)

argue from causation (254)

argue from sign (255)

hasty generalization (257)

false cause (257)

ad hominem argument (258)

statement of reasons (259)

comparative advantages (259)

criteria satisfaction (259)

problem solution (260)

INFOTRAC COLLEGE EDITION EXERCISE

To learn more about the psychology of persuasion, use your Challenge of Effective Speaking CD-ROM to access InfoTrac College Edition and conduct a subject search on the word "persuasion." Locate the citations under "persuasion, psychology of" in the Subject Guide, and choose two articles to read that you believe will help you understand how to be a better persuasive speaker. Choose two key points from the articles you have chosen and plan to incorporate them in your next persuasive speech.

SPEECH PLANNING ACTION STEPS

Access the Action Step activities for this chapter online at the Challenge of Effective Speaking Web site. Select the chapter resources for Chapter 13, then click on the activity number you want. You may print out your completed activities.

7A Writing a Specific Goal as a Persuasive Proposition (245–246)

7B Selecting Reasons (248)

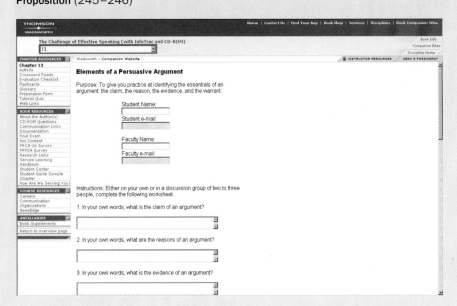

14

Persuasive Speaking: Motivating the Audience

© David Young-Wolff/PhotoEdit

There can be no knowledge without emotion. We may be aware of a truth, yet until we have felt its force, it is not ours. To the cognition of the brain must be added the experience of the soul.

Arnold Bennett, *The Journals of Arnold Bennett*, entry for March 18, 1897

As he finished his speech on "Taking Back the Neighborhood: Get Out the Vote!" the audience rose to their feet and began to chant, "No more, No more, No more, No more. . ." It was clear to him that he had made an impact. Not only had he convinced his audience, but also he could see that they were visibly angry and ready for action. As he was leaving the platform, he heard a member of the audience shout out, "You heard him. It's time! Voting won't do any good. Let's go take what is ours. Take to the streets! Get yours!" In the riot that ensued, three neighborhood shops were ransacked, ten cars set on fire, and twenty-three people were arrested. The next day as he toured the neighborhood and saw firsthand the wreckage his speech had led to, all he could think was, "This wasn't what I meant. This isn't what I wanted."

As this vignette suggests, speeches can be powerful catalysts for action. As speakers we have an awesome responsibility to ensure that we use reasoning, emotional appeals, and our credibility in ethical ways.

In the previous chapter you studied how to use reasoning to build a speech whose logic can convince an audience. But to get members of an audience to act requires additional speech making skills. In this chapter we will focus on motivating your audience to think, increasing audience involvement through emotional appeals, cueing your audience through credibility, motivating your audience to act, following ethical guidelines, and organizing your speech with a motivated sequence.

Motivating Your Audience to Think: The Elaboration Likelihood Model (ELM)

Can you remember times when someone tried to convince you to believe or do something and you really listened to and carefully thought about what the person was saying in order to make a decision about what you wanted to believe or do? Can you remember other times when you only half listened to what was being said and made up your mind quickly based on just a few "feelings" that you got about what was said? Why in some cases are we motivated to listen carefully and in other instances decide without really thinking? Understanding the answers to these questions will help you as you develop your persuasive speeches.

An explanation that has received scholarly attention and research support is known as the elaboration likelihood model (ELM), developed by social psychologists Richard Petty and John Cacioppo. In the newest edition of his textbook on persuasion, Charles Larsen asserts that the ELM model "has changed how persuasion is viewed,"[1] a view that is supported by nearly everyone who discusses theories of persuasion. The purpose of the theory is to explain what determines the *likelihood* that people will choose to spend time evaluating information (such as arguments they hear in a speech) in an *elaborate* way, using their critical thinking skills, rather than processing information in a simpler, less critical manner (hence the name *elaboration likelihood model*).[2] Let's look at what the model says.

Petty and Cacioppo believe that people can process information through one of two routes (one of two ways). One way is to use what they call the **central route,** in which people carefully listen to, think about, evaluate, and even mentally elaborate on what has been said before making up their minds. The second way, which they call the **peripheral route,** is a "shortcut" that relies on simple cues. Instead of listening to, thinking about, evaluating, and elaborating on what is said, people base their judgments on impressions rather than actual arguments. Chief among the cues that people use when taking the peripheral route is what they think about the speaker—in other words, the speaker's credibility.

According to the ELM model, when an issue is really important to us—when we are involved with it and have an emotional stake—we are willing to travel the central path and put a great deal of time and energy into determining what we think and how we should behave. Under these circumstances, we exert the mental energy it takes to evaluate the reasons and evidence used in the speaker's arguments. When we are less involved with the issue, however, we don't take the time or energy to really "dig into" the issue; instead, we'll take the peripheral route and accept what is said on the basis of simple cues, such as the credibility of the source or the appeal of motivational techniques (so well known and used by advertising agencies). So, according to ELM, what determines whether your audience takes the central or peripheral route in evaluating your arguments depends on how involved they feel with your topic.

Let's look at an example. Suppose you belong to a union and you are listening to your union rep present the new medical benefits policy that the union has negotiated and wants you to vote for. How closely will you listen to what is said, and how much study are you likely to make prior to your vote? Well, according to this model, if you and your family are young, have always been healthy, and have never had trouble having your health care needs met, you are likely to take the peripheral route. You reason, "This is my union rep, she has my best interest in mind, so if she says it's a good deal, I guess it must be." But suppose that you or someone in your family has a chronic disease that is expensive to treat and that you have had to fight to have expenses covered. How will you evaluate what is said? According to ELM, you are unlikely to take what the union rep has to say on face value because you are more involved with this subject. You will choose the central route, listening carefully to the information about the new policy, thinking through its implications for you and your family, and maybe even doing additional research before deciding whether to vote "yes."

The ELM model also posits that when attitudes are formed as the result of central route processes (critical thinking), they are less susceptible to change than when attitudes are formed on the basis of peripheral route processes (using simple cues such as the credibility of the source or emotional response). Can you recall times when you listened to a persuasive message, seemed totally drawn to the power of the message, yet within a day or two forgot why you were so enthralled and changed your mind? This is a sign that you were affected through the peripheral route. Likewise, can you think of times when you listened to a persuasive message, thought about the strengths of the reasons and evidence, changed your mind, and days later could still echo the reasoning you heard in that message? This is a sign of being affected through the central route of critical thinking. It is important to note that the peripheral route of persuasion, although short-term, is still very effective. This is why advertising repetition and use of emotional appeals are very successful.[3] But as Herman Simons points out, "Central and peripheral processing are not mutually exclusive; much of the time we use them in combination depending on how much we truly care about a matter."[4]

The speech planning process and what you have learned about the reasoning process in previous chapters will help you provide audience members with sound reasons and solid evidence as the basis for their change of belief or decision to act. Now we want to explore how you can increase the likelihood that your audience members will feel involved with your proposition and so take the central route in processing what you say. Then, we will explain how to establish your credibility for those whose interest cannot be piqued so that they are likely to agree with you.

Increasing Audience Involvement through Emotional Appeals

When we are involved with something, we care about it and have an emotional stake in it. **Emotions** are the buildup of action-specific energy.[5] We can see simple examples of this when we observe how people's facial expressions change as they receive good or bad news. Smiling is one way to release our built-up feelings of happiness. Crying is a way to release our built-up feelings of sadness. People who are experiencing the tension associated with any emotion look for a way to release the energy. So as a speaker, if you can involve your audience (give them an emotional stake) in what you are saying, they are more likely to travel a central route and use their energy to listen carefully to your speech. Let's look at how research from Robin Nabi shows you can increase involvement by stimulating both negative and positive emotions in your speeches.[6]

emotions the buildup of action-specific energy

Evoking Negative Emotions

Negative emotions are disquieting, so when people experience them, they look for ways to eliminate them. During your speech, if you can help your audience experience negative emotions, they will be more involved with what you are saying. As a result, they will be motivated to use their energy to listen carefully to you to see if your arguments give them a way to reduce their feelings of discomfort. There are numerous negative emotions that you could tap; in the discussion below, we describe five of the most common.

When people are involved with the message, they listen attentively and process using the central route. Emotional appeals create involvement.

FEAR

We experience fear when we perceive that we have no control over a situation that threatens us. We may fear physical harm or psychological harm. Fear is reduced when the threat is eliminated or when we escape. If as a speaker you can use examples, stories, and statistics that create fear in your audience, they will be more involved in hearing how your proposal can eliminate the source of their fear or allow them to escape. For example, in a speech whose goal was to convince the audience that they were at risk of developing high blood pressure, the speaker might begin by personalizing the statistics on heart disease.

> One out of every three Americans age 18 and older has high blood pressure. It is a primary cause of stroke, heart disease, heart failure, kidney disease, and blindness. It triples a person's chance of developing heart disease, and boosts the chance of stroke seven times and the chance of congestive heart failure six times. Look at the person on your right, look at the person on your left. If they don't get it, chances are, you will. Today, I'd like to convince you that you are at risk for developing high blood pressure.

GUILT

We feel guilt when we personally violate a moral, ethical, or religious code that we hold dear. Guilt is especially keen in situations where the violation is associated with how we believe we should conduct ourselves in relationship to others. We experience guilt as a gnawing sensation that we have done something wrong. When we feel guilty, we are energized or motivated to "make things right" or to atone for our transgression. As a speaker, you can evoke feelings of guilt in your audience so that they pay attention to your arguments. To be effective, your proposal must provide a way for the audience to repair or atone for the damage their transgression has caused or to avoid future violations. For example, in a speech designed to motivate the audience to take their turn as designated drivers, a speaker might evoke guilt like this:

> Have you ever promised your mom that you wouldn't ride in a car with someone who had been drinking? And then turned around and got in the car with your buddy even though you both had had a few? You know that wasn't right. Lying to your mother, putting yourself and your buddy at risk . . . (pause) but what can you do? Well, today I'm going to show you how you can avoid all that guilt, live up to your promises to Mom, and keep both you and your buddy safe.

SHAME

We feel shame when we have violated a moral code and it is revealed to someone we think highly of. The more egregious our behavior or the more we admire the person who has found out, the more shame we experience. When we feel shame, we are motivated to "redeem" ourselves in the eyes of that person. Likewise, we can be convinced to refrain from doing something in order to avoid feelings of shame. If in your speech you can evoke feelings of shame and then demonstrate how your proposal can either redeem someone after a violation has occurred or prevent feelings of shame, then you can motivate the audience to carefully consider your arguments. For example, in a speech advocating thankfulness, the speaker might use a shame-based approach by quoting the old saying, "I cried because I had no shoes until I met a man who had no feet."

ANGER

When we are faced with an obstacle that stands in the way of something we want, we experience anger. We also experience anger when someone demeans us or someone we love. As with all emotions, the intensity of what we feel varies. We can be mildly annoyed, or we can experience a level of anger that short-circuits the reasoning process and leads to blind rage. Speakers who choose to evoke anger in their audience members must be careful that they don't incite so much anger that reasoning processes are short-circuited. You will recall that in the opening vignette, the speaker left the audience so riled up that instead of using their energy to thoughtfully probe their own beliefs, the audience responded to a rabble-rouser's call and rioted.

When we feel anger, we want to strike back at the person or overcome the situation that is thwarting our goals or demeaning us. So in your speeches, if you can rouse your audience's anger and then show how your proposal will enable them to achieve their goals or stop or prevent the demeaning that has occurred, you can motivate them to listen to you and think about what you have said. For example, suppose you want to convince the audience to support a law requiring the active notification of a community when a sex offender is released from prison and living in the neighborhood. You might arouse the audience's anger to get their attention by personalizing the story of Megan Kanka:

> She was your little girl, just seven years old, and the light of your world. She had a smile that could bring you to your knees. And she loved puppies. So when that nice man who had moved in down the street invited her in to see his new puppy, she didn't hesitate. But she didn't get the puppy, and you didn't ever see her alive again. He beat her, he raped her, and then he strangled her. He packaged her body in an old toy chest and dumped it in a park. Your seven-year-old princess would never dig in a toy chest again or slip down the slide in that park. And that hurts. But what makes you really angry is, she wasn't his first. But you didn't know that. Because no one bothered to tell you that the guy down the street was likely to kill little girls. The cops knew it. But they couldn't tell you. You, the one who was supposed to keep her safe, didn't know. Angry? You bet. Yeah, he's behind bars again, but you still don't know who's living down the street from you. But you can. There is a law pending before Congress that will require active notification of the community when a known sex offender takes up residence, and today I'm going to tell how you can help to get this passed.[7]

SADNESS

When we fail to achieve a goal or experience a loss or separation, we feel sad. Unlike other negative emotions, whose energy is projected outward, when we feel sad, we tend to withdraw and become isolated. Because sadness, like the other negative emotions, is an unpleasant feeling, we look for ways to end it. This can happen through the actions of others when they notice our withdrawal and try to comfort us. Because we withdraw when we are sad, sadness helps us to focus inward, pondering what has happened and trying to make sense of it. As a result, when we are sad, we are already "looking for answers." So, speeches that help us understand and find answers for what has happened can comfort us and help relieve this unpleasant feeling. For example, after 9/11 many Americans were sad. Yes, they were also afraid and angry, but overlaying it all was profound sadness for those who had been lost, and what had been lost. The questions "Why? Why did they do this? Why do they hate us so?" capture the national melancholy. So when politicians suggest that they understand the answers to these questions and can repair the relationships that led to 9/11, Americans listen and think about what they say.

Evoking Positive Emotions

Just as evoking negative emotions can cause audience members to take a central processes path and think about what you are saying, so too can you increase audience involvement with your proposal by tapping positive emotions. With negative emotions, our goal is to show how our proposal will help the audience to reduce or avoid the feeling. With positive emotions, our goal is to help the audience sustain or develop the feeling. Five of the positive emotions that can motivate the audience to become involved in listening to your arguments are discussed below.

HAPPINESS/JOY

Happiness or joy is the buildup of positive energy we experience when we accomplish something, when we have a satisfying interaction or relationship, or when we see or possess objects that appeal to us. Think of how you felt when you won that ribbon in grade school, or when you found out that you got an "A" on that volcano project in fourth grade. Think of how you felt when you heard that special someone say "I love you" for the very first time. Or think about that birthday when you received that toy that you had been dreaming about. In each of these cases you were happy, maybe even so happy that you were joyous. As a speaker, if you can show how your proposal will lead your audience members to be happy or joyful, then they are likely to listen and to think about your proposal. For example, suppose that you want to motivate your audience to attend a couples encounter weekend where they will learn how to "rekindle" their relationship with a partner. If you can remind them about how they felt early in the relationship and then prove how the weekend can reignite those feelings, they will listen.

PRIDE

When you experience self-satisfaction and an increase to your self-esteem as the result of something that you have accomplished or that someone you identify with has accomplished, you feel pride. "We're number one. . . . We're number one. . ." is the chant of the crowd feeling pride in the accomplishment of "their" team. Whereas happiness is related to feelings of pleasure, pride is related to feelings of self-worth. So, if in your speech you can demonstrate how your proposal will help your audience members to feel good about themselves, they will be more involved in hearing what you have to say. For example, suppose you want to convince your audience to volunteer to work on the newest Habitat for Humanity house being constructed in your community. You might involve them by alluding to the pride they will feel when they see the house they have helped to build standing where there was once a vacant lot.

RELIEF

When a threatening situation has been alleviated, we feel the positive emotion of relief. In relief, the emotional energy that is experienced is directed inward, and we relax and put down our guard. Thus, relief is not usually accompanied by overt action. As a speaker, if you want to use relief as a way to motivate audience members to be involved in your arguments, then you will want to combine it with the negative emotion of fear. For example, suppose your goal is to convince the audience that they are not at risk for high blood pressure. You might use the same personalization of statistics that was described in the example of fear appeals, but instead of proving that the audience is at risk, you could promise relief. Your audience would then listen and evaluate whether they believed your arguments in order to experience relief from the fear of high blood pressure.

HOPE

The emotional energy that stems from believing you can beat the odds is called hope. When you yearn for better things, you are feeling hope. Like relief, hope is a positive emotion that has its roots in a difficult or problem situation. Whereas relief causes you to relax and let down your guard, hope energizes you to take action to overcome the situation. Hope empowers. As with relief, hope appeals are usually accompanied by fear appeals. So, you can get audience members to listen to you by showing them how your proposal provides a plan for overcoming a difficult situation. In this problem solution organization, you can embed both fear and hope appeals. For example, if your proposal is that adopting a low-fat diet will reduce the risk of high blood pressure, you can use the same personalization of statistics that were cited in the example of fear, but change the ending to state: "Today, I'm going to explain to you how you can beat the odds by adopting a low-fat diet." This offer of hope should influence your audience to listen to and adopt your plan.

COMPASSION

When we feel selfless concern for the suffering of some other person that energizes us to try to relieve that suffering, we feel compassion. Speakers can evoke audience members' feeling of compassion by vividly describing the suffering being endured by someone. Then the audience will be motivated to listen to the speaker to see how the speaker's proposal plans to end that suffering. For example, throughout the sample speech on corneal donations at the end of this chapter, the speaker works to elicit strong feelings of compassion. The introduction invites the audience to imagine themselves as victims of corneal disease. The particular examples depict a wide cross section of people who have been blinded by problems that this proposal can remedy. Even the section transitions echo the theme with the mantra, "No one who has seen the . . . caused solely by corneal . . . can doubt the need or the urgency." Throughout, this speech uses vivid language to generate feelings of compassion that will allow audience members to seriously consider the proposal that implicitly requires them to acknowledge their own mortality.

As you prepare your speech, especially when you are creating introductions and conclusions and selecting supporting material, you will want to consider how you can use emotional appeals to increase audience members' involvement with your proposal. In this way, you can influence the likelihood that members of your audience will use the emotional energy that you have generated to use the central processing route. This means that they will listen closely and evaluate your arguments, internalizing what you have said as they make a careful decision. To explore one speaker's use of emotional appeals, use your Challenge of Effective Speaking CD-ROM to access Web Resource 14.1: Terrorism and Islam: Maintaining the Faith. To see a video clip of a student speaker appealing to her audience's emotions, use your Challenge of Effective Speaking CD-ROM to access the chapter resources for Chapter 14 at the Challenge Web site. Click on "Environmental Racism (1)" in the left-hand menu.

Cueing Your Audience through Credibility: Demonstrating Goodwill

Although you may try your best to emotionally involve your audience with what you are advocating, not all audience members will choose the central processing route. Some will choose to pay minimal attention to your arguments and will instead use simple cues to decide whether or not to accept your proposal. The most important cue that people use when they process information by the peripheral route is the credibility of the speaker. In Chapter 5 we discussed three characteristics of a speaker (expertise, trustworthiness, and personableness) that audience members pay attention to when evaluating the speaker's credibility. We also described how, as you were speaking, you could demonstrate being expert, trustworthy, and personable. You may want to go back to Chapter 5 and review our suggestions. A fourth characteristic of credibility is especially important in persuasive settings, influencing whether audience members who are processing the speech on the peripheral route believe what the speaker is advocating. This is called goodwill.

Bono

Credibility and the Rock Star

Does fame derived from being a rock star give someone credibility to speak on third world debt, AIDS, or free trade? Well, there is certainly no question that Bono, the lead singer for the band U2, arguably one of the most celebrated rock bands of our time, has used his fame to gain an audience for his views on these and other issues.

In fact, most of his time these days is spent not so much performing on stage with his *rock* group, but speaking on behalf of his *humanitarian* group, DATA.org (Debt, AIDS, Trade, Africa). DATA.org raises awareness—and dollars—to fight hunger and disease, and to advocate for changes to fair trade policies and for third world debt relief. It's almost commonplace to see a news clip of Bono speaking about his relief efforts, such as those he undertook in Malawi: "I've seen the eyes of the people dying three to a bed—it's children they leave behind . . . eighteen million AIDS orphans by the end of the decade in Africa alone."[1]

While Bono's fame certainly gives him visibility, his credibility to speak on these issues derives not simply from his fame that gives him "personableness," but more importantly stems from his trustworthiness. In the lyrics that Bono writes we see reflected the same deeply held beliefs he advocates through his nonprofit organization: "And today the millions cry / We eat and drink while tomorrow they die / The real battle just begun."[2] We see a consistency between what he sings and what he says. Finally, Bono's advocacy is powerful because in it he demonstrates goodwill. He chooses to use his voice and the power of his fame not to further his own ambitions, but rather to help those who are voiceless and powerless. So in Bono we see how fame coupled with credibility can be a powerful tool for effecting change.

---

[1] Bono, "Make AIDS a Crucial Topic at Both Conventions" [Op-Ed], *Boston Globe,* 25 July 2004.

[2] U2, "Sunday, Bloody Sunday," 1982.

---

goodwill a perception that the audience forms of a speaker who they believe understands them, empathizes with them, and is responsive to them

It was the Greek philosopher Aristotle (384–322 B.C.E.) who first observed that a speaker's credibility was dependent on the audience's perception of the speaker's goodwill. Today, we define **goodwill** as a perception that the audience forms of a speaker who they believe understands them, empathizes with them, and is responsive to them.[8] In other words, goodwill is the audience's take on the speaker's intentions toward them. When audience members believe in the speaker's goodwill, they are willing to believe what the speaker says. Especially in situations where the audience may not have high personal involvement with the topic, their perceptions of the speaker's goodwill helps determine their response to the message.

Recall the union contract example that we discussed as we explained the ELM model. Suppose you are one of the people who has had little direct experience with the union health insurance benefit plan and don't really expect to need it in the foreseeable future. Because you have low involvement with this issue, you are likely to be processing what the union rep is saying along a peripheral route. Under these circumstances, you may either accept or reject the union rep's recommendation based on what you think of the rep. Key to your decision will be whether you believe that this union rep has your best interests at heart. If you think that the union leadership is out of touch with the membership, doesn't really identify with their day-to-day experiences, or isn't responsive to them, then you will be suspicious of the proposal and may decide to vote against it because

Throughout the September 11 crisis, then Mayor Rudy Giuliani was seen as credible because of the goodwill he displayed.

you don't perceive that the union leadership really cares about you. On the other hand, if, as she speaks, the rep demonstrates that she understands you and your situation, empathizes with it, and has openly listened to and accommodated the wishes of the membership, then on this basis alone, you are likely to vote to accept the plan.

When you speak, then, in addition to establishing your expertise, trustworthiness, and personableness, you will want to demonstrate your goodwill toward your audience. Just as with the other dimensions of credibility, it is unethical to fake goodwill. So you should only advocate for proposals that you believe are in the best interest of the audience.

Let's take a closer look at what goodwill entails. The better you know audience members' experiences, circumstances, and desires, the better able you will be to formulate proposals that they will see as in their best interests. A thorough audience analysis will help you. For example, as she explains the proposal, the union rep can build goodwill by demonstrating her understanding of the membership. By referencing membership facts, she can personalize one aspect of the proposal:

> I know that about 40% of you have little use for eye care, which is a new part of the health plan, but for the 60% of you who wear glasses or have family members who wear glasses, this plan will not only pay for your annual eye exam, but it will also pay 30% of the cost of new glasses or 25% of the cost of new contact lenses. This will mean about $250 in your pocket each year and with less overtime predicted for this year, that's a real benefit.

Not only must you understand your audience, but speakers who are able to show goodwill also empathize with their audience. **Empathy** is the ability to see the world through the eyes of someone else. When we empathize, we put aside our own ideas and feelings and try to experience something from another's point of view. If you do not understand your audience, you will be unable to empathize with them. But empathizing requires you to go beyond understanding to identify emotionally with your audience members' views.

Empathizing with the views of the audience doesn't mean that you accept them as your own. It does mean that you acknowledge them as valid. Although

empathy the ability to see the world through the eyes of someone else

your speech may be designed to change audience members' views, the sensitivity you show to audience members' feelings will demonstrate your goodwill. For example, the union rep might demonstrate empathy during her presentation as she says:

> I can imagine what it will be like for some of you who, under this plan, will go to the drugstore and find that there is a high co-pay required for a drug you take that is not on the formulary of this plan. But I also guarantee the plan formulary will have drugs that your doctor can prescribe that are direct substitutes, or you will be able to appeal.

Finally, to demonstrate goodwill, you will want to be responsive to the audience. Speakers who are **responsive** show that they care about the audience by acknowledging feedback from the audience, especially subtle negative cues. This feedback may occur during the presentation, but it also may have occurred prior to the speech. For example, during her presentation, the union rep can demonstrate responsiveness by referencing feedback that the membership provided to the negotiating team before negotiations began:

> Before we started negotiations, we surveyed you, our membership, asking what changes you wanted to see to health care in the new contract. The number one concern for 75% of you was keeping the co-pay on office visits at $10 per visit, and we were able to get management to agree to that.

Or if, as she speaks, she notices that some members of the audience are looking disgusted and shaking their heads, she might respond,

> I can see that some of you are disappointed with the increase in premiums, and I understand that. I wish we could have done better on this issue. But the fact is, health care costs have gone up 15% nationwide.

By establishing goodwill, you enhance your credibility with the audience. This is especially important for persuading those who are not personally involved with your proposal.

Motivating Your Audience to Act: The Speech to Actuate

In speeches in which your specific goal is to convince, you affect your audience members' attitudes by using emotional appeals to involve the audience so that it listens to, evaluates, and internalizes your well-reasoned arguments. Just because your audience intellectually agrees with your arguments, however, doesn't mean that they will choose to act on what you have said. Appeals to emotion can prompt audience members to be involved with your topic and to think carefully about your arguments. Demonstrating your credibility can cue audience members when they are uninvolved. But when your goal is to motivate audience members to take action, you will have to provide them with incentives to act that outweigh the costs. That is, you will have to demonstrate how, by behaving as you advocate, they can increase the likelihood that they will fulfill their unmet needs. For example, if you want your audience to vote for candidate A, you will have to show how the election of candidate A will meet needs the audience feels and will leave them better off than if they didn't vote or voted for another candidate.

In this section we turn our attention to a particular type of persuasive speech, the **speech to actuate,** which moves beyond affecting audience beliefs and attitudes and motivates the audience to act. In the speech to actuate, you not only present convincing arguments for your audience to consider, but go beyond this, motivating the audience by explaining how taking the action you recommend offers incentives that will satisfy their unmet needs. We begin by discussing how

responsive showing care about the audience by acknowledging feedback from the audience, especially subtle negative cues

speech to actuate a speech that moves beyond affecting audience beliefs and attitudes and motivates the audience to act

incentives work in helping people meet their needs. Then we use this framework to explain how you can identify and articulate incentives for your audience. Finally, we will describe the motivated sequence organizational pattern, a fifth way you can arrange the arguments in your persuasive speeches that is especially suited to speeches to actuate.

Understanding How Incentives Motivate Behavior

An **incentive** is a reward that is promised if a particular action is taken or goal is reached.[9] Incentives encourage us to act. Incentives can be physical rewards such as food, shelter, money, and sex. They can be psychological rewards such as positive self-concept and peace of mind. They can be social rewards such as acceptance, status, and popularity. Regardless of the type of incentive offered, if a person values it, that person will be motivated to take goal-related action. Suppose you hear a speech whose goal is to motivate you to recycle aluminum cans. The speaker uses the incentive that you can earn a penny a can by taking aluminum cans to the local recycling center. Would hearing that you could earn a penny per can be an incentive for you to recycle? It depends. If you were really destitute and you were hungry, you might go home, disassemble the soda pop can pyramid you and your roommate have built in the living room, take the cans to the recycling center, and head to the local market to get some food. In this case, the money offered for recycling was an effective incentive that motivated your action. Suppose, however, that you're not destitute. Even if you have lots of easy access to cans, a penny a can may not be enough to propel you into acting.

As we evaluate the incentives that are meant to motivate us to act, we usually balance them against the costs that we think we will incur. **Costs** are expenditures that we incur when we act. Like incentives, costs can be physical (time, money, energy), psychological (uncertainty, confusion), or social (ostracism, humiliation). Costs are deterrents to action.

Obviously, then, people are more likely to be motivated to act by incentives if they perceive that the incentives outweigh the costs. The greater the costs associated with an action, the less likely we are to act, even if we value the incentive. According to Thibaut and Kelley, who wrote about social exchanges, each of us seeks exchange situations with a favorable cost/reward ratio (where rewards outweigh costs).[10] So we will continue our present behavior unless we are shown that by changing our behavior we can either lower our costs or raise our rewards. Let's look at an example. Suppose that you are asking your audience to use some of their free time to volunteer an hour a week to help adults learn to read. The time you are asking them to give would be perceived as a cost because they would have to give up time that they usually spend relaxing. So, if you are going to motivate your audience to actually do this, you will have to describe to them the rewards that they will experience if they volunteer. For these to be incentives, the promised rewards must be perceived to outweigh the cost of giving up free time.

incentive a reward that is promised if a particular action is taken or goal is reached

costs expenditures that we incur when we act; may be physical, psychological, or social

When Bill Gates talks about using Microsoft products, he is likely to give the audience incentives to motivate their behavior.

© Gary Nolan/Corbis

As a speaker, then, you must show your audience that the time, energy, or money investment for behaving as you suggest is small when compared to the rewards to be gained from acting.

Using Incentives to Meet Needs

Why was the penny a can an incentive to the hungry person and not an incentive to the sated person? Because we make our cost/reward decisions based on our needs. Incentives are more likely to motivate people when they satisfy a strong but unmet need. Various ways of categorizing needs have been developed to help us understand types of needs. One of the most widely recognized is Maslow's hierarchy of needs. Abraham Maslow divided people's needs into five categories, illustrated in Exhibit 14.1: (1) physiological needs, including food, drink, and life-sustaining temperature; (2) safety and security needs, including long-term survival and stability; (3) belongingness and love needs, including the need to identify with friends, loved ones, and family; (4) esteem needs, ego gratification including the quest for material goods, recognition, and power or influence; and (5) self-actualization needs, including the need to develop one's self to realize one's full potential and engage in creative acts.[11] Maslow believed that these needs were hierarchical; that is, your "lower-order" needs had to be met before you would be motivated by "higher-order" needs. In theory, then, a person cannot be motivated to meet an esteem need of gaining recognition until basic physiological, safety, and belongingness and love needs have been met.

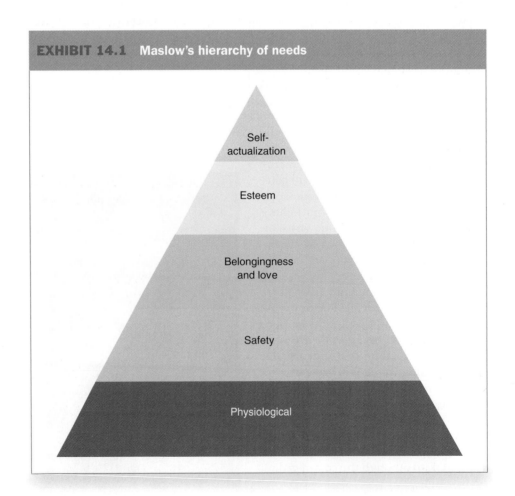

EXHIBIT 14.1   Maslow's hierarchy of needs

The hierarchical nature of needs is still debated because there is evidence that at times some people will sacrifice lower-order needs to satisfy higher-order ones. Nevertheless, as a speaker, if you can tie the incentives that accompany your proposal with unmet audience needs, you will increase the likelihood that the audience will take the action you are proposing. Let's see how this could work in the volunteering for literacy speech with a college student audience. Suppose that during the speech you point out that people who volunteer thirty hours or more a year receive a recognition certificate and are invited to attend a private dinner with the stars of the hot band that will be headlining the big spring campus concert. After announcing this, you add, "I know that while most of you care about literacy, you're thinking about what else you could do with that hour. But the really cool part of spending your time as a literacy volunteer is that not only will you feel good about yourself because you have improved someone's life, but you also will be able to list this service and recognition on your resúmé. And as a bonus, you'll get to brag to your friends about having dinner with several celebrities." In the first part of this short statement, you have enumerated three incentives that are tied to volunteering: a physical incentive (an award certificate), a psychological incentive of enhanced self-concept (I feel good about myself because I have helped someone else), and a social incentive (having dinner with an elite group and meeting celebrities). In the second part, you have also tied each incentive to a need that it can satisfy. With an enhanced resúmé, people are more likely to be able to get jobs that provide money for food and shelter. If by helping someone else we feel better about ourselves, then we have met a self-actualization need. And by attending the private dinner, we might satisfy both esteem needs and belongingness needs.

As you prepare your speech, you not only want to understand the needs of the audience and the incentives that are attached to acting as you suggest, but you also need to understand what the action you are proposing will cost the audience and how this cost may result in increasing a need. In your speech, you will want to address how the incentives you highlight will compensate for the cost or will result in the need that is threatened being fulfilled in an alternative way. For example, in the literacy speech, one obvious cost is the hour of free time each week that might take away from time audience members currently spend with their friends. This could threaten their belongingness need. To address this concern, you might point out, "Now I know you might be concerned about the time this will take away from your friends, but rest your mind. Not only will your friends understand and admire you (esteem need substitute for belongingness), but at the Literacy Center you're going to have time before the tutoring starts to meet other volunteers (belongingness) and they are some really cool people (esteem). I know a couple who just got engaged, and they met through their volunteering (big-time belongingness).

If you discover that you cannot relate your material to basic audience needs, then you probably need to reconsider what you are asking the audience to do. For example, if you discover that most of your audience members are overcommitted and have no time to take on an additional volunteer activity, then it is unrealistic to ask them to volunteer an hour a week. But you may be able to persuade them to donate a book or money to buy a book for the literacy library.

Finally, if your incentives are to motivate your audience, the audience must be convinced that there is a high likelihood that if they act as you suggest they will receive the rewards. It is important, therefore, that you discuss only those incentives that you have strong reason to believe are closely tied to the action you are requesting and are received by almost all people who act in the recommended way. Although there is an annual award given to the literacy volunteer who has donated the most time that year, mentioning this in your speech is unlikely to motivate the audience because only one person receives it, and the cost is very high.

So, when you want to move an audience to action, you need to understand their needs and explain the rewards they can receive by taking the action you suggest. You also need to make sure that the incentives you mention fulfill unmet needs in the audience.

The Motivated Sequence Persuasive Speech Pattern

motivated sequence a form of persuasive organization that combines a problem solution pattern with explicit appeals designed to motivate the audience

In the previous chapter we explained four of the five organizational patterns that can be used in persuasive speeches. Having read this chapter, you now understand how to use emotion to motivate audience members to listen to and really think about your arguments. In addition, you know how to use incentives to motivate people to act. The fifth pattern, the **motivated sequence,** is a form of persuasive organization that combines a problem solution pattern with explicit appeals designed to motivate the audience. Allan Monroe articulated the motivated sequence as a distinct speech pattern in the 1930s. In the motivated sequence, the normal introduction, body, and conclusion are unified into a five-step sequence, described below.

1. The Attention Step. The attention step replaces the traditional introduction. Like an introduction, it should begin with a statement that can generate attention. Startling statements, rhetorical questions, quotations, or short narratives will all serve this purpose. Then you should pique the audience's curiosity by talking about the value of what you are going to say. During the attention step you might also refer to the knowledge and experiences you have that build your credibility. Finally, just as in a traditional introduction, you will want to state your purpose and preview the rest of the speech.

2. The Need Step. The need step should explore the nature of the problem that gives rise to the need for change. In it you will point out the conditions that are unsatisfactory, using statistics, examples, and expert opinion to bolster your argument. Then you will describe the implications or ramifications of this problem. What is happening because the condition is allowed to continue? Finally, you will allude to how the audience might be instrumental in changing the situation.

3. The Satisfaction Step. Having developed a rational argument that there is a need for change, in the satisfaction step you explain your solution to the problem. In this step you will show, point by point, how what you are proposing will satisfy each of the needs that you articulated in the step before. If there are other places where your proposal has been tried and has been successful, you will want to mention these. In addition, you will want to present and refute any objections to the proposal that you can anticipate.

4. The Visualization Step. In the visualization step you will ask your audience to imagine what will happen if your proposal is implemented and is successful. Alternatively, you can ask the audience to visualize how things will be if your proposal is not adopted, or you can do both and have the audience experience the comparison. Obviously, the more descriptive and graphic your visualization step, the more likely it is to have an impact on the audience.

5. The Action Appeal Step. In this final step, which functions like a conclusion, you might quickly review your main ideas, but then you will emphasize the specific belief or action that you are directing your audience toward. You will also state or restate your own commitment and action that you have taken. Finally, you will want to conclude with a quote, story, or other element that is emotionally compelling.

Let's look at a short outline of what a speech asking the audience to support a school tax levy would look like if it were organized using the motivated sequence.

Proposition: I want the audience to vote in favor of the school tax levy that is on the ballot in November.

I. **Attention Step**

    A. Comparisons of worldwide test scores in math and science show the United States continues to lose ground.

    B. I've made an extensive study of this problem, and today I'm going to tell you how you can help stop this decline.

    C. I'll start by describing the problem, then I will tell you what you should do and why it will help.

II. **Need Step:** The local schools are underfunded.

    A. The current funding is insufficient and has resulted in program cuts.

    B. Qualified teachers leave because of stagnant wages.

    C. A threatened state takeover of local schools would lead to more bureaucracy and less learning.

III. **Satisfaction Step:** The proposed local tax levy is large enough to solve these problems.

    A. Programs will be restored.

    B. Qualified teachers will be compensated so they will stay.

    C. We will retain local control.

    D. You'll once again have pride in your community.

IV. **Visualization Step:** Imagine the best and imagine the worst.

    A. What it will be like if we pass the levy. How will you feel?

    B. What it will be like if we don't. How will you feel?

V. **Action Appeal Step:** Vote "yes" for the levy in November.

    A. If you want to see schools improve and the United States catch up to the rest of the world, vote for the levy.

    B. Come join me. I'm registered, I'm ready, I'm voting for the levy.

    C. It costs to be the best in the world. Where there is pain, there is gain.

    D. They say it takes a village, so you can make a difference.

All persuasive speeches, regardless of organizational pattern, use emotional appeals, include demonstrations of speaker credibility, and can be used to change attitudes and behavior. But as you can see from the description and the sample outline, in the motivated sequence the use of emotion, credibility, and incentives is built into the structure of the speech. To see a video clip of a student speaker motivating her audience to act, use your Challenge of Effective Speaking CD-ROM to access the chapter resources for Chapter 14 at the Challenge Web site. Click on "Environmental Racism (2)" in the left-hand menu.

Guidelines for Developing an Ethical Persuasive Speech

We hope that in this chapter we have motivated you to consider the various ways of motivating your audience to believe and to act. Unfortunately, some speakers get so involved in the process of motivation that they fail to remember that use of all of these forms must still meet ethical standards. In Chapter 1 we discussed the fundamental ethical behaviors of truthfulness and crediting the ideas that are used in the speech. At this point, we want to look at six additional ethical guidelines that speakers should follow when their specific goal is to convince the audience to believe a certain way or to move the audience to action.

1. Ethical persuasive speeches aim to improve the well-being of the audience by advocating the honest belief of the speaker. If you have reason to believe that the members of the audience will be hurt or disadvantaged if they believe what you say or do what you ask, then you should not give the speech. At times we can get excited about seeing what we can do as a devil's advocate—that is, argue for a belief or action that is totally counter to anything we really believe in just to stir up discussion. Although this can be fun when we're dealing with a few friends who just enjoy the spirit of debate, in the real world it is unethical for you to give a speech that calls for the audience to believe something that you do not believe. So, for your persuasive speech, phrase a proposition that you enthusiastically endorse.

2. Ethical persuasive speeches provide choice. In any speech, you are free to provide the audience with reasoning that supports your position in a way that encourages them to think about and evaluate what you have said before making up their own mind. Although it is possible to persuade an audience by manipulating their emotions, using smear tactics to attack opposite points of view (or advocates of those points of view) or coercing them with serious threats is unethical.

3. Ethical persuasive speeches use supporting information that is representative. In your persuasive speech, you will use evidence in the form of statistics, expert opinion, and examples to support your claims. You can probably find an item of "evidence" to support any claim, but ethical speakers make sure that the evidence they cite is representative of all the evidence that might be used. Although you may use an individual item to show that something is possible, or can happen, you do not want to give the impression that the item is commonplace. In short, it is unethical to misrepresent what a *body* of evidence (as opposed to a single item) would show if all of it were presented to the audience.

4. Ethical persuasive speeches use emotional appeals to engage the audience in the rational thought process. Emotional appeals are a legitimate part of a persuasive speech when they are used to increase the involvement of the audience so that audience members choose the central processing route to listen to, think about, evaluate, and personally decide whether to believe or act. When excessive emotional appeals are used as the basis of persuasion instead of logical reasons, then although the speech might be effective, it is unethical.

5. Ethical persuasive speeches honestly present the incentives and costs associated with an advocated action. Because the goal of ethical speaking is to equip

Ethical persuasion requires that the audience have free choice to accept or reject the ideas of the speaker without fear of retribution. Under totalitarian political systems, coercion rather than persuasion is the norm.

© Reuters/Corbis

the audience with the information that it needs to make a rational choice, ethical speakers are careful to present honestly all the known costs and incentives associated with a recommended action. It is unethical to downplay costs or overstate incentives.

6. Ethical persuasive speeches honestly present the speaker's credibility. Because some audience members will process what you say along a peripheral route, using your credibility as the primary factor that determines what they will believe or how they will act, as an ethical speaker you will want to present your expertise and trustworthiness honestly. It is unethical to act as if you know a great deal about a subject when you do not. In fact, most people believe that it is unethical to try to convince others of something on which you are not extremely well informed because you may inadvertently misrepresent the arguments and information. Finally, ethical speakers disclose interests that may have inadvertently biased their arguments and may place their interests and those of their audience at odds. You might say, for example, "I think you should know that I work for the Literacy Project as a paid intern, so even though I will do my best to give you the most accurate information possible on this subject, I may not be totally objective in my comments."

As you work on your speech, you will want to continually remind yourself of your ethical responsibilities. It's easy to get caught up in trying to build arguments and lose sight of your bigger ethical responsibility to your audience.

REFLECT ON ETHICS

Alexandro, a student who had worked full-time for three years before returning to college for his sophomore year, decided that for his final speech he would motivate the members of his class to donate money to the Downtown Food Bank. He was excited about this topic because he had begun volunteering for the Food Bank during those last three years and had seen firsthand the face of hunger in this community.

He planned to support his speech with three reasons: (1) that an increasing number of people in the community needed food; (2) that government agencies were unable to provide sufficient help; and (3) that a high percentage of every dollar donated to the Food Bank went into food. As he researched these points, he discovered that the number of families who were in need in the community had not really risen in the past two years and that government sponsorship of the Food Bank had increased. Then, when he examined the Food Bank's financial statements, he discovered that only 68 percent of every dollar donated was actually spent on food. Faced with this evidence, he just didn't think his reasons and evidence were very strong.

Yet, because of his experience, he still thought the Food Bank was a cause that deserved financial support, so he decided to focus his entire speech on the heart-warming case of the Hernandez family. Ineligible for government assistance, over the years this family of ten had managed to survive because of the aid they received from the Food Bank. Today, several of the children had graduated from college, and one was a physician working in the barrio. By telling this heart-wrenching story of the struggle to survive, Alexandro thought he would be successful in persuading the class.

1. Would it be ethical for Alexandro to give his speech in this way? Why or why not?
2. If not, what would he need to do to make the speech ethical?

Speech to Actuate

1. Prepare a four- to seven-minute persuasive speech in which your goal is to persuade the audience to act. To help you prepare your speech and your outline, use your Challenge of Effective Speaking CD-ROM to access Speech Builder Express and complete the Speech Planning Action Step Activities.

2. As an addendum to the outline, write a persuasive speech adaptation plan in which you describe:

   a. The reasoning process for your arguments.

   b. How you will use emotional appeals to involve your audience so that they process what you are saying on the central route. List the emotions you plan to appeal to, and explain why you chose these.

   c. How you will establish your credibility by demonstrating your expertise, trustworthiness, personableness, and goodwill.

   d. The incentives for action and the needs that they will satisfy.

   e. The persuasive organizational pattern that you will use, and why you chose it.

Speech to Actuate Evaluation Form

Primary Criteria

_____ 1. Did the speaker use statistics, expert opinion, and examples that had emotional impacts on the audience?

_____ 2. Did the speaker appeal to negative emotions? If so, check all that were tapped: ___ fear ___ guilt ___ anger ___ shame ___ sadness

Were the appeals ___ very effective ___ somewhat effective ___ ineffective?

_____ 3. Did the speaker appeal to positive emotions? If so, check all that were tapped:

___ happiness/joy ___ pride ___ relief ___ hope ___ compassion

Were the appeals ___ very effective ___ somewhat effective ___ ineffective?

_____ 4. Did the speaker establish credibility?

___ Did the speaker establish expertise?

___ Did the speaker demonstrate trustworthiness?

___ Did the speaker demonstrate personableness?

___ Did the speaker demonstrate goodwill?

_____ 5. Did the speaker identify the incentives for taking action?

___ Did the speaker show that incentives outweighed costs?

___ Did the speaker show how incentives would satisfy unmet audience needs?

_____ 6. If the speaker used the motivated sequence, was each of the steps clearly evident?

General Criteria

_____ **1.** Was the specific goal clear?

_____ **2.** Was the introduction effective in creating interest and involving the audience in the speech?

_____ **3.** Was the speech organized using an appropriate persuasive pattern?

_____ **4.** Was the language clear, vivid, emphatic, and appropriate?

_____ **5.** Was the conclusion effective in summarizing what had been said and mobilizing the audience to act?

_____ **6.** Was the speech delivered enthusiastically, with vocal expressiveness, fluency, spontaneity, and directness?

Based on these criteria, evaluate the speech as (check one):

_____ excellent _____ good _____ satisfactory _____ fair _____ poor

You can use your Challenge of Effective Speaking CD-ROM to access this checklist online under student resources for Chapter 14 at the Challenge of Effective Speaking Web site.

SAMPLE SPEECH

Open Your Eyes

by Kathleen Sheldon Verderber

The speech that follows was developed and presented by Kathleen (Sheldon) Verderber, one of the authors of your textbook, in a public speaking class she took as an undergraduate student in 1970. It appeared as a sample speech in earlier editions of this textbook. The speech is an excellent example of a speech to actuate using motivated sequence and is being reprinted here in response to requests by instructors who use the text. Unfortunately, the original references have been lost. An adaptation plan was not required by the instructor, so the one provided here has been created for instructional purposes.

You can also use your Challenge of Effective Speaking CD-ROM to watch a video clip of another student, Raimone, presenting the persuasive speech "Become an Entrepreneur." Click on the Speech Interactive icon in the menu at left, then click on Speech Menu in the menu bar at the top of the screen. Select "Become an Entrepreneur" to watch the video (it takes a minute for the video to load).

Audience Adaptation Plan

AUDIENCE ANALYSIS: My audience is composed of traditional-age college student with varying majors and classes. Most are European Americans from working- or middle-class backgrounds.

BACKGROUND KNOWLEDGE: My perception is that my audience knows little about corneal disease and corneal transplants and donation. I think they are an uninformed audience.

CREATING AND MAINTAINING INTEREST: I will involve my audience with heavy use of personalization, appealing to several emotions including guilt, sadness, relief, hope, and most of all, compassion. I will use representative examples as short stories.

ORGANIZATION: I have organized my speech using the motivated sequence.

(continued)

BUILDING CREDIBILITY: (Because the speaker didn't create an adaptation plan, she did nothing to establish her credibility. This was a serious oversight).

MOTIVATION: The incentive that I will offer is that the audience members can act compassionately by signing up to donate. This will fulfill their self-esteem needs—the need to feel benevolent. I will try to overcome the cost of recognizing one's own mortality by presenting two philosophies that put this gift into a positive light.

Outline

SPEECH GOAL: I want my audience to donate their corneas to the local eye bank.

ATTENTION

I. Visualization
   A. Close your eyes and imagine what it would be like not to see
      1. Colors of the sunset
      2. Crisp green of the world after a rain
      3. The faces of those you love
   B. Now open your eyes to see what you couldn't have if you couldn't have opened your eyes.

NEED

II. Describe the appearance and function of corneas.
   A. They are dime-size tough transparent semi-elastic tissue.
   B. Their function is to allow light to enter the lens and retina.
   C. Normally they are so clear that we don't know they are there, but when they are damaged they blur or blot out light.
      1. Imagine looking through a rain-slashed windowpane.
      2. Imagine trying to see while swimming underwater.

(Transition: Shakespeare quote: "To see the world through another man's eyes.")

SATISFACTION

III. Donated corneas are needed for implantation.
   A. Medical science has made the restoration of sight possible.
   B. This generation is the first to have this potential.
   C. There is an urgent need.
   D. The operation must occur within 72 hours and can be 100% effective.

VISUALIZATION

(Transitional refrain: No one who has seen the human tragedy caused solely by corneal disease can doubt the need or the urgency.)

IV. See how donated corneas can return sight to the blind.
   A. Sight was restored to a young mother with corneal disease. (transition refrain)
   B. Sight was restored to a young boy blinded by flying glass. (transition refrain)
   C. Sight was restored to Dr. Belding H. Scribner, inventor of the artificial kidney, the modern dialysis machine. (transition refrain)

V. See the different philosophies for donating corneas:
   A. Philosophy of minister and wife
   B. Philosophy of woman with cancer

ACTION

VI. Donate your corneas by signing the card (or checking box on driver's license).
   A. Donating in your will won't help.
   B. You need to sign the card or check the box.

VII. Repeat Visualization

    A. Close your eyes . . . .

    B. Direct ask: Now open your eyes, look all around you, won't you give some-
one else the chance to open their eyes?

Speech

Read the following speech aloud. Then, analyze it on the basis of primary criteria in
the Speech to Actuate Evaluation Form on pages 286–287.

It is important to note that some of the information in the speech is dated. For
example, today organ donation is widely accepted and corneal transplants are performed on about 40,000 people in the United States each year, making it one of the
most common transplant surgeries around. Today, one eye donor can help up to 10
people through transplanted tissue, and tissue shelf life has been increased. Now, in
most states, you can donate by marking the space provided on your driver's license.
For the past several years, U.S. eye banks have been able to meet the need in the
United States and have been exporting corneas to other countries. But there continues to be no substitute for corneal transplant, and the threat of bioterrorism could
quickly create a shortage.

Speech

Would all of you close your eyes for just a minute? Close them very tightly so that all
of the light is blocked out. Imagine what it would be like to always live in a world of
total darkness such as you are experiencing right now, though only for a moment—
never to see the flaming color of the sunset or the crisp green of the world after the
rain, never seeing the faces of those you love. Now open your eyes, look all around
you, look at all of the things that you couldn't have seen if you couldn't have opened
your eyes.

The bright world we awake to each morning is brought to us through two
dime-sized pieces of tough, transparent, semi-elastic tissue. These are the corneas,
and it is their function to allow light to enter the lens and the retina. Normally,
they are so clear that we don't even know that they are there. However, when they
are scratched or scarred either by accident or disease, they tend to blur or blot out
light. Imagine peering through a rain-slashed windowpane or trying to see while
swimming underwater. This is the way the victims of corneal damage often describe
their vision.

"To see the world through another man's eyes." These words are Shakespeare's,
yet today, it can literally be true. Thanks to the miracle of modern medicine, the operation known as a corneal transplant or a corneal graft has become a reality, giving
thousands of people the opportunity to see. No other generation has had such a profound legacy in its possession. Yet, the universal ignorance on the subject of cornea
donation is appalling. The operation itself is really quite simple; it involves the
corneas of the donor being transplanted into the eyes of the recipient. And if this operation takes place within seventy-two hours after the death of the donor, it can be
100 percent effective.

(continued)

Analysis

*Much of the strength of this speech
results from the speaker's ability to
involve members of the audience
personally and get them to feel
what she is saying. This opening
is a striking example of audience
involvement. She doesn't just tell
them what it would be like—she
has them experience the feeling.
The speaker very successfully lays
the emotional groundwork for total audience attention.*

*In this section the speaker begins
to explain the need. Because most
audience members won't know
much about the cornea and
corneal disease, she has to provide
basic information. Notice how her
vivid word choice helps to quickly
describe the basics and sustains
an emotional tone through this
description. Again, she uses personalization to create involvement: "Imagine peering . . ."*

*Interesting quotation used as a
transition from need step to satisfaction step. Notice how the
speaker uses indirect language as
she begins to draw the audience
into her argument. "No other generation . . ." rather than "we"
gradually introduces the audience
to her solution.*

Her indirectness continues as she moves into the visualization step.

The real effectiveness of this section is the result of the parallel structure and repetition of the key phrase, "No one who has seen . . ." Notice the diverse examples, which meet the test of representativeness: a young New Jersey mother stricken by corneal disease, a young California boy with accident-related corneal damage, and a groundbreaking medical inventor. Also notice how the examples are phrased so as to evoke sadness, relief, and compassion.

The first two examples show the personal effect of successful transplant, but the Scribner example demonstrates a more universal effect. Again, the choice of language is highly evocative.

In this section the speaker anticipates one of the most difficult "costs" associated with corneal donation: the recognition and acceptance by audience members that they are mortal.

Notice how the rationale offered by the minister indirectly addresses concerns about the religious implications of donation. Both examples appeal to the hope for meaning in death.

The speaker now begins the action step. Even in this nuts and bolts section, she continues to use evocative language like "the abyss of darkness." Notice how she starts by explaining what won't work, which narrows the choice she would have the audience make. She minimizes the difficulty ("All you have to do . . .") of complying with her request through her words and through providing the cards to be completed. Wisely, she waits until she is finished to hand these out. She misses several opportunities to establish credibility, including stating that she has already done what she is asking the audience to do. Given the nature of what is being asked, this is a serious oversight.

No one who has seen the human tragedy caused solely by corneal disease can doubt the need or the urgency. Take the case of a young woman living in New Jersey who lost her sight to corneal disease. She gave birth to a baby and two years ago, thanks to a corneal transplant, she saw her three-year-old baby girl for the first time. And no one who had seen this woman's human tragedy caused solely by corneal disease or her great joy at the restoration of her sight can doubt the need or the urgency.

Or take the case of the five-year-old boy in California who was playing by a bonfire when a bottle exploded, flinging bits of glass which lacerated his corneas. His damaged corneas were replaced with healthy ones in an emergency operation, and no one who had seen this little boy's human tragedy caused solely by corneal laceration or the great joy to his young life of receiving his sight back again can doubt the need or the urgency.

Or take the case of Dr. Belding H. Scribner of the University of Washington School of Medicine. Dr. Scribner's eyesight was damaged by a corneal disease that twisted the normally sphere-shaped corneas into cones. A corneal transplant gave Dr. Scribner twenty-twenty corrected vision and allowed him to continue work on his invention—the artificial kidney machine. And no one who has seen this man's human tragedy caused solely by corneal disease, or the great joy brought not only to Dr. Scribner but also to the millions of people that kidney dialysis has saved, can doubt the need or the urgency.

There are many philosophies behind such a gift. One of them was summed up by a minister and his wife who lost their daughter in infancy. They say, "We feel that a part of her goes on living." Or take the case of the young woman who was dying of cancer. She donated her eyes and did so with this explanation: "I want to be useful; being useful brings purpose and meaning to life." Surely if being useful is important, there are few better ways than to donate your corneas to someone who lives after you.

But no matter which philosophy you do adopt, I hope each of you will consider donating your corneas to another who will live after you and who otherwise would have to survive in the abyss of darkness. It will do no good for you to leave your corneas in a regular will if you have one, for as I mentioned earlier there is a seventy-two-hour critical period. If you wish to donate your eyes, it's simple. All you have to do is fill out the form that I will hand out when I am done (*or* take out your wallet, extract your driver's license, turn it over, and check the appropriate organ donation box). Then when you die and no longer have need for your sight, someone who desperately wants the chance to see will be able to.

Will all of you close your eyes again for just a moment? Close them very tightly so that all of the light is blocked out. And once more, imagine what it would be like to live always in a world of total darkness such as you are experiencing right now, though only for a moment—never to see the flaming color of the sunset or the crisp green of the world after the rain, never seeing the faces of those you love. Now open your eyes, look all around you—won't you give someone else the chance to open theirs? ■

Her concluding remarks bring the audience full circle. Although she could have chosen different images, the repetition of the same ones takes the emphasis off the sensory experience and allows the audience to focus on how the experience must feel to the blind. The last line of the speech is a little abrupt, but the "direct ask" given in the context of the emotional tone set throughout the speech is simple but powerful. ■

Summary

Persuasive speeches are based on logical reasons but must also present those reasons in a way that motivates the audience to listen and to think about what the speaker is saying. The elaboration likelihood model (ELM) suggests that when people hear an argument, they can process it in either of two ways. One is a central route, in which they listen carefully, think about the arguments, and then make conscious decisions about what they believe or will do. The second is a peripheral route, in which they make decisions based on simple cues about the speaker's credibility. According to this model, when people are personally involved with a proposition, they are more likely to process it using the central route.

Because audience members become involved with an issue when they have an emotional stake in it, speakers need to use emotional appeals to create involvement. Speakers can evoke negative emotions, including fear, guilt, anger, sadness, and shame, or positive emotions such as happiness/joy, pride, compassion, relief, or hope.

Because some audience members will choose the peripheral route, persuasive speakers need to establish their credibility. In addition to demonstrating their expertise, trustworthiness, and personableness, they also need to demonstrate goodwill—the perception that they have the best interests of the audience at heart.

One type of persuasive speech, the speech to actuate, moves beyond affecting audience beliefs and asks audience members to take action. When you want to move your audience to action, you need to show them the incentives for acting and how these incentives outweigh the costs. You also need to point out how incentives meet audience members' needs. One way to understand needs is through Maslow's hierarchy, which suggests that needs can be classified as physical, safety, belongingness, esteem, and self-actualization.

The fifth persuasive organizational pattern, the motivated sequence, is designed for moving audiences to action. The motivated sequence has five steps: attention, need, satisfaction, visualization, and action.

Finally, persuasive speakers must bear in mind that they have special ethical responsibilities. These include advocating the honest belief of the speaker, providing choice for the audience, using supporting information that is representative, using emotional appeals to engage audience rational thought process, presenting incentives and costs accurately, and honestly presenting speaker credibility.

Now that you've read Chapter 14, use your Challenge of Effective Speaking CD-ROM for quick access to the electronic study resources that accompany this text. Your CD-ROM gives you access to the sample persuasive speech described on pages 287–291, the evaluation checklist shown on pages 286–287, the video of Raimone's speech described on page 287, InfoTrac College Edition, Speech Builder Express, and the Challenge of Effective Speaking Web site. When you get to the Challenge of Effective Speaking home page, click on "Student Book Companion Site" in the Resource box at the right to access the online study aids for this chapter, including the video clips described on pages 275, 283, and 287, a digital glossary, review quizzes, and the chapter activities.

KEY TERMS

At the Challenge of Effective Speaking Web site, select chapter resources for Chapter 14. Print a copy of the glossary for this chapter, test yourself with the electronic flash cards, or complete the crossword puzzle to help you master the following key terms.

central route (270)	**responsive** (278)
peripheral route (270)	**speech to actuate** (278)
emotions (271)	**incentive** (279)
goodwill (276)	**costs** (279)
empathy (277)	**motivated sequence** (282)

INFOTRAC COLLEGE EDITION EXERCISE

Use your Challenge of Effective Speaking CD-ROM to access InfoTrac College Edition. Under the subject "attitude change," click on periodical references. Look for articles that discuss how audiences process information. Make a special effort to find an article or articles by Richard Petty.

WEB RESOURCE

Access the Web resource for this chapter online at the Challenge of Effective Speaking Web site. Select the chapter resources for Chapter 14, then click on "Web Resources."

14.1 Terrorism and Islam: Maintaining the Faith (275)

Ceremonial Speaking: Speeches for Special Occasions

© Susan Van Etten/PhotoEdit

*A society emphasizing social rituals and
manners requires a certain reverence
for words to adequately express
sentiment and feeling.*

William Van O'Connor. "Robert Penn Warren, 'Provincial Poet',"
A Southern Vanguard: The John Peale Bishop Memorial Volume, 1945

The wedding had gone off without a hitch. Now all that stood between the best man and a great night of partying with the bride and groom was one little speech. Who would have thought that it would be so difficult to find exactly the right words to express his feelings when he toasted his best friend from childhood and the woman he had just married?

On special occasions such as weddings and funerals, we may be called on to "say a few words." On these ceremonial occasions, your audience has distinct expectations for what they will hear. So, although the speech plan action steps you have learned will help you prepare your remarks, you also need to understand how the occasion affects what the audience anticipates. This chapter describes six common types of ceremonial speeches given on special occasions—welcomings, introductions, recognition presentations, acceptances, toasts, and tributes and eulogies—as well as speeches for other ceremonial occasions. For each speech type, we describe the normal expectations for the speech and provide some cautionary guidance for you to consider as you prepare.

Welcomings

welcoming speech a brief ceremonial address that greets and expresses pleasure for the presence of a person or an organization

A **welcoming speech** is usually a very brief ceremonial address that greets and expresses pleasure for the presence of a person or an organization. You can welcome someone on your own, but more frequently you will give a welcoming speech as the representative of a group.

Expectations

You must be familiar with the group that you are representing and the occasion for the welcoming. It is surprising how little some members of an organization, a community, or a college or university really know about their organization or community. As you prepare your welcome, you may need to do some research so you can accurately describe the group and the circumstances or occasion to the person you are welcoming.

After expressing appreciation on behalf of your group for the presence of the person or organization, you are expected to provide a brief description of the group and setting to which he or she is being welcomed. The conclusion should briefly express your hope for the outcome of the visit, event, or relationship.

A typical welcoming speech might be as simple as this:

> Today I want to welcome John Sheldon, who is joining us from the North Thurston Club. John, as you are aware, we are a newer club, having been established in 2000. At that time, we had only ten members. But we had big hopes. Today we are 127 members strong, and we raised more than $250,000 last year to support local children's organizations. We hope that our talks here today will lead to closer cooperation between the North Thurston Club and ours here in Yelm.

Considerations

Speeches of welcome should be brief and should set the tone for what is to follow. A humorous welcoming speech is inappropriate if the main focus of the occasion is to be serious. At times you may be asked to give a speech that both welcomes and introduces the speaker or organization. When this is the case, the speech can be longer and should include the type of information described next.

Introductions

A **speech of introduction** is a ceremonial speech that familiarizes the audience with biographical information that establishes the credibility of the person being presented.

Expectations

A speech of introduction often precedes a longer speech. It is expected to establish the credibility of the main speaker by letting the audience know the education, background, and experience of the speaker related to the topic of the speech, and to suggest why the audience should listen.

At times you will be given a resúmé or brief biography of the speaker; at other times you may need to research the speaker's background yourself. Regardless of what you have learned, before you prepare your remarks you should try to contact the speaker and ask what points in the biography the speaker would like you to emphasize.

In general, the better known the person is, the less you need to say about him or her. For instance, simply saying "Ladies and gentlemen, the President of the United States" is usually all it takes to let the audience know whom they will be hearing. The average speech of introduction should last between two and three minutes; on rare occasions, it may extend to three or four. Although the person you are introducing may have impressive credentials, the audience is interested in hearing the speaker, not the introducer.

The beginning of the speech of introduction should quickly establish the nature of the occasion, the body of the speech should focus on three or four things about the person being introduced that are critical for the audience to know, and the conclusion should briefly identify the speaker's topic or the title of the speech. If the person being introduced is not scheduled to present a speech, the introducer might invite the audience to talk with the person at a later time.

Considerations

Speeches of introduction should honestly represent the person being introduced. Do not hype a speaker's credentials or overpraise the speaker. If you set the audience's expectations too high, even a good speaker may have trouble living up to them. For instance, an overzealous introducer can doom a competent speaker by saying, "This man [woman] is undoubtedly one of the greatest speakers of our time. I have no doubt that what you are about to hear will change your thinking." Although this introduction is meant to be complimentary, it does the speaker a grave disservice.

A second consideration is to familiarize yourself with the person you are introducing and what you are going to say so that you present accurate and relevant information and are fluent in doing so. It is awkward and embarrassing for speakers to have to correct an inaccurate introduction, or to have to reintroduce themselves in order to have the audience understand the authority and credibility that they bring to their subject. Introducers who are so unfamiliar with the person they are introducing that they have to read the introduction or search through notes to find the person's name also undermine the prestige of the person being introduced.

"What's the matter, Chet—you really look as if something is bothering you!"

"Well, you know I'm introducing Rick at the University Convocation for those running for offices. He's my friend, and I told him I'd be happy to introduce him. So I asked him to give me some information that he'd like me to include. I thought he'd summarize some of the stuff he's done, but instead he wrote out an introduction that includes stuff about him that's largely fiction! I really feel like I'm in a pickle, Ken."

"So, he's the one who's running for office. You're just giving the introduction he wants you to give. Don't worry about it—nobody's going to pay attention to what you're saying anyway."

"Still, I'm giving the speech. I'm afraid that I'm going to be the one who gets blamed when and if people find out that what I've said isn't true."

"I'm telling you—your job is to do what Rick wants. You asked him to give you information, and he did."

"I guess you're right—but I'm not going to like doing it."

1. Is Chet violating ethical principles by agreeing to give the opening Rick wants as written?
2. If so, what should Chet do about it?

A typical speech of introduction might look like the following:

Today, it is my pleasure to introduce our speaker, Ms. Susan Wong, the new president of the finance club. I've worked with Susan for three years and have found her to have a gift for organization, insight into the financial markets, and an interest in aligning student organizations with leaders in our community. Susan, as you may not know, has spent the last two summers working as an intern at Salomon Smith Barney, and has now laid the groundwork for more college internships for students from this university. She is a finance major, with a minor in international business. Today she is going to talk with us about the benefits of summer internships. Let's give a warm welcome to Susan Wong!

SPEECH ASSIGNMENT

Speech of Introduction

Prepare a two- to three-minute speech of introduction. Assume that you are introducing the featured speaker for a specific occasion. Criteria for evaluation include creativity in establishing speaker credibility and presenting the name of the speaker and the speech title.

speech of recognition a ceremonial presentation that acknowledges someone and usually presents an award, a prize, or a gift to the individual or a representative of a group

Recognition Presentations

A **speech of recognition** is a ceremonial presentation that acknowledges someone and usually presents an award, a prize, or a gift to the individual or a representative of a group. Usually, the speech is a fairly short, formal recognition of an accomplishment. Sometimes, a presentation is accompanied by a longer tribute to the individual or group.

Expectations

A recognition speech is expected to discuss the nature of the recognition or award, including its history, donor, or source, and the conditions under which it is made. Although the tangible award may be a certificate, plaque, trophy, or check symbolizing an achievement, the recognition may have a long history and tradition that you are responsible for recounting.

Because the audience wants to know why the recipient is being recognized, you must know the recognition criteria and how the recipient met them. If the recognition is based on a competition, this might include the number of contestants and the way the contest was judged. If the person earned the award through years of achievement, you will want to describe the specific milestones that the person passed.

Ordinarily, the speech begins by describing what the recognition is for, then states the criteria for winning or achieving the recognition, and finally describes how the person being recognized won or achieved the award. In some cases a recognition is meant to be a surprise, so you will deliberately omit the name of the recipient in what you say, building to a climax when the name is announced.

Considerations

For the speech of recognition, there are two special considerations. First, as in a speech of introduction, you should refrain from overpraising; do not explain everything in superlatives that make the presentation seem to lack sincerity and honesty. Second, in the United States it is traditional to shake hands with recipients as recognitions are received. So, if you have a certificate or other tangible award that you are going to hand to the recipient, be careful to hold it in your left hand and present it to the recipient's left hand. In that way you will be able to shake the right hand in congratulations. With practice, you will be able to present the award and shake the person's hand smoothly and avoid those embarrassing moments when the recipient does not know what he or she is supposed to do.

When presenting an award, discuss the nature of the award and the recipient's accomplishments.

A typical speech of recognition may look like this:

I'm honored to present this year's Idea of the Year Award to Rebecca Goldbloom from the installation department. As you may remember, this is an award that we have been giving since 1985 to the employee who has submitted an idea that resulted in the largest first-year cost savings for the company. Rebecca's idea to equip all installation trucks with prepackaged kits for each type of job has resulted in a $10,458 savings in the first twelve months. And in recognition of this contribution to our bottom line, I am pleased to share our savings with Rebecca in the form of a check for $2,091.60, one-fifth of what she has saved us. Good work, Rebecca.

SPEECH ASSIGNMENT

Speech of Presentation

Prepare a three- to five-minute speech in which you present a gift, a plaque, or an award to a member of your class. Criteria for evaluation include showing what the award is for, the criteria for winning, and how the person met the criteria.

Acceptances

speech of acceptance a ceremonial speech given to acknowledge receipt of an honor or award

A **speech of acceptance** is a ceremonial speech given to acknowledge receipt of an honor or award.

Expectations

In this speech, speakers should briefly thank the person or group bestowing the honor, express their feelings about receiving the recognition, and acknowledge any help they received that contributed to the honor or award.

Considerations

Most acceptance speeches are brief. Rarely, as in the case of a politician accepting a nomination, a professional accepting the presidency of a national organization, or a person receiving a prestigious award that is the focus of the gathering, an audience will expect a longer speech. As the Academy Awards program graphically illustrates, when people are honored, they can give overly long and occasionally inappropriate speeches. So, when you have the opportunity to give an acceptance speech, you will want to practice it so that you are confident that you can accomplish your purpose quickly. It is also important that you focus your remarks on the recognition you have been given or on the position you are accepting. It is inappropriate to use an acceptance speech to advocate for an unrelated cause. The following is an example of an appropriate speech of acceptance:

On behalf of our board of directors, thank you for this award, the Largest Institutional Benefactor in Second Harvest's 1998 Food Drive. It is an honor to be a part of such a worthwhile cause, and it is really our board who should be thanking you, Second Harvest, for all the wonderful work you have done over the years. You continue to collect and distribute food to thousands of needy families and individuals, especially to our senior citizens and single mothers. Without your work, many would otherwise go hungry. You are a model of community sharing and caring.

Daniel Inouye

Duty, Honor, Country

Each year West Point Military Academy gives an award to an American who has served the United States with distinction. Recipients of the Thayer Award, named after a celebrated West Point alum and academy superintendent, have included Colin Powell, Walter Cronkite, Barbara Jordan, and Ronald Reagan. In 2002, Hawaii senator Daniel Inouye joined the list of those who have received this honor.

Of course, being honored with an award typically necessitates honoring, in turn, a request to give an acceptance speech. A master public speaker, Senator Inouye's speech to a sea of West Point cadets and spectators received a standing ovation and media accolades.

Inouye's warm reception was perhaps a response to his skillfully crafted use of audience-involving language. Because West Point's motto, "Duty, Honor, Country," is ingrained among the cadets, Inouye deliberately weaves their recognizable, cherished creed into his speech. In the excerpts that follow, notice the many ways he emphasizes the motto. (For a full transcript, visit http://www.aogusma.org/aog/awards/TA/01speech1.htm.)

> In the introduction: "The sacred words of West Point—'Duty, Honor, Country'—have been a part of the history of this land since the time of its birth."
>> As a transition: "'Duty, Honor, Country' are words that are also important in my life."
>> In the body: ". . . if only to prove our loyalty and demonstrate our commitment to the essence of your three sacred words: 'Duty, Honor, Country.'"
>> As reinforcement: "We Americans should not be reluctant or afraid to use the words, 'Duty, Honor, Country,' because they are necessary if we are to continue enjoying the good life we have become accustomed to."
>> In closing: "I envy you because I believe you will live in a better America, a better America where the sacred words of 'Duty, Honor, Country' will have meaning and relevance."

In accepting the Thayer Award, Senator Inouye honored the traditions of the institution while challenging the audience to fully embrace "duty, honor, and country."

I would also like to thank our company staff—Juanita Alverez, Su Lin, Al Pouzorek, Linda Williams, and Jesus Washington—for their efforts in organizing the collection of food and money to go to Second Harvest. They were tireless in their work, persistent in their company memos and meetings requesting donations, and consistent in their positive and upbeat attitudes throughout the drive! We could not have won this award without them! Let's give them a round of applause, too.

Finally, thank you, Second Harvest, for this honor—and we hope to be back next year to receive it again!

Speech of Acceptance

This assignment can be paired with the speech of recognition assignment. Prepare a one- to two-minute speech of acceptance in response to another speaker's speech of recognition. The criteria for evaluation are how well you express your feelings about the recognition and your acknowledgment of the contribution of others.

Toasts

toast a ceremonial speech offered at the start of a reception or meal that pays tribute to the occasion or to a person

A **toast** is a ceremonial speech offered at the start of a reception or meal that pays tribute to the occasion or to a person. It usually concludes with the speaker and audience raising glasses and drinking to acknowledge what has been honored.

Expectations

On most occasions a toast is expected to be very brief (lasting less than a minute), consisting of only a few sentences, and focuses on a single characteristic of the person or occasion. Usually a short example is used to support or illustrate the characteristic.

Wedding toasts, given at a rehearsal dinner or reception by family members and members of the wedding party, are generally longer speeches (three to four minutes) that may use humor but should not embarrass the person at whom they are directed.

Considerations

A toast should be sincere and express a sentiment that is likely to be widely shared by those in attendance. The person giving the toast stands or in some other way separates from the rest of the people. Generally the person giving the toast and all other attendees have a drink in hand, which they raise and sip from at the conclusion of the toast. So, before offering a toast it is customary to make sure that drinks are refreshed so that all can participate. If particular people are being toasted, the toast is drunk in their honor, so they do not drink.

A typical toast by a daughter given to honor her mother's college graduation might be:

> Tonight I'd like to offer a toast to a woman that I admire and respect. My mom has always supported my brother and me. So when she told me that she wanted to go back and finish college, I was worried about how we'd all manage. But I shouldn't have worried. Mom not only finished her degree in less than two years, but she also continued to work full-time, and what's more, she's even had time to coach my brother's Little League team. Here's to you, Mom—you're amazing!

Special occasions such as weddings, birthdays, and retirements call for toasts that are presented with sincerity and sensitivity to the situation.

© Amy Etra/PhotoEdit

Toast

Prepare a one-minute toast to a specific person or persons on a specific occasion. Criteria for evaluation include how well you illustrate a quality or behavior of the person you are celebrating.

Tributes and Eulogies

A **speech of tribute** is a ceremonial speech that praises someone's life and accomplishments. You might be asked to pay tribute to a person or persons on the occasion of their birthday, anniversary, oath of office, or retirement. A speech of tribute given at the memorial or funeral for a person who has died is called a **eulogy.**

speech of tribute a ceremonial speech that praises someone's life and accomplishments

eulogy a speech of tribute given at the memorial or funeral for a person who has died

Expectations

Audiences expect that a tribute to someone will highlight important aspects of the person's character, supported by in-depth biographical information, often presented in short narratives. The keys to an effective tribute are intimate knowledge of the person you are honoring and sincerity.

You may have had the unfortunate experience of attending a funeral presided over by a cleric who obviously didn't know the deceased and who didn't take the time to talk to family and friends in order to get an accurate picture of the person and good material to use. As a result, the speech was a disaster that portrayed the deceased inaccurately and failed to comfort the mourners. So, when you are asked to pay tribute or to eulogize someone you don't know well, you must begin by collecting biographical information and interviewing people with close relationships to the person you are to honor.

Based on what you know about the person, you can then select three or four positive personal characteristics of the person to use as the main points in your tribute, and the stories you have collected about the person will provide support. Your audience will enjoy hearing new stories that exemplify the characteristics as well as revisiting widely shared stories. Incidents that reveal how a personal characteristic helped the person overcome adversity will be especially powerful.

Considerations

How detailed you make the speech will depend on how well the audience knows the person. We expect that most people who attend a funeral know the person being eulogized, but audience members do not always know the person who is the topic of a tribute. If the person is little known to the audience, you will need to provide many more biographical details so that the audience has enough background to appreciate the characteristics and the supporting narratives. If the audience knows the basic biographical facts, then there is no sense in rehashing them.

Remember, however, that no one is perfect. Although you don't want to dwell on the person's character flaws or failures, some allusion to them may be honest and appropriate. If you need to speak about someone's shortcomings, humor can be an effective means to soften what otherwise might be perceived as inappropriate criticism.

Speech of Tribute or Eulogy

Prepare a four- to six-minute speech paying tribute to a person, living or dead. Criteria for evaluation include how well you identify and develop the person's laudable characteristics and accomplishments.

Other Ceremonial Speeches

Other occasions that call for ceremonial speeches include graduations, conferences or conventions, and holidays or events.

commencement address a speech that recognizes graduation

Nearly every educational institution includes a **commencement address** that recognizes graduation. Commencement speakers range from political, business, or community leaders to prominent alumni to members of the graduating class. Although a commencement speech may begin by praising the educational accomplishment of the class, the purpose is to inspire the graduates about their place in the future. Although in some instances a commencement speech becomes a platform for a major political figure to make a major policy statement, the best commencement speeches are ones that are directed to the specific graduating class.

keynote address a speech that begins a conference or convention

Most major organizations schedule a **keynote address**—a speech that begins a conference or convention. Most of us are familiar with the keynote addresses presented at the national Democratic and Republican Party conventions. The word *keynote* gives us insight into the primary goal of the speech: to present a significant idea intended to set the tone for the rest of the meeting and inspire participants in their work. Some keynotes, like those at national political conventions, are given as much or even more for the benefit of the television or radio audience. In these cases, the goal is to inspire listeners to support the particular political party and its candidates for office. Although there are no set guidelines for a keynote speech, the goal is to inspire—to generate enthusiasm among participants and those watching television or listening to the radio.

commemorative addresses speeches presented to celebrate national holidays or anniversaries of important dates or events

Commemorative addresses are presented to celebrate national holidays or anniversaries of important dates or events. Thus, national holidays like the Fourth of July, Cinco de Mayo, and Bastille Day are the occasion for countless speeches across the globe. We also hear speeches commemorating the tenth, twenty-fifth, or fiftieth anniversary of significant events such as D-Day, Nakba, or "The Catastrophe," or the founding of organizations such as the United Nations. The goals of such speeches often include reminding the audience of the background for the particular holiday, date, or event and then, ultimately, drawing some conclusion about its significance that inspires the audience.

Summary

In addition to informative and persuasive speeches, you are likely to have occasion to give speeches of welcoming, introduction, recognition presentation, acceptance, toasting, tribute, and eulogies. You may also have occasion to present a commencement address, a keynote address, or a commemorative address.

A welcoming speech expresses pleasure at the presence of a person or an organization. A speech of introduction serves to introduce a speaker. In a speech of presentation, you present an award, a prize, or a gift to an individual or to a group. A speech of acceptance is a response to a speech of presentation. A toast, offered before a meal or reception, pays tribute to the occasion or to a person. A tribute or eulogy praises someone's life and accomplishments.

Speeches for other ceremonial occasions include commencement addresses, keynote addresses, and commemorative addresses. Commencement speeches praise the graduating class and turn them toward the future. A keynote address, as its title indicates, offers a keynote for a conference or convention. Commemorative speeches celebrate national holidays or anniversaries of important dates.

CHALLENGE ONLINE

Now that you've read Chapter 15, use your Challenge of Effective Speaking CD-ROM for quick access to the electronic study resources that accompany this text. Your CD-ROM gives you access to InfoTrac College Edition, Speech Builder Express, and the Challenge of Effective Speaking Web site. When you get to the Challenge of Effective Speaking home page, click on "Student Book Companion Site" in the Resource box at the right to access the online study aids for this chapter, including a digital glossary, review quizzes, and the chapter activities.

KEY TERMS

At the Challenge of Effective Speaking Web site, select chapter resources for Chapter 15. Print a copy of the glossary for this chapter, test yourself with the electronic flash cards, or complete the crossword puzzle to help you master the following key terms.

welcoming speech (294)	**speech of tribute** (301)
speech of introduction (295)	**eulogy** (301)
speech of recognition (296)	**commencement address** (302)
speech of acceptance (298)	**keynote address** (302)
toast (300)	**commemorative addresses** (302)

INFOTRAC COLLEGE EDITION EXERCISE

The goal of most commencement speeches is to praise members of the graduating class and to inspire them in their future work. Use your Challenge of Effective Speaking CD-ROM to access InfoTrac College Edition. In "subject guide," type in either Jeanne Hey or "Inheritance of the Past" to bring up

Jeanne Hey's commencement speech, *Vital Speeches*, July 1, 2002. Read the speech and then answer these questions: What does she do to (1) praise members of the graduating class and (2) inspire them in their future work? Based on these two criteria, how would you evaluate this commencement speech?

Increasing the Effectiveness of Problem Solving Discussions

Men are never so likely to settle a question rightly as when they discuss it freely.

Thomas Babington, Lord Macaulay, *Southey's Colloquies*

Members of the Alpha Production Team at Meyer Foods were gathered to review their hiring policies. As the meeting began, Kareem, the team leader, said, "You know why I called you together. Each production team has been asked to review its hiring practices. So, let's get started." After a few seconds of silence, Kareem asked, "Drew, what have you been thinking?"

"Well, I don't know," Drew replied, "I haven't really given it much thought." There were nods of agreement all around the table.

"Well," Jeremy said, "I'm not sure that I even remember what our current policies are."

"When I sent you the email notice of this meeting, I attached a preliminary analysis of our practices and some questions I hoped each of us would think about before this meeting," Kareem replied.

"Oh, is that what that was?" Byron said. "I read the part about the meeting, but I guess I didn't get back to look at the attachment."

"Kareem, anything you think would be appropriate would be OK with me," Dawn added.

"Well, how about if we each try to come up with some ideas for next time," Kareem suggested. "Meeting adjourned."

As the group dispersed, Kareem overheard Drew whisper to Dawn, "These meetings sure are a waste of time, aren't they?"

Perhaps you have been a part of a problem solving discussion at school, at work, or at your church. If so, the opening dialogue probably sounds familiar. But as the opening quote suggests, when problem solving discussions are effective, they usually result in decisions that are useful. Because most of us take part in problem solving discussions, we need to learn how group process works and how to participate in ways that maximize effective problem solving.

In this chapter, we explain how problem solving discussions can be structured to be both effective and efficient. We begin by examining the characteristics of effective problem solving discussions. Next we consider the steps in an effective problem solving discussion. Then we describe the essential responsibilities of both leaders and group members before, during, and after the discussion. Finally, we describe four formats used in public problem solving discussions.

Characteristics of Effective Problem Solving Discussions

problem solving discussion
a structured dialogue among individuals who interact with and influence one another in order to develop a plan that will overcome an identified difficulty

A **problem solving discussion** is a structured dialogue among individuals who interact with and influence one another in order to develop a plan that will overcome an identified difficulty. Effective problem solving discussions are characterized by clearly defined goals to which members are committed; an optimum number of members who have diverse personalities, knowledge bases, skills, and viewpoints; appropriate levels of cohesiveness; rules and norms that facilitate the open exchange of information, ideas, and opinions; and a working environment that encourages interaction.

Developing Clearly Defined Goals to Which Members Are Committed

A **problem solving goal** is a future state of affairs desired by enough members of the group to motivate the group to work toward its achievement.[1] Goals become clearer to members, and members become more committed to goals, when they are discussed. Through these discussions members are able to make problem solving goal statements more specific, consistent, challenging, and acceptable. To read about various methods that can be used to arrive at group goals, use your Challenge of Effective Speaking CD-ROM to access Web Resource 16.1: Setting Group Goals.

problem solving goal a future state of affairs desired by enough members of the group to motivate the group to work toward its achievement

Optimum Number of Diverse Members

Effective discussion groups are composed of enough members to ensure good interaction but not so many members that discussion is stifled. In general, as the size of a discussion group grows, so does the complexity it must manage.

So what is the "right" size for a problem solving discussion group? It depends. In general, research shows that the best size for a group depends on the goal. If the goal is quality of the decision, then a moderate-size group of seven or so is advisable. If the goal is speed of decision, then a group of three or four is advisable.[2] As the size of the group increases, the time spent discussing and deciding increases as well. This argues for very small groups because they will be able to make decisions more quickly. However, as the goals, problems, and issues become complex, it is unlikely that very small groups will have the diversity of information, knowledge, and skills needed to make high-quality decisions. For many situations, then, a group of five to seven or more might be most desirable.

More important than having a certain number of people in a group is having the right combination of people in the group. Notice that the heading of this section was "Optimum Number of *Diverse* Members." Effective groups are likely to be composed of people who bring different but relevant knowledge and skills into the group discussion.[3] In homogeneous groups, members are likely to know the same things, to come at the problem from the same perspective, and consequently, to overlook some important information or take shortcuts in the problems solving process. In contrast, heterogeneous groups are likely to discuss ideas more thoroughly, to have different information, perspectives, and values, and consequently, to discuss issues more thoroughly before reaching a decision.

Cohesiveness

Cohesiveness is the degree of attraction that members have to one another and to the problem solving goal. In a highly cohesive group, members genuinely like and respect one another, work cooperatively to reach the group's goals, and generally perform better than in noncohesive groups.[4] Research has found that several factors, including attractiveness of the group's purpose, voluntary membership, freedom to share opinions, and celebration of accomplishments, tend to enhance group cohesiveness.[5]

cohesiveness the degree of attraction that members have to one another and to the problem solving goal

Rules and Norms

norms shared expectations for the way that group members will behave during discussions

Norms are shared expectations for the way that group members will behave during discussions. Effective groups develop norms that achieve effectiveness and cohesiveness.[6] Norms begin to develop early in the life of the group. They grow, change, and solidify as people get to know one another better. Group members usually comply with norms or are sanctioned by the group when they do not.

ground rules prescribed behaviors designed to help the group meet its goals and conduct its conversations

Norms can be developed through formal discussions or informal group processes.[7] Some groups choose to formulate explicit **ground rules**—prescribed behaviors designed to help the group meet its goals and conduct its conversations. Such rules may include sticking to the agenda, refraining from interrupting others, actively listening to others, participating fully, focusing arguments on issues rather than personalities, and sharing decision making. To read a list of group norms that contribute to group effectiveness, use your Challenge of Effective Speaking CD-ROM to access **Web Resource 16.2: Setting Group Norms**. In most groups, however, norms evolve informally. When group members violate a group norm, they are usually sanctioned.

The Working Environment

working environment a physical setting that is conveniently located for most members, has a comfortable temperature, and has enough space of appropriate size for the size and work of the group

A good **working environment** includes a physical setting that is conveniently located for most members, has a comfortable temperature, and has enough space of appropriate size for the size and work of the group. Most important, the space should be comfortably furnished with all the resources the group needs to perform its tasks, and seating should be arranged to facilitate group interaction.

The temperature of the room in which a group meets affects the way in which the group interacts. People in rooms they perceive to be too warm not only feel uncomfortable but may feel crowded, resulting in negative behaviors. When the temperature of a room or meeting place is too cold, group members tend to become distracted.

The space in which a group meets should be appropriate for the size and composition of the group and the nature of what they are trying to accomplish during their time together. When the space is too big for the group, members will feel overwhelmed and distant from one another. In some cases, they may have trouble hearing one another. When the space is too small, the group will experience feelings of crowding. We've all found ourselves in situations in which room size contributed to negative experiences.

Seating arrangements can affect both group interaction and decision making. Seating can be too formal when it approximates a board of directors style, as illustrated in Exhibit 16.1a. In this style, a dominant/submissive pattern emerges that can inhibit group interaction. People who sit at the head of the table are likely to be looked to for leadership and are seen as having more influence than those members who sit on the side. People who sit across the table from each other interact more frequently, but also find themselves disagreeing with each other more often than they disagree with others at the table.

Seating that is excessively informal can also inhibit interaction. For instance, in Exhibit 16.1b, the three people sitting on the couch form their own little group, the two people seated next to each other form another group, and two members have placed themselves out of the main flow. In arrangements such as these, people are more likely to discuss with the people adjacent to them than with others. In such settings, it is more difficult to make eye contact with every group member. Johnson and Johnson maintain that "easy eye contact among members enhances the frequency of interaction, friendliness, cooperation, and liking for the group and its work.[8]

The circle, generally considered the ideal arrangement for group discussions and problem solving, is depicted in Exhibit 16.1c. Circle configurations increase participant motivation to speak because sight lines are better for everyone and everyone appears to have equal status. When a round table is unavailable, the group may be better off without a table or with an arrangement of tables that forms a square, which approximates the circle arrangement, as in Exhibit 16.1d.

The Problem Solving Discussion Process

Research shows that groups follow many different approaches to problem solving. Whether groups move in something approximating an orderly pattern or go in fits and starts, those groups that arrive at high-quality decisions are likely to accomplish certain tasks during their deliberations. These tasks include identifying a specific problem, analyzing the problem, arriving at criteria that an effective solution must meet, identifying possible alternative solutions to the problem, comparing the alternatives to the criteria, determining the best solution or combination of solutions, implementing the chosen solution, and monitoring the results.

Define the Problem

Much wheel-spinning takes place during the early stages of group discussion as a result of members' not understanding their specific goal. Although it is the duty of the person, agency, or parent group that forms a particular discussion group to give the group a charge, such as "Work out a new way of selecting people for merit pay increases," rarely will the charge be stated in such a way that the group does not need to clarify its precise goal. Even when the charge seems clear, effective groups will want to make sure that they are focusing on the real problem and not just symptoms of the problem.

Even when a group is given a well-defined charge, it will need to gather information before it can accurately define the specific problem. Accurately defining the problem requires the group to understand and discuss the background, history, and status of the problem. This means collecting and understanding a variety of information. Some groups, however, rush through defining the problem and end up working to solve symptoms, not root causes. To read an article suggesting that later states of problem solving move more quickly if the group has thoroughly studied, discussed, and agreed on the problem, use your Challenge of Effective Speaking CD-ROM to access **Web Resource 16.3: What's Your Problem?**

As early as possible, the group should develop a formal written statement of the problem. Unless the group has a formal definition of the problem, its discussion may be inefficient because each member is looking at a slightly different problem. Effective problem definitions have the following characteristics.

1. They are stated as questions. Because problem solving discussions begin from the assumption that solutions are not yet known, problems should be stated as questions to be answered. For example, "What are the most important criteria for determining merit pay increases?"

2. They contain only one central idea. If the charge includes two questions—"Should the college abolish its foreign language and social studies requirements?"—the group should break it down into two separate questions for discussion: "Should the college abolish its foreign language requirement? Should the college abolish its social studies requirement?"

3. They use specific and precise language to describe the problem. For instance, the problem definition "What should the department do about courses that aren't getting the job done?" may be well intentioned, and participants may have at least some idea about their goal, but such vague wording as "getting the job done" can lead to problems later. Notice how this revision of the preceding question makes its intent much clearer: "What should the department do about courses that receive low scores on student evaluations?"

4. They can be identified as a question of fact, value, or policy. How we organize our problem solving discussion will depend on the kind of question we are addressing.

Questions of fact are concerned with discovering what is true or to what extent something is true. Implied in such questions is the possibility of determining truth through the process of examining facts by way of directly observed, spoken, or recorded evidence. "Do the sales figures from last year support our introduction of a new model next year?" is a question of fact. The group will discuss the validity of the evidence it has to determine what is true.

Questions of value concern subjective judgments of what is right, moral, good, or just. Questions of value often contain evaluative words such as *good, reliable, effective,* or *worthy.* For instance, the program development team for a TV sitcom aimed at young teens might discuss the question "Is the proposed series of ads too sexually provocative?" Although we can establish criteria for "too sexually provocative" and measure material against those criteria, the criteria we choose and the evidence we accept depend on our judgment. A different group of people using different values might come to a different decision.

Questions of policy concern what course of action should be taken or what rules should be adopted in order to solve a problem. "Where should the new landfill be built?" is a question of policy. The inclusion of the word *should* in questions of policy makes them the easiest to recognize and the easiest to phrase of all problem statements.

questions of fact questions concerned with discovering what is true or to what extent something is true

questions of value questions that concern subjective judgments of what is right, moral, good, or just

questions of policy questions that concern what course of action should be taken or what rules should be adopted in order to solve a problem

As early as possible, the group should develop a formal written statement of the problem.

Analyze the Problem

Analysis of a problem entails finding out as much as possible about the problem and determining the criteria that must be met to find an acceptable solution. Just as in speech making, three types of information can be helpful in analyzing problems. Most groups begin by sharing the information that individual members have acquired through their experience. The second source of information that should be examined includes published materials available through libraries, electronic databases, and the Internet. The third source of information about a problem can be gleaned from other people. At times the group will want to consult experts for their ideas about a problem. Or the group may want to conduct a survey to gather information from a particular target group.

Once group members have gathered information, it must be shared with other members. It is important for group members to share new information they have

© LWA–Dann Tardif/corbisstockmarket.com

found in order to fulfill the ethical responsibility that comes with participating in a problem solving discussion. A study by Dennis revealed that groups tend to spend more time discussing information that is common to all group members if those members with unique information don't work to get the information heard.[9] The tendency to discuss common information while ignoring unique information leads to less effective decisions. To improve the group's ability to consider the information effectively, members should discuss the information that they have uncovered that seems to contradict their personal beliefs about the issue or the beliefs that have been discussed so far by the group. When addressing complex issues, groups should separate information sharing from decision making by holding separate meetings, spaced far enough apart to enable members to think through their information.

Determine Solution Criteria

Once a group understands the nature of the problem, it is in a position to discuss the tests a solution must pass in order to solve the problem. The criteria that are selected should be ones that the information gathered has suggested are critical to solving the problem. These criteria will be used to screen alternative solutions. Solutions that do not meet the test of all criteria are eliminated from further consideration. For example, suppose a local citizens' committee is charged with selecting a site for a new county jail. The group arrives at the following phrasing for the problem: "Where should the new jail be located?" After the group agrees on this wording, they can then ask the question, "What are the criteria for a good site for a new jail?"

Suppose that in discussion, members contribute information related to the county's budget, the need for inmates to maintain family contact, concerns about proximity to schools and parks, and space needs. After considering this kind of information, the group might then select the following criteria for selecting a site:

1. Maximum cost of $500,000 for purchasing the land
2. A location no more than three blocks from public transportation
3. A location that is one mile or more from any school, day-care center, playground, or youth center
4. A lot size of at least ten acres

Author Kathryn Young and her colleagues suggest that when groups discuss and decide on criteria before they think about specific solutions, they increase the likelihood that they will be able to avoid becoming polarized and will be more likely to come to a decision that all members can accept.[10]

Identify Possible Solutions

For most policy questions, many solutions are possible. The trick is to tap the creative thinking of group members so that many ideas are generated. At this stage of discussion, the goal is not to worry about whether a particular solution fits all the criteria, but to come up with a long list of ideas.

brainstorming an uncritical, nonevaluative process of generating alternatives by being creative, suspending judgment, and combining or adapting the ideas of others

One way to identify potential solutions is to brainstorm for ideas. **Brainstorming,** you'll recall, is an uncritical, nonevaluative process of generating alternatives by being creative, suspending judgment, and combining or adapting the ideas of others. It involves verbalizing your ideas as they come to mind, without stopping to evaluate their merits. Members are encouraged, however, to build on the ideas presented by others. For a more detailed discussion of the brainstorming process, use your Challenge of Effective Speaking CD-ROM to access Web Resource 16.4: Rules for Brainstorming. In a ten- or fifteen-minute brainstorming session, a group may come up with twenty or more possible solutions, depending on the nature of the problem.

Evaluate Solutions

Once the group has a list of possible solutions, it needs to compare each solution alternative to the criteria that were developed. During this phase, the group must determine whether all of the criteria are equally important or whether certain criteria should be given more weight in evaluating the alternative solutions. Whether a group weights certain criteria more heavily or not, it should use a process that ensures that each alternative solution is thoroughly assessed against all of the criteria.

Decide

A group brought together for problem solving may or may not be responsible for making the actual decision, but it is responsible for presenting its recommendation. **Decision making** is the process of choosing among alternatives. The following five methods differ in the extent to which they require that all members agree with the decision and in the amount of time it takes to reach a decision.

decision making the process of choosing among alternatives

    1. The expert opinion method. Once the group has eliminated those alternatives that do not meet the criteria, the group asks the member who has the most expertise to make the final choice. Obviously, this method is quick and useful if one member is much more knowledgeable about the issues or has a greater stake in the implementation of the decision.

expert opinion method asking the group member who has the most expertise to make the final choice

    2. The average group opinion method. In this approach, each member of the group ranks each of the alternatives that meet all the criteria. Their rankings are then averaged, and the alternative receiving the highest average ranking becomes the choice. This method is useful for routine decisions or when a decision needs to be made quickly. It can also be used as an intermediate straw poll that enables the group to eliminate low-scoring alternatives before moving to a different process for making the final decision.

average group opinion method accepting the alternative receiving the highest average ranking as the choice

    3. The majority rule method. In this method, the group votes on each alternative, and the one that receives a majority of votes (50% + 1) is selected. Although this method is considered democratic, it can create problems. If the majority voting for an alternative is slight, then there may be nearly as many members who do not support the choice as there are those who do. If these minority members strongly object to the choice, they may sabotage implementation of the solution either actively or passively.

majority rule method selecting the alternative that receives the majority of votes (50% + 1)

    4. The unanimous decision method. In this method, the group must continue deliberation until every member of the group believes that the same solution is the best. As you would expect, it is very difficult to arrive at a truly unanimous decision, and to do so takes a lot of time. When a group reaches unanimity, however, it can expect that each member of the group will be fully committed to selling the decision to others and helping to implement the decision.

unanimous decision method deliberating until every member of the group believes that the same solution alternative is the best

consensus method deliberating until all members of the group find an acceptable solution, one they can support and are committed to helping implement

5. The consensus method. This method is an alternative to the unanimous decision method. In consensus, the group continues deliberation until all members of the group find an acceptable solution, one they can support and are committed to helping implement. Some members of the group may believe there is a better solution than the one that has been chosen, but they feel they can "live with" the one they have agreed to. Arriving at consensus, though easier than reaching unanimity, is still difficult. Although the majority rule method is widely used, going with the consensus method is a wise investment if the group needs everyone's support to implement the decision successfully.

 For a fuller comparison of the advantages and disadvantages of various decision-making methods, use your Challenge of Effective Speaking CD-ROM to access Web Resource 16.5: Decision-Making Methods.

Implement and Monitor Decisions

In some cases, a decision made by a group requires some or all members of the group to take action to implement it. When this is the case, the group continues to use the problem solving process to determine how action will be taken and who will be responsible for specific acts. In other cases, decisions made by the group may not require it to take action but may direct the work of others. For example, the citizens' site selection committee's choice for locating the new jail will not be implemented by the committee, but by county officials. In either case, however, the group retains an ethical responsibility for monitoring how well the alternative that was chosen has been implemented and whether the original problem has been resolved. This monitoring responsibility can be delegated to one member of the group, or in the case of an ongoing group, the results of decisions can be scheduled for regular review.

REFLECT ON ETHICS

"You know, Sue, we're going to be in deep trouble if the group doesn't support McGowan's resolution about dues reform."

"Well, we'll just have to see to it that all the arguments in favor of that resolution are heard—but in the end it's the group's decision.

"That's very democratic of you, Sue, but you know that if it doesn't pass, you're likely to be out on your tail."

"That may be, Heather, but I don't see what I can do about it."

"You don't want to see. First, right now the group respects you. If you would just apply a little pressure on a couple of the members—you'd get what you want."

"What do you mean?"

"Look, this is a good cause. You've got something on just about every member of the group. Take a couple aside and let them know that this is payoff time. I think you'll see that some key folks will see it your way."

Heather may well have a point about how Sue can control the outcome. Should Sue follow Heather's advice? Why or why not?

Leader Responsibilities

How many times have you complained that a meeting you attended was a waste of time? Good problem solving discussions don't just happen. Rather, they are intentionally planned, facilitated, and followed up. One of the principal duties that formal discussion leaders perform is to plan and run effective problem solving sessions. The following guidelines can help leaders make discussions productive.

Preparing for the Meeting

1. Prepare the agenda. An **agenda** is an organized outline of the items that need to be covered during a meeting. Items for the agenda come from where the group is in its problem solving process and can be determined by reviewing the minutes of the last meeting. What steps did the group agree to take? What new issues have arisen since the last meeting? Effective discussion leaders make sure that the agenda is appropriate for the length of the meeting. Exhibit 16.2 shows an agenda for a group meeting to decide which one of three courses to offer over the Web next semester.

agenda an organized outline of the items that need to be covered during a meeting

2. Decide who should attend the meeting. In most cases, all of the members of a problem solving group will attend meetings. But at times, one or more members of the group may not need to attend a particular meeting but may only need to be informed of the outcomes of the meeting.

3. Arrange for an appropriate location and meeting time. Be sure that the location has all of the equipment and supplies that the group will need to work effectively. This may include arranging for audiovisual equipment, computers, and other specialized equipment. Because discussion groups become less effective in long meetings, ideally a meeting will last no longer than ninety minutes. If a meeting must be planned for a longer period of time, then hourly breaks should be planned.

4. Distribute the agenda. The agenda should be in the hands of participants several days before the discussion. Unless group members get an agenda ahead of time, they won't be able to prepare for the meeting.

5. Speak with each participant prior to the meeting to understand his or her positions and personal goals. Spending time preworking issues helps the leader anticipate the conflicts that are likely to emerge during discussion and to plan how to manage them so that the group makes effective decisions and maintains cohesiveness.

Leading the Discussion

1. Review and modify the agenda. Begin the meeting by reviewing the agenda and modifying it per member suggestions. Because things can change between the time an agenda is distributed and when the discussion is held, reviewing the agenda ensures that the group is working on items that are still important and relevant. Reviewing the agenda also gives members a chance to control what is to be discussed.

2. Provide task direction and manage interpersonal dynamics. The role of the leader during a discussion is to provide the task or procedural direction and relationship management that the group lacks. Leaders need to maintain awareness of what the group needs at a specific time in order to facilitate productive discussion. For example, if the leader notices that some people are

EXHIBIT 16.2 Agenda for Web course committee meeting

March 1, 2004

To:	Campus commuter discussion group
From:	Janelle Smith
Re:	Agenda for discussion group meeting
Date:	March 8, 2004
Place:	Student Union, Conference Room A
Time:	3:00 to 4:30 P.M. (Please be prompt)

Meeting Objectives

We will familiarize ourselves with each of three courses that have been proposed for Web-based delivery next semester.

We will evaluate each course against the criteria we developed last month.

We will use a consensus decision process to determine which of the three courses to offer.

Agenda for Group Discussion

Review of Philosophy 141

    Report by Justin on Philosophy 141 proposal

    Committee questions

    Comparison of PHIL 141 to criteria

Review of Art History 336

    Report by Marique on Art History 336 proposal

    Committee questions

    Comparison of ARTH 336 to criteria

Review of Communication 235

    Report by Kathryn on Communication 235

    Committee questions

    Comparison of COMM 235 to criteria

Consensus building discussion and decision

    Which proposals fit the criteria?

    Are there non-criteria-related factors to consider?

    Which proposal is most acceptable to all members?

Discussion of next steps and task assignments

Set date of next meeting

---

talking more than their fair share, and no one else is trying to draw out quieter members, the leader should act as gatekeeper by asking a reluctant member to comment on the discussion.

3. Monitor the time so that the group stays on schedule. It is easy for a group to get bogged down in a discussion. Although a group member may serve as an expediter, it is the leader's responsibility to make sure that the group stays on schedule.

4. Monitor conflicts and intervene as needed. A healthy level of conflict should be encouraged in the discussion so that issues are fully examined. But if the conflict level becomes dysfunctional, the leader may need to mediate so that relationships are not unduly strained.

Leaders of formal discussions should begin meetings by reviewing the goals and agenda for the session.

5. Periodically check to see if the group is ready to make a decision. The leader of the group should listen for agreement and move the group into its formal decision process when the leader senses that discussion is no longer adding insight.

6. Implement the group's decision rules. The leader is responsible for seeing that the decision-making rule that the group has agreed to is used. If the group is deciding by consensus, the leader needs to make sure that each member feels that the chosen alternative is one that he or she can support. If the group is deciding by majority rule, the leader calls for the vote and tallies the results.

7. Before ending the meeting, summarize decisions, task responsibilities that have been assigned, and next steps that have been planned. To bring closure to the meeting and to make sure that each member leaving the meeting is clear about what has been accomplished, the leader should summarize what has happened in the meeting.

8. Ask the group to decide if and when another meeting is needed. Continuing groups should be careful not to meet just for the sake of meeting. So, leaders should clarify with members when and if future meetings are necessary. The overall purposes of future meetings will dictate the agenda that will need to be prepared.

Following Up

1. Review the discussion outcomes and process. A good leader learns how to be more effective at running discussions by reflecting on and analyzing how well the previous meeting went. Leaders need to think about whether the discussion accomplished its goals and whether group cohesion was improved or damaged in the process.

2. Prepare and distribute a summary of discussion outcome. Some groups have a member who serves as the recorder and who distributes minutes, but many groups rely on the leader. A written record of what was agreed to, accomplishments, and next steps serves to remind group members of the work they have to do. If the group has a recorder, the leader should check to make sure that minutes are distributed in a timely manner.

3. Repair damaged relationships through informal conversations. If the debate during the discussion has been heated, it is likely that some people have damaged their relationships with others and left the meeting angry or hurt. Leaders can help repair relationships by seeking out these participants and talking with them. Through empathetic listening, we can soothe hurt feelings and spark a recommitment to the group.

4. Follow up with participants to see how they are progressing on items assigned to them. When participants have been assigned specific tasks and responsibilities, the leader should check with them to see if they have encountered any problems in completing what was assigned.

Member Responsibilities

Members of effective problem solving groups also assume common responsibilities for making their meetings successful. The following guidelines, prepared by a class of university students, describe how problem solving group members should prepare for, behave in, and follow up the discussion so that problem solving effectiveness is increased.[11]

Preparing for the Meeting

As the chapter opening vignette illustrated, too often people think of group discussions as something that require attendance but no particular preparation. Countless times we've observed people who bring the packets of material about a discussion with them, but have spent little if any time studying the material. The reality is that problem solving discussions should not be treated as impromptu events, but as activities that pool information from well-prepared individuals.

1. Study the agenda. Determine the purpose of the discussion and what you need to do to be prepared. Consider the agenda as an outline for preparation.

2. Study the minutes. If this is one of a series of meetings, study the minutes and your own notes from the previous discussion. Each meeting is not a separate event. What happened at one meeting should provide the basis for preparation for the next meeting.

3. Prepare for your contributions. Read handouts and do the research you need to become better informed about items on the agenda. If no handouts are given, it is up to you to find sources of information that you will need to be a contributing member of the discussion. Bring any materials that you have uncovered that will aid the group in reaching a decision. If appropriate, discuss the agenda with others who will not be attending the meeting and solicit their ideas concerning issues to be discussed in the meeting.

4. List questions. Make a list of questions related to agenda items that you would like to have answered during the discussion.

Participating in the Discussion

Go into the discussion with the expectation that you will be a full participant. If there are five people in the group, all five should be participating.

1. **Listen attentively.** Concentrate on what others are saying so that you can use your material to complement, supplement, or counter what has been presented.

2. **Stay focused.** In a group setting, it's easy to get the discussion going in nonproductive directions. Keep your comments focused on the specific agenda item under consideration. If others have gotten off the subject, do what you can to get people back on track.

3. **Ask questions.** "Honest" questions whose answers you do not already know help to stimulate discussion and help to build ideas.

4. **Play devil's advocate.** When you think an idea has not been fully discussed or tested, be willing to voice disagreement or encourage further discussion.

5. **Monitor your contributions.** Especially when people are well prepared, they have a tendency to dominate discussion. Make sure that you are neither dominating the discussion nor abdicating your responsibility to share insights and opinions.

6. **Take notes.** Even if someone else is responsible for providing the official minutes, you'll want notes that help you follow the line of development. Also, these notes will help you remember what has been said.

Following Up

Too often, when discussions end, people leave and forget about what took place until the next meeting. But as we said, what happens in one discussion provides a basis for what happens in the next.

1. **Review and summarize your notes.** Try to do this shortly after you've left the meeting while ideas are still fresh in your mind. Make notes of what needs to be discussed next time.

2. **Evaluate your effectiveness.** How effective were you helping the group move toward achieving its goals? Where were you strong? Where were you weak? What should you do next time that you didn't do in this discussion?

3. **Review decisions.** Make note of what your role was in making decisions. Did you do all that you could have?

4. **Communicate progress.** Inform others who need to know about information that was conveyed and decisions that were made by the group.

5. **Follow up.** Make sure that you complete any assignments you received in the meeting.

6. **Review minutes.** Read the official minutes of the meeting, compare them to your own notes, and report any significant discrepancies that you find.

When the Discussion Goes Public

Although most of your group problem solving will be done in private, without the presence of an onlooking or participating audience, occasionally a discussion takes place in a public forum. At times this means conducting your discussion with nonparticipating observers present; at other times this means presenting your group's conclusions to another group. In a public discussion, the group's discussion provides information for the listening audience as much as it provides the basis for members to analyze or solve a problem. As such, public discussions have much in common with traditional public speaking. Four common forms of public discussion are the symposium, the panel discussion, the town hall meeting, and the public hearing.

Symposium

A **symposium** is a discussion in which a limited number of participants (usually three to five) present individual speeches of approximately the same length dealing with the same subject. After delivering their planned speeches, the participants in the symposium may discuss their reactions with one another or respond to questions from the audience. Despite the potential for interaction, a symposium is often characterized by long, sometimes unrelated speeches. Moreover, the part designated for questions is often shortened or deleted because "our time is about up." A symposium often omits the interaction necessary for a good discussion. If the participants make their prepared speeches short enough so that at least half of the available time can be spent on real interaction, a symposium can be interesting and stimulating. A good symposium that meets the goals of discussion is much more difficult to present than it appears; as a public speaking assignment, however, the symposium may be beneficial. Rather than solving a problem, a symposium is more effective in shedding light on or explaining various aspects of a problem.

Panel Discussion

A **panel discussion** is a problem solving discussion in front of an audience. After the formal discussion, the audience is often encouraged to question the participants. The discussion can thus be seen and heard by the audience. The group is seated in a semicircle, with the chairperson in the middle, to get a good view of the audience and the panelists. Because the discussion is for an audience, the panelists are obliged to make good use of traditional public speaking skills. And because a panel discussion encourages spontaneity and interaction, it can be stimulating for both the audience and the panelists. The panel works as a form of problem solving discussion.

Town Hall Meeting

A **town hall meeting** is an event in which a large number of people who are interested in a topic are convened to discuss, and at times to decide, an issue. In the New England states, many small towns use town hall meetings of residents to decide community issues. In a town hall meeting, one person who is respected by other participants is selected to lead the discussion. The leader announces the ground rules for the discussion, introduces the issues to be discussed, calls on participants for comments, ensures that divergent opinions are expressed, periodically summarizes the discussion, and oversees the decision making. Because town hall meetings involve large numbers of people, turn taking is strictly controlled by the leader. Many town hall meetings follow *Roberts Rules of Order* so that the discussion remains focused and all participants' views are heard.

Public Hearing

A **public hearing** is a meeting of an elected or appointed government group for the purpose of explaining a pending change in policy (or a new policy), answering questions, and receiving public comments. Sometimes members of the pub-

Town hall–style meetings are often used by communities to discuss controversial issues that affect the well-being of residents.

lic must sign up prior to the meeting in order to speak. The meeting usually begins with a member of the government group giving a speech that explains the rationale for the policy or policy change and the specifics of the policy. Then members of the audience are invited to ask questions. Finally, members of the audience who wish to comment on the policy are given the opportunity to speak.

At a public hearing, the government representatives generally sit at a table facing the audience of community members. The government official who is leading the hearing should ensure that adequate time is allocated for audience questions and comments. In order to hear comments from all community members who would like to speak, the leader should survey the audience to find out who wants to speak and then set and enforce a time limit for each speaker. If you plan to speak at a public hearing, you will want to plan a speech that you can adapt to comply with various time limits.

SPEECH ASSIGNMENT

Public Discussion

Divide the class into groups of four to six. Each group will prepare to conduct either a symposium, a panel discussion, a town hall meeting, or a public hearing of approximately thirty to forty minutes. Each group must determine an appropriate issue, prepare for the public discussion, and participate in it.

Summary

Effective problem solving discussion groups share five characteristics: They develop clearly defined goals, have an optimum number of diverse members, work to develop cohesiveness, establish rules and norms, and meet in an appropriate working environment.

Problem solving is a process that includes defining the problem as a question of fact, value, or policy; analyzing the problem; determining solution criteria; identifying possible solutions; evaluating solutions; deciding; and implementing and monitoring decisions.

Both members and leaders can improve the effectiveness of the meetings they attend through pre-meeting preparations, during-meeting behaviors, and post-meeting activities.

Four common forms of public discussion are the symposium, the panel discussion, the town hall meeting, and the public hearing.

CHALLENGE ONLINE

Now that you've read Chapter 16, use your Challenge of Effective Speaking CD-ROM for quick access to the electronic study resources that accompany this text. Your CD-ROM gives you access to InfoTrac College Edition, Speech Builder Express, and the Challenge of Effective Speaking Web site. When you get to the Challenge of Effective Speaking home page, click on "Student Book Companion Site" in the Resource box at the right to access the online study aids for this chapter, including a digital glossary, review quizzes, and the chapter activities.

KEY TERMS

At the Challenge of Effective Speaking Web site, select chapter resources for Chapter 16. Print a copy of the glossary for this chapter, or test yourself with the electronic flash cards, or complete the crossword puzzle to help you master the following key terms.

problem solving discussion (306)
problem solving goal (307)
cohesiveness (307)
norms (307)
ground rules (308)
working environment (308)
questions of fact (311)
questions of value (311)
questions of policy (311)
brainstorming (312)

decision making (313)
expert opinion method (313)
average group opinion method (313)
majority rule method (313)
unanimous decision method (313)
consensus method (314)
symposium (320)
panel discussion (320)
town hall meeting (320)
public hearing (320)

INFOTRAC COLLEGE EDITION EXERCISE

Use your Challenge of Effective Speaking CD-ROM to access InfoTrac College Edition. Under the subject "problem solving discussion," click on periodical references. Select two articles that talk about guidelines for effective group problem solving. In what ways does the information support material in this chapter?

WEB RESOURCES

Access the Web Resources for this chapter online at the Challenge of Effective Speaking Web site. Select the chapter resources for Chapter 16, then click on "Web Resources."

16.1 Setting Group Goals (307)

16.2 Setting Group Norms (308)

16.3 What's Your Problem? (310)

16.4 Rules for Brainstorming (313)

16.5 Decision-Making Methods (314)

Notes

Chapter 1 Introduction to Public Speaking

1. Daniel Golman, *Working with Emotional Intelligence* (New York: Bantam Books, 1998), 12–13.

2. "More than three quarters of Americans have a pessimistic view of the current state of ethics and morality, and even fewer see it getting better according to a new Gallup poll," *Christian Century*, 28 June 2003, 17.

3. Supid K. Das, "Plagiarism in Higher Education: Is There a Remedy? Lots of Instruction and Some Careful Vigilance Could Work Wonders," *Scientist*, 20 October 2003, 8.

4. "Web Plagiarism Keeps Rising," *Curriculum Review*, November 2003, 5.

5. Caroline McCullen, "Tactics and Resources to Help Students Avoid Plagiarism," *Multimedia Schools*, November–December 2003, 40–43.

6. Brian Spitzberg, "A Model of Intercultural Communication Competence," in *Intercultural Communication: A Reader,* 9th ed., ed. L. A. Samovar and R. E. Porter (Belmont, CA: Wadsworth, 2000), 375.

7. Gerald M. Phillips, *Communication Incompetencies: A Theory of Training Oral Performance Behavior* (Carbondale: Southern Illinois University Press, 1991).

Chapter 2 Developing Confidence through the Speech Planning Process

1. Virginia P. Richmond and James C. McCroskey, *Communication: Apprehension, Avoidance, and Effectiveness,* 4th ed. (Scottsdale, AZ: Gorsuch Scarisbrick, 1995), 98.

2. R. R. Behnke and L. W. Carlile, "Heart Rate as an Index of Speech Anxiety," *Speech Monographs* 38 (1971): 66.

3. Michael J. Beatty and R. R. Behnke, "Effects of Public Speaking Trait Anxiety and Intensity of Speaking Task on Heart Rate during Performance," *Human Communication Research* 18 (1991): 147–176.

4. Michael J. Beatty, James C. McCroskey, and Alan D. Heiser, "Communication Apprehension as Temperamental Expression: A Communibiological Paradigm," *Communication Monographs* 65 (September 1998): 200.

5. James C. McCroskey and Michael J. Beatty, "Communication Apprehension," in *Communication and Personality: Trait Perspectives,* ed. James C. McCroskey, John A.

Daley, Michael M. Martin, and Michael J. Beatty (Cresshill, NJ: Hampton Press, 1998), 229.

6. John A. Daly, John P. Caughlin, and Laura Stafford, "Correlates and Consequences of Social-Communicative Anxiety," in *Avoiding Communication: Shyness, Reticence, and Communication Apprehension,* 2d ed., ed. John A. Daly, James C. McCroskey, Joe Ayres, Tim Hopf, and Debbie M. Ayres (Cresskill, NJ: Hampton Press, 1997), 27.

7. Gerald M. Phillips, "Rhetoritherapy versus the Medical Model: Dealing with Reticence," *Communication Education* 26 (1977): 37.

8. Michael Motley, "COM Therapy," in *Avoiding Communication: Shyness, Reticence, and Communication Apprehension,* 2d ed., ed. John A. Daly, James C. McCroskey, Joe Ayres, Tim Hopf, and Debbie M. Ayres (Cresskill, NJ: Hampton Press, 1997), 382.

9. Phillips, "Rhetoritherapy," 37.

10. Motley, "COM Therapy," 382.

11. Ibid., 380.

12. Joe Ayres and Theodore S. Hopf, "The Long-Term Effect of Visualization in the Classroom: A Brief Research Report," *Communication Education* 39 (January 1990): 77.

13. Phil Scott, "Mind of a Champion," *Natural Health* 27 (January–February 1997), 99.

14. Joe Ayres, Tim Hopf, and Debbie M. Ayres, "An Examination of Whether Imaging Ability Enhances the Effectiveness of an Intervention Designed to Reduce Speech Anxiety," *Communication Education* 43 (July 1994): 256.

15. Richmond and McCroskey, *Communication*, 98.

16. Lynne Kelly, Gerald M. Phillips, and James A. Keaten, *Teaching People to Speak Well: Training and Remediation of Communication Reticence* (Cresskill, NJ: Hampton Press, 1995), 11.

17. Ibid., 11–13.

18. Karen Kangas Dwyer, "The Multidimensional Model: Teaching Students to Self-Manage High Communication Apprehension by Self-Selecting Treatments," *Communication Education* 49 (January 2000): 79.

19. Delivered in speech class, University of Cincinnati. Used with permission of Eric Wais.

Chapter 3 Effective Listening

1. Judi Bownell, *Listening: Attitudes, Principles and Behavior*, 2nd ed. (Boston: Allyn & Bacon, 2002), 48.

2. John A. Kline, *Listening Effectively: Achieving High Standards in Communication* (Upper Saddle River, NJ: Prentice Hall, 2003), 1.

3. International Listening Association. *Listening Factoid* [Online, 2003]. Available at http://www.listen.org/pages/factoids/html.

4. "Sharpening Your Listening Skills," *Teller Vision* 0895–1039 (October 2002): 7.

5. Roni S. Lebauer, *Learning to Listen, Listen to Learn: Academic Listening and Note-Taking*, 2nd ed. (White Plains, NY: Longman, 2000), 49.

6. Andrew Wolvin and Carolyn Gwynn Coakley, *Listening*, 4th ed. (Dubuque, IA: Brown & Benchmark, 1996), 69, 239.

7. Charles U. Larson, *Persuasion: Reception and Responsibility*, 8th ed. (Belmont, CA: Wadsworth, 1998), 12.

Chapter 5 Adapting to Audiences

1. *The World Almanac and Book of Facts* (New York: World Almanac Books, 2004), 798, 850.

Chapter 6 Researching Information for Your Speech

1. M. Miller, *The Lycos Personal Internet Guide* (Indianapolis: Que Corporation, 1999), 187.

2. S. B. Barnes, *Computer-Mediated Communication: Human-to-Human Communication across the Internet* (Boston: Allyn & Bacon, 2003), 7.

3. Craig Tengler and Frederic M. Jablin, "Effects of Question Type, Orientation, and Sequencing in the Employment Screening Interview," *Communication Monographs* 50 (1983): 261.

4. Shirley Biagi, *Interviews That Work: A Practical Guide for Journalists*, 2d ed. (Belmont, CA: Wadsworth, 1992), 94.

5. David Munger, Daniel Anderson, Bret Benjamin, Christopher Busiel, and Bill Pardes-Holt, *Researching Online*, 3rd ed. (New York: Longman, 2000), 5.

6. Ibid.

7. Using Cyber Resources [Web page], DeVry/Phoenix, 3/15/2000, http://www.devry-phyx.edu//rnresrc//dowsc/integrity.htm [Accessed 17 October 2001].

8. Jim Kapoun, "Teaching Undergraduates web evaluation: A Guide for library instruction" [Web page], 1/25/2000, http://www.ala.org/acrl/undwebev.htm [Accessed 17 October 2001].

9. Munger et al., *Researching Online*, 17.

10. John Ahladas, "Global Warming," *Vital Speeches* (1 April 1989): 382.

11. Donald Baeder, "Chemical Wastes," *Vital Speeches of the Day* (1 June 1980): 497.

12. J. A. Howard, "Principles in Default: Rediscovered and Reapplied," *Vital Speeches* (1 August 2000): 618.

13. Steven Trachtenberg, "Five Ways in Which Thinking Is Dangerous," *Vital Speeches* (15 August 1986): 653.

14. G. Michael Durst, "The Manager as a Developer," *Vital Speeches* (1 March 1989): 309–310.

15. Hans Becherer, "Enduring Values for a Secular Age: Faith, Hope and Love," *Vital Speeches* (15 September 2000): 732.

16. Cynthia Opheim, "Making Democracy Work: Your Responsibility to Society," *Vital Speeches* (1 November 2000): 60.

Chapter 8 Completing the Outline: Creating the Introduction and the Conclusion

1. Wendy Liebermann, "How America Shops," *Vital Speeches*, 15 July 1998, 595.

2. Earnest W. Deavenport, "Walking the High Wire: Balancing Stakeholder Interests," *Vital Speeches*, 15 November 1995, 49.

3. Dana G. Mead, "Courage to Grow: Preparing for a New Commercial Century," *Vital Speeches*, 15 May 1998, 465.

4. Susan Morse, "The Rap of Change: A New Generation of Solutions," *Vital Speeches*, 1 January 2001, 186.

5. Nancy W. Dickey, "Packing My Bag for the Road Ahead: Everyone's Access to Medicine," *Vital Speeches*, 15 September 1998, 717.

6. H. R. Ettinger, "Shattering the Glass Floor: Women Donors as Leaders of Fundamental Change," *Vital Speeches*, 15 September 2000, 730.

7. Chester Burger, "Sooner Than You Think: Technology Pulling the World Together," *Vital Speeches*, 15 September 2000, 712.

8. S. D. Trujillo. "The Hispanic Destiny: Corporate Responsibility," *Vital Speeches*, 15 April 2002, 406.

Chapter 9 Constructing and Using Visual Aids

1. Michael E. Patterson, Donald F. Danscreau, and Dianna Newbern, "Effects of Communication Aids on Cooperative Teaching," *Journal of Educational Psychology* 84 (1992): 453–461.

2. Barbara Tversky, "Memory for Pictures, Maps, Environments, and Graphs," in David G. Payne and Frederick G. Conrad, eds., *Intersections in Basic and Applied Memory Research* (Mahwah, NJ: Laurence Erlbaum, 1997), 257–277.

3. Joe Ayres, "Using Visual Aids to Reduce Speech Anxiety," *Communication Research Reports* (June–December 1991): 73–79.

4. Judith Humphrey, "Executive Eloquence: A Seven-Fold Path to Inspirational Leadership," *Vital Speeches of the Day,* 15 May 1998, 470.

Chapter 10 Practicing Speech Wording

1. C. K. Ogden and I. A. Richards, *The Meaning of Meaning* (London: Kegan, Paul, Trench, Trubner, 1923).

2. Adam Robinson, *Word Smart: Building an Educated Vocabulary,* 3rd ed. (Princeton, NJ: Princeton Review, 2001).

3. W. B. Gudykunst and Y. Matsumoto, "Cross-Cultural Variability of Communication in Personal Relationships," in W. B. Gudykunst, S. Ting-Toomey, and T. Nishida, eds., *Communication in Personal Relationships Across Cultures* (Thousand Oaks, CA: Sage, 1996), 21.

4. G. Hofstede, *Cultures and Organizations: Software of the Mind* (New York: McGraw-Hill, 1991), 67.

5. D. Levine, *The Flight from Ambiguity* (Chicago: University of Chicago Press, 1985), 28.

6. C. W. Hensley, "Speak with Style and Watch the Impact," *Vital Speeches of the Day* (1 September 1995): 703.

7. Robert H. Schertz, "Deregulation: After the Airlines, Is Trucking Next?" *Vital Speeches of the Day* (1 November 1977):40.

8. D. D. DuFrene and C. M. Lehman, "Persuasive Appeal for Clean Language," *Business Quarterly* 65 (March 2002): 48.

9. J. V. O'Connor, FAQs #1 Cuss Control Academy [Online], Available at http://www.cusscontrol.com/faqs.html, 2000.

10. L. P. Stewart, P. J. Cooper, A. D. Stewart, and S. A. Friedley, *Communication and Gender,* 4th. ed. (Boston: Allyn & Bacon, 2003), 63.

11. S. B. Gmelch, *Gender on Campus: Issues for College Women* (New Brunswick, NJ: Rutgers University Press, 1998), 51.

Chapter 11 Practicing Delivery

1. Judee K. Burgoon, Deborah A. Coker, and Ray A. Coker, "Communicative Effects of Gaze Behavior: A Test of Two Contrasting Explanations," *Human Communication Research* 12 (1986): 495–524.

2. K. E. Menzel and L. J. Carrell, "The Relationship between Preparation and Performance in Public Speaking," *Communication Education* 43 (1994): 23.

3. Delivered in speech class, University of Cincinnati. Used with permission of Rebecca Jackson.

Chapter 12 Informative Speaking

1. Ice Man, http://www.digonsite.com/drdig/mummy/22.html.

2. Vegan Society's Web site, http://www.vegansociety.com.

3. Based on "Narrative" by Diane Baerwald, Northshore School District, http://ccweb.norshore.wednet.edu/writingcorner/narrative.html.

4. Delivered in speech class, University of Cincinnati. Used with permission of John Mullhauser.

5. Delivered in speech class, University of Cincinnati. Used with permission of Lindsey Degenhardt.

Chapter 13 Persuasive Speaking: Reasoning with Your Audience

1. Richard E. Petty and John Cacioppo, *Attitudes and Persuasion: Classic and Contemporary Approaches* (Boulder, CO: Westview, 1996), 7.

2. Bill Hill and Richard W. Leeman, *The Art and Practice of Argumentation and Debate* (Mountain View, CA: Mayfield, 1997), 135.

3. Stephen Toulmin, *The Uses of Argument* (Cambridge, England: Cambridge University Press, 1958).

4. Ibid.

5. Delivered in speech class, University of Cincinnati. Used with permission of Tobias Varland.

Chapter 14 Persuasive Speaking: Motivating the Audience

1. Charles U. Larson, *Persuasion: Reception and Responsibility,* 10th ed. (Belmont, CA: Wadsworth, 2004), 13.

2. Stephen W. Littlejohn, *Theories of Human Communication,* 7th ed. (Belmont, CA: Wadsworth, 2002), 132.

3. Gary C. Woodward and Robert E. Denton, Jr., *Persuasion and Influence in American Life,* 4th ed. (Prospect Heights, IL: Waveland Press, 2000), 168.

4. Herbert W. Simons, Joanne Morreale, and Bruce Gronbeck, *Persuasion in Society* (Thousand Oaks, CA: Sage, 2001), 35.

5. Herbert L. Petri and John M. Govern, *Motivation: Theory, Research, and Application,* 5th ed. (Belmont, CA: Wadsworth, 2004), 376.

6. Nabi, Robin L., "Discrete Emotions and Persuasion," in James P. Dillard and Michael Pfau, eds., *The Persuasion Handbook: Developments in Theory and Practice* (Thousand Oaks, CA: Sage, 2002), 291–299.

7. "Megan's Law." http://www.parentsformeganslaw.com/html/questions.lasso.

8. James C. McCroskey and Jason J. Teven, "Goodwill: A Reexamination of the Construct and Its Measurement," *Communication Monographs* 66 (March 1999): 92.

9. Herbert L. Petri, *Motivation: Theory, Research, and Applications,* 4th ed. (Belmont, CA: Wadsworth, 1996), 3.

10. John W. Thibaut and Harold H. Kelley, *The Social Psychology of Groups* (New York: Wiley, 1959), 10.

11. Abraham H. Maslow, *Motivation and Personality* (New York: Harper & Row, 1954), 80–92.

Chapter 16 Increasing the Effectiveness of Problem Solving Discussions

1. D. Johnson and F. Johnson, *Joining Together: Group Theory and Group Skills,* 8th ed. (Boston: Allyn and Bacon, 2003), 73.

2. J. Dan Rothwell, *In Mixed Company: Communicating in Small Groups and Teams,* 5th ed. (Belmont, CA: Wadsworth, 2004), 44.

3. J. S. Valacich, J. F. George, J. F. Nonamaker, Jr., and D. R. Vogel, "Idea Generation in Computer Based Groups: A New Ending to an Old Story," *Small Group Research* 25 (1994): 83–104.

4. C. Evans and K. Dion, "Group Cohesion and Performance: A Meta-analysis," *Small Group Research* 22 (1991): 175–186.

5. W. N. Widmer and J. M. Williams, "Predicting Cohesion in a Coacting Sport," *Small Group Research* 22 (1991): 548–570; P. R. Balgopal, P. H. Ephross, and T. V. Vassil, "Self Help Groups and Professional Helpers," *Small Group Research* 17 (1986): 123–137.

6. John F. Cragan, David W. Wright, and Chris R. Kasch, *Communication in Small Groups: Theory, Process, Skills,* 6th ed. (Belmont, CA: Wadsworth, 2004), 11.

7. Johnson and Johnson, *Joining Together,* 27.

8. Ibid., 171.

9. A. R. Dennis, "Information Exchange and Use in Small Group Decision Making," *Small Group Research* 27 (1996): 532–550.

10. K. S. Young, J. T. Wood, G. M. Phillips, and D. J. Pederson, *Group Discussion: A Practical Guide to Participation and Leadership,* 3rd ed. (Prospect Heights, IL: Waveland Press, 2001).

11. "Guidelines for Meeting Participants," developed by students in BAD 305: Understanding Behavior in Organizations, Northern Kentucky University, Fall 1998.

Glossary

accent the inflection, tone, and speech habits typical of the natives of a country, a region, or even a state or city

active listening identifying the organization of ideas, asking questions, silently paraphrasing, attending to nonverbal cues, and taking notes

ad hominem argument attacking or praising the person making the argument, rather than addressing the argument itself

adaptation reaction the gradual decline of your anxiety level that begins about one minute into the presentation and results in your anxiety level's declining to its prespeaking level in about five minutes

agenda an organized outline of the items that need to be covered during a meeting

anecdotes brief, often amusing stories

anticipation reaction the level of anxiety you experience prior to giving the speech, including the nervousness you feel while preparing and waiting to speak

antonym a word that is directly opposite in meaning

apathetic uninterested, unconcerned, or indifferent to your topic

appeal describes the behavior that you want your listeners to follow after they have heard the arguments

argue from analogy to support a claim with a single comparable example that is significantly similar to the subject of the claim

argue from causation to cite events that have occurred that result in the claim

argue from example to support your claim by providing one or more individual examples

argue from sign to cite information that signals the claim

arguments the process of proving conclusions you have drawn from reasons and evidence

articulation using the tongue, palate, teeth, jaw movement, and lips to shape vocalized sounds that combine to produce a word

attending paying attention to what the speaker is saying regardless of extraneous interferences

attitude a general or enduring positive or negative feeling about some person, object, or issue

audience the specific group of people to whom the speech is directed

audience adaptation presenting ideas verbally, visually, and vocally in a way that will help the audience relate to them; the process of tailoring your information to the specific speech audience

audience analysis a study made to learn about the diverse characteristics of audience members and then, based on these characteristics, to predict how audience members are apt to listen to, understand, and be motivated to act on your speech

audience feedback nonverbal and verbal cues that indicate audience members' reaction to what the speaker is saying

average group opinion method accepting the alternative receiving the highest average ranking as the choice

bar graph a diagram that uses vertical or horizontal bars to show relationships between two or more variables at the same time or at various times on one or more dimensions

brainstorming an uncritical, nonevaluative process of generating associated ideas and alternatives by being creative, suspending judgment, and combining or adapting the ideas of others

central route a way of processing information in which people carefully listen to, think about, evaluate, and even mentally elaborate on what has been said before making up their minds

chart a graphic representation that distills a lot of information and presents it to an audience in an easily interpreted visual format

claim the proposition or conclusion to be proven

closed questions narrow-focus questions that require only very brief answers

cohesiveness the degree of attraction that members have to one another and to the problem solving goal

commemorative addresses speeches presented to celebrate national holidays or anniversaries of important dates or events

commencement address a speech that recognizes graduation

common ground the background, knowledge, attitudes, experiences, and philosophies that are shared by audience members and the speaker

communication competence the perception that communication behavior is appropriate and effective

communication orientation viewing a speech as just an opportunity to talk with a number of people about a topic that is important to the speaker and to the audience

communication orientation motivation (COM) techniques designed to reduce anxiety by helping the speaker adopt a "communication" rather than a "performance" orientation toward the speech

comparative advantages an organization that shows that a proposed change has more value than the status quo

comparison illuminating a point by showing similarities

comparison and contrast a method of informing that explains something by focusing on how it is similar to and different from other things

concrete words words that appeal to the senses or conjure up a picture

confrontation reaction the surge in your anxiety level that you feel as you begin your speech

connotation the feelings or evaluations we associate with a word

consensus method deliberating until all members of the group find an acceptable solution, one they can support and are committed to helping implement

context the physical, cultural, historical, and psychological factors in the setting in which your speech is presented; the position of a word in a sentence and its relationship to other words around it

contrast illuminating a point by highlighting differences

conversational style an informal way of presenting a speech so that your listeners feel that you are talking with them

costs expenditures that we incur when we act; may be physical, psychological, or social

creativity a person's ability to produce new or original ideas and insights

credibility the confidence that an audience places in the truthfulness of what a speaker says; the perception that the speaker is knowledgeable, trustworthy, and personable

crediting ideas giving the sources of information you use

criteria satisfaction an indirect organization that seeks audience agreement on criteria that should be considered when evaluating a particular proposition and then shows how the proposition satisfies those criteria

critical analysis the process of evaluating what you have heard in order to determine a speech's completeness, usefulness, and trustworthiness

cultural setting the values, beliefs, meanings, and social mores of specific groups of people to which your audience members belong

decision making the process of choosing among alternatives

definition a method of informing that explains something by identifying its meaning

demonstration a method of informing that explains something by showing how something is done, by displaying the stages of a process, or by depicting how something works

denotation the explicit meaning a language community formally gives a word

description the informative method used to create an accurate, vivid, verbal picture of an object, geographic feature, setting, or image

emotions the buildup of action-specific energy

empathy the ability to see the world through the eyes of someone else

emphasis the weight or importance given to certain words or ideas

emphasize give different shades of expressiveness to

enthusiasm excitement or passion about your speech

ethics a set of moral principles that are held by a society, group, or individual that differentiate right from

wrong and good behavior from bad behavior

eulogy a speech of tribute given at the memorial or funeral for a person who has died

evaluation of speech effectiveness how well you believe a speaker meets key criteria

examples specific instances that illustrate or explain a general factual statement

expert opinion method asking the group member who has the most expertise to make the final choice

expert opinions interpretations and judgments made by authorities in a particular subject area

expository speech an informative presentation that provides carefully researched in-depth knowledge about a complex topic

extemporaneous speech a speech that is researched and planned ahead of time but whose exact wording is not scripted and will vary from presentation to presentation

eye contact looking directly at the people to whom you are speaking

facial expression eye and mouth movement

factual statements information that can be verified

false cause a fallacy that occurs when the alleged cause fails to be related to, or to produce, the effect

flipchart a large pad of paper mounted on an easel

flowchart a chart that uses symbols and connecting lines to diagram the progressions through a complicated process

fluent speech that flows easily without hesitations and vocal interferences

follow-up questions questions designed to pursue the answers given to primary questions

general criteria criteria that we can use as a starting point for evaluating any speech

general goal the overall intent of the speech

generic language using words that may apply only to one sex, race, or other group as though they represent everyone

gestures movements of hands, arms, and fingers

goodwill a perception that the audience forms of a speaker who they believe understands them, empathizes with them, and is responsive to them

graph a diagram that presents numerical comparisons

ground rules prescribed behaviors designed to help the group meet its goals and conduct its conversations

hasty generalization a fallacy that presents a generalization that is either not supported with evidence or is supported with only one weak example

hate speech the use of words and phrases to demean another person or group and to express the speaker's hatred and prejudice toward that person or group

historical setting events that have already occurred that are related to your speech topic, to you as a speaker, to previous speeches given by you with which audience members are familiar, or to other encounters that audience members have had with you

hypothetical examples specific instances based on reflections about future events

impartial having no opinion

impromptu speech a speech that is delivered with only seconds or minutes of advance notice for preparation and is usually presented without referring to notes of any kind

incentive a reward that is promised if a particular action is taken or goal is reached

informative speech a speech whose goal is to explain or describe facts, truths, and principles in a way that stimulates interest, facilitates understanding, and increases the likelihood of remembering

initial audience attitudes predispositions for or against a topic, usually expressed as an opinion

intellectually stimulating information that is new to audience members and is explained in a way that piques their curiosity and excites their interest

internal transitions words and phrases that emphasize the relationships between ideas within a main point

Internet an international electronic collection of thousands of smaller networks

interviewing the skillful asking and answering of questions

jargon technical terminology; meaningless talk, gibberish

keynote address a speech that begins a conference or convention

knowledge and expertise how well you convince your audience that you are qualified to speak on the topic

leading questions questions phrased in a way that suggests the interviewer has a preferred answer

line graph a diagram that indicates changes in one or more variables over time

listening the process of receiving, constructing meaning from, and responding to spoken and/or verbal messages

logical reasons order organizing the main points of a persuasive speech by the reasons that support the speech goal

main points complete-sentence statements of the two to five central ideas that will be used in the thesis statement

majority rule method selecting the alternative that receives the majority of votes (50% + 1)

marking the addition of sex, race, age, or other group designations to a description

metaphor a comparison that establishes a figurative identity between objects being compared

monotone a voice in which the pitch, volume, and rate remain constant, with no word, idea, or sentence differing significantly from any other

motivated sequence a form of persuasive organization that combines a problem solution pattern with explicit appeals designed to motivate the audience

movement the motion of the entire body

multiple-response items survey items that give the respondent several alternative answers from which to choose

narration a method of informing that explains something by recounting events

narrative/personal experience speech a presentation in which you recount an experience you have had and the significance you attach to that experience

narratives accounts, personal experiences, tales, or lengthier stories

neutral questions questions phrased in ways that do not direct a person's answers

newsgroup (bulletin board) an electronic gathering place for people with similar interests

nonparallel language language in which terms are changed because of the sex, race, or other group characteristics of the individual

norms shared expectations for the way that group members will behave during discussions

open questions broad-based questions that ask the interviewee to provide perspective, ideas, information, or opinions

open-ended items survey items that encourage respondents to elaborate on their opinions without forcing them to answer in a predetermined way

panel discussion a problem solving discussion in front of an audience

parallel when wording of points follows the same structural pattern, often using the same introductory words

paraphrase a statement in your own words of the meaning you have assigned to a message

performance orientation viewing public speaking as a situation demanding special delivery techniques in order to impress an audience aesthetically or viewing audience members as hypercritical judges who will be unforgiving about even our minor mistakes

periodicals magazines and journals that appear at fixed periods

peripheral route a "shortcut" way of processing information that relies on simple cues

personableness the extent to which you project an agreeable or pleasing personality

personal pronouns "we," "us," and "our"—pronouns that directly link the speaker to members of the audience

personalize to present information in a frame of reference that is familiar to the audience

persuasive speech a speech whose goal is to influence the beliefs and/or behavior of audience members

physical setting the location, size of room, seating arrangement, distance between audience and speaker, time of day, room temperature, and lighting

pie graph a diagram that shows the relationships among parts of a single unit

pitch the scaled highness or lowness of the sound a voice makes

plagiarism the unethical act of representing another person's work as your own; using a created production without crediting the source

poise assurance of manner

posture the position or bearing of the body

precise words words that narrow a larger category

primary questions questions the interviewer plans ahead of time

problem solution an organizational pattern that provides a framework for clarifying the nature of some problem and for illustrating why a given proposal is the best solution

problem solving discussion a structured dialogue among individuals who interact with and influence one another in order to develop a plan that will overcome an identified difficulty

problem solving goal a future state of affairs desired by enough members of the group to motivate the group to work toward its achievement

productive thinking working to think about something from a variety of perspectives

pronunciation the form and accent of various syllables of a word

proposition a declarative sentence that clearly indicates the position that the speaker will advocate in a persuasive speech

proposition of fact a statement designed to convince your audience that something is or is not true, exists, or happens

proposition of policy a statement designed to convince your audience that they should take a specific course of action

proposition of value a statement designed to convince your audience that something is good, bad, desirable, undesirable, sound, beneficial, important, or unimportant

proximity relevance to personal life space

psychological setting the feelings, attitudes, and beliefs of individual audience members that affect how your speech message is perceived

public hearing a meeting of an elected or appointed government group for the purpose of explaining a pending change in policy (or a new policy), answering questions, and receiving public comments

public speaking apprehension a type of communication anxiety; the level of fear a person experiences when anticipating or actually speaking to an audience

public speaking skills training systematic teaching of the skills associated with the processes involved in preparing and delivering an effective public speech with the intention of improving speaking competence as a means of reducing public speaking apprehension

quality the tone, timbre, or sound of your voice

questions of fact questions concerned with discovering what is true or to what extent something is true

questions of policy questions that concern what course of action should be taken or what rules should be adopted in order to solve a problem

questions of value questions that concern subjective judgments of what is right, moral, good, or just

rate the speed at which you talk

reasoning the mental process of drawing inferences (conclusions) from factual information

reasons main point statements that summarize several related pieces of evidence and show *why* you should believe or do something

rehearsing practicing the presentation of your speech aloud

relevance adapting the information in the speech so that audience members view it as important to them

remembering being able to retain and recall information that you have heard

responsive showing care about the audience by acknowledging feedback from the audience, especially subtle negative cues

rhetorical questions questions phrased to stimulate a mental response rather than an actual spoken response on the part of the audience

scaled items survey items that measure the direction and/or intensity of an audience member's feeling or attitude toward something

scripted speech a speech that is prepared by creating a complete written manuscript and delivered by reading a written copy

section transitions complete sentences that show the relationship between, or bridge, major parts of a speech

setting the location and occasion for a speech

simile a direct comparison of dissimilar things using *like* or *as*

skimming a method of rapidly going through a work to determine what is covered and how

slang informal, nonstandard vocabulary

speaker the source or originator of the speech

speaking appropriately using language that adapts to the needs, interests, knowledge, and attitudes of the listener and avoiding language that alienates audience members

specific goal a single statement that identifies the exact response the speaker wants from the audience

specific language words that clarify meaning by narrowing what is understood from a general category to a particular item or group within that category

speech effectiveness the extent to which audience members listen to, understand, remember, and are motivated to act on what a speaker has said

speech goal a statement of what you want your listeners to know, believe, or do

speech making the process of presenting a speech to the intended audience

speech notes a word or phrase outline of your speech, plus hard-to-remember information such as quotations and statistics, designed to help trigger memory

speech of acceptance a ceremonial speech given to acknowledge receipt of an honor or award

speech of introduction a ceremonial speech that familiarizes the audience with biographical information that establishes the credibility of the person being presented

speech of recognition a ceremonial presentation that acknowledges someone and usually presents an award, a prize, or a gift to the individual or a representative of a group

speech of tribute a ceremonial speech that praises someone's life and accomplishments

speech plan a strategy for achieving your goal

speech planning process the system that you use to prepare a speech

speech to actuate a speech that moves beyond affecting audience beliefs and attitudes and motivates the audience to act

spontaneity a naturalness that does not seem rehearsed or memorized

statement of reasons a straightforward organization in which you present your best-supported reasons in a meaningful order

statistics numerical facts

subject a broad area of expertise, such as movies, cognitive psychology, computer technology, or the Middle East

supporting material developmental material that will be used in the speech, including personal experiences, examples, illustrations, anecdotes, statistics, and quotations

survey a questionnaire or a canvassing of people in order to get information directly from them about their ideas and opinions; the information gathered is then analyzed for trends

symposium a discussion in which a limited number of participants present individual speeches of approximately the same length dealing with the same subject, then discuss their reactions to what others have said and answer questions from the audience

synonym a word that has the same or a similar meaning

systematic desensitization a method that reduces apprehension by gradually having people visualize increasingly more frightening events

thesis statement a sentence that states the main points of the speech

time order organizing the main points of the speech in a chronological sequence or by steps in a process

timeliness showing how information is useful now or in the near future

toast a ceremonial speech offered at the start of a reception or meal that pays tribute to the occasion or to a person

topic some specific aspect of a subject

topic order organizing the main points of the speech by categories or divisions of a subject

town hall meeting an event in which a large number of people who are interested in a topic are convened to discuss, and at times to decide, an issue

transitions words, phrases, or sentences that show a relationship between, or bridge, two ideas

trustworthiness the extent to which the audience can believe that what you say is accurate, true, and in their best interests

two-sided items survey items that force the respondent to choose between two answers, such as yes/no, for/against, or pro/con

unanimous decision method deliberating until every member of the group believes that the same solution alternative is the best

understanding the ability to assign accurate meaning to what was said

uninformed not knowing enough about a topic to have formed an opinion

visual aid a form of speech development that allows the audience to see as well as hear information

visualization a method that reduces apprehension by helping speakers develop a mental picture of themselves giving a masterful speech

vivid language language that is full of life—vigorous, bright, and intense

vocal expressiveness vocal contrasts in pitch, volume, rate, and quality that affect the meaning audiences get from the sentences you speak

volume the degree of loudness of the tone you make

warrant the logical statement that connects the support to the claim

welcoming speech a brief ceremonial address that greets and expresses pleasure for the presence of a person or an organization

word chart a chart used to preview, review, or highlight important ideas covered in a speech

working environment a physical setting that is conveniently located for most members, has a comfortable temperature, and has enough space of appropriate size for the size and work of the group

Index